To: Dea Daulna

Swami

A Biography

Asha Prasad

DIAMOND BOOKS

ISBN : 978-81-288-3180-5

© Publisher

Publisher	:	**Diamond Pocket Books (P) Ltd.**
		X-30, Okhla Industrial Area, Phase-II
		New Delhi-110020
Phone	:	011-40712100, 41611861
Fax	:	011-41611866
E-mail	:	sales@dpb.in
Website	:	www.dpb.in
Edition	:	2016
Printed by	:	Laxmi Enterprises, Okhla

SWAMI VIVEKANAND : A BIOGRAPHY
By - *Asha Prasad*

Foreword

Swami Vivekanand enjoys a unique position among the leaders of the Indian National Movement during the second half of 19th century. Historians accept the contributions made by Swamiji in terms of his work and the message spread by him during the Indian National Movement that took a significant turn in the beginning of the 20th century. During the period of revolutionary movements that Bengal witnessed after the partition of Bengal in 1905, the revolutionary leaders of Bengal had in their possession the books containing the speeches of Vivekanand along with the Bhagvat Gita. Mention of Swami Vivekanand can be found in Jawaharlal Nehru's book – "Story of India." Subhash Chandra Bose had made a thorough study of all the works of Swami Vivekanand at a very young age. Almost all major contemporary leaders during the Gandhian era were mainly inspired by the thoughts and philosophies of Swami Vivekanand. Even 99 years after his death, Indians continue to uphold and cherish his thoughts and ideals. Even now his life is a source of inspiration for the young generation.

The efforts made by Swami Vivekanand to reawaken the lost glory of India was not solely meant to end India's political dependence. He showed the way to escape the state of, mind of Indians brought about by years of slave-like existence. Vivekanand was a great dreamer. He always imagined of a society which did not differentiate between human beings on the basis of caste, creed, religion, etc. He presented the philosophies inherent in Vedanta in such a manner without getting entangled in the debate between spirituality and physicality, one can say that there can be no other strong basis for the philosophy of equality laid down by Swami Vivekanand.

The philosophy of equality was a source of inspiration and trust for all the activities undertaken by him. He always tried his level test to enhance the living standards of the poor and miserable lots. He always used to tell his followers that the real India resides in huts and as long as their conditions remain unimproved, it is impossible for our country to develop.

In his view the only possible means of improvement of our country was dissemination of education. He wanted his followers to spread themselves in every village and educate the poor. A literate person can search a decent livelihood on his own.

The most powerful message by Swamiji was his own life. This young saint who left this earthly abode even before attaining the age of 40 years, instilled a new life throughout the whole nation and displayed such a social philosophy which is meaningful even today.

Vivekanand pinned all his hopes on the youth. This biography on such a glorious personality is dedicated to today's youths. My attempt has been to recount each and every facet of Swami Vivekanand's social philosophy as well as his humanitarian personality.

The overwhelming personality and his thoughts have always been a source of inspiration for each and every Indian. Today as we have entered into the 21st century, it is becoming increasingly evident that there is no other source of inspiration.

—Asha Prasad

Contents

The Worshipper in Dakshineswar

Four miles away from Calcutta, on the eastern banks of the Ganges, there situated a very majestic temple of Goddess Kali. Outside the temple, within its boundary walls sat a young 'pujari' in the yogic padmasana pose. He was normally tall, his complexion wheatish, brood forehead there under two half closed long eyes. Full of love, calm and unusually bright eyes, seemed able to fathom both the inner and outer world of the people with its slight glance. In between the half open lips, the white teeth and the childish smile beamed. On the face with sweat shining there was a brightness that resembled an aura. Eyes kept on getting attracted towards this saint who was hiding an unending ocean of love towards humanity.

The story of this saint begins way back to Kamarpukur. Kamarpukur – a triangular shaped beautiful village in Bengal. Nature's beauty is embedded in the palm tree, lakes and the green fields that are spread all over the village. Khudiram Chattopadhyay, a poor Brahmin devotee of Lord Vishnu was an old resident of the village. At the age of 60, he went to Gaya to have oblation for his long dead forefathers and ancestors. There he offered worship for his ancestors at a temple of Vishnu. That day he experienced a strange kind of happiness and satisfaction. He felt that his forefathers have accepted his offerings whole heartedly and have blessed him.

That night, he dreamt of Lord Vishnu "I take birth in this universe again and again to redeem it from sins. This time I will take birth in your small hut and will make you my father." Did he actually hear this voice of Lord Vishnu or was this a mere deception of his mind? Who knows? But Khudiram was in a puzzled state when he somewhat regained a balanced state of mind he said, "No my Lord! I am not worth this blessing. You have showered me more blessings that I actually deserve. I am very poor to serve you and look after you."

That very night at Kamarpukur his wife Chandramani while worshipping Lord Shiva at the temple received a shock. She felt that the idol has suddenly become lively. A spot of light emerged from the idol and entered into the body of Chandramani. She could not withstand the brightness of that light and fell down on the ground unconscious.

That day the sound of couch shell emerged from the house of Chattopadhyay couple on that auspicious day was 18 February, 1836. On an auspicious day the Chattopadhyay was blessed with a boy baby in memory of the strange experience he had at Gaya. Khudiram named the child Gadadhar. Days transformed into months and months gave way to years. Gadadhar was now five years old. The child was healthy, handsome and at the same time well-mannered smiling face and childish pranks were his characteristic features. People used to feel surprised at his sharp intellect beyond his age. His father sent him to the school in Kamarpukur. There his simple behaviour attracted other students and teachers alike. He learnt to read and write very easily. But he was not much interested in mathematics from the very beginning. In fact he was not ready to learn even the basics of Mathematics.

Gadadhar's personality was different from other children of his age. His father, due to his past vision, was able to envision his son's great future. The shlokas that he recited during his worship of Gods and Goddesses, the religious stories that he used to tell to Gadadhar, everything got embedded in Gadadhar's memory at the very first instance. During those days, wandering saints used to tell religious tales to the villagers. Gadadhar never missed any such occasion and listened to them very attentively. He observed them minutely – the manner in which they told the stories and the expression thereof. Then later, while playing along with his friends, without any assembly or stage, he, in the very style and manner of the saint, told those very stories. Though very naughty in nature, sometimes he observed the beauty of nature in a calm and serious manner. He used to be so engrossed in watching the minute details of nature that he almost forgot his actual existence. During those days of Gadadhar's childhood, nobody was aware of the depth and philosophy underlying this small body and mind.

In 1842, when he was six years old, people experienced this blessing of goddess on him. One day, he was walking through the narrow path in between the paddy fields. As he walking through the paddy fields, chewing sweetmeat, suddenly he looked up towards the sky. He saw that a grayish clouds had suddenly enveloped the whole sky and behind those clouds came out a group of snow white herons which flew over his head to nowhere. The colour difference between the cloud and the herons was such a beautiful sight that his soul was so overwhelmed that it left his body and got drifted away for. He lost his consciousness and fell on the ground. The sweetmeat that he was relishing was strewn all over the ground. Somebody carried him to his home. That day the happiness and devotion that he experienced was unlimited. This was his first feeling of ecstasy. Later his life kept on experiencing fulfilment with such kind of ecstacies again and again.

When Gadadhar attained the age of seven, his father left this worldly abode. The Chattopadhyay family was as if in the midst of a disaster. Chandramani, who considered her husband to be the epitome of God on earth, now seemed to be in a bewildered state of mind. She stayed away from worldly things and spent her days and nights in worship and prayers. The responsibility of the whole Chattopadhyay family now fell on the shoulders of the eldest son of Khudiram and Chandramani – Ram Kumar. It became his responsibility to look after his old mother and the younger siblings education and other requirements. Gadadhar was very much attached to his father. After the loss of his father many changes became evident in his behaviour. The seriousness that had been inherent in his character gave way to contemplation sitting in the mango groves or in the cremation grounds, he kept on meditating, making small idols of gods and goddesses or reciting the prayers etc other than thus he made efforts to keep his mother happy in the given circumstances. After some days he underwent the ritual of formally wearing the sacred threat – the *yagyopavit* ceremony – wherein a child is initiated to learning Vedas and religious texts. From then onwards, he was entrusted with the task of offering daily prayers and worships to their household deity – 'Raghuvir'. He performed the daily worship of the deity with complete devotion and was very much excited about it.

He felt that the idol of Lord Raghuvir resembled with his own father's image.

The land of Bengal has been solemnized by the birth of saints like Chaitanya, Chandidas and Vidyapati. All of them were devotees of Lord Krishna and sang sweet and melodious songs in praise of Lord Krishna. And the melody of those songs were embedded in the very air of this land. Gadadhar was born in this very land. It was obvious that he was very much influenced by melody of this music which had a great impact on his life. Gadadhar's loving heart had the qualities of an emotional artist. His mind got attracted towards the subtle beauties of nature music and even silent emotions. He envisioned the image of God in them.

Once, the festival of Shivratri was being celebrated in Kamarpukur with great pomp and éclat. A drama based on the life of Lord Shiva was to be played at night. Suddenly, at the time when the play was to begin, the main protagonist who was to play the role of Lord Shiva, feel ill. Now who will play the role of Lord Shiva? People began to worry. Somebody suggested the name of Gadadhar. Some people went to Gadadhar's house. He was engrossed in offering prayers to Lord Shiva. He was not ready to leave his worship to act in a play. But people insisted and kept on convincing him that in such a situation he should help them and that playing the role of Lord Shiva is also like worshipping him. While acting, he can strike a chord with Lord Shiva by thinking of the Lord. Soon he got convinced and was ready to play the role of Lord Shiva.

On the stage he walked with reserved steps and a serious countenance, the audience was spellbound by his appearance and performance. His body covered with ash, the garland of rudraksha beads around his neck, Mutted hair rolled up into a knot over the head, the crescent shaped moon drawn on the forehead, the large earrings hanging on his ears, the skin of lion wrapped around the waist – the real Kamdeva would not have looked so handsome. Soon Gadadhar was totally transformed into Lord Shiva. It seemed as if he had totally become one with the Lord. His co-actors, viewers and the whole world itself got dissolved and disappeared away from his eyes. He was so overwhelmed with emotions that he fainted on to the ground. Tears were rolling down incessantly from his closed eyes. People thought that he was about to die. They tried to bring him back to

Swami Vivekanand: A Biography

consciousness but to no avail. The play had to be packed up in the middle. Gadadhar was taken to his home. He regained his consciousness next day in the morning. He was looking very happy and pleased. After this, during such occasions, he experienced such kind of rapture.

Some residents of Kamarpukur identified the great soul hidden inside child Gadadhar. A low caste fellow of the village, named Sriniwas adored Gadadhar. One day while Sriniwas was busy making garlands for gods, Gadadhar came near him. He at once went to the market and bought some sweetmeats. He took Gadadhar to an isolated place in an open ground and made him sit under a tree. He glanced here and there and began to worship Gadadhar in a clandestine and scared manner. He first garlanded Gadadhar and then offered him sweets. Sriniwas considered Gadadhar to be an impersonation of God and a great saint.

Now Gadadhar was on the threshold of teenage. His heart was feminine and his physique very tenderly. Women of all ages got attracted towards him. His simplicity, his true devotion to God and his heart, everything were a source of admiration. None of the womenfolk's in his village had any kind of hesitation in interacting with him. They all considered him to be somebody related to them and very close to them. Almost every day, in the afternoon, after completing their daily chores, the women folk in the village assembled in front of Chandramani's house and listened to Gadadhar's talks relating to God.

Gadadhar had no interest in studying in the village school. Most of the time he along with other children formed a group and enacted the play of Gopi Krishna. He used to play the role of Radha, head-over heels in love with Krishna and in the process of enacting Radha he felt ecstatic and lost consciousness. His elder brother Ram Kumar had been running a school in Calcutta. He thought of calling Gadadhar over to Calcutta so that he was able to get modern education. One fine morning Gadadhar left Kamarpukur. The images of incidents that took place in his life for the past seventeen years past his memory. The thought of bidding adieu to the village where he was born and spent seventeen years of his life was a really difficult task for him. But the future in the form of Calcutta was calling him. How could have he overcome the call of destiny?

In Calcutta, Ram Kumar admitted Gadadhar to his school. Modern education was imparted in this school. This modern system of education could not quench his thirst for knowledge. He saw some different kind of light deep inside life. He saw only one objective in life and that was godly devotion. One day he asked Ram Kumar, "What will I do by attaining this kind of education which will help me achieve only livelihood. I want to attain such kind of knowledge that would enlighten my mind." Ram Kumar tried to reason out with Gadadhar but he failed in his attempt to convince him.

A widow belonging to the Vaishya community – Rani Rasmani established a temple dedicated to Goddess Kali at Dakshineswar. Every religious person irrespective of caste, colour or birth had easy access to this temple. With the construction of this temple, people who experienced prejudice due to their lowly birth felt a sense of happiness. But during those days, howsoever popular the deity or goddess was, if she stayed in a temple having access to people of all caste and creed, it was difficult to get a Brahmin priest to offer daily worship in such a temple. And if the priest does not belong to a high caste Brahmin community then he is no priest at all. Ram Kumar after much apprehension took over the responsibility as priest to this temple. He was compelled to take up this job as he had a huge family to look after and he was not financially sound. But with in a short period he died. Now Gadadhar had to take up the vacant position.

This way the youthful Gadadhar who later earned name and fame as Swami Ramakrishna Paramahansa, devoted his whole life in the worship and prayer of 'Goddess Kali' at the temple of Dakshineswar. He was a true servant of mother Kali. He worshipped and served the idol of mother Kali from down to dusk in such a devoted manner that he forgot that he was worshipping a mere idol which was devoid of any life. He used to search life in that idol. Many nights he spent in meditation. But he failed to behold the real Goddess. In the evening at the time of sun set he stood near the bank of river Ganga and used to shout like a lunatic - "Today another day has gone away waste. I could not see you mother. Another day from this small life has passed and I was not able to witness the truth. Mother, if you are the embodiment of truth, if you are indeed present somewhere, why am I not able to see you?"

Once his pain of not able to see Goddess Kali became unbearable. Without beholding the goddess he felt his life to be a total failure. He was overcome with frustration and decided to end his worthless life. His eyes fell on the sword hanging in front of the idol of Goddess Kali, inside the temple. 'Sword! Only you can help me end my life.' No sooner than this thought came to his mind he like an insane fellow ran towards the sword and took hold of the sword. At the very same moment a bright light enveloped around him. He felt as if he was getting drowned in that luminous light. His whole self, then temple, its door, window everything got merged with that illumination. He lost his consciousness and fell on the ground. After this how days and nights lapsed he had no idea. The goddess was there in front of him in flesh and blood and he experienced an ocean of joy.

After this incident, Ramkrishna became all the more engrossed with the goddess. Time and again, Goddess Kali appeared before him. His devotion kept on increasing day by day. This way he stroke a chord with the mother goddess and he experienced the heights of ecstacy. As he performed the daily rituals of worship, the stone idol of goddess Kali transformed into a lively goddess smiling and showering blessings on him. He felt as if he was able to experience the very breathe of the goddess on his hands. He used to hear the tingling sound of anklets of the goddess. Now there was no more gulf between himself and the goddess. He used to be or engrossed in his meditation and worship of the goddess that, for him every woman that he saw resembled to the mother goddess. Even in his dreams he beheld every woman considering her to be the mother.

His first meeting with Goddess Kali has such a great impact on him – that he became weak and began to keep ill health. His mother and other relatives compelled him to undergo a weather change and under their compulsion he went to Kamarpukur. After so many days when Gadadhar's mother saw him, she was surprised and sad to find that her son had lost his old happiness and glow on his face. He was no more interested in the natural beauty of his village, company of his old friends or old mother's love and affection. He looked physically weak and engrossed with some sorrowful and deep thoughts. Many a time he used to moan with some internal pain and sometimes incessant tears came rolling down from his eyes and he kept on calling "Mother...mother".

Chandramani was not familiar with this new image of her son. She felt as if her beloved son has been lost somewhere in the city of Calcutta and this was somebody else, a look alike of his beloved son Gadadhar. Her heart wept at the present condition of her son. Nobody was able to find out a possible reason for Gadadhar's new ailment. She employed every possible treatment to cure his son's illness – both traditional and modern – but to no avail. Most of the time he sat in the loneliness of cremation grounds and kept on meditating for hours together. To divert his attention towards worldly and materialistic affairs, people tried to arrange his marriage. Considering it to be the wish of mother Kali, Gadadhar gave his consent for marriage very happily. But nobody was ready to give their daughter's hand in marriage to such an ascetic. His family members lost all hopes of getting a bride for him after a long search. At last one day Ramakrishna in a semi-conscious state said, "All your search is futile. You people go to 'Jayaramvati' village and my bride there in safe custody in the house of Ram Chandra Mukhopadhyay."

A messenger was sent in person to the house of Ram Chandra Mukhopadhyay at Jayaramvati village. What Ramkrishna had said proved to be true. Ramchandra Mukhopadhyay had a five-year old daughter and he accepted the marriage proposal. Chandramani was a bit hesitant due to the minor age of the bride. But there was no other way out. Eventually the marriage between Ramakrishna and Sharda Devi was fixed. The marriage ceremony was accomplished at an auspicious time. About one and a half year after marriage, Ramakrishna returned back to Dakshineswar along with his bride.

Returning back at Dakshineswar, once again he forgot his mother, wife and other relatives and got engaged in offering prayers and worship to mother Kali. Days, weeks and months kept on passing, in search of truth. One day Ramakrishna saw a saintly woman in the temple precincts. She was wearing cloth made from tree bark, she had long thick hair, looked mature and her beautiful face reflected the glory of knowledge. She carried a small cloth bundle in which there were two-three dresses and two-three books.

Ramakrishna was greatly surprised to see her. The woman saw Ramakrishna and suddenly she turned emotional and began to weep. "My dear, you were here. Since many days I had been searching you. Oh! Its now that I have found you." It seemed that her voice drenched in tears flowed from her lips.

She was a woman belonging to a Bengali Brahmin family and a true devotee of Lord Vishnu. She had deep knowledge about religion and philosophy. People knew her as Bhairavi Brahmani. She was able to assess Ramakrishna's state of mind as soon as she met him. She felt that God had sent her to him to convey His message. She experienced a strange kind of affection towards him. Soon a mother-son relationship took birth between the two. Ramakrishna like a small school going kid, put forth many questions relating to god and worship before Bhairavi Brahmani. Brahmani slowly and gradually lent a philosophic basis to Ramakrishna's love and devotion. She also guided him towards tantric devotion.

Ramakrishna was totally immersed in the colours of love and devotion. He considered Bhairavi Brahmani as his mother and teacher. He gained knowledge from Bhairavi Brahmani through the path of love. The first step towards the path of love is to make any one God, the centre of worship or thought. Ramakrishna had already chosen Mother Kali as his chosen deity. Hence, he remained engrossed in the love and devotion. Slowly his prayers became so strong that he was able to see Mother Kali in person, touch her and could even converse with her. Then he attained the knowledge that there existed God in one form or the other in everything on the earth. To see them one should possess a sight full of love. After this Ramakrishna experienced that images of all other gods and goddesses reflecting the image of mother Kali. With this he was also able to see the different images of God before his mind's eye. To witness various images and incarnations of the God he remained totally engrossed in the emotions of love. Now he could establish different kinds of relationship with God like that of master-servant, mother-son, lover, friend etc. He experienced fulfillment in life after beholding every form and image of the god almighty. His life did not even give a slight space for worldliness or materialism. His love, devotion, worship and tantrik meditation became popular far and wide.

Ramakrishna was still undergoing the process of attainment of knowledge and was learning things from Bhairavi Brahmani. One day, a wandering yogi reached Dakshineswar. He was tall and was having strong rock-like physique. His looks were primitive and it was quite evident from iron body that he had never detracted any disease or even a slight fever in his life. He was popular among people in the name Totapuri. He had taken initiation from a Naga saint. He started a nomadic life at a very young age and before that he was the chief of an ashram in Punjab consisting of 400 saints. All the saints in this ashram after undergoing tough practices of meditation had made themselves very strong and stoic. They were able to easily endure extreme hot and cold climatic conditions as well as happiness and sorrow. Totapuri had attained proficiency in proving truth on the basis of Vedanta philosophy. According to the Advaita philosophy, *Param Brahma* is the ultimate and eternal truth. Through the means of yoga one can merge his soul with the *Param Brahma*. But myth is something untrue and impermanent. He was against the belief that one can attain ultimate truth and conjoin the Supreme being on the basis of myth.

At Dakshineswar, when Totapuri was walking towards the Kali temple, he saw young priest sitting on the stairs and lost in some unworldly thoughts. Totapuri was surprised and asked to see the young man. What an aura? Not aura but something magnetic which was attracting his attention towards the young man. He felt like beholding the young man continuously. Totapuri's footsteps unknowingly led him towards Ramakrishna. He was a seasoned wanderer. He never stayed at a place for more than three days. But after seeing the transcendental image of Ramakrishna, overflowing with love and devotion he could not make an easy exit from Dakshineswar. He spent eleven months just talking to Ramakrishna.

Ramakrishna worshipped his formal deity through the medium of love whereas Totapuri used the medium of yoga to worship his formless *Brahma* – the Supreme Being. Two celestial source of lights on two entirely opposite poles. But both had the same aim. Slowly and gradually, the gulf between them kept on narrowing. Both the saints possessing opposite thoughts about worship and devotion came near each other. They influenced each other with the knowledge they possessed. Ramakrishna, who was ignorant about the magical attributes of formless Brahma was unable to imagine that it was possible to identify God without the help of an idol. Totapuri said – "My son, you have already crossed a long way towards truth. If you are desirous of attaining knowledge regarding what is left then I may guide you with the help of Vedanta." Ramakrishna did not give him any answer. He like an innocent child stood before the idol of mother Kali and awaiting her permission for practicing such kind of worship. After getting permission, he took initiation in Advaita Vedanta from Totapuri in a humble manner. The first phase of learning of Advaita Vedanta included controlling the senses, freeing oneself from all kinds of pomp and show associated with worship and offering prayers, and to forget one's ego. Ramakrishna was quickly able to win over all these. But when he tried to indulge in meditation sitting in a pose as instructed by Totapuri, the image of Mother Kali came before his closed eyes time and again. He, in a despaired manner, told Totapuri that everything is futile and it is impossible for him to raise his soul unconditionally to conjoin it with the Supreme Being.

When Totapuri heard there words from Ramakrishna, he glanced at the latter furiously and in a harsh tone said – "What? What did you say? You cannot do this? You will have to do this." Saying this, he took out a piece of mirror and placed it in front of Ramakrishna and asked him to concentrate on any single point on the mirror. Ramakrishna, later on recounting his experience said – "I employed all my strength in focusing my attention. When the image of the mother goddess came in front of my eyes I used my intellect to cut the image into two pieces. I was able to overcome the last and only hindrance and I was just lost in my samadhi." Samadhi reached as its peak and the soul merged with the supreme being. He experienced a complete void all over where there was no God and no worshipper. This unhindered samadhi is inexpressible, devoid of any emotion or language. To reach this situation, Totapuri spent 40 difficult years of his life. But Ramakrishna overcame every difficulties inherent in this samadhi within a day and emerged victorious in conjoining his soul with the *Param Brahma*. After this episode, Ramakrishna experienced that Goddess Kali is the supreme truth as well as the supreme truth as well as the supreme being. She is the beginning as well as the end and she is the zero which is above one and many. One day, he heard mother goddess saying – "I am the universal mother. I am the supreme being mentioned in the Vedanta. I am the soul of Upanishads. I am the supreme being who created a world of variety. You can attain me through devotion, knowledge and action. If you want to achieve perfection then come to me. Those who have attained complete samadhi, they have achieved it because of my will."

Totapuri who was a scholar in Vedanta and a great intellect could not accept the fact that God can be attained through the medium of love. He was all condemnation for Ramakrishna's act of prayers and worship and dances full of devotion. The manner in which he chanted the name of God in a weeping sound exuded sarcastic smile on Totapuri's face and he asked – "Are you begging or what?" But when Totapuri concentrated a bit he was swayed by the melody and sweetness of Ramakrishna's chantings of slokas. Tears of love filled Totapuri's eyes. Ramakrishna in a childish innocence smilingly said – "See, see you are also getting defeated by the indomitable power of strength." Totapuri was unable to say anything. Strength was taking control over his heart. He felt that both Shakti and Brahma were one and the same. He felt the impact of shakti everywhere in life. He took leave from his disciple, learned teacher and again embraced the path of wandering life.

In this way Totapuri's visit to Dakshineswar helped Ramakrishna achieve wholeness and perfection in the field of knowledge. He saw a singular image of God in everything in the universe. He realized that every religion has a single aim or end but the means or the ways are different. Now he wanted to study each religion in depth and follow the means mentioned in them to attain and behold the gods of those religions.

He first of all chose the path of Islam. Many Muslim saints frequented the Kali temple on daily basis. Rani Rasmani had constructed accommodation for Muslim travellers also along with low caste Hindu travellers beneath the temple premises. One day Ramakrishna came across a Muslim lying on the ground and engrossed in chanting praises of God. His countenance displayed a unique brightness of fulfillment and happiness as if he was enjoying a face to face conversation with God. His name was Govind

Rai. Ramakrishna took initiation in Islamic religion from that person. The worshipper of Goddess Kali, forgot to worship his mother Goddess. He did not perform any prayer or worship in the name of Goddess Kali and not even once the image of the Goddess came to her mind. He sat outside the temple, wearing Muslim outfit and kept on chanting the name of "Allah'. He was even ready to eat cow flesh which was a sin according to Hindu religious striptures. Seeing this, his disciples and well-wishers were totally scared and tried to discourage him from such kinds of acts. But Ramakrishna was least affected by them all. At last as a last resort they clandestinely made arrangement of a Brahmin cook to prepare food for Ramakrishna under the supervision of a Muslim cook. In this manner they saved Ramakrishna without any second thoughts, smoothly gave his body and soul to the religion of Islam. As he was totally engrossed in this heavenly journey, one day a fair, hardworking and serious looking fellow came in front of him. As he moved towards that radiant figure, he felt as if he had totally merged with it. After this celestial experience he was overwhelmed with excessive joy. He was blessed to have a glimpse of the God, the Allah of Musalman, who had all the qualities of the Supreme Being *(Brahma)* inherent in him.

After about 8 years of this experience, in 1874, Ramakrishna started his prayers in Christianity. A Hindu person read out the Bible for him. For the first time he came to know about Jesus Christ. His heart and soul were totally lost in the life story of Jesus Christ. One day, he was awaiting for a meeting with a very influential and wealthy person at his beautifully decorated office. A painting of Mother Mary holding the child Christ was hanging on the wall. His thirsty eyes fell on the painting and he felt that the painting has suddenly become lively. He felt that the austere shape of Jesus Christ came near him and merged inside his soul. The splendour of Jesus Christ spread all over Ramakrishna. Its impact was deeper than what he experienced while practicing Islam.

This unparallel brilliance totally enveloped Ramakrishna's soul. All other connections of life began to crumble. The thoughts and ideologies of Hinduism got lost somewhere. Ramakrishna experienced a fear deep within and his heart shivered. He was totally confounded and screamed – "Mother

Kali! What are you doing? Why don't you help me?" But all this to no avail. This new emotional experience had erased all his prior experiences. Now nobody else other than Jesus Christ had space left in his heart. For days together he did not feel like going to the Kali temple. He always remained immersed in thoughts relating to Jesus Christ and his thoughts. One day as he was strolling around in the garden at Dakshineswar, he saw a handsome looking person with brilliant eyes and a peaceful countenance walking towards him. Ramakrishna experienced a feeling of attraction towards him. Suddenly a sound echoed from within Ramakrishna: "Behold Jesus Christ, who in order to free the world from sins, fled his heart and suffered many hardships for the sake of love amongst humanity. This learned saint merged into union with the image of God. This is Jesus Christ – Incarnation of love." Then Jesus Christ hugged the priest of Dakshineswar and hid himself in his body. Once again Ramakrishna reveled in ecstacy. He had once again beheld the Supreme Being. Now he was sure that Jesus Christ is also an incarnation of God. Jesus Christ also began to be counted one among the class of Lord Buddha and Sri Krishna.

Once Ramakrishna told his disciples – "I have followed every religion – Hinduism, Islam, Christianity, etc. I have also closely followed different castes within Hinduism. I have found that God whom people belonging to different religions are trying to search through different means in one and the same. Wherever I put my glance I see Hindus, Muslims, Brahma Samajis, Vaishnavites and other religious followers fighting with one another. But they are unaware of the fact that one who is called Krishna, He himself is Shiv, He is the Supreme Power, He is Jesus Christ and He is Allah also. The one who is known by thousands of name is Ram also. A lake has banks on all sides and from one bank Hindus drown water in a kalash and calls it 'jal', from the other Muslims draw water in a bag made from hide and calls it 'pani', from the third, the Christians draw water and calls it 'water'. Do we think that 'water' or 'pani' are not 'jal'? How ironic it is? A single entity behind all the varied names and all are searching for that one entity. Every individual should follow the correct path. If he tries to know the Almighty with truth, then only he will be able to gain peace of mind. Then he will be able to meet the Supreme Being at all costs."

Swami Vivekanand: A Biography

When Ramakrishna found the same celestial personality and irrepressible strength inherent in gods worshipped by different religious entities, he felt inner peace of mind and his thirst subdued. But the rigorous methods of prayers and penance that he employed resulted in deterioration of his health. To regain his lost vigour and health he was compelled to take rest. Again he went back to his native village Kamarpukur for six to seven months.

A saint at heart, a yogi at mind, Ramakrishna, once at Kamarpukur, turned into an innocent child. The news of his becoming a recluse agitated the simple village folks. But when they found the old Gadadhar like behaviour in Ramakrishna, their happiness knew no bounds. Ramakrishna's wife Sharda Devi was now awaiting her fifteenth birthday. Hearing the arrival of Ramakrishna at Kamarpukur, her parents had sent her to Kamarpukur. Sharda Devi's pious soul was even more mature in comparison to her age. At the first glance itself, she was able to measure the great objective that Ramakrishna wanted to fulfill in his life. She took a firm decision that she would be instrumental in fulfilting her husband's objectives in life. An urge for an unconditional love towards husband devoid of any physical desires. But Ramakrishna was aware that being married, his wife had complete right on him. She can transform him according to her will. His mind was full of hesitation and apprehension and he wanted to free himself from them. Hence, one day he opened up his heart before his wife. His voice was distressed as he said, "Mother Kali had told me that she is present in every woman and hence, I behold every woman in the form of mother. And my feelings towards you is also that same. But we are united with each other, hence if you want to drag me to the worldly mundane life, I am ready to do so, at your will."

Sharda Devi was not surprised to hear all this. She was already aware of the thing that her husband presented before her. This trustworthy behaviour on the part of the husband won the wife's heart. She was the life long companion of her husband and hence, it is her duty to enlighten her husband's ambitious path at any cost whether through sacrifice or rigorous penance. Lost in all these thoughts, the young wife, in a sweet but confident voice replied – "Why should I drag you to worldly physical life?...I want to stay at your feet and serve you and learn more things from you."

Hearing such a mature reply from Sharda Devi, Ramakrishna was very happy. In his view the basis of love between husband-wife was not physical relationship. Marital love becomes meaningful only when two souls conjoin with each other. In this consummation of love there was no excitement nor any sorrows of separation, there was complete peaceful happiness. Such kind of joy was possible only for those who have encountered the real God. Both Ramakrishna and Sharda Devi have understood the permanence of this kind of love. During his stay at Kamarpukur, Ramakrishna taught Sharda Devi regarding household management, reading and writing and religious thoughts and philosophies. At the end of 1867 he returned back to Dakshineswar.

In the beginning of new year Ramakrishna set out on a pilgrimage. He was accompanied by Mathur Babu. Being the son-in-law of Rani Rasmani, Mathur Babu was the co-ordinator of the Kali temple. He had a great sense of affection towards Ramakrishna and both of them were like friends. He enjoyed his trip to Shivdham, Varanasi, Prayag (place were the Ganga and the Yamuna confluenced), Vrindavan that reverberated with the dance of Radha and Krishna. But the experience that he had while he was in Deoghar in Bihar had a great impact on him. He was greatly perturbed by the condition of Santhal inhabitants who were leading the life of poverty and hunger, as if on the brink of death. Moreover, the place was under the grip of dangerous disease which was spreading rapidly. Ramakrishna asked Mathur Babu to arrange food for these unfortunate lots. But Mathur Babu did not pay any heed to him. He clearly stated that he did not have the capability to care for the hardships of the whole world. Ramakrishna was very sad and he sat amidst those miserable people and began to cry. He said that he would not leave the place and that God will decide his fate like that of those hungry lots. At last, Mathur Babu was compelled to give in. Ramakrishna from the very beginning had the belief that God resides in every thing in this universe. Now his belief got reaffirmed that the service of poor is the most appropriate worship of God.

There, on the other hand, Sharda Devi had been spending a life of hardship at her parental home. Sufferings and discomfort had been her constant companions. She was humble and thoughtful hear and longed to do selfless service for the society. The news about Ramakrishna's penance and love for Mother Kali had spread all over the village of Jayaramvati. Ramakrishna's reclusive lifestyle and mad-man like behaviour was a constant topic of discussion. Sharda Devi also heard all these rumours. But she had complete trust on her husband. She expressed her desire to go to Dakshineswar and serve her husband.

When Sharda Devi's father came to know about his daughter's will, he began arrangements to send her to Dakshineswar. During those days there were no rail services from Jayaramwati to Dakshineswar. Women belonging to the higher strata of society used to travel in 'palkis' (hand drawn carriages). Since Sharda Devi belonged to a poor family, her father could not make any such arrangement for her. Hence, at last she along with her father travelled all the way from Jayaramvati to Dakshineswar on foot. They had completed only half the way of their journey that she became ill. Due to fever, they had to discontinue their journey. They were staying in an inn. As she was lying unconscious in the grip of fever. She dreamt that a dark complexioned woman had come to her and sat near her. The woman touched her body with her soft and cold hands and her temperature suddenly came down. Sharda asked the woman – 'From where have you come?' The woman answered – 'From Dakshineswar'. 'From Dakshineswar?' Sharda Devi exclaimed in surprise and said – "I also want to meet him and serve him for which I would like to go to Dakshineswar. But this fever has played havoc with all my desires."At this the woman said, "You would soon again regain your health and go to Dakshineswar and will meet him. I have left him there for your sake." Next day, in the morning Sharda Devi felt that her fever has gone and she was perfectly alright. This time her father made arrangements to transport his daughter on Palki and she resumed her journey and reached the door of her husband's residence at Dakshineswar.

The first phase of night in the month of Phagun. The winds of the spring season spread the fragrance of incense. The atmosphere was totally pure and dear. Palki was kept near the temple. A disciple came near the Palki and entered into short conversation with the girl's father and back inside his room. Sharda Devi's eyes reflected her curiosity and longingness to meet her husband. At the same time, somewhere deep in her heart, she had a sense of doubt too. She was not sure whether her husband would let her or accept her to serve him. Suddenly he saw two forms emerging from inside the temple and alighting the stairs. Due of them held a lamp and with its light fell on the other person's face and she identified him. That was her husband. Yes, that very same, simple and peaceful countenance. He was wearing a knee-length dhoti a part of which was hung on his shoulders covering his chest. He walked towards the Palki, paid respect to his father-in-law and looked towards his wife. But what is this?

His Sharda was beyond recognition. The severity of fever had withered her beautiful rose flower like face. Her face was looking pale as if devoid of blood. A mixed emotion of suffering and happiness on her face. Dusty untidy clothes on a tired body. Ramakrishna felt pity for her. In a sad voice he said – "Oh! You should have come here much earlier." Ramakrishna helped her out from the Palki and took her to his room. He himself took care of his wife and after some days Sharda Devi regained her health completely. Ramakrishna allotted his mother's room for her stay. Sharda Devi's father stayed at Dakshineswar for three-four days. When he got thoroughly assured about Ramakrishna's devotion towards his wife and that her daughter was happy with him, he returned back to Jayaramwati. Now Ramakrishna began to give religious education to his wife.

Once a strange kind of desire took birth in Ramakrishna's heart. It was in the year 1872 in the month of May. It was a full moon night. An auspicious time to offer worship to Kali. Ramakrishna was setting up a beautiful altar for Goddess Kali. His countenance and activities were completely like that of a true devotee. One of his disciples was assisting him in the arrangement for puja (worship). All the primary arrangements for the puja were made. He ordered his disciple to bring Sharda Devi. When Sharda Devi came near him, he signalled her to sit on the altar. She was surprised. He looked at her husband in a questioning manner. She felt that her husband was only physically present, his mind was wandering somewhere in the heavenly abode. Devotion spilled once from his half opened eyes as if he was beholding the real goddess Kali, not his wife. Sharda Devi understood her husband's mental feelings and as desired by her husband sat on the altar of worship. No sooner than she sat on the attar the magic of devotion enveloped her. In the beginning, she watched the manner of worship with full concentration but slowly she entered into meditation and sat on the altar ignorant of what was happening around. Ramakrishna was engrossed in offering flowers and prayers. This was not his wife Sharda Devi who was sitting before him. That was Mother Goddess Kali in real. With the help of another priest he made up Sharda Devi from head to tow and after chanting mantras for hours together he entered into complete meditation and lost physical consciousness. At this time both worshipped and worshipper had reached the heights of ultimate truth above the mundane world and was witnessing the eternal image of God. The next day Ramakrishna gained consciousness after much efforts.

One day, Sharda Devi, while serving at the feet of her husband in a simple straight forward manner asked him – "Tell me, what is my image in your eyes?" Soon came the reply, "A mother, who is being worshipped in a temple. I have always looked upon you as a lively symbol of Mother Kali." This answer on the part of his husband and his day to day behaviour turned her also into a recluse. Still those days of his stay with his wife are days of acid test for him. A worship, wherein there is no presence of woman to create hindrance will be successful at any cost. But it is very difficult as well as surprising to achieve victory in one's worship in the presence of a young woman who is your wife also. Ramakrishna always used to praise his wife – "After marriage I used to humbly pray goddess Kali to uproot all emotions of physical pleasure from Sharda Devi's heart. My association with her during this period has proved that my prayers have been accepted." Both husband and wife were totally immersed in the world of spirituality. Sharda Devi stayed with her husband at Dakshineswar for almost one-and-a-half years and then returned to Kamarpukur.

In the first half of nineteenth century the religious life of India was in a topsy-turvy state. The educated people were greatly influenced by the teachings of Raja Ram Mohan Rai (1772-1832) and his Brahma Samaj and Swami Dayanand Saraswati (1824-1853). The followers of Brahma Samaj advocated learning of Hindu religious books as well as of attaining western education. They believed in single God and were against idol worship. They were greatly influenced by Christianity. They wanted to improve Indian society on lines of western thoughts. They had realized that British rule had spread its roots all over the country, hence, we should take this opportunity of our association with them and improve our condition. On the other hand, the founder of Arya Samaj, Swami Dayanand Saraswati was strictly against English education and culture. After spending so many years in learning Vedas and Vedantas he came to the conclusion that there is only one God which is formless. Hence, it is futile to perform idol worship. On the basis of Vedas, he wanted to reawaken the lost glory of Hindu culture and civilization. He fully supported the Hindu theory of 'Karma' (action), safeguarding the purity of cows who were considered as mother and even accepted the four caste theory. Along with this, he raised voice against the evil practices that were existent in the then society.

But Ramakrishna's religious field was much wider and all embracing in comparison to theirs. He advocated equality of all religions. He believed in both the single God theory as well as multiple God theory. According to him, Ram, Rahim and Christ were the different images of a single entity. To attain them, one has to travel on the path of love and devotion. The contemporary Bangla society – whether educated or uneducated – both revered Ramakrishna and followed his principles. General public, yogis and saints, scholars who were influenced by western thoughts, philosophers who have learned Vedas and Vedantas in depth, renowned social workers, litteratures, and students raising voice against fundamentalists – every one came to Ramakrishna to seek advise and share their thoughts. Some major leaders of Brahma Samaj like Keshav Chandra Sen, famous novelist Bankim Chandra Chatterjee, popular playwright Girish Chandra Ghosh all revered him and considered him a great personality. How could a simple priest of a small village, who was totally unaware of western thoughts and ideals, attract such a huge crowd of intellectuals and scholars to him? This is a very significant question.

The then highly intellectual people considered Ramakrishna to be a symbol of national awakening on the basis of culture. Along with yoga and meditation, he practiced worship with devotion, unity of all religions and worship of men and women. Born in a Brahmin family, he grew up in a circumstances of fundamental beliefs still he was totally opposed to strong rituals like untouchability deep rooted in the society. Secondly, the intellectual society considered the secretive personality to be a rebellion against English culture and civilization. They had realized that they have unknowingly taken a turn towards a direction which is not good for themselves and for their country. They were engrossed in the western culture that they had lost their actual self, existence and Indianism. Ramakrishna's association with scholars like Keshav Chandra Sen and Girish Chandra Ghosh had made him aware of the mindset of contemporary educated Indian society. They discussed with him the new developments taking all over the world. Ramakrishna was least embarrassed about his ignorance regarding the outside world. He welcomed new thoughts and views too happily. This way he was able to change his view points. His quality, humility, large-heartedness, ability to assess good and evil was able to understand the problems faced by educated Indians and felt empathetic towards them. The bright side of his personality left his opponents armless and he gave necessary guidance in order to guide them. Ramakrishna was able to win over the heart and mind of the educated class because the foundation of their hope was very weak. There was a wide gulf between the society they were born in, grown up and the views they owned through their education. To solve a problem, they required a power which was an image of ancient and modern thoughts and excellent ideologies.

Ramakrishna's teachings were based on the ideology that by worshipping God in the traditional methodology one an attain God. Christians considered it a total superstition. For the national awakening that was taking birth during that period, this Indian ideology put forth by Ramakrishna became a major weapon. People understood the fact that they can very well stand tall in front of westerners and say to them that in Mutters pertaining to religious beliefs, they did not. require the help of westerners.

In this way slowly and gradually, Ramakrishna began to occupy space in the hearts and minds of both literate and illiterate Indians. Among his disciples there was one student studying in Calcutta University whose name was

Narendranath. For the first time when he visited Dakshineswar along with his friends to meet Ramakrishna, Ramakrishna had identified him to be a person totally different from other. He was in search of such a person. He was the right person who will prove to be instrumental in spreading his message to all corners of the world. And Ramakrishna's judgment about Narendranath proved to be true. The person who attracted the attention of a saint like Ramakrishna so strongly, later became world famous in the name of Swami Vivekanand. The entry of Narendranath in the life of Ramakrishna paved the way for a new history of India.

■■

Young Narendra
In Search of Truth

In the beginning of nineteenth century, a Dutt family in Calcutta was very famous due to their cultural affinity. The head of this family Shri Durgacharan Dutt followed the footstep of Siddharth after the birth of a son. After his father embraced Sannyasa, his son Vishwanath Dutt grew up in the shadow of his mother. He later on became a clerk in the Calcutta High Court. He accumulated wealth to a great extent. His family led a very luxurious life. His overspending ways gained him the title a of royal spender. No poor person who came to his door returned empty handed. He had great love for music. His religious thoughts never accepted the fundamentalism inherent in Hinduism. His study of Bible gave him complete knowledge regarding Christianity. He was well aware of the contemporary educated society. His wife Bhuvaneswari Devi was a simple hearted and religious woman. Her wisdom, dexterity in work and patient behaviour had made her lovable to all.

For days together no son was born to Vishwanath – Bhuvaneswari couple. She was very keen to have a son. Bhuvaneswari was an ardent devotee of Lord Shiva and during her worship she always sought God to bless her with a son. She desired to visit the Lord Vishwesvar temple at Varanasi and make offerings. But during those days there were no proper modes of transportation and it was not easy to travel all the way from Calcutta to Varanasi especially for ladies. Hence she wrote to one of her relatives staying in Kashi to make offerings to Vishwanath on her behalf and seek blessings for a son. The female relative was too happy to fulfill Bhuvaneswari Devi's wishes. When the offering was made to Lord Vishwanath at Kashi, Bhuvaneswari Devi was fully sure and confident that her prayers have been accepted and she will get the desired result at an appropriate time. Once she spent the entire day in worshipping and offering prayers to Lord Shiva. At night she dreamt that the lord of the universe. Lord Shiva has taken the form of a child and got conceived in her womb. When she woke up she was not able to believe what she had dreamt. Still her inner heart was happy and she again began worshipping Lord Shiva. Deep within the heart she heard an inner voice which kept on saying that her dream will prove to be true. After a few months on January 12, 1863, early morning on a Monday she gave birth to a handsome boy baby. Bhuvaneswari Devi's dream had taken a realistic form. That day was the festival of Makar Sankranti – the holy festival of Hindus. Innumerable men and women were indulged in offering prayers to Lord Shiva after taking a holy dip in the Ganges. It seemed as if their subconscious mind was calling the name of this child form of Shiva. Considering the new born to be a blessing from Lord Shiva, the mother named the child Vireswar. Later on Vireswar's name changed to Narendranath. But mother called him 'Nitu' (short form of Vireswar).

During his childhood days, Narendra was a very naughty child. People were fed up of his naughtiness. All efforts were made to instill a sense of discipline but all became futile. At last Bhuvaneswari Devi adopted a strange methodology. Whenever he used to indulge in irritating pranks, she made him stand outside the house and chanting 'Shiv-Shiv' threw cold water on him and used to tell him that if he does not improve his behaviour then he won't be a favourite with Lord Shiva and he will never call him to Mount Kailasha. After this for some times he used to become very calm and peaceful. Sometimes the mother used to be get so fed up by his naughty acts that she would say – 'I had sought a son from Lord Shiva and he has sent his demon for me'.

Young Narendra had a special kind of attraction towards saintly people. Whenever a saintly person paid a visit to his home he used to be very excited and never let them go back empty handed. One day, he was playing outside in front of his home, when a sadhu came. Narendra was wearing a new 'dhoti' at that time, he gifted the sadhu his dhoti itself. The sadhu tied it around his head and went away. When he was questioned he gave the reply that, "Sadhu asked for alms and I gave him my cloth." Then onwards whenever any saintly persons came near the door, Narendra was kept locked inside his room. But it was of no use. He threw the articles kept inside his room one by one through the window. What kind of prank was this? Narendra's elder sisters were very much perturbed by his naughtiness. Whenever they chased him to catch and punish him he would hide himself in an open drain and would teasingly ask them how they will touch him. A mark of naughty act during his childhood remained on his body throughout his life. Once, while fighting with his friends he fell down from the Varandah and his forehead got against a rock. The wound bled and the cut mark remained on his forehead above his right eye till his death.

Narendra had a great attraction towards birds and animals. He used to play with the cows and calves at his home. In addition to mainah, parrot, pigeon, peacock he had pet animals like goats, monkeys and horses. He behaved with his servants in a friendly manner. He used to be attracted towards those who behaved with him in a loving manner.

It is well said that the first school of children is their mother's laps. This was true with Narendra also. His early education took place in that very school. His mother, Bhuvaneswari Devi used to tell him stories from Ramayana and Mahabharata. She was the one who taught him the Bangla and English alphabets. The story of Ramayana had a special impact on young Narendra. Wherever people organized the reading of Ramayana, he would attend it at all cost. If he missed any such opportunity he used to feel restless. The episode pertaining to Hanuman was more interesting to him. Once he heard that Hanuman spent a whole night in a banana grove in Lanka and relished the bananas. After hearing the story he went and spent the whole night in a banana grove to have a glimpse of Hanuman eating bananas. One day Narendra bought an idol of Lord Rama and Mother Sita and brought it home. Almost everyday while offering prayers and worshipping the idol he would enter into meditation. Once Narendra along with his friend took the idol and went to the topmost floor of the house. Both the friends closed the door from inside and decorated the idol with flowers and leaves and sat in meditation. There a search had begun for Narendra. Everybody searched inside-outside, garden and grove but failed to find Narendra out. At last, they went to the roof top and found the room locked from inside. They tried to make open the door by knocking it hard but no sound could be heard from inside. At last they broke the door open. As they stepped inside, they saw Narendra and his friend sitting in meditation in front of the decorated idol of Ram and Sita unaware of anything.

To concentrate his mind and enter into meditation was the favorite game of Narendra. He always played this game of entering into meditation with his friends. For other children it was a sheer game but Narendra's heart filled with the light of spiritual ecstasy after this. Once Narendra was busy playing this game of meditation with his friends in an open field. All of them stood with closed eyes and were trying to concentrate. Suddenly a thick and long snake came wriggling in front of them. Those children who after closing their eyes, could not concentrate and enter into a meditative state, saw the snake and ran away from the place. They stood at a distance and called Narendra and tried to make him alert about the presence of snake near him. But he remained engrossed in deep meditation. People saw that the snake was moving towards Narendra. It came near to him and stopped near him for a while and returned back. People were greatly surprised by this incident. When his parents asked him why he did not run away on being warned by his friends he answered – "I was not aware of the snake or anything else. Being in the meditative state I was in a total rapture indulged in this game of meditation time and again. He kept the idol of Sita-Ram in a very safe manner as he loved it more than his life. One day, he overheard an argument between two people regarding marriage. One was talking against marriage in very tough terms. He was presenting a dark picture of marital life stating it to be full of hardships and hindrances. After hearing this, Narendra was greatly hurt, one question kept on haunting his mind – "If marriage is so bad then why did Lord Ram marry Sita?" His soft heart experienced a kind of shivering. He threw away the idol of Sita Ram which was so dear to him. In place of that he brought home an idol of Lord Shiva.

At night when he lied down to sleep and closed his eyes he used to see a strange kind of light between his bow-like eyebrows. The colour of that strange light kept on changing and after some time it took a big circular form. In the end Narendra felt as if his whole body has taken a bath in that

Swami Vivekanand: A Biography

light. He experienced this almost every day. While sleeping, both during day and night, this process took place in his brain. Considering it to be natural, he did not discuss it with anyone during childhood. After many days, he took up the topic with his classmate – "Do you see a light between your eyebrows when you go to sleep at night?" When his friend replied in negative, Narendra said – "I see a light, you also try to think. Do not sleep as soon as you go on to bed. Remain awake for sometime then you will see it surely." After some years, his teacher also asked him the same question – 'Narendra, my son, do you see a light when you go for sleep." People guessed that Narendra's all these experiences were related to his past birth. After some time, this process kept on reducing gradually but not completely.

At the age of six, he was sent to school for primary education. Students belonging to different classes, caste and creed took admission in schools. Narendra mingled with every student within a short span of time. In the company of bad children he learnt bad behaviour and foul language. This kind of behaviour alerted his parents and they withdrew him from that school. A teacher was arranged to teach Narendra at home itself. Some more children from the neighbourhood joined with him. Narendra was an intelligent child. When other children were learning alphabets, Narendra had already started learning to read and write. His memory power was par excellent.

Whatever the teacher spoke, it got embedded in his brain. For him, it was sufficient to read a book only once. With just one reading he was able to tell what he learnt. At the age of 7, he memorized the Sanskrit grammar book titled 'Mugdaboth' and even many questions from 'Ramayana' and 'Mahabharata'. Once some saints came to his house reciting hymns from 'Ramayana' for alms. Narendra pointed out mistakes from the verses sung by them. People were surprised to see the young genius.

From his childhood, Narendra had leadership qualities inherent in him. He had many friends. He played different kinds of games with them. One of his favourite games was enacting the scene of a king and his courtiers. On the topmost stair of the verandah he himself sat and that was the throne of the king. Nobody else could take up the role of the king in his presence. After taking his seat on the throne he himself chose his queen, adviser, cashier, army general and other subordinates of the king. After making the appointments, he allotted them stairs in the declining order of their position. In this court he meted out law and justice on the basis of appropriate arguments as per rationale and honour of the king. This game was building up the foundation of the greater and more significant role he had to play in the future days to come.

People belonging to different castes came to meet Narendra's father at home. Separate smoking pipes (Hukkas) were kept for different castes. A separate hukka was kept for Muslims also. Narendra was not able to understand the reason behind this differentiation. After all what was the secret or a logic behind this? Why cannot people belonging to one caste eat or drink or exchange their hukkas with people belonging to other caste. If I go against this rule what will happen? This question kept on haunting Narendra. At last he firmly took up the decision that he will chart out a different way for himself. One day turn by turn, he took puff from each hukka even the one meant for Muslims. What a surprise? Nothing happened. Later on, describing about the incident he said – "I am unable to understand, what difference will it make?"

In the year 1870, when Narendra was seven years old, he went to the institute of Pt. Ishwar Chandra Vidyasagar to get education. Within a very short span of time the teachers at the institute realized the unearthly talent inherent in him. But Narendra was still so naughty that he was not very keen about his studies. He had great attraction towards games. When he was engrossed in games he forgot everything else. He was very competent in all sorts of games. He liked toy vehicles and motorized toys. During the half time breaks in school he was the one to run towards the ground and reach there first. He was the one who interfered and tackled the quarrels between his friends during the game. He overlooked his life to safeguard the interest of students belonging to the weaker section. His practice and knowledge in wrestling helped him to a great extent in such kind of situations. Even inside the classroom, he indulged in childish pranks, as a result of which other children were unable to concentrate on what the teacher had been teaching. In the classroom, he discussed about games and told stories from the 'Ramayana' and 'Mahabharata' to other students. Whenever any kind of debate arose among students, he used to be the winner due to his argumentative power.

Once the teacher was giving lecture on certain topic. Narendra was talking to children sitting near him regarding some game. The teacher noticed it and became angry. He asked Narendra and his group who were discursing questions pertaining to the topic he had been teaching. Every other student except Narendra stood silent. Narendra stood up and answered every question correctly. Narendra's memory power was indeed very sharp. Even while talking he had the capacity to retain what was being taught in his memory. The teacher once again tried to find out the real culprit who had been talking during his lecture. All the students pointed towards Narendra but the teacher could not be convinced. He asked all the students who were indulged in talking to stand up. All of them stood up and Narendra was also one among them. The teacher said – "You need not stand up." But Narendra replied – "I am supposed to standup because I was also talking" and he continued standing along with others.

During the days of his study, his teachers informed him that he has to study English too. Narendra was not ready for this because English was a foreign language and what was the need to learn it. When teachers made learning of English compulsory, he approached his parents crying. After much reasoning and convincing by his parents he got ready to learn English. Once the subject began to be taught to Narendra, he surprised his teachers and parents alike. Within a few months of studying English he made a marked improvement in the language.

Narendra remained always in the front fighting against injustice. There was a teacher in his school who was very cruel in nature. One day he gave a harsh punishment to a boy who did not minor prank. The helpless boy kept on weeping and the teacher kept on beating him. Narendra saw the scene and was taken aback. His whole body shivered with both fear and anger. He lost his patience and began to laugh loudly. The teacher when saw Narendra laughing, he turned all the more furious. He pulled Narendra's ear and began beating him with no sense of remorse. Narendra's crying and wailing had no effect on the teacher. His ear was pulled in such a manner that blood began to ooze out. But the teacher was least perturbed or moved. Narendra pained and angered and released himself from the teacher's clutches and shouted – "Don't pull my ears. Who are you to beat me? Look! Don't even try to touch me again." Fortunately, Ishwar Chandra Vidyasagar came that way. Narendra kept on weeping and related the whole incident to him. Vidyasagar took Narendra to his office and tried to pacify him. When he returned back and his mother saw this and heard about the whole incident, she restrained him from going to school. But in spite of the wound in his ear, still afresh, he went to school daily without fail. After this incident, a strict restriction was imposed on physical punishment in that school.

Narendra was least affected by any fear factor or superstitious beliefs. He applied his reasoning power and tried to dig out the fact behind any such beliefs before believing them or following them blindly. There stood a huge tree near Narendra's house on which beautiful and attractive flowers bloomed. Narendra's favourite pastime was to climb that tree. He always used to climb the tree not just to pluck the flowers but to play a strange game. Plucking the flowers was a mere excuse. In fact the extra energy that his body possessed did not let him sit idle. He used to climb the tree and entangle both his legs crossing then across the branch and hung himself upside down swinging himself in that position. He enjoyed swinging in this manner.

But his old father, who watched Narendra's this act, sitting on the verandah did not like this. In order to divert his attention from such a risky game, he told Narendra that a demon resides in that tree and the demon throttles the throat of those who climbs it and hence Narendra should never climb the tree. Narendra listened to his Baba with utmost humility but it did not have any impact on him. In the absence of Baba he continued with his endeavour of climbing on the tree and hanging upside down and swinging to his heart's fill. His other friends who also heard about the presence of demon on the tree, never ever again climbed it and discouraged Narendra also from doing so. But Narendra laughed and said – "You all are donkeys. If what Baba said was true, the demon would have throttled my neck much before." This very Narendra when became world famous in as Swami Vivekanand while addressing his audience always used to say – *"Never believe anything considering it to be something you have read in a book. Never believe anything considering someone have told it to you. You search for the truth yourself and find it out."*

Narendra was irritant towards a stagnant lifestyle. He formed a drama troupe along with his friends. Almost always they enacted plays in a big room at his house. It was but natural that they talked loudly and shouted during the course of the play. Narendra's uncle disliked all this. He went to the room where the play was in progress and destroyed the stage and other articles and strictly ordered them not to create any noise. After this, as per the instructions of Narendra his friends set up a gym in front of his house. There they exercised and indulged in all sorts of games. Narendra's uncle felt disturbed by this gym also. Hence, within a few days he destroyed the gym also. But Narendra was not at all discouraged by all this. Soon he along with his friends opened a gym at his friend's place. There they attained proficiency in many games such as fighting with long sticks, wrestling, boxing, etc. All this helped him in achieving first position in various competitions.

Once Narendra and his friends together planned to set up a huge swing in a ground. Articles were accumulated for it. Narendra and his friends were totally engrossed in accomplishing their plan. A British navigator, seeing the children trying to set up the swing came to them and extended his assistance. But as luck would have it, as they were trying to set the structure of the swing in place, the Englishman received serious injuries. People saw that he had lost his consciousness. Those were the days when Britishers enjoyed domination and Indians remained afraid of English. Except for Narendra and his two to three friends, rest of them disappeared from the scene. People were afraid that the navigator had died. But in such a dangerous situation, Narendra commanded the situation. He was a person who was deeply concerned about others and always ready to help out others. He instantly tore his dhoti and tied it around the wound and sprinkled water on his face to regain back his consciousness. After a while, the navigator regained his consciousness. Then he took him to the nearby rest house and let him sleep. Doctor was also called to check the patient. Narendra served the person for almost a week and he fully regained back his health. When he became hale and hearty,

Narendra gifted him a purse along with some money which he and his friends had pooled in.

Narendra was the favourite of his family as well as neighbours. All had equal right on his love and friendship. He never showed any distinction between rich or poor, higher caste or lower caste. He behaved with all of them equally. He was always ready to help those in distress. He was also famous among the female community. As per the age he addressed them as aunt or sister as appropriate.

At school, he sometimes indulged in a special kind of pastime. He collected money from his friends and added more amount of money from his own pocket and indulged in cooking meals. Their preparations somehow turn out to be very delicious and tasty. Later all of them together relished the food cooked by them in a playful manner.

Narendra used to lead his friends in every game. Many a time he used to organize trips and take his friends to the famous tourist spots in Calcutta such as museums, zoo, gardens, the Ganges etc. Once, he along with his friend, after one such trip was returning home by a boat. Suddenly one of his friends took ill and vomitted inside the boat. The boatman became furious and asked the children to clean the boat. But the children bluntly refused. When the boat approached the bank, he did not allow any of them to alight from the boat and kept on scolding them and using foul languages. Narendra somehow managed to escape from the boat without being noticed by the boatman. He saw two British soldiers loitering near the river bank. He approached them and in whatever English that he could speak, he recounted the whole tale to them. The soldiers listened to young Narendra affectionately and accompanied him to the spot where the boat was ashore. Seeing the British soldiers with Narendra, the boatman was intimidated and before they said anything he let the children alight from the boat without any delay or arguments. The soldiers were pleased with the courageousness of young Narendra. They invited Narendra to attend a play. Narendra thanked them for the invitation and expressed his inability to attend the same.

In this context, another incident is worth mentioning. Narendra was about eleven years old. At that time, son of the late British Emperor Edward VII, Prince of Wales, had been on a visit to India. His ship stopped at the Calcutta port.

Many people used to go to the port to have a glimpse of the ship. For this they had to take prior permission of the chief officer. Narendra had gone to meet the chief officer along with a request application and considering him a child, the sentry did not allow him to go inside. Narendra did not lose his heart. He noticed that people were going upstairs through the middle staircase towards the British officer's room. Narendra strolled around the premises of the building and chalked out a plan to reach that particular room. There was a narrow staircase at the backside of the building. He went upstairs through that staircase and found himself in front of the officer's room. He was very happy and stood behind the people standing in a queue. When his term came the officer kept his application and issued him the entry pass. He returned back from the officer's room through the main gate. The sentry recognized him when he came out and asked in surprised manner – "How did you get inside?" Narendra smiled and answered – "I am a magician."

As days passed by his childish pranks kept on diminishing. After the age of eleven to twelve years, his interest was diverted towards reading books, magazines and daily newspapers. After reading those articles he put forth his views before his friends.

Narendra inherited love for music from his father. His father had a special love for music. Once after listening to a rendition by his friend, he expressed his opinion regarding music.. "Music does not take birth with mere 'Ragas' and 'Talas'. It is an expression of emotion. Is it so that only a song sung in proper notes and beats gets recognition? The emotion inherent in the song awakens the innermost feeling of the singer. The lyrics should be suitably measured along with beats and notes. A song whose inner emotion does not spring from within the heart of the singer is not music.

In 1877, when Narendra was 14 years old, his father got transferred to Raipur, Madhya Pradesh. After some days, his father called over the family to Raipur. Narendra was entrusted the task of safe and secure transportation of the family members to Raipur. During those days, there were not direct trams to Raipur from Calcutta. From Nagpur, he made arrangement for an one-cart. The cart passed through lonely stretches and thick jungles. The climate was very pleasant and the nature spread a heavenly beauty all around. Below the vast stretch of sky this journey on the cart was an interesting and novel experience for young Narendra. He did not experience any tiredness or boredom during the journey. He was so engrossed in enjoying the beauty of nature that he lost his senses. He felt ecstatic, looking at the nature's bliss once their cart passed through an extremely beautiful place. On the way on both sides there were the Vindhya mountain ranges, huge trees laden with flower borne creepers. Every corner of Narendra's heart was overwhelmed with this sight. He closed his eyes and lied down on the cart. The celestial beauty of nature seeped deep into his heart through his eyes that he remained lost in that and for hours together he was unaware of the physical realities. He began to sink in a special kind of godly luminosity. He wanted to remain in that state for more time period. When the mystical frame of mind he was in disappeared, the ox cart had covered a pretty good distance.

When Narendra reached Raipur, he realized that his studies were likely to run into bad weather because there was no school in Raipur. Hence, he spent most of his time in the company of his father as he assisted him in his work. His father entered into conversation with him and Narendra had great interest in such kinds of conversations. The father made proper assessment of his son's brain and mental abilities and provided the necessary nutritious food required for its nurture and development. Vishwanath strongly believed that the main objective of education is to strengthen one's thinking capability and thereby formation of a point of view. Narendra's brain had always been busy thinking and assessing different topics. Intellectuals and scholarly people assembled at Vishwanath Dutt's house on regular basis. Narendra listened to their debates and took part in them. Within a few days people recognized his sharp intellect. Wherever he failed to gain intellectual superiority, his ego remained perturbed and restive. In such circumstances he displayed aggression and went to any extent to prove his point as correct. In order to calm him down people sometimes even sought him. He had such a towering personality that people were compelled to bow down before him. In Raipur, he chose friends in a careful manner. He chose only those boys as his friends, who possessed excellent intellectual abilities and who had the capability to enter into a debate with him. He was least

Swami Vivekanand: A Biography

interested in becoming friends with boys who were dumb and readily accepted his superiority and followed him.

Since his childhood, Narendra believed in the philosophy of rebirth. Many a time, he discussed the concept of rebirths and past births with his friends. During his childhood days whenever he saw some special objects or met some special persons, he felt as if he had got across them ever before. He tried to recollect when and where he had seen that object or met that person before but he was not able to find any outcome. All his efforts to tap his memory proves to be a fortune. Later on he described above it – "Once at a particular place I was talking with my friends. Suddenly we began to discuss on certain topic and its memory flashed over my mind. I felt that in the past also I had discussed the topic in that very place, in that very house, with the very same persons he had been talking then. I felt that it was because of the concept of rebirths or previous births. But when I again thought about it I felt that no conclusion fits appropriate in this context. Now I believe that before my birth, I had a glance of those things or people at one time or the other – with whom I am related to in this birth. These kind of memories have been coming to my mind throughout my life."

In Raipur, though Narendra did not attend any school or attain any formal education. His mental development took place constantly, rather faster. He never felt bored with his life. After almost two years, in 1879 Vishwanath Dutt returned back to Calcutta with his family. Narendra was once again admitted to school. School authorities did not express any opposition in granting him admission because they were well aware of Narendra's mental ability. Just after one year, Narendra had to appeal for the entrance exam. Hence, he had to finish three years study in one year. Narendra concentrated on his work. The lessons taught in the classroom did not satisfy his thirst for knowledge. In addition to reading his course books, he was busy reading books pertaining to English and Bangla literature and books on Indian history. As a result, his normal class syllabus received a setback. He could not properly concentrate on the books referred for the exams. Later on he said – "Just two days before the entrance exam I realized that I have a very little knowledge about 'Geometry'. Then I spent the whole night learning the subject. In this way, within a short span of 24 hours I achieved proficiency in four books pertaining to 'Geometry'." He appeared for the entrance exam and passed out in first class. That year, from the school, Narendra was the only student who attained first class. His father was very proud of his son. As a gift for his achievement he gifted his son a wrist watch.

During the whole year, while studying books pertaining to different subjects, Narendra had searched out a new methodology of learning. He easily understood the view point of the author of the book without reading each line. As a result of profuse reading, he had attained a special kind of capability – just by reading the first and last line of any quotation or passage he understood the meaning of the entire paragraph. Later on, his grasping power became so sharp that by reading the first and last line of a page he understood the whole meaning or concept. Talking about this strange mental ability he said – "Whenever the author, with the help of argument or counter argument, tries to clarify his point and for which he takes four, five or even more pages, then by reading two-three lines in between I used to understand his argument and bent of mind."

This way Narendra took a very little time in completing reading of even hefty books. By total concentration of mind he was able to develop this unusual brain power. It was because of this that within a short span of his life he attained such a deep knowledge in every subject that even elderly scholars were surprised.

Narendra's school life had come to an end. His childhood gave way to youthful seriousness. His strong physique reflected his youthful exuberance. After completing his school education, he studied in Presidency College for a year. Then he joined the Scottish Church College run by Scottish priests. While appearing for the entrance exam, he underwent great hardship to complete three years study in one year, which had a negative impact on his health. He began to remain ill and unwell. Hence, he was sent to Gaya for change of weather. There he stayed for few months to regain his health and returned back to Calcutta to appear for the first college exams. He stood second in the exam.

Narendra never kept himself within the bounds of school or college syllabi. His mind wandered freely in the arena of knowledge. During the first two years in college he made a thorough study of all major books pertaining to western rationale thinking. During last two years in college he read the western philosophical thoughts and the ancient as well as modern histories of different European countries. He had complete confidence on his sharp memory power. Hence, he kept aside his college books and studied them only two days before the exam.

Only one month was left for the graduation exam and it was at that time that Narendra thought about his books pertaining to college books. Suddenly he realized that he had not read the book 'History of Europe' authored by Greene which was recommended for them. Unfortunately, he did not have the book in his possession. Later when he somehow managed to grab a copy of the book, he took a firm decision that it won't come out of his room unless and until he attains complete proficiency in the book. Within three days, he mastered the book totally. This way before the exams, he kept himself awake throughout the night, taking tea and coffee and kept on studying continuously.

At last, the last day of graduation examination came. But that day a strange kind of thought overtook his mind. The meaningless endeavour behind college examination kept on haunting him. How are these exams connected to one's life? What is the significance of these exams? Is the sole aim of our life to follow the exams? A kind of duel was going on deep inside Narendra's heart – whether to appear for the exam or not? After sometimes the storm going on in his mind became calm and an echo came out from deep within – 'No'. "The knowledge which is not instrumental in revealing the truth of life is no knowledge. The truth of life gets its illumination from the love for God." Narendra was standing in front of the door of the hostel room of one of his classmates. His enchanted vision was trying to look beyond its capacity, searching to sight something invisible. The strings of his heart gave out the musical beats of God's greatness. He began to sing a devotional song in praise of the Almighty, Omnipresent God. The lyrics of the devotional song was springing out deep from his soul. The voice was full of emotions. He was so engrossed and emotional that he was not aware of his environment or circumstances nor time. He continued with his singing till 9 o'clock. His classmates sensed something mysterious in his changed behavioural pattern. After much apprehension they reminded him about the exam that was to begin after sometimes. But their attempt proved to be futile. Narendra did not pay any heed to what his friends had said. That day, his friends could not achieve success in taking him to the examination hall. But the next day, his friends compelled him to appear for the exam. Somehow Narendra answered the questions in the question paper. In this way, Narendra completed his graduation examination unwillingly. Still then when the results came he had passed the exam with flying colours.

The senior lecturers of Narendra's college were greatly influenced with the personality of Narendra. These lecturers whether Indian or British, all had witnessed at one point of time or the other, his mental ability which was beyond any comparison. The Principal of the college Mr. Hasty said, "Narendra was indeed a talented student. I have travelled far and wide, but I have not seen anyone as talented as this boy, not even among the students of philosophy, in German University. He will of course, make his life invincible." Narendra trusted everything in life only after weighing and balancing it on the basis of rational thinking. If he had begun discussion on any topic during the study time then even during the game time debate on the topic continued. He was full of unlimited energy. It seemed as if his strength and energy never diminished. He had innumerable topics to discuss over. According to one of Narendra's friends, "It gave enjoyment to listen to Narendra's talking. His voice had the melody of music. To hear him speak we began discussion on any topic. His thoughts were very basic and at the same time interesting. He was a admirer of Napoleon and he used to convince others that in order to accomplish a great mission a follower need to be ready to obey the directions of the leader in the same manner as Marshal obeyed his emperor's order."

Narendra was in possession of a sentimental heart along with a powerful mind. He had deep rooted love for his friends. He was always ready to help his friends physically, mentally and financially. Once during the last exam of the graduate level examination, one of his classmates didn't have money to deposit as examination fee. The boy was hailing from a poor background. When Narendra came to know about it he tried to find out a way to help him out. At last, he came to know that with the chairperson's will a fee concession can be considered and thereby his friend can appear for the exam without remitting the fees. Hence, he wrote an application seeking to consider fee concession. But it proved to be futile. No result came out. But Narendra was not the kind of person who easily accepted failure. One day when the chairman came out of his room, Narendra confronted him and discussed the problem with him and somehow convinced him and sought permission to appear for the exam.

He was an epitome of truth and purity from the very beginning. This invaluable quality, he inherited from his mother. His mother had always been very cautious regarding her responsibilities. This kind of dedication towards duties was the result of purity of heart. Purity of heart is an unlimited thing. With its help one can reach God – it is able to redeem the soul from its ignorance. In the future Narendra felt that without the purity of heart and soul he cannot make any achievement in his spiritual endeavours. In his view, purity was not an inactive opposition towards evil but a very bright spiritual power.

In the first half of his university life, Narendra's father took up the question of marriage with him. Many fathers were ready to accept Narendra as their prospective son in-law. The girls family were even ready to take up the expenses of his higher education abroad. His father became all the more attracted towards such kinds of attractive dowry offers. But when Narendra came to know about this, his soul revolted against such endeavours. He felt so miserable that he said – "Where are you people dragging me? After entering into a wedlock, everything will be over for me. From his childhood days, he was against the institution of marriage. His ambition was to enter into the field of social service. Still he was not willing to hurt the sentiments of his parents by employing any arguments against the topic. A deep thought into the issue made him feel that there was some disturbance somewhere in his mind – a sort of duel, on the issue of marriage.

When he went to sleep two kinds of images came in front of his mind's eye alternatively. The first image was that of worldliness – a beautiful, well mannered wife and a family, honour, glory. The second image was that of spirituality – a denouncer who has won over every desires existent in the world, has attained the experience of the almighty supreme being, has realized the truth of life, has spent his whole night in the jungles or the valleys in between high mountains and has left the responsibility of providing him with food for existence to fate.

Narendra was a cunning painter of both these images. During his peaceful times he kept them before him and filled colours of his choice in them. Both the pictures have different attractions of their own. In both the pictures the role of Narendra was unimitable. But due to some unknown reasons as he thought about it again and again, the depth he entered, the role in the second image – role of a saint, appealed him. An image of a person with a materialistic bent of mind kept on diminishing and finally got disappeared.

As fate would have it, whenever talks regarding Narendra's marriage began there occurred some kind of problem or other within the family and the discussion regarding his marriage got stalled. And Narendra experienced a sense of relief due to such kind of developments.

With his university life coming to an end his spiritual journey began. His eyes were keen to see the realities hidden behind nature. His heart was impatient to find the truth of the world. The temporary happiness of life never had any kind of attraction for him. Outwardly he wore a simple look and led a very normal life, but deep inside his objective was something else which kept on poking him saying that you are different from others and your life-path is unique. He was confident that with ardent devotion he will be able to attain his objective. In the beginning, he was attracted towards Brahma Samaj. At Brahma Samaj, they discussed ideology and philosophy, they taught the formless image of the supreme being through Upanishad and gave the feeling of its existence. They prayed the purity of mind and heart. People felt satisfied with it. But Narendra's doubts never got satisfied. He always remained thirsty to gain more and more knowledge. One thing always haunted him – if no power in the world could show him the image of the Supreme Being then everything is futile. The whole philosophy, Vedanta, prayers and worship – nothing has any significance. The Supreme Being who has created this universe, even if it is without form, if present anywhere, could be seen if one has true feeling of devotion in his heart. God will surely listen to the prayer of his devotee. Slowly this thinking took deep roots within Narendra's mind that without experiencing envision of the Supreme Being life is but meaningless.

Swami Vivekanand: A Biography

During those days among the leaders of Brahma Samaj, Maharishi Devendranath Thakur had achieved great renown. During his past years of life, he was leading a life of recluse in a house boat in the river Ganges. Narendra had met him once earlier along with his friends. During his last days of study in university, when Narendra felt a heartfelt desire to attain knowledge regarding the truth of existence, he decided to meet Maharishi once again.

Narendra went to the boat where Maharishi stayed alone. His heart was burning with the desire to envision the truth. Maharishi was surprised to find Narendra in his boat at an odd time and that too behaving in an impatient and overtly emotional manner. Narendra could not maintain his calm before Maharishi and the question darts out from his mouth – "Sir, have you seen God?" Maharishi's both calm eyes rested on this young fellow for a while. He was unable to give a proper answer. He just said, "My dear son, you have been blessed with the eyes of a saint." Narendra's face got withered. He was very sad. But he was not the one to sit quiet. His curious mind was not ready to sit idle. If Maharishi Devendranath Thakur had not seen God then what, he will meet some other spiritual men of renown and will witness the ultimate truth. Was it possible that all these godly and saintly men belonging to various sects have not seen the God almighty? No, it is not at all possible.

Many such emotions and questions came to Narendra's mind. He met many spiritual saints belonging to various sects. But his thirst for attaining a glimpse of truth remained unquenched. One day, a past incident got enlivened in front of his eyes. That day his English lecturer in college was absent. Hence, the principal of the institute, Prof. William Hasty who himself was a renowned scholar of English literature came to Narendra's class to deliver a lecture on English literature. Explaining the poem 'Excursion' written by the great English Romantic poet William Wordsworth, he said that enjoying the beauty of the nature, he reaches such a blissful state that he loses his conscious and achieves an ecstatic feeling. The students were not able to understand it. The principal once again explained it – "When one meditates on any particular thing with a pure mind he experiences this kind of feeling, though such kinds of people are very rare these days. I have seen only one person who have attained this rapturous feeling of mind and that is Shri Ramakrishna Paramahansa of Dakshineswar. If you go there and see on your own, then only you will be able to understand it."

Now Narendra remembered that a few months ago there was a meeting at the residence of Surendranath's friend and there Shri Ramakrishna was also invited. On the occasion, Narendra had sung a Bhajan and Ramakrishna had listened to it very intently. He was overwhelmed with emotions, had praised Narendra's song and had invited him to Dakshineswar. After hearing what the Professor had said, Narendra decided, "I have to go to Dakshineswar definitely and meet Ramakrishna who knows, by meeting him I will be able to attain peace." He decided to go to Dakshineswar along with his friend Surendranath. This visit opened a new chapter in Narendra's life.

■■

The Disciple Meets His Guru

The temple of Goddess Kali at Dakshineswar. The main door of the hallway was open. On reaching the gate itself one is able to identify the lean figure of Shri Ramakrishna. In the centre of the room sitting on a mat he was exchanging thoughts and views with his students. They heard the footsteps of people coming to them. Some students entered into the hall from the western door. One among them was a graduate from Calcutta University. Ramakrishna identified him at the very first sight. He had seen this student earlier at a meeting and had listened to him singing. He beheld the young man without even winking his eyes for a long time. Yes, the same image, normal height, fair complexion with a healthy body, innocent countenance with two shining but calm eyes. He seemed careless about his clothes and body as if he had no concern with the physical world. Eyes were lost somewhere as if he was entangled in the thoughts of the inner world more than the outside one. The friend who was accompanying him seemed to be a normal young man fascinated by and attracted towards the materialistic pleasures of the world.

Ramakrishna was surprised. In a city like Calcutta with a materialistic outlook, how such an unworldly personality came out. But his minute vision was well aware of the fact that this was the very person whom his soul was searching. He was to become the closest of his disciples and will eternalize his teachings. Ramakrishna signalled the quests to sit on the mat spread in front of him. Narendra sat in front of Ramakrishna along with his friends. Ramakrishna asked him to sing a song. He sung a devotional song in an extremely emotional and touching manner. Hearing the song, Ramakrishna felt extremely emotional. He could not control himself and slowly relapsed into rapturous feeling as if he was not having any knowledge regarding the outside world.

As soon as the song ended his rapture broke. He suddenly stood up and took hold of young Narendra's hand and took him to the verandah towards the north and closed the door. Narendra could not understand this sudden behaviour on the part of Ramakrishna. He thought that Ramakrishna would give him some secret advise, but nothing as such happened. Something extremely opposite took place. Ramakrishna displayed the personality of an ignorant child. He took hold of Narendra's hand and tears came rolling down his eyes incessantly, his throat was heavy and in a very loving manner he addressed Narendra as if he had an intimate relationship with him, "Oh Narendra, you have exercised great delay in coming over here. How could you be so cruel and keep me waiting for you for such a long time? I am almost fed up of listening to people talking about worldly and materialistic things. I am very keen to lighten up my mind by expressing my innate experiences to someone who would understand them and praise them. He was weeping as he said all these things. Then he became calm and silent for a moment and with folded hands began to say – "Lord, you are the incarnation of Narayan, you are an ancient saint who has taken birth on this earth to dominate the sufferings and hardships of mankind." In an emotional outburst he kept on mumbling such things.

In Narendra's view, Ramakrishna was a spiritual fellow. He was a saintly fellow who had won control over all his senses. But that day Narendra saw an altogether different picture of Ramakrishna – a person overwhelmed with emotions. Narendra was shocked by his behaviour. "Who is this man whom I have come all long to meet? He is definitely a mad person. I am just the son of Vishwanath and still he is addressing me like this." But he did not say anything to Ramakrishna. He just listened to what Ramakrishna was saying. After sometime Ramakrishna returned back to his room in a hurried manner as if he had recollected something that he had forgotten. After a while when he returned from his room he carried some sweetmeats and butter in his hands. He made Narendra eat the sweets with his own hands. He was not at all bothered about Narendra's taste and Narendra kept on eating it in a mechanical manner and kept on saying in a futile manner – "Please give the sweets to me, I will eat them with my friends." But Ramakrishna did not pay any heed to what he said. He simply said, "They will also get something behind. When the sweets finished he again took hold of Narendra's hand and said, "Promise me that you will return back to me all alone very soon." Narendra could not bluntly refuse this loving wish expressed by Ramakrishna. He was compelled to say 'yes'.

After this, Ramakrishna led Narendra to the main hall. There Narendra's friends and many others were waiting for Ramakrishna. As he stepped into the halt addressing those who were sitting there he said, "Look, how Narendra's face is glowing with the divine glory of the goddess of knowledge, Goddess Saraswati. Hearing these words, those who were present there began to behold Narendra in a surprised manner. Turning towards Narendra, Ramakrishna again asked, "Do you see a light in between your eyebrows before going to sleep?" Narendra answered in affirmative. Ramakrishna again said, "Yes, it is true. It is a meditative capability one gains by birth."

When Ramakrishna took his seat, Narendra also sat down. A duel was going on in Narendra's mind as he was trying to form an opinion about Ramakrishna. His conversation, behaviour and personality was something that Narendra was not able to assess properly. He sat and perceived Ramakrishna's behaviour and conversational style. Different kinds of thoughts kept on haunting his mind. Ramakrishna's interaction, behaviour and activity with others had nothing abnormal in them, everything looked normal. He was recounting his spiritual experiences and meditative position, etc. There was a deep connection between his words and life. It seemed as if with his great efforts he had bridged the gap between himself and God. In the eyes of others, he was an incarnation of God in the image of human being.

Narendra was analyzing the personality of Ramakrishna in his mind. The language used by Ramakrishna was very simple—easy to comprehend by the common people. The tough and secretive views of spirituality were described by him in a quite simple language. He had all the necessary qualifications of a teacher. Narendra thought that he has reached the right place and approached the right person. He was not wrong in coming there. One question was constantly haunting Narendra and making him heart impatient. And when he got an opportunity he shot the question, "Sir, have you seen the God?"

Ramakrishna instantly answered in a normal manner, "Yes I see him in quite the same manner as I see you now. In fact, you can experience God even more intensely than this. Anybody can see him, can talk with him in the same manner as I am talking to you now. But who wants to have that experience or value it. People spent tonnes of tears for money, wealth and their children but nobody has got time for God. If somebody cries for Him with a true heart, He will be surely attained. Narendra felt excited. His surprised eyes just rested on Ramakrishna. His heart was lost to some kind of magical chants. After so many days he had come across a person who had the guts to say that he had seen God. Narendra was sure that whatever Ramakrishna had said was based on his personal experiences. But he felt very strange about Ramakrishna's behaviour with him. In the end, Narendra came to the conclusion that Ramakrishna has some kind of madness. At the same time he readily accepted the fact that Ramakrishna was a great saint. Narendra kept on thinking that Ramakrishna might be an excited person, but how many people are lucky to have an opportunity to see God and experience that feeling to have a direct contact with God. This person inspite of his madness is a true saint and a pure soul. Just because of this he deserves the honour and reverence of the entire humanity. With all these contradictory thoughts in his mind, Narendra paid obeisance to Ramakrishna and took leave from him to return back to Calcutta.

Once back in Calcutta, Narendra concentrated on his studies. He had almost forgotten the promise he had made to Ramakrishna that he will soon return to Dakshineswar. But how long could have his sub conscious mind let him sit peacefully? Almost after a month, one day he had an innate desire to go to Dakshineswar. He went to Dakshineswar temple on feet. First time, he had gone there on vehicle. This time he did not even think of a vehicle. An invisible force was pulling him towards Dakshineswar. The journey from Calcutta to Dakshineswar was very long. He kept on walking and walking. At last, by the time he reached Dakshineswar his whole body was tired. His feet automatically moved towards the room occupied by Ramakrishna.

In the room, Ramakrishna was sitting on a small cot. No sooner he saw Narendra than his face brightened up with happiness. He lovingly called Narendra near him and made

Swami Vivekanand: A Biography

him sit near his feet. Within a moment, he was overwhelmed with emotions. He mumbled something on his own and slowly drew himself to Narendra and began looking at him with total concentration. Narendra was a bit embarrassed by this act on the part of Ramakrishna as he thought perhaps he might behave in a somewhat strange manner. But he did not speak a word with Narendra. He just reclined his right leg on Narendra's body. This touch was quite wondrous. Narendra experienced a strange kind of feeling. He saw that the walls of the room and other articles began to rotate at a fast speed and in the end dissolved into a vacuum. The whole world along with his personality and ego merged with the mysterious zero. He was overcome with fear and was afraid that his end was near. But with the dissolution of his personality, this kind of feeling kept on reducing. He could not exercise control over himself at any cost. At last, he cried out, "What are you doing to me? My parents are there at my home." At this, Ramakrishna began to laugh loudly and patting on his chest – "Let us leave if for now. You will learn everything with time." Surprisingly, the moment he said so, the strange feeling he had been experiencing disappeared all of a sudden. He regained back his previous self. His innermost self became calm. The things belonging to the outside world returned back to its original position and became still. All this happened within a second's time. But this incident kept on haunting his mind for quite sometime.

Narendra was wonderstruck with the incident. But now his heart had become very weak. Ramakrishna had now become a sort of enigmatic personality for him. Narendra kept on thinking – "After all what does this man has in his possession, what kind of magic he has that he totally enticed me? Is it the kind of magic that makes a person unconscious? It effects a weak mind. But my mind is very strong and stable. I am not going to be affected by it. Then what a man he is? Tell now I have been considering him to be a fake fellow. But he has some strange power which has tantalized me for even a second." His intellect was unable to provide a rational answer. He took a strong resolve that he would not be influenced by Ramakrishna. Narendra was thinking all these when Ramakrishna assumed the image he had shown in the first instance of their meeting. He took the form of an affectionate motherly figure. He behaved with Narendra in such a manner as if he was meeting a close relative or a friend after a long gap. He was not satisfied with the hospitality he extended to Narendra. He wanted to do something more and more. This kind of affectionate and caring attitude on the part of Ramakrishna attracted Narendra towards him. At last in the evening when he took his leave, his brightened up face suddenly lost its glow. He was in despair. Then after some thoughts, he extracted a promise from Narendra to return back soon and gave him permission to leave.

Narendra reached back Calcutta late in the night. The promise he had given to Ramakrishna kept on coming back to his mind. He could not keep himself away from Ramakrishna for too long. An inner desire to meet Ramakrishna kept on creeping him and he could not control himself any more. Again after three to four days, he went to Dakshineswar. He felt that unwillingly he was getting drawn towards that saint in Dakshineswar.

From cultured and spirit was point of view, Ramakrishna was the epitome of ancient India. He had attained God or established a direct contact with God by exercising severe penance and unwavering faith. Goddess Kali could not withstand his painful wail and emotional cry and was compelled to appear before him. But a person like Narendra who had developed his thoughts on the basis of modern education was not ready to accept anything relating to God without proper and satisfactory rationale. His mind stormed with many doubtful thoughts. His mind was totally agitated. He experienced peace of mind in the company of Ramakrishna. He felt that solution for all the doubts that enveloped his mind, was there only in the hands of Ramakrishna. Meditation and renunciation, became the two most significant objectives of his life. He dreamt of freeing his soul in the company of Ramakrishna. Slowly and gradually, a deep rooted belief was taking shape in his heart that the role of a teacher was significant in every person's life. Before meeting Ramakrishna, he could not have imagined that this much of spiritual power could be inherent in a person like Ramakrishna and he will deeply influence his strong mind. But with just meetings with Ramakrishna, his whole world had changed.

This time Narendra took a strong resolve before going to Dakshineswar that he will not let his mind swayed by the touch of Ramakrishna. Ramakrishna, on the other hand, could not control his happiness at seeing Narendra before him for the third time. He along with Narendra strolled towards the garden adjacent to the temple. After walking there for a while both of them sat on a mounted platform. They kept on talking with each other and in the course of conversation Ramakrishna entered into a trance and in that very condition he touched Narendra minutely. Despite his preparedness and resolve, Narendra could not exercise control over himself. The kind of joy he experienced with that simple touch was beyond description and slowly he began to lose his consciousness. He felt as if he had dissolved himself into a big void. After sometime when he regained back his consciousness, he saw that Ramakrishna was patting on his shoulders. Narendra could not recollect anything that had happened a while ago. When Narendra was in the unconscious situation, Ramakrishna hypnotized him and heard everything about Narendra in his own word.

During such resolute trance, Ramakrishna experienced a heavenly feeling. The whole world dissolved like bubbles of water in front of his eyes. Past, present and future – all the three ages got enlivened before his eyes. In this way, he was aware that many of his devotees had already taken birth or will be born in this universe who will later assist him in his mission. With the help of his yogic power, he had known everything regarding Narendra, his previous birth, even before meeting him. Whatever Narendra told about himself about his present and previous birth in his semi conscious state. Ramakrishna was already aware of them. Many days before he met Narendra for the first time, Ramakrishna felt as if a ball of light from Varanasi moving across the sky at a great speed, like an arrow, towards Calcutta. At that very moment he cried out in happiness – "God heard my prayers. My person will definitely come to me." Ramakrishna was totally sure that his representative was indeed Narendra himself and will be instrumental in fulfilling his objectives. This person will remain with him as a true devotee always.

Narendra was not aware as to what all he blurted out Ramakrishna in his unconscious state. In his previous birth, he was a perfect saint complete in all respects. Ramakrishna thought that Narendra should not be informed about his greatness of previous birth so early. He had before him a whole world for action. India, our motherland needs his service, the world requires his light when he takes up his responsibilities as a Karma yogi – a person who works for the society in a selfless manner – then he will realize his internal yogic powers. Hence, Ramakrishna kept all those things relating to his previous life away from his subconscious mind.

Narendra was an atheist from the very beginning. He used to make fun of the prohibitions mentioned in religious texts and theologies. He was not ready to suppress the doubts and inquisitiveness with the arguments given in those religious texts. His logical intellect always remained alert and logically reasoned out things before arriving at a conclusion. Ramakrishna was well aware of Narendra's best of mind — his hesitation to be drawn towards Ramakrishna, his own faith and keenness to find out the truth on his own. It was perhaps due to this that Ramakrishna had a kind of attraction towards Narendra.

Ramakrishna's love for Narendra was so deep that whenever Narendra's visit to Dakshineswar got delayed, he used to become impatient and longed for Narendra's presence near him. He used to cry like a child and pray before the idol of Goddess Kali with folded hands to enable an early meeting with Narendra. He remained restive till Narendra came over to Dakshineswar to meet him. Narendra and his other disciples were not able to assess the condition of Ramakrishna. Many a time, Narendra considered him to be a psychic but when he saw the immense love showered on him by Ramakrishna he used to feel overwhelmed with emotions. This irrepressible love on the part of Ramakrishna was responsible for exercising control over a literal thinker like Narendra. Once Narendra had made it clear that – "It is his love towards me that is binding me to him." Once Narendra did not pay visit to Ramakrishna for a long time. Ramakrishna was becoming impatient at this. When his two disciples Ram Dayal and Babu Ram came to meet him, he told them – "Naren has not come to meet me since long. I am longing to see him. Will you ask him to come here at the earliest possible? Hope you won't forget?" Both of them had planned to spend the night there itself and around 11 o'clock at night they went to sleep at their respective places. Just after midnight, Ramakrishna went to the place where Ram Dayal was sleeping with a cloth under his arms and called Ram Dayal, "Have you slept?" Hearing Ramakrishna's voice he woke up saying "No sir."

"Look here, please go and ask Naren to come quickly. I am having a feeling as if somebody is twisting my throat like a towel", Ramakrishna said this twisting the cloth he was holding in his hands. Ram Dayal was well aware of Ramakrishna's habits. He somehow assured his teacher that he will make all arrangements of calling Narendra at the earliest. That night Ramakrishna remained disturbed. All the other students who were present there were surprised by such a behaviour on the part of Ramakrishna.

Once Ramakrishna was praising the qualities of Naren sitting with other disciples. As he was talking he turned very emotional and expressed his keenness to meet Naren. He could not suppress his desire and began to wail loudly. He went out to the verandah and began to shout – "Oh goddess! Oh mother, I cannot live without seeing him." After sometime he returned to his room where his disciples were sitting and said, "I am crying for him, but Naren has not come. My heart is longing and weeping. I am suffering greatly being not able to see him but he is least bothered about me." Instinctively he again went out and came inside at a great speed saying – "An old fellow is undergoing all these suffering for the sake of a young boy. He is weeping and wailing. What will people think about me?" You people are my own. Hence, I am not ashamed to accept my weakness in front of you people. But what will others think? They will think that I have no control over myself and my emotions." Later when Narendra came to Dakshineswar, his joy knew no bounds.

Once, Ramakrishna's devotees were celebrating the birthday of their Guru and till afternoon when his favourite disciple did not turn up, he kept on asking others about Naren. At last, when Narendra reached there and came in front of him to pay obeisance, while he was blessing him by bowing once his shoulders he entered into a trance at the very next moment. When he regained back his original self he began to enquire about Narendra and made him sit near him and entered into a conversation with him and lovingly made him eat with his own hands. On seeing Narendra he used to become so overwhelmed with emotions that he used to go into a trance. Once Narendra paid visit to Dakshineswar after so many days. He had just reached near the banks of river Ganges and Ramakrishna heard about his arrival from someone and he himself went towards the banks on the river to welcome him. On seeing Narendra, he felt so satisfied and joyous that he began to touch his face livingly and began to chant mantras from the Vedas and entered into a trance. During the five years of his education, Narendra came to meet his teacher once or twice in a week. In the last few years, he was so much involved in familial problems that he was not able to pay as much visits as he desired to make at Dakshineswar. During those days he exercised restraint and patience thinking that it is good that Narendra has not come otherwise I would have experienced turmoil. Whenever he comes here it becomes a long issue.

Ramakrishna used to call Narendra and some of his chosen disciples as 'Nityasidh' (those who are perfect by birth). In his opinion, they are complete in all respects in their own rights. They require no teaching or learning. Whatever they learn while in contact with their teachers that turns out to be for the good of the society, the good of the world not of themselves.

Ramakrishna was never hesitant to shower praises on Narendra in front of others. Praises more than due sometimes have its negative impact. The one who is being praised becomes egotistic but it is true in case of common men. Narendra was much above all the complexities associated with a normal human being and Ramakrishna was well aware of this. Once Ramakrishna was conversing with some members of Brahma Samaj and its leader Keshav Chandra Sen and Vijay Krishna Goswami. Narendra was also present there. While talking, once he looked towards Keshav Chandra, once towards Vijay Krishna and once towards Narendra. His sharp glance was able to look across the present, beyond their present into their future. The image of Narendra's bright future enlivened before Ramakrishna's mind's eye. He glanced at him lovingly. When the meeting with the members of Brahma Samaj concluded, he turned towards his disciples and said, "If Keshav possesses one point which has made him great and renowned, then Narendra has in his possession eighteen points. I have seen the light of knowledge equivalent to an earthern lamp inherent in Keshav and Vijay but Narendra has in him knowledge equivalent to that of a sun which is destroying the leftovers of ignorance and disillusionment." Narendra heard all this but it had no respect on him. If somebody else would have been in his place, he would have puffed up with pride.

In comparison to Keshav Chandra and Vijay Krishna he considered himself nothing. He opposed Ramakrishna's views saying:– "Oh great soul, why are you speaking such things? People would consider you mad. How could you compare world renowned Keshav and sent Vijay Krishna with a mere student like me? Please do not say such things again." Hearing this, Ramakrishna felt happy from within and said, "I am helpless. Do you think those were my words. Mother Goddess has shown me all these. I have just repeated them. She does not show anything other than truth."

Narendra was least affected by the future forecast made about him by goddess kali. He expressed his doubts before Ramakrishna quite openly.

Who knows that the words of the Goddess are indeed of the mother goddess Kali or your mind's imagination. If I had been in your place, I would have considered it an outcome of sheer and pure imagination. Western scientific knowledge and philosophy have already proved these things beyond doubt that our senses deceive us sometimes and where there is personal leniency such kind of illusions are quite common. You love me and want me to become a great person, hence this kind of imagination took birth in your brains. It is but quite natural." Narendra's such kinds of reaction and views some times hurt Ramakrishna but this time he was in a state of extreme spirituality. Hence, he ignored Narendra's views. Earlier whenever Narendra made comments of such types, he used to go in front of Goddess Kali's idol for a judgment in this regard and the mother God used to pacify him saying – "Why are you bothered about what he says? After sometimes he himself will accept the truth. The words of praise bestowed by the Guru has its magical effect. It is a chant which not only enamours the person but takes the person to the ultimate level of confidence."

Ramakrishna's frequent showers of praise on Narendra had this very outcome. It gave him great support and was a source of inspiration throughout his life when Narendra, in the image of Swami Vivekanand had been spreading the great message throughout the world, the words of his Guru were charging his courage, strength and confidence. But in the beginning Narendra was unable to assess the value of his Guru's words.

Sometimes Narendra used to get fed up of Ramakrishna's overt show of love. He disliked all this. Once he said, "I never hesitated using strong words against showing blind love towards me. Once I warned him by saying that if he keeps on thinking about me then he will become like me as it happened in the ancient story of King Bharat who was so attached to his pet deer that while on his death bed he could not think of any one else and as a result he was born a deer in his next birth." At this Ramakrishna said, "What you are saying is quite true. What if I am reborn as Narendra. I cannot even think of getting separated from you. The very thought is unbearable for me. Sad and despaired, he went to Kali temple. After sometimes he returned back with a smile on his face and said, "You are a cruel fellow. Now I won't listen to you any more. Mother says that she is projecting God in you. That is way I love you. The day I cease to find God in you, I won't be able to withstand you." Thus in a single stroke Ramakrishna disproved or defeated the reasonings put forth by Narendra. In Ramakrishna's view, his love towards Narendra was much above human relations and human emotions.

Once, as usual, Narendra did not pay visit to Dakshineswar for many days. Ramakrishna became impatient after waiting for him. He sent a representative to bring Narendra but due to some reason he could not come. At this, Ramakrishna himself set off on a journey to Calcutta to meet his favourite disciple. He knew that Narendra was busy in some work associated with Brahma Samaj. Ramakrishna himself had a kind of fascination for Brahma Samaj. Many a time he used to attend the meetings of Brahma Samaj. Hence, he was well acquainted with many important leaders of Brahma Samaj. When Ramakrishna reached the office of Brahma Samaj, the evening programme were going on. In a semi conscious state his footsteps moved towards the place where his young disciple was present. Seeing the newly arrived guest in such a condition the person who was preaching, stopped his preaching. All the people present there slowly began to assemble around Ramakrishna. But he was east aware or bothered about the people surrounding him.

Swami Vivekanand: A Biography

His concentration was elsewhere. His longing eyes were searching for some one. When he reached in front of Narendra his consciousness regarding the outside world got completely erased. The members of Brahma Samaj were greatly perturbed by Ramakrishna's arrival. Some of them did not like his presence there because two of their senior members – Keshav Chandra and Vijay Krishna were slowly changing their views as a result of the influence of Ramakrishna and they were afraid that his presence there would influence other members also. In order to calm down the stir they switched off the lights. This instead of solving the problem increased the difficulty. People began to shove and push others in a bid to go out from the hall. Narendra understood the reason behind Ramakrishna's visit. He was furious at Ramakrishna for creating such an awkward situation. He thought that what will the people present in the meeting think of Ramakrishna's behaviour with him. What meaning will they assume. Still he sympathized with Ramakrishna and came forward to extend him a helping hand. With great care he lead Ramakrishna out of the hall through the crowd and later on accompanied him to Dakshineswar. When Ramakrishna regained back his consciousness he scolded him for what he had done. But all this had no effect on Ramakrishna. Yes, he became fascinated by Narendra's caring and affection.

Such kind of incident took place once again. Narendra had not come to Dakshineswar for long. In Calcutta, he was sitting in his room talking with his friends. Suddenly he heard someone calling him. All his friends stood up in surprise. Narendra ran downstairs and came out and to his surprise found his Guru standing in front. His face was sorrowful and his eyes were filled with tears. He in a very sad tone said, "Naren, Why did you not come to me all these days!" The disciple saw an innocent child in his teacher. Narendra took Ramakrishna to his room. Ramakrishna had brought some sweets along with him. He started making Narendra eat those sweets with his own hands. His countenance displayed a divine shine. His half opened eyes looked like waves of love – "Sing any of your songs to me." Narendra set his Tanpura and began rendering a song on the mother goddess. Hearing the song Ramakrishna lost his consciousness. His heart went into another world free from worldly happiness and sorrows.

Ramakrishna was totally sure that in the image of Narendra, Lord Shiva was standing in front of him. At the time Narendra was about to be born he had a strange dream, which had been re-emphasizing his belief. With Narendra, his relationship was that of a teacher and student but still it was somewhat different from other teachers and students. During the ancient days, serving of the Guru by the disciple was mandatory. That disciple's life was thought to be pure who served his Guru whole heartedly. In those days, massaging the Guru's feet, fanning him, etc were the usual jobs of the disciples. Narendra used to extend his hands to serve his Guru in a very humble manner but Ramakrishna instantly refused any sort of such service. 'Taking service from Lord Shiva! It is a shame.' Ramakrishna used to say, "Narendra is different from others and hence, his way is also different." Once Ramakrishna had told Narendra, "See Lord Shiva is inherent in you and Shakti is inherent in me and both of them are same." Narendra who was just on the threshold of youth at that time was unable to comprehend the meaning of what his Guru was saying.

From the very beginning Ramakrishna was aware that Narendra was 'Nityasiddh' and 'Dhyansiddh'. He knew that the great source of fire was inherent inside Narendra, so powerful and bright, which was able to destroy any kind of physical or mental feelings within seconds. He can never be attracted by any kind of illusions. Devotees used to make offerings of dry fruits, fruits and sweets at the temple of Goddess Kali. Ramakrishna gave instructions to his other disciples to keep them safe. He accepts those offerings only when he becomes totally sure that the one who had made those offerings have made it without any selfish interest and has pure feelings. Otherwise he gave orders to reject or dispose off those offerings.

But no such prohibitions were applicable on Narendra. Whenever he came to Dakshineswar he was compelled to eat them because he was not going to be affected by pure or impure food. Whenever Narendra's visit to Dakshineswar got delayed he used to send all these eatables to Calcutta for Naren. Once, after intaking meals from the eating place, Narendra straightaway came to Ramakrishna and said, "Sir today I have partook the food which is prohibited." Thinking that whatever Narendra is talking about is devoid of any obstinacy. Ramakrishna said in a calm tone, "You are not going to be affected by it. Even if a person's thoughts are fully concentrated on the almighty God inspite of consuming cow or pig meat, then these are no less than 'Satvik' (pure) food. But even the vegetables partook by a person totally indulged in worldliness are not less than the meat of cow or pig. Even if you have consumed prohibited food, that is not going to make any difference as far as I am concerned. Indicating towards other students he further said, "But had any of them done such an act, I would not have stood even a touch on their part." In that age of rigid thoughts and beliefs, such kind of courageous works on the part of a Brahmin priest surprised Narendra. How Ramakrishna assessed the character of strangers was a mystery for Narendra. He used to think – Is it true that the character of a strange fellow becomes evident to his Guru from the form or shape of that fellow? Earlier Narendra was in a state of disbelief. Many a time he made an enquiry about the people who made offerings and found that the statement made by his Guru was indeed true. Wonderstruck he used to exclaim, "What a surprising person he is! How does he assess the things going on in others brain. His purity is beyond my level of understanding.

Narendra was a prominent member of Brahma Samaj. It was not so that being a Brahma Samaj member he did not believe in formal image of God. Whatever things or thoughts that was beyond his rationale, he never believed in it and his heart did not accept it. He expected such sort of behaviour from others also. One of his friends who was also a follower of Brahma Samaj – Rakhal when came into contact with Ramakrishna was greatly impressed with him. Seeing the idol of Goddess Kali he became very emotional. Many a time he stood in front of the idol of the goddess with folded hands. This kind of behaviour on the part of Rakhal was against the principles of Brahma Samaj. Once Narendra saw him doing so and he scolded him for that. Rakhal was a very humble fellow. He could not argue with Narendra about his views regarding the philosophy of formal worship. After the incident, he began to stay away from Narendra and avoided him.

Once Ramakrishna convinced Narendra that Rakhal believed in idol worship and hence, Narendra should not become an obstructive force in his worship of God. He also made him understand about the difficulties of worshipping a formless God in the beginning. Whosoever wants to worship in whatever ways should be let free to do so. After this Narendra never interfered with Rakhal's religious choice. But during those days, Narendra displayed a strange kind of obstinacy. Whatever he thought or whatever path he had chosen, he considered them to be correct. He was in the clutches of such a thought. Ramakrishna sometimes used to softly condemn his views but in spite of the arguments put forth by him he never used to accept it. Once Ramakrishna became furious and questioned him, "If you do not have faith in my mother, why you are here?" Narendra replied courageously – "Is it so that I have come here just to accept 'Her'?" Guru replies, "Okay. In future, you will not only believe in my mother Goddess but will also shed tears for her sake." Then he put his glance on other students and said, "This boy does not believe in formal image of God and he considers my spiritual ecstasies as my mental illusions. But his boy who has pure emotions inherent in him is a very good boy. He never believes in anything without proper evidence. He has learnt many things and his mind is filled with his own intellectual thinking and decisions."

One of the major topics of argument between Ramakrishna and Narendra used to be the content of Radha-Krishna's *Ras Lila* in religious texts. Earlier, Narendra had his doubts on its historical evidence. He considered the relationship between Radha and Krishna as unethical and improper. Ramakrishna employed various methods to make him understand the concept of their relationship but Narendra could not be convinced nor was he able to change his views. At last, Ramakrishna said, "I agree that historically Radha and Krishna have no base or existence and their story is a mere imagination of some God lover. But why are you ignoring the emotional rapture or curiosity on the part of Radha and her friends to meet the supreme one. Why are you sticking yourself to their expression of love? It would be natural for you to see their longingness. Consider this imagination, this dream as something divine and heavenly."

Ramakrishna used to feel happy with his arguments with Narendra on religious Mutters. He knew that Narendra won't accept anything without proper rationale. There was no dearth of learning or knowledge in Narendra. What he lacked was a teacher who was capable of quenching his curiosities or uprooting his doubts. Ramakrishna's thoughts, his expressions, his whole and many more things related to him used to make Narendra curious and doubtful. Many questions relating to Ramakrishna haunted his mind and made him excited. Narendra's intellectual conflict kept on increasing. But Ramakrishna solved his problems patiently and slowly.

Ramakrishna, first of all, tried to teach him the Advaita Vedanta and he asked Narednra to read some chapters from Ashtavakra code and Advaita philosophy. Narendra, who was greatly influenced by the principles of Brahma Samaj and his soul became agitated after reading Advaita philosophy. He could not believe the philosophy. He used to try out – "This is all degradation of God because there is no difference between this philosophy and atheism. There is no sin in this world than equalling ourselves to the creator of this universe. I am God, you are God, all the things made by God are God, what more rubbish is possible than such a thought. All those eminent people who have written all these might be mad people. Hearing such rebellious words on the part of Narendra, Ramakrishna said, "It is alright if you do not accept the thoughts of these saints but how can you scold them or limit the unlimited power or existence of God. Worship God in its image of truth. Believe in any of God's form which. He shows in your heart." But Narendra could not get influenced. He went out of Ramakrishna's room in an excited manner and began to say, "This water jug is God, this glass is 'God and we people are also God. Nothing more improper is possible in this world than such a thought. His words were filled with satire, disbelief and anger. Ramakrishna was lying in his room in a semi conscious state and hearing his laugh, he came out from his room and touching Narendra asked, "What topic you are talking about?"

Saying this, he once again entered into Samadhi. That touch had a great impact on Narendra – "That touch by Gurudev on that day brought about surprising changes in my mind. I was enlightened by the knowledge that there is nothing else in this universe other than God. I envisioned it very clearly but I remained silent about it thinking that whether the thought is permanent or not. But this understanding did not end in a day. Even after reaching home, I felt the presence of God in everything. When I sat down to have my meals, but each and everything – the food, the plate, the person who was serving the food and I myself were nothing but an extension of God. Hearing my mother I was surprised. She said, "Why are you sitting idle, finish your food." Then I again began to eat. But always while eating, while sleeping, while going to college I saw motor vehicles moving across, but I did not feel like giving way to them. I felt that both the motor vehicle and I have been made with the same ingredients. I did not experience any life in my body parts. I felt as if they were devoid of any strength. I found no appeal for food. I felt as if someone else was eating. Sometimes while in the process of eating I used to lay down and suddenly got up and sat to continue with my eating. As a result of this for some days I took more food than usual but it did not do any harm to me. My mother became worried by my behaviour and said that something was definitely wrong with me. She felt afraid that I may not stay alive for more days. When this situation changed I felt the world to be a dreamland. While strolling on the Cornwallis Square, I sometimes hit my head on the iron wall just to check whether it was a dream or a reality. This situation continued for some days. When I regained back my health, then the thought came to me that perhaps I was having a glimpse of Advaita. Then it dawned upon me that the words given in religious texts were not false. After this, I never considered the philosophy of Advaita to be wrong.

The way Ramakrishna's teaching methodology was unique, similarly Narendra's technique of acquiring knowledge was also beyond comparison. Slowly in Narendra's life faith overcame doubt, concentration took the place of duel, joy in place of tension and light in place of darkness. The differences that existed in the world disappeared. Now he was convinced that everything was singular built from one basic being. Ramakrishna always used to tell Narendra to thoroughly check and test his Godly experiences. In fact, he himself was ready to face any test. He used to say, "In the manner, the person who collects change properly tests the coins, similarly you can also test me. Till the time you test me you should not accept me." Once when Narendra came to Dakshineswar and went to Gurudev's room, he found the room vacant. The room was found vacant. Later on, he was informed that Ramakrishna had gone to Calcutta. Narendra quickly hid a coin under Gurudev's Muttress and went for meditation at Panchvati. After sometimes Ramakrishna returned back to Dakshineswar. He went to his room and sat on the bed. Unknowingly, he came into touch with the coin hidden by Narendra. With that mere touch he experienced great pain and began to write in pain. Narendra had, by then, returned back from Panchvati and was watching Gurudev's reaction towards the coin in a clandestine manner. Seeing Ramakrishna's sufferings, another disciple went near his bed and spread the bed sheet in a proper manner and as he did so a one rupee coin dropped on the ground. Narendra went out of the room without uttering a word. But Ramakrishna soon realized that Narendra was testing him. Ramakrishna felt satisfied at the fact that Narendra accepted anything after proper test and trial. On Narendra's view, the teacher should also be subjected to a trial before acceptance.

Ramakrishna also subjected Narendra to many such tests. Once Ramakrishna conducted a bodily checkup o۱ Narendra and said, "Your physical condition is quite perfect. Only I find one fault in you and that is you snore while sleeping and in the opinion of saintly men such kind of men die young." Once Ramakrishna took a harsh test of Narendra. Although Ramakrishna nursed deep love for Narendra in his heart and a mere glimpse of Narendra from a distance took him to a state of ecstasy, once when Narendra came to Dakshineswar to meet him he just ignored him and did not speak a word to him. Narendra thought that his Guru was lost in some other world hence, he went out, sat near other disciples and entered into a conversation with them. Then he heard Ramakrishna's voice talking to somebody.

Narendra once again went to Ramakrishna's room but he once again turned away his face and did not reciprocate to his obeisances. Narendra spent some time there and returned back to Calcutta. Again after a week, he made a visit to Dakshineswar and found Gurudev's behaviour still very cold and arid. In this manner, once in three-four days Narendra paid a visit to Dakshineswar, many a times met the Guru, sat near him and talked with others and in the evening returned back to Calcutta. But still Guru's heart remained harsh. In the absence of Narendra, Ramakrishna sent one of his representaties to seek the whereabouts of Narendra. Narendra was not aware of all this. Even after a month. Narendra continued with his visits to Dakshineswar without any fail, in spite of such a behaviour on the part of his Guru, one day

Ramakrishna called him and asked – "Even though I did not talk to you all these days, still you kept on coming here, how?" Narendra replied, "Do you think that I come here just to listen to you or talk to you! I am devoted to you and want to have a glimpse of you. That is why I come here." Narendra's reply satisfied him and made him extremely happy. "I was assessing whether you will continue to come here even if I do not pay attention to you or spend time with you."

Ramakrishna had attained strange godly powers by practicing severe yoga. He wanted to utilize these powers for the welfare of the universe. He was imparting training to Narendra for this very purpose. One day he called Narendra to Panchvati and said, "I have practised many spiritual exercises and made myself discipline and acquired great spiritual powers. But what use are they to me? I cannot even cover my body properly. Hence, with the permission of Mother Kali I am going to transfer these powers to you. From 'Her' I have come to know that you will have to do so many things for her. If I pass on those powers to you, you will make use of them as per the requirements of this society. What do you say? Narendra was aware of the fact that Ramakrishna had such spiritual power in his possession. After a second's thought he said, "Will this power be helpful to me in experiencing God? No, they won't be of any help towards that. But after understanding God properly and when you will be involved in that work, then you will get help from them", replied Gurudev. Narendra said, "I do not want them. Let me first worship and concentrate on God first. Possibly after that I will gain knowledge as to whether those powers would be useful for me or not. If I accept them now, then perhaps I might forget my ideals and utilize those powers for selfish interests and become a sinner." Hearing Narendra's clear cut views Ramakrishna was very happy Perhaps this was a test. Narendra was a person of independent thoughts. In spite of his deep love for Narendra, Ramakrishna never interfered with his freedom. This increased Narendra's confidence. The heart of his Guru was laid bare before Narendra. Ramakrishna shared every secret pertaining to his life with Narendra. He was Ramakrishna's close confidante. It is said that love is a kind of shackle but in Narendra's case, Ramakrishna's love towards him was freedom from all shackles. The freedom, in a hidden manner enlightened Narendra's entire life. ■■

Beginning of a New Life

Narendra was not able to even breathe freely in the tension free environment of his youth because the complete responsibility of his family fell suddenly on his young shoulders. In those days (year 1884), he had just appeared for his graduation examination. The results were still to be out. One day, Narendra had gone to meet one of his friends in Bara Nagar about two miles from Calcutta. There he got engaged in discussions with his friends and soon it was night. Then they began music and orchestra. The music reached the heights of ecstasy. At that moment, a person entered the room. He had come from Narendra's house and he informed the tragic news of the death of Narendra's father due to heart failure. The news sent shock waves in Narendra's heart. Narendra soon set off for Calcutta. When he reached home, he found the whole environment immersed in sorrow. His two younger sisters and brothers were waiting inconsolably with his mother. Narendra felt scared at the situation and was unable to respond properly – neither he was able to cry nor talk. People tried to console him. Somehow he got control over his mind and performed the last rites of his father.

Narendra's father Vishwanath Dutt was a very large hearted person. His expenses were more than his income. Because of his royal spending ways he was not able to save anything for himself or his family. His friends and relatives were burdened with his help. But as the ways of the world is no sooner than Vishwanath Dutt closed his eye, all his friends and relatives turned their face away from the bereaved family. Perhaps they were afraid that if they showed more sympathy to the family then they will have to extend a helping hand to them. Even before the rituals were complete, money lenders queued up before his house. Narendra had no source of income before him. Still he had the responsibility of seven-eight family members before him. Nothing but the irony of fate – the young boy who had grown up in the midst of all comforts had suddenly been thrown out in the midst of discomfort and difficulties. In the midst of all these sufferings, sometimes Narendra's self-confidence lit up like lightning. Narendra led himself ahead on the path of life with the help of that very light. He transformed himself into an opponent of his fate. After a few days, the result of his graduation exams were out. He had passed his graduation and rejoined the college to study law. Now Narendra was the poorest student in his college. His wore dresses made of coarse cloth and very simple and cheap shoes. Many a time, he went to college empty stomach. Many a time, due to hunger, he fell unconscious. His friends used to invite him for meals at their homes. There he spent hours together talking, singing etc but whenever his friends ask him to have meals he replied in negative. At that moment, the images of his hungry mother and siblings came before his eyes. His heart cried from within. In such a situation, he was unable to continue with his conversation and left the company at some pretext or the other and returned back home.

Narendra's household was famous for its luxurious ways. After the death of Vishwanath Dutt they had to continue with their luxurious ways to a certain extent so that the hardships and poverty were not evident for the outsiders. Narendra's family hid their miserable condition behind show off. Nobody was even able to see the follies of a royal household and the same was the case with Narendra. Nobody was able to see the real situation they were in. His rich friends came in luxurious vehicles and took him along for long rides. When he returned back his mother gave him food to eat. He partook only a part of the food so that his siblings and mother could also have some food. And whenever he felt that there was utter shortage of food he used to completely refuse saying that he had had food from his friend's house. He partook only that much food that was necessary for his existence. Because of less eating his health deteriorated day by day. But Narendra's friends were unable to understand the reason behind this.

Day after day, disaster befell on Narendra's family now the hidden secret began to be disclosed publicly. Relative of Narendra was also staying in one portion of his house. After the death of Vishwanath Dutt that relative made upon the effort to divide the house. Even though legally Narendra's family was supposed to get the maximum portion of the property, but the thought of shame and infamy compelled them to keep the will a secret. But in spite of their efforts, once the secret was out it slowly reached the court. It became a topic of discussion for the outsiders. Narendra and his mother felt ashamed of this. Fortunately, the decision of the court was in favour of Narendra's family. The major portion of property came under Narendra's control. With this, Narendra's mental tension got reduced to a certain extent. The question of fulfilling the food and clothing needs appeared before him assuming an enormous form. To solve this problem, he took up the job of a teacher in an educational institute run by Ishwar Chand Vidyasagar. But the job did not continue for more than a month. The problem of providing proper food and clothing for the family constantly haunted Narendra.

Later in his life, he had mentioned this dark period of life – "Before the days of bereavement were over, I was compelled to knock the doors for opportunities, wandering in hot weather with empty stomach and bare foot carrying application. I went from one office to other. Two of my best friends, who supported him in his condition of misery and misfortune, sometimes went along with him. But at every place, doors were closed for me. In the first realization of the realities of life, I understood very well that selfless sympathy was a rare thing in this world." "There is no place for poor, miserable and weak people in this world. I saw that those who offered prompt help a few days ago just turned away their faces now, even though they were capable of giving many things. After confronting such people I felt this world to be a home of satans." Once feeling tired and helpless, I sat under the shade of a monument in the garden. Some of my friends were also there. One of them, perhaps with the intention to revive my mood, began to sing a song praising the beauty of God's creation. It gave me a fearful fright. The helpless situation of my mother and my siblings suddenly came to my mind and out of deep despair and pain I cried out, 'Stop this song. This emotion will please only those who are lying on a bed of flowers and who do not have any of his loved ones or relatives in a miserable situation at home. Yes, there was a time when I used to think so, but today I am confronting the harsh truths of life and in face of it all this seems to be a serious joke.' My friend might have surely felt bad at this kind of reaction on my part. How could have my friend understood my real feelings which compelled me to speak in such a rude manner? Sometimes when I felt that there was no sufficient food left to fill the stomach of all the family members, I used to make excuses to my mother that I have been invited for lunch or dinner by someone and on that day I remained without eating a grain of food for the whole day. Because of self-respect, I never disclosed my actual situation before others. My rich friends sometimes invited me to there house or elsewhere and asked me to sing. When I was unable to avoid them, I went along with them. Some of them sometimes enquired why I am looking so weak. One of them realized the actual situation at my household and time and again provided provisions to my mother anonymously without my knowledge. The kind act on his part made me grateful to him and I felt burdened by his obligations.

During this period of hardship in his life many profitable offers came to him. But none of them could attract him or distract him from his path. "Some of my old friends, who were earning their livelihood through wrong means invited me to join them, some of them were compelled to take up the wrong means because misfortune had befallen on them like it had befallen on me. They had true feelings of sympathy towards me. Many difficulties and many challenges came my way. One rich lady put forth a very unbecoming proposal before me of staying in relationship with her. I rejected all of them in a harsh manner."

These days of hardship had a significant role in the spiritual development of Narendra. Later on, he said, "In spite of all their worst experiences, my belief in God or his blessings never wavered. Every morning, I woke up uttering his name and left home in search of an appropriate job. One day my mother heard my prayers to God and said in a harsh tone – 'You are a stupid fellow. Since childhood you had been uttering the name of God but what had he done for you?' A severe pain arose in my brain. A kind of doubt crept into my brain. 'Does God exist in reality? And if He is existent, does He hear the heart rending prayers of human beings? If it is so, then why is there no reaction towards my requests? Why is there so much turmoil in his blissful kingdom? Why is Satan reigning Supreme in the kind world of God. The words of Pt.

Ishwar Chandra Vidyasagar resounds in my ear like a Satan. If the God is kind and glorious why is it so that crores of people are dying for meals to fill their stomach I became very angered with God. This was an opportune time when doubts mushroomed in my mind. It was against my character to do anything secretively. Moreover, I was not habitual of hiding my views from others either out of fear or any other reasons from my childhood. Hence, I came to the conclusion that God is just an imagination and even if He is omnipotent, there is no room for any kind of appeal in his kingdom. It was but natural on my part to go habitual of hiding my views from others either out of fear or any other reasons from my childhood. Hence, I came to the conclusion that God is just an imagination and even if He is omnipotent, there is no room for any kind of appeal in His kingdom. It was but natural on my part to go ahead in proving this to the outside world."

Soon, Narendra's real views became explicit before the society and became a topic of discussion. Not only that people began to believe that Narendra was no more reluctant to use intoxicating drinks or any prohibited articles. Such kind of rumours polluted the air in such a manner that it reached Dakshineswar also. All these rumours reached Ramakrishna's ears too, but he did not trust what his ears had heard. But his other disciples wanted to go to Calcutta and see the truth for themselves because they knew that, whatever be the Mutter, Narendra would give them a satisfactory answer. Narendra did what was expected of him. He later on said, "In an intense mental state, I just made them understand that it is cowardice to believe in God just out of fear of attaining hell. Quoting the thoughts of many western philosophers I argued with them claiming the non-existence of God. As a result of my arguments they left me thinking that I have gone dangerously astray. But I was happy. I thought, most probably, Ramakrishna would also believe all this. This thought created excitement in my heart in an uncontrollable manner. I pacified myself saying that no Mutter, if good or bad thoughts relating to a person is based on such a weak foundation, then I am least bothered about that.

When these disciples of Ramakrishna went back to Dakshineswar and recounted everything before Ramakrishna, it seemed that Ramakrishna heard nothing even after hearing everything. The expression on his face remained unchanged. There was no change evident in his activities. But his disciples were very aggressive. When one of his favourite disciples Bhavnath said in a highly sentimental and distressed tone that he had never imagined that Narendra would disgrace himself to that extent, Ramakrishna could not restrain himself any more. He roared furiously – "Shut up you idiot! 'Mother' had told me that such a thing will never happen. If you speak out anything like this ever again to me I will not even look at you. In Ramakrishna's view, Narendra's personality was totally different from that of others. He considered Narendra to be pure and reverent like Lord Shiva. He was not prepared to hear anything derogatory against Narendra at any cost. Once one of his disciples made some derogatory remarks about Narendra. When Ramakrishna heard this, he scolded that fellow saying – "You are disgracing Lord Shiva. Nobody can come to a permanent conclusion about Narendra. Nobody can understand him completely."

At that moment actually a duel was going on in Narendra's mind. In such a turbulent situation, he was so lost that he was unable to understand himself. The harsh realities of the situation had made him an atheist indeed. But in the inner most layers, deep in his heart the spark of experiencing God laid suppressed. The wind of changing time would have at any moment of time caused that spark to transform into a huge fire. "But even while embracing these atheistic thoughts out of compulsion, my childhood experiences especially my relations with Ramakrishna which led me to envision the Goddess compelled me to think that there exists a kingdom of God and there are indeed some ways and means to witness God. Otherwise our life is meaningless and diminutive. I have to search out a way to attain God travelling through difficult and miserable paths. Days passed by and my mind oscillated between belief and disbelief."

Day followed night and night followed day. Many months and seasons passed one by one in this manner. But Narendra did not get a permanent job. One day, he was returning home drenched in rain, his stomach tearing with hunger. His mind was enveloped with the darkness of despair. His eyes though open were not able to see anything. His body had become totally devoid of any life. He found it difficult to put even a step forward. He saw a building in front of him and automatically entered into its lonely verandah and sat at a corner. Many thoughts came into his mind like waves. He felt as if he were unable to take hold of any one of them. His intellect turned in the whirlpool of thoughts. In that situation, he suddenly felt as if some supernatural power was removing the curtain of the myths in his mind. Slowly and gradually, his heart became devoid of any doubts. A strange kind of light took position there. In the glory of that light he found that all doubts inherent in his mind have disappeared and his mind once again developed trust in the superiority of God. Narendra's mind achieved calm slowly and gradually. The tiredness that his body had been experiencing suddenly disappeared. When he reached home both his mind and heart were calm and peaceful.

Narendra was a changed man now. Lots of changes had come over him. Praise or condemnation by people had least impact on him. He became sure that his life was different from that of others. He was not born just to indulge in worldly comforts or to look after his family members. Narendra's grandfather had embraced sannyasa and he himself had an attraction towards sannyasa from his childhood. Now that thought became old the more rooted in his mind that he should leave his home and family to embrace sannyasa. He always used to tell his friends – the life of a saint is indeed great because it pushes away the strength of death and stress ahead. When the whole world is trading in an environment of change, is immersed in it, at that time a saint is immersed in the reach of the permanent truth.' After much thinking one day, he finally decided to leave his home. As destiny would have it that very day Ramakrishna came to Calcutta. Narendra thought it would be beneficial to seek the blessings of Gurudev before leaving home. Hence, he went to meet Ramakrishna at the place where he was camping in Calcutta. But Ramakrishna forced him to accompany him to Dakshineswar for a night. The auspicious time was passing by but he was unable to say 'No' to his Guru so he accompanied him to Dakshineswar under compulsion. No conversation took place between the teacher and disciple on the way. After reaching Dakshineswar, Ramakrishna made Narendra sit with other disciples and went into a samadhi. After a long gap, he broke his samadhi and went to Narendra and touched him in a loving manner. His eyes were filled with tears and he began to sing a song. Narendra had been exercising control over himself. But now he was unable to control himself. He was deeply hurt and tears came rolling down his eyes in an uncontrollable manner. That meeting between the teacher and the disciple was rather unusual and strange. Those present there were also saddened by such a heart rending scene. When Ramakrishna regained back normally the people who witnessed the scene asked him what had happened to both of them. He smiled and replied, "It is something between me and him." It was almost midnight. After seeing off the visitors Ramakrishna turned to Narendra and said, "I know that you have come to this world for the sake of fulfilling the 'Mother's' work and will not be involved in worldly things but till the time I am alive stay here for my sake." Saying this, Gurudev began to wail in an uncontrollable manner. The next day Narendra returned back home after seeking Gurudev's permission.

The moment he stepped into his house many thoughts came into his mind. The problem of looking after his family stood before him as a big question. He felt that he will be able to do something only after making his family members self-dependent. With great difficulty he was able to get a job in an office. He got a little bit of money from book translation. This way somehow he managed to look after his family. But without a regular income for the family Narendra's problem was unlikely to get solved. To solve this problem Narendra kept on making one plan or the other. One day, the idea to consult Ramakrishna for a solution to this problem struck him. "Ramakrishna considers me something. He is even ready to give up his life for my sake. Many a time he had said that 'Mother Kali' has listened to his prayers then why won't he convey this small prayer on my part to 'Mother Kali'! Why have I been bothered by this problem for such a long time? Narendra went towards Dakshineswar. He had full faith in Ramakrishna that he will never ignore his wish. After reaching Dakshineswar, he requested Ramakrishna to pray 'Mother Kali' on his behalf to provide a decent livelihood to his family. Ramakrishna tried to evade him at first. Then after thinking something he replied –

"My dear, I cannot make such kind of demands. But why don't you yourself go there. You can speak to the Mother on your own. You do not severe her, nor have respect for her that is why you are in the midst of all these sufferings."

"I do not know the Mother. Please you tell her about me", said Narendra.

Again Ramakrishna replied in a soft voice – "My dear child, I have told her many a time. But you do not accept her that is why she is not listening to my prayers. O.K. Today is Tuesday. At night, go inside the temple of Kali. Supplicate before the 'Mother'. Then seek whatever blessings you need you will of course get the blessings. She is complete and is the great strength of creation. The universe has been constructed because of her small desire. Every thing is within the precincts of her power. She is capable of doing anything."

Narendra's heart filled up with joy. He believed in every word that his Guruji had said. He began to wait for night to come impatiently. At around 9 P.M. Ramakrishna gave him permission to enter inside the temple. Excited about seeing the vivid image of mother Goddess and hearing her sweet voice, he stepped inside the temple and the very next moment he was in a sort of rapturous state. He felt as if his legs were shaking. He took a good view of the idol of the goddess and felt that the Mother Goddess looked real and vivid. He later on recounted his experience, "I was overwhelmed by the waves of love and devotion. Intoxicated by happiness I kept on supplicating before the image of the goddess and prayed to be blessed with wisdom, detachment, knowledge and devotion. Bless me to have an uninterrupted vision of you, my Mother. A gentle power overpowered my soul. I forgot the entire world. The image of Mother Goddess was the only thing I could see before my eyes."

But the problems with which Narendra had appeared before the Mother Goddess remained untold. After getting a sight of the goddess when he returned back to the Gurudev, he was in complete ecstasy. Gurudev asked, "Have you put up all your worldly needs before the mother."

Hearing the question Narendra was surprised. He was embarrassed at his failure to present his actual prayers, "No Gurudev, I forgot about that. Now what will happen? Is there any other solution?"

"Go again and tell her about your needs", Ramakrishna said.

Narendra again went towards the temple. Mother Kali stood there in the same expression as before. The sight of the Goddess once again made him forget his actual objective and he just supplicated before the idol of the Goddess Mother and prayed her to bless him with love and reverence. The second time again Gurudev asked Narendra whether he had accomplished his work. Narendra bowed down his head humbly and recounted what happened inside the temple. Gurudev scolded him in a harsh manner, "You are such a fool. What? You were not able to control yourself and tell those few words? Yes, try once again and put your actual prayers before her. Do it quickly."

Narendra went inside the temple for the third time. The moment he stepped inside the door he felt ashamed. He began to think – with how silly a prayer I have come in front of the Goddess. It is like asking for some vegetables from a great emperor. How stupid I am! He felt ashamed and guilty. Just one thing came out from his mouth – "Mother, I need nothing more than knowledge and devotion."

When he came out of the temple he understood that all this happened because of Gurudev's wishes. Otherwise how could he fail in his objective for the third time? He went near Ramakrishna and expressing sorrow over his repeated failure he said, "Gurudev, you are the one who had mystified my brains and made me forgetful. Now please bless me that my family members will never ever suffer due to poverty any more."

Ramakrishna answered in a serious tone, "This kind of prayer will never come to my lips. That is why I asked you to pray on your own. But you could not do that. This proves that you do not have the luck to enjoy materialistic comforts. In such circumstances tell me what can I do?"

But Narendra was not ready to leave Gurudev so easily. He compelled Gurudev to listen to his prayers. At last Ramakrishna said, "Okay, now onwards your family members will no more bother about food and clothing."

From here begins the second chapter of Narendra's life. Till now he had been experiencing an invisible godly rapture. After this episode, he experienced such heavenly ecstatic state many a time later on whenever he beheld the image of Goddess Kali he experienced a motherly affection. From then onwards he started having faith and devotion towards idol worship. He understood that idol worship is the same as worship of Brahma. With this knowledge, Narendra's spiritual life became fulfilled. This sudden change in Narendra's view point surprised Ramakrishna. He was innately happy with this transformation on the part of Narendra.

The very next day after this episode another disciple of Ramakrishna, Baikunthanath Sanyal came to Dakshineswar. Whatever he saw at Dakshineswar surprised him – "When I reached Dakshineswar in the afternoon I saw that Ramakrishna was alone inside his room and Narendra was fast asleep outside. Ramakrishna was in a very joyous state. When I paid my obeisance to Ramakrishna, he indicating towards Narendra said – "Look here, this boy is extremely good. His name is Narendra Nath. Before this, he never accepted the Mother Goddess, but yesterday he accepted the Goddess. These days he is in a difficult situation, so I asked him to seek money from the Mother but he could not do so. He said that he is ashamed of asking money from the Goddess. After returning back from the temple he asked me to teach him a song for Mother Goddess. I taught him a song. Yesterday, he had been singing the song overwhelmed with emotions for the whole night. That is why he is asleep till now." After a brief silence, he in a joyous state again said, "Is it not surprising that Narendra has accepted Mother?" I replied 'yes'. After a moment, he again repeated the same things."

That day Narendra got up from his sleep at around 4 in the evening. He had to return back to Calcutta in a hurry. Before leaving for Calcutta, Narendra went to Ramakrishna's room. Seeing Narendra, Ramakrishna went near him in an impatient manner and sat very near to Narendra. Then pointing his finger first towards himself and then towards Narendra he said, "Hear, I feel that I who am sitting here is there also. It is true, I do not find any difference. The way in which the log floating in the Ganga river water looks as if dividing the water but in reality it is unified. Are you able to understand what I am saying. See after all this what remains – only 'Mother'. What do you think?

For sometime, he kept on talking like this and then expressed his desire to smoke 'hukka'. One of his disciples got the hukka ready and landed it over to Guruji. After puffing twice or thrice he directed the pipe of the hukka towards Narendra and said, "You also take some puff from me."

Narendra was hesitant. How could he let Gurudev touch his lips. "How stupid your thoughts are? Am I different from you? This is me and that is alone", first indicating towards himself and then towards Narendra he said. He took the pipe of the hukka towards Narendra's lips. Narendra was in a dilemma and he had no other way left than to fulfill his Gurudev's wishes. Narendra took three puffs. When Ramakrishna was about to take the puff, Narendra said, "Gurudev, first wash your hands."

But Gurudev did not pay any heed to Narendra's opposition. "You have been nursing such wrong thoughts of inequality." Saying this, he began to blow the pipe of the hukka without washing his hands.

Ramakrishna's meals were got prepared and served in a very disciplined manner. If somebody partook the meal meant for him before he partook it he considered it be the leftover food and refused to eat it. But his behaviour with Narendra proved the fact that his relationship with Narendra was not only inseparable but heavenly. Ramakrishna's selfless, unwavering and unlimited love had tied up Narendra's life. Narendra once said, "Shri Ramakrishna trusted me in every situation alike. Even my mother and brother lacked trust in me. This unwavering trust and love towards me on the part of Ramakrishna tied me to his company for ever. He just knows how to love others. Those interested in worldly life only acts love to fulfill their selfish interests.

In the summer of year 1885, signs of ailment became evident in Ramakrishna's body. He was greatly troubled by the persistent pain in his throat. The pain aggravated day by day and his health deteriorated. His disciples were greatly worried by his condition. To give him proper treatment, he was taken to Calcutta. Experienced doctors checked him and diagnosed that he was suffering from throat cancer. Doctors recommended to take him out of Calcutta for change of weather. They were unable to find a suitable accommodation in Calcutta. Hence, some of his disciples took initiative and took a rented accommodation in a small town adjacent to Calcutta known as Kashipur. The house was small one in the middle of a garden. Ramakrishna was taken to that house. To look after and serve Gurudev some of his main disciples also stayed there. Narendra was teaching in the school established by Ishwar Chandra Vidyasagar during those days also left his job and came over to Kashipur to serve Gurudev. Some of his disciples extended financial help from outside. Narendra earlier used to go to his home

Swami Vivekanand: A Biography

twice for his meals but whenever his condition deteriorated he stayed back and did not go to his house. But Ramakrishna never used to take any kind of service from him. In his view, Narendra was entirely different from other disciple.

In the garden house of Kashipur along with the looking after of the patient, imparting knowledge to the disciples, meditation and daily prayers and worship were also held regularly. As per the instructions of Gurudev, Narendra practised prayer and meditation with most concentration. He experienced that the flow of spiritual powers within him had become quite forceful. He knew that Ramakrishna was the actual force behind it. He was slowly and gradually filling him up with spiritual powers. He was sure that Narendra will utilize these powers in a positive and beneficial manner for the welfare of the world.

An incident in this context is worth recounting. That was the day of Shivaratri. Narendra and some of his friends were on complete fasting that day and decided to spend the whole night in prayer, worship and meditation. After offering prayers to Lord Shiva it was time for meditation. By that time all others went out of the room due to some reason. Only Narendra was left alone in the room along with one another person Kali. Narendra's heart became curious to put the spiritual powers being attained by him to test. Before entering into meditation Narendra asked Kali, "After a few minutes touch me."

Kali touched his right hand on Narendra's right knee. With that mere touch Kali's right arm began to shiver at great speed as if he had been electrocuted. After two minutes Narendra opened his eyes and asked, 'Are you alright? How was the experience?'

Describing his experience, Kali said that in spite of his continuous efforts, he could not exercise control over himself or become normal. Hearing this, Narendra's curious heart became happy and satisfied. He began to think – "It means I have also attained the power inherent in Gurudev." With a pleased countenance, he went to the adjacent room of the Gurudev. No sooner than he stepped inside Gurudev's room he said in a furious tone – "See, you have begun to waste your power without harnessing it wholly and properly. First accumulate it properly and then you will understand how much to utilize it for what purpose."

Hearing Ramakrishna's words Narendra became silent. He felt surprised that how Guruji came to know what happened in the next room. In fact, he was aware of the hidden powers possessed by Ramakrishna.

One day, Ramakrishna called his disciples and gave them an insight into the life of saints in a 'Mutt' (Ashram). The person who has left his household and family in search of truth and for the welfare of the universe, he does not worry about his stomach. He never accumulates anything for himself. He has to stay alive not for himself but for others. Ramakrishna ordered his disciples to go from house to house and beg for alms. The disciples obeyed his order. Whatever little rice they got, they cooked them. Ramakrishna took a grain of cooked rice and said to his disciples, "Very well cooked. How pure this rice is?"

In Ramakrishna's view that rice was pure because it was devoid of any possessiveness or affection and all the disciples had equal right on it. Secondly, it came from the household belonging to the higher class as well as the lower caste.

By then Narendra had totally detached himself from college education. Even in his ill-health condition, once Ramakrishna reminded him to complete his college education but Narendra in a highly excited manner replied, "Gurudev, whatever I had learnt till today if I get some medicine to forget then I will be too eager to have that medicine."

By now Narendra had developed a totally indifferent attitude towards the educational system meant for earning a livelihood. Especially after embracing sannyasa he was normally busy in reading the biography of saints and indulged himself in discussions relating to the teachings of those saints. He was more attracted towards the teachings of Lord Buddha and remained lost in such thoughts. One night, Narendra along with two other disciples went to Bodh Gaya in a secretive manner. After visiting the temple of Bodhisattva, he entered into meditation under the Bodhi tree. The other two disciples also sat in meditation under the same tree. After some times when their meditation broke they saw that Narendra's body looked like a stone statue. They waited for quite long but Narendra was totally immersed in meditation. After many hours, he opened his eyes.

At Kashipur, the inmates of the garden house were worried when they were unable to find Narendra and two others in the morning: They searched everywhere. When Ramakrishna heard about it he laughed and said, "You people don't worry, he will return. Is there any other place other than this where he can remain stagnant?"

And actually Narendra could not stay at Bodh Gaya for long time. After hours of stringent meditation that he practiced under the Bodhi tree he realized that he will not be able to attain peace away from Ramakrishna's feats. He returned back to Kashipur at the earliest.

Ramakrishna's situation was deteriorating day by day. As a result his disciples and well-wishers were afraid and worried. Because of pain in the throat he was unable to even gulp down the boiled barley water. His tone had become weakened. But his courage and excitement remained as before. He kept on imparting some kind of learning or the other to his disciples and initiated those who performed prayer and devotion for the sake of affection for entertaining his disciples. He emphasized on the importance of developing the power of soul. Once he said, "If you keep on saying that you are a sinner then you will remain a sinner throughout. In addition you should also keep on repeating that I am not under any shackles, who can keep me under shackles? I am the son of the Supreme Being. I am the king of kings." If you accomplish your work with will power then you will be free. The one who always says that I am an humble servant', he is a fool. He will remain a slave till the end. The unhappy person who always mumbles that "I am a culprit" becomes a culprit in real but that person who persistently says that 'I am free from all shackles of the world, I am independent. Is the Almighty not my father? Dependence is something of the mind but freedom is the result of one's own mindset", is always free.

Narendra used to listen to Gurudev's teachings with great concentration and used to follow them. He was well versed with the Advaita philosophy being discussed in the Upanishads. He wanted to experience the feeling of becoming one with Supreme Being. He wanted to know the basis of a yogi's confidence in telling that he is one with Brahma. He was longing to have this feeling.

One day, he went to Ramakrishna's room with the view to clarify some of his doubts. Gurudev was alone at that time. Narendra stood in front of Gurudev with head bowed in reverence. There was sense of affirmation in his eyes. Gurudev asked – "Naren, what you want?"

"I want to remain in the ocean of almighty in intermittent meditation." Narendra replied in an hesitant manner.

Ramakrishna showed an expression of discomfort, but said in a serious manner, "Don't you feel ashamed saying the same thing again and again. At an opportune time where are you going to extend your shadow of peace to millions of people like a huge tree, right now you are impatient to find freedom for your soul, how indifferent are your ideal?" Tears came to his eyes. His throat became heavy and was unable to speak properly, "Without achieving unhindered Samadhi, my mind can never be calm. And if I did not attain peace of mind then I won't be able to do anything."

"You will do things according to your wishes? Mother Goddess will compel you to do things...okay go, you will be able to achieve unhindered Samadhi." Gurudev said with a natural smile on his face.

The next day in the evening Narendra was doing meditation in his room. Another disciple was also present there. Suddenly Narendra felt that a source of light has suddenly opened at the backside of his brain and that light was brightening up gradually. In the end, the light took such a wild form that he felt as if his brain was breaking into pieces and getting merged with those rays of light. Narendra's body began to lose his consciousness. Suddenly crying out in the meditative state, Narendra said, 'Gopal da, where is my body?' Frightened at this question, Gopal touched his body and said, "Why Narendra? Your body is here. Here itself."

When Gopal touched Narendra's body, he felt that it has become hard and devoid of life. He quickly went to the other room where Gurudev was lying and told him the whole incident and asked him to help Narendra. But Gurudev remained calm as if he had prior knowledge of everything. He said, "Let him remain in that position for some time." At around 9 o'clock Narendra regained back his consciousness. His countenance was calm and he was happy. He had attained the ultimate joy of Brahma. It was an ultimate condition which cannot be expressed in words. He felt as this very condition epitomized the whole philosophy of Vedanta. When he went to Gurudev and stood before him with his head bowed down in obeisance, Gurudev as if measuring the depth of his eyes stared at him and smilingly said, "Yes, now the Mother has showed you everything. In the same manner as harnessed energy is kept safe inside a box. This experience will remain locked and the key will remain with me. Now you have to do some work. Once the work gets finished then the lock will be opened."

Narendra who was overwhelmed with this ecstatic experience remained involved in prayers and devotional songs as if in an unconscious state. Seeing his condition, Ramakrishna made a heart rending appeal to Mother Kali – "Mother, hide this Advaita experience that he had enjoyed with your power of Maya. 'Mother' you have to make him do so many works."

During those days, Ramakrishna's health conditions had deteriorated miserably. Neither was he able to speak properly nor eat properly. He was only able to speak in a weak voice and that too with great difficulty. Seeing his miserable condition, all his well-wishers were greatly perturbed and sad. Once one of his devotees who was also a philosopher came to Kashipur to meet him. He said that many yogis free themselves from their ailments by concentrating the heavenly power inherent in their brains on the particular portion where the ailment exists. "You are such a great saint. If you make efforts you will surely gain back your health." Hearing his view Ramakrishna in a very soft tone replied, "You are such a scholarly person and you are putting forth such a foolish proposal. I have entrusted my brain to the Supreme once forever. How is it possible to get it back and concentrate it on this cage of blood and flesh."

The scholar was silenced at this reply and went away from there. But Narendra and the other disciples were unable to see the sufferings of the Guru. It seemed that every treatment for this incurable disease proved futile. The light of life of Gurudev was getting blown off slowly and gradually. With no rays of hope from anywhere, Narendra and other disciples accumulated some strength and expressed the same desire as expressed by the philosopher scholar – "Gurudev you should free yourself from this disease especially for own sake."

Ramakrishna replied, "Do you think that I am suffering all this pain out of my own sweet will. I want to save myself from this. Still I am suffering from this cruel disease.

Everything is happening due to the sweet wish of Mother Goddess."

Narendra – "Then for God's sake ask the mother to make you well. She will not refuse your prayers."

Ramakrishna – "It is but natural for you to talk like this but I can never say all this."

Narendra insisted – "But nothing will happen with your principles. You should tell this to the Mother, at least for own sake."

Ramakrishna gave his nod – "Okay, let me think, what I can do about this."

After the lapse of few hours Narednra and some of his friends entered his room again and asked –

"Have you told everything to this 'Mother'?"

Ramakrishna replied – "Yes, I showed my throat to the Mother Goddess and told her that due to this injury I am unable to eat anything. Please do something so that I am able to eat something. At this the 'Mother' indicating towards all of you said why I am not eating with the help of all these mouths. I was so ashamed with this that I could not ask her anything else."

Narendra was surprised. He had never seen or experienced such a lively example of Advaita. Seeing Ramakrishna's deep rooted faith in Advaita, Narendra could not say anything further.

Days were one by one lapsing into invisibility behind the past. For Narendra, in addition to worship, prayer, meditation and Samadhi, the job of looking after Guruji was increasing. He was also shouldering the additional burden of being a path bearer for other disciples. He sat on meditation and Samadhi along with others almost everyday. Day by day his capacity to concentrate and power of meditation increased. One evening, Narendra sat under a huge tree in the Kashipur garden of Guru brother Girish Babu. There due to disturbance of mosquitoes, Girish Babu could not concentrate on his meditation. With the increasing disturbance of the mosquitoes, he became helpless and was compelled to open his eyes. To his consertation he saw an extremely surprising scene. The body of Narendra who was sitting in meditation along his side was completely enveloped by innumerous mosquitoes. It looked as if his body had been covered by a blanket made of infinite number of mosquitoes. But Narendra was lost deep in his Samadhi unaware of all this.

Swami Vivekanand: A Biography

During his last days Ramakrishna was able to talk only in a low tone and with hand indications. In such a difficult situation, overwhelmed with emotions he used to pat on the back of his disciples and tell them that Naren will look after them after he leaves this worldly abode. He will impart knowledge to them. Narendra hearing all this would lose control over himself and say that nothing like that would happen. At this, Gurudev would say, "You will have to do this. At a ripe time, all my powers would be expressed through you." Narendra used to be overwhelmed with a feeling of regret. In the evenings, almost everyday, Ramakrishna used to call Narendra to his side and used to give him advise. Two-three days before the Mahasamadhi he called Narendra near him. Then looking into his eyes in an affectionate manner for sometime he entered into Samadhi. Narendra felt as if he had come into contact with electric current, as if some pointed thing has priced into his body. Narendra could not withstand it and became unconscious. When he regained back his consciousness he saw that tears were rolling down from Gurudev's eyes continuously. He said, "Naren, today I have given every possession of mine to you; now I am just a pauper who is devoid of any possession. With this power you will be able to do innumerous good things for this world." After this handover of power and strength, it seemed that there remained no difference between the teacher and the disciple. Both of them became a single entity.

There were only two days left for the Mahasamadhi. The pain in Gurudev's throat was just intolerable. His intake of food and water had stopped. His voice had become very low. Doctors were called but they also expressed helplessness and hopelessness. Ramakrishna's disciples and well wishers wore greatly distressed but Ramakrishna's countenance displayed a unique kind of peace and calmness. There was an ocean of love in his eyes and a smile on his lips. His strange personality was attractive like a setting sun. People who looked at his face just kept on staring at him. He pacified all of them in a whispering tone.

'Only the body is suffering pain. When the brain has conjoined with the God, it cannot experience anything.'

After a brief silence, he continued, 'Let the body and its sufferings remain involved with each other. Oh my mind, you remain in ultimate joy. Now I am completely unified with the Mother Goddess forever.'

Sunday 15 August, 1886 was Ramakrishna's last day. In spite of unbearable pain in his throat, in the afternoon he talked with his disciples with great excitement and affection for about two hours. By evening his condition deteriorated which became a cause of concern for everyone. The pain kept on increasing rapidly and it created obstruction in breathing too. Doctors expressed their inability to do anything. Ramakrishna's well wishers, worried and helpless, kept on surrounding him. If at all they could do something to soothe down the sufferings of their Gurudev. Gurudev looking towards his favourite disciple Narendra, went into a Samadhi lying on the bed. All who were present there began to weep. Some of them thought that Ramakrishna will not wake up from this Samadhi. He went into a deep slumber but at midnight he opened his eyes. There was an unending calm on his face, resembling a calmness that prevailed after an earth-rending storm. The black clouds of suffering had vanished from his eyes. In their place was the brightness of spiritualism and a natural smile on his lips. He expressed his desire to eat something. He was given a small quantity of sweet dish (kheer). One disciple gave support to Gurudev by keeping two-three pillows behind his back. Narendra was massaging Gurudev's feet. But Gurudev signalled him to come near him and till the end kept on giving him some lessons in an unclear tone. After some time he stopped. He took rest for a while. Then pronounced the name of Goddess Mahakali for thrice and fell back on the pillows. His vision fell on the tip of his nose. The upper portion of his body began to shiver slightly as if the soul imprisoned inside the cage like skeleton and bones was longing to free itself. The time was 1:02 A.M. midnight. Ramakrishna's body became motionless for ever. He entered into everlasting sleep. Narendra's heart became impatient. Along with other disciples, tears came rolling down his eyes incessantly. Their patience broke. They were unable to find any bank. They felt as if the boat of life without a row man was becoming a toy at the hands of an invisible force.

The sad morning of 16 August. People crowded the garden house in Kashipur. The body of Ramakrishna was covered with saffron cloth. The portion above the throat was kept open, sandalwood paste was applied on the forehead and innumerous floral garlands around his neck reaching over to his head. People bowed before the dead body of their Guru and paid the last tribute. After some time arrangements were made to take the body of their Guru to the banks of the Ganges to perform the last rites. All the disciples turnwise shouldered the bodily remains to the Ganges. The early morning wind carried the fragrance of sandalwood and incense and the environment reverberated with chantings and devotional songs. The disciples and devotees carried the bodily ashes which signified purity in a kalash. Their hearts were heavy and footsteps slow as they walked back to Kashipur with earthly remains of their beloved Guru. All of them stepped inside the garden house shouting 'Bhagwan Shri Ramakrishna Ki Jai' which echoed all over. But who was there to hear that. The house was empty, the courtyard empty, the plants and trees sad and all the directions were weeping. But Gurudev's last words which remained eternal – "I am going from one to another" echoed within the minds of all those young saints and imparted them a sense of satisfaction.

■■

Bharat Darshan
A Journey of India

The earthly body of the worshipper of Dakshineswar was no more there but he was spread with all strength in the hearts of all the saints staying in the Mutt. Those people who felt themselves in the middle of the sea also could experience an invisible support. All the disciples, especially Narendra felt the presence of their beloved Guru in their vicinity. Mother Sharda many a time felt that Ramakrishna was telling her something in a very much life-like manner. Sometimes after Ramakrishna left this earthly abode, when she got ready to remove all signs that signified matrimony according to the Hindu customs. But from somewhere she heard the voice of her husband saying, "You cannot do this. I am not dead." Mother Sharda once again wore the gold bangles on her empty arms and wore red bordered sari usually worn by a married woman.

Just ten-fifteen days after the passing away of Sri Ramakrishna, the contract of rent of the garden house was about to expire. Narendra, on whose shoulders, the responsibility of looking after other disciples was entrusted, began to worry about finding another place of stay. Due to Gurudev's illness, all the disciples were compelled to stay together at one place to look after and serve their Guru. They joined the workshop of spirituality. All these disciples had a single objective in their minds and so they were all tied together in a single strand of love. But after Gurudev left them and with no proper place to stay this string began to break slowly. Some unmarried youths who had broken their relations with their homes and families to embrace Sannyasa under the supervision of Gurudev found themselves without any shelter and support. During the last moments of Sri Ramakrishna, they had undertook an oath to remain a saint renouncing family life throughout life. Now they were not wishing or willing to return back to their homes. But in such a difficult situation parents of some of them compelled them to return back. They were not willing to support their children's desire to lead a saintly life. some of them had actually left their college education in the middle and had joined the ashram of Ramakrishna to offer their services to their beloved Guru. The problems of Narendra's family had also not been resolved fully. Hence, he was unable to stay with the Guru brothers in the garden house day and night. The problem of leaving the Mutt haunted him continuously and he was greatly perturbed with that. Narendra was even unable to imagine the situation wherein all these disciples who had united together for the welfare of the country, renouncing their family, getting scattered here and there.

Among the devotees of Ramakrishna, four of them i.e. Shri Balram Bose, Shri Surendranath Mitra, Shri Mahendra Gupta and Shri Girish Chandra Ghosh belonged to affluent families. They were people with responsible, glorious and unwavering ideals. Narendra consulted all the four of them. It was Surendranath who took care of the expenses of Gurudev and his disciples stay during the days of his serious illness at Kashipur. Once again he extended a helping hand to redeem the situation. He acquired a dilapidated house in Bada Nagar on rent. This act on the part of Surendranath was in fact like a blessing for Narendra.

Exactly during this time some of Sri Ramakrishna's devotees who were leading a familial life took up the question of keeping the bodily remains of Guru under their control. They reasoned out that the sanryasis were generally wanderers who had no permanent place to stay. In such a situation, it is impossible to choose a proper place for its safekeeping. If the devotees who are leading a familial life is handed over the kalash containing the holy ashes of their reverential Guru, they will establish it at an appropriate place and build a temple in memory of Sri Ramakrishna. But the disciples of Ramakrishna were not ready to accept this proposal. They were not ready to part with that sole invaluable possession at any cost. Differences of opinion and argument and counter argument took place between the two groups over the issue. At last, Narendra convinced his Guru brothers that everyone had equal right on Gurudev. Such kind of antagonism after the passing away of their Guru was unbecoming of them. The sannyasis have with them the ideal of Ramakrishna's teachings which in itself is an asset and their lives are devoted for the welfare of the world. In such a situation, it would be an honourable act on their part to hand over a part of Guruji's bodily remains to the devotees who are family men. The Guru brothers accepted Narendra's proposal. They kept some part of ashes and bones of their beloved Guru with themselves and handed over the rest to them along with the kalash. One devotee Sh. Ramachandra Dutt donated a plot of land at Kakargachi some distance away from Calcutta for this noble work. The devotees who were leading a family life were very happy to obtain the bodily remains of their Guru. On an auspicious day, Sri Ramakrishna's devotees and disciples together buried the kalash at the Kakargachi plot and after a few months they built a beautiful temple also. The place was unanimously named as 'Yogodhyan'. With the accomplishment of this noble work the indifferences that had cropped up between the devotees and disciples ended for ever. They once again got united with love and responsibility.

After this, Narendra diverted his attention to the building that was hired for them by Surendranath Mitra at Baranagar. All the Guru brothers together cleaned the premises and kept the central room aloof to keep their Guru's memories alive. The day specified to leave the Kashipur garden house was near. Many emotional memories were connected to that house. At the time of taking leave from that place Narendra's heart wept from within. But it was inevitable for them to leave the place. With past memories accumulated in their eyes and carrying the Gurudev's bodily remains Narendra and other disciples left the place and moved to Baranagar.

Now the first thing for Narendra was to take care of the strength of the Mutt. He made frequent visits to those Guru brothers who had distanced themselves after the passing away of·Ramakrishna. He tried to reason out with them that they should get themselves out from their trivial family life and should stand in front of the world, for the welfare of mankind. Till the time they do not return back to the Mutt permanently, the Mutt cannot acquire strength. The success that Narendra achieved in this endeavour was beyond his expectations. Many of Gurudev's disciples sacrificed their parents and home and followed Narendra's advise. Some of them promised to return back to the Mutt after appearing for their final exams. They considered Narendra as their leader from the very beginning not because Gurudev had told them to do so but because Narendra's personality had a kind of attraction or some magic which drew people towards him automatically.

The financial condition of Narendra's family had improved to some extent by then. Hence, he also left his home for a permanent stay at Baranagar ashram along with other disciples. The narrow affection that he had for his family had acquired a broader dimension – affection for the whole world. In place of solving the trivial family problems, he had before him the challenging task of solving the problems of the entire human kind. He had now a broader area of work in front of him. The main room of the Mutt, where the bodily remains of Gurudev was kept, was the place where all the disciples assembled for worship, prayers and meditation. Narendra taught the disciples here itself. In addition to western and Indian philosophy, he taught foreign history, sociology, literature, art and science also. Discussion about existence of God used to come up. Narendra, on the basis of science and rationalism would prove that the existence of God is a mere thought of imagination. But the same time with his reasoning he would prove that God is the only truth and reality of this universe. That is the only acceptable fact that gives mankind the ultimate happiness. His style of reasoning was so appealing that those who listened to him got easily convinced and became drawn towards his view. Debates and discussions of various facets of philosophy such as Sankhya, Yog, Nyay, Vaiseshi, Mimansa and Vedanta were held regularly. Comparison between Buddhist ideology and Vedanta were also done. Many a time Christian fathers also participated in those debates. But none of them were able to endure in face of Narendra's deep knowledge and sharp intellect. They were compelled to accept their defeat. In the end, Narendra would tell them about the greatness of Jesus Christ. Narendra's arguments and counter arguments were based on some rationale. Inspired by the life and teachings of Gurudev, each word spelt by Narendra had a special fervour. Even people having views opposed to him used to get spellbound by him.

All the disciples staying in the Mutt once again embraced saffron outfits and took the form of sannyasis. The fire of spiritualism had brightened up in their hearts. In the light of this fire, all their doubts and dilemmas got completely dissolved in darkness. Many bodies but single soul, one sect and one mission. There was no force left in the world that could lead them astray from their path. All of them unified together in brotherhood and took oath to move ahead together to work for the welfare of the world.

Even after taking such a bold decision some parents of some disciples visited the Mutt to ask their children to return back to their homes. But the heart of the sannyasis had acquired rock-like qualities. They could not be lured towards worldly comforts. They had wholly embraced a new personality, after freeing themselves from the materialistic pleasures. A naming ceremony was organized with a view to forget the old memories and began life anew. The word 'Anand' was suffixed to the names of all disciples to reiterate their singularity of mission.

How mysterious was the path towards this objective? How much penance and penitence involved in it? Begging for alms not for the sake of stomach. To live the life with the support of luck. If some charitable person offered something in charity then only something got cooked on the stove in the ashram, otherwise not. Sh. Surendranath Mitra and another benevolent devotees were the basic support of this Ashram. Without their support, half the life of the inhabitants of the Mutt would have been wasted in earning a livelihood to remain alive at least. Still there used to be days when they had rice with them, they did not have salt and when they had salt with them, they did not have rice. Still they were so immersed and indulged in prayers, singing of devotional songs, meditation, worship and debates on philosophy that they hardly heard the call of their stomachs. The mat spread on the floor of the main room was the only bed spread on which they slept and sat. In the name of cloth all of them just had a loin cloth and a piece of cloth covering them till the knee. Only one sheet was hooked on the peg on the wall, which was used by all of them – whosoever happens to go out covered his body with that and when he returned back he again hung it on the peg.

In the field of worship of Goddess, Badanagar had become synonymous with Dakshineswar. Its importance was no less than that of Dakshineswar at any level. The land of Dakshineswar had become pure because of the vigorous yoga and meditation practised by Sri Ramakrishna Paramahansa. But for all those young sannyasis who took shelter under Ramakrishna, the land of their penance, yoga and meditation was Baranagar. The words spoken by Gurudev at his death bed – "Look after these children" could never be forgotten by Narendra. He remembered it till his end. His love and affection for the Guru brothers were same as that of Sri Ramakrishna hearing-teaching, argument-counter argument, prayer-meditation, yoga-penance practised by them as per the directions of Narendra made his co-sannyasis completely lose the subtle emotions of their heart and made them like pure and shining gold. Sometimes, seeing the harsh meditative practices by the Guru brother, Narendra would make fun of them saying – "Do you think that by doing all this you would become Sri Ramakrishna Papramahansa? No…never, it is impossible. One Ramakrishna Paramahansa takes birth only once in an era."

After Sri Ramakrishna left the earthly abode. Mother Sharda went on a pilgrimage to Vrindavan along with two disciples. The mundaneness of the daily activities of Baranagar Mutt caused boredom in the minds of some sannyasis. They longed to go on a tour or pilgrimage. One day, Narendra had to go to Calcutta for some work. When he returned back from there he heard that three sannyasis have left the Mutt. Narendra was the leader of the Mutt. He was shouldering the responsibility of taking care of the sannyasis. Hence. on receiving this information he became sad and at the time worried. It was but natural on his part to feel sad at hearing that the sannyasis left the Mutt without consulting him. He was worried about the hardships the sannyasis were likely to face on their way with no money in their hands. At that moment, a Guru brother handed a piece of paper over to him in which it was written – "I am going to Vrindavan on foot. It has become impossible for me to stay here any more. Who knows when the mind will change. Sometimes my house, my relatives, my parents come in my dream. In my dreams, I am being lured by materialistic comforts. I have suffered much. Twice I was compelled to visit my home and meet my near ones due to this attraction. Hence, it is no more appropriate to stay here. To free myself from the clutches of materialistic attractions there is no other way left than to leave this place and go to a far flung place." This letter was written by Shardaprasann (Swami Trigunatitanand) who had left the Mutt in a secretive manner.

This letter proved to be an eye opener for him. "Oh! What have I done? I have embraced renunciation by breaking all ties with my family. But have I really been able to free myself from the worldly attractions? Now I am under the shackles of affection for the Mutt and the Guru brothers. When I was freed from one, the other one fell on my shoulders. I must surely break them all. Otherwise I won't fit to any slot. My home is the whole country, my family is all the citizens of this country, the area of my activity is quite broad and I have to look after the whole country. I have to understand the situation of people here. If I am being offered with different kinds of new experiences then only I would be able to assess the strength on the basis of action undertaken by me. By restraining myself within the four walls of this house in Baranagar neither am I able to make my life meaningful nor am I able to create self confidence and self-dependence in the minds of Guru brothers. Is it possible for the small trees to grow under a huge tree. To strengthen this Mutt, for the welfare of this country I should leave this Mutt. Narendra's decision was firm. One-day after entrusting the whole responsibilities of the Mutt with the other Guru brothers, Narendra left for Kashi.

At Kashi, he stayed at the Ashram of Shri Dwarkadas. There his daily routine was to beg alms for the sake of his stomach, visit the temple of God, meditation, worship etc. Shri Dwarkadas introduced him to a Bangali scholar Sant Bhudevchandra Chattopadhyay. His interaction and exchange of knowledge with Bhudev Babu made him happy. Bhudev Babu also got spellbound by Narendra's views on religion, morals, society etc. Talking about another person about Narendra, Bhudev said – "I am surprised that how this young man at this young age could gain such serious perspective and unlimited knowledge. I am sure that he will become a great person in the future." At Varanasi, Narendra met many yogis and saints. During those days, Swami, a renowned saint was sitting in deep meditation. Sri Ramakrishna Paramhansa had also met him once. Narendra also met him and had discussions with him. One day,

Narendra was returning from the temple of Mother Durga when a group of monkeys followed him. Seeing so many monkeys together, he became afraid and began to run. At that moment, a voice came from behind – "Stop and face the cruel beings." An old sannyasi was ordering Narendra to do so. Narendra stopped. The fear had disappeared from his mind. When the monkeys saw his courageous and strong countenance they backed away. This incident got registered itself in his mind. After many years, during his addresses in New York and other places he always used to cite and describe this incident and drew the attention of people towards the ideal behind it. To face nature, to face ignorance to face the myths within the mind is the greatest of all human religions. One should not back out from that duty.

Narendra's sensitive heart was not able to keep away from the attraction towards Baranagar Mutt. He soon returned back to Baranagar and resumed the earlier routine of teaching. Learning, prayer and meditation. But this time he could not continue to stay there for long. The company of sadhus in Kashi tried to draw him towards them. This time Shri Akhandanandji (one of Sri Ramakrishna's beloved disciples) introduced him to Shri Premdas Mitra. This man was a great scholar of Sanskrit language, literature and Vedanta philosophy. With them, Narendra usually had debates on religious theologies. Narendra was so impressed by his knowledge that whenever he used to have any doubt in religious texts he used to consult him through letters and clarify his doubts.

After this, Narendra toured many places in North India. The holy city of Ayodhya ruled by Lord Rama, settled in the lap of Saryu river, where every speck of the soil pervaded by the memories of Lord Rama. The Agra city which showered the incomparable art of the Mughal era. The night of full moon in the Hindu month of Kartik. The Taj Mahal built from white marble stood shining in the bright moonlight. The strange monument of Mumtaz Mahal's love story. A single glance at this monument, refreshes the age old memories of the Mughal Emperor Shahjahan. Lost in deep thoughts, Narendra wandered around Taj Mahal for a long time unaware of the time. The glorious mosques in Lucknow, beautiful palaces of Nawabs and their colourful gardens. The glories lost in the past, were still speaking volumes about their honour. The complete picture of Mughal era, whizzed past in front of his mind's eye.

After this, the Vrindavan inhabited by Surdas, Vidyapati, Jaidev and Chandi Das attracted Narendra. The banks of river Yamuna, the shadow of Kadamb tree and above all the magic of Krishna's flute passed before his eyes and reverberated his ears. Narendra was not ready to stop with this. To enjoy the natural beauty of Vrindavan, Narendra left the vehicle he had hired about 30 miles before and began to walk on foot. He had embraced the form of a complete saint wearing saffron dress, carrying a Kamandal (a container carried by saints) in one hand and two books in the other. He kept on walking and whenever he felt tired he took short breaks. If some generous person gave something to eat, he ate it. During his journey he saw that a person sitting on the road side was smoking pipe in a relaxed manner. "If I also take two-three puffs I will also feel relaxed", thought Narendra. He spread his hand in front of the person in a begging posture. He at once dragged himself away and hesitatingly said, "I am low caste 'Bhangi' belonging to the sweeper class. According to the traditional culture prevalent during those days, he withdrew his hands and stepped behind and without saying anything walked ahead to his destined direction. He must have just taken two-three steps ahead that something striked his mind – "What am I doing this? I have embraced Sannyasa. I have undertook to the oath of living a life above caste, creed, untouchability and familial status. Then why did I draw myself away from that man, refusing to touch his pipe or smoke it when he said that he was of low-caste birth. This is the outcome of the culture we have been following all through the ages. The internal duel going on within the mind of Narendra had ended as if somebody had awakened his inner soul which was in deep slumber by hitting with a hunter. He turned back his direction and walked towards the man who was still sitting there enjoying the pipe. As soon as he reached near the man, he said, Son, please let me smoke it." The man was taken aback in surprise and was at the same time in a dilematic situation – "What the hell has happened to this saint. He is not listening to me at all. How can I be a sinner by letting him smoke the pipe used by me." In spite of his negative answers, he continued enjoying the pipe and kept on constantly looking at this God like saint in an intimidated manner. After this, Narendra felt happy and satisfied and resumed his journey towards Vrindavan.

Once after reaching Vrindavan he stayed at a temple. The temple was famously known as 'Kala Babu Ka Kunj'. The forefathers of Balram Bose who was one of the disciples of Sri Ramakrishna had constructed this temple. No sooner than he reached there he experienced an ecstatic feeling of the supreme love between Radha and Krishna and the infallible connection between the soul and the Almighty. He began to wander here and there lost in the imagination of this celestial love. Once he went on a walk towards Govardhan mountain and felt unconscious due to hunger and tiredness. When he regained back his consciousness he got up and be_ _n to walk towards the temple. As he was walking, he heard someone calling him from behind. But he did not pay any attention to that and kept on walking ahead. But that person continued calling Narendra from behind. The person had to run about a mile to catch up with Narendra. He very humbly requested Narendra to partake the food he had brought for him. When Narendra quenched his hunger by partaking that food, the person felt satisfied and happy and returned back. Narendra never saw that man again in the vicinity. Whenever the thought of this unexpected godly help that he received came to his mind he became ecstatic.

After Vrindavan, his next destination was Haridwar. Railway station – Hathras. Narendra was tired after wandering extensively. So he sat at the station itself for taking rest. The station master was a very religious person. He suddenly saw the young saint sitting. Spiritualism reflected on his face. He went near the sannyasi perhaps with the view to extend his help. After the initial 'Namaskar' and all Sharat Babu took Narendra to his home and served food to him very lovingly. He was so impressed and influenced by Narendra's views that he resigned from the job of station master and embraced the kamandal and the saffron dress. Narendra's fame spread all over Hathras especially the Bengalis settled there who assembled to hear and have a glimpse of Narendra. They wanted Narendra to stay there for some more days. But Narendra had to complete his mission. He found it inappropriate to stay at one place for long. He said, "I cannot stay here for any longer. We sannyasis should not stay at one place for many days.

Moreover, I am developing a feeling of affection towards you all. This is also a kind of boundation for spiritual life. Do not compel me too much." Sharat and other people tried to reason out with them but he stuck to his words. At last Sharat and one of his friends put forth the proposal of becoming his disciples. At this, Narendra said, "Why! Don't think that only by becoming a disciple you will be able to achieve something in the life of spirituality. Remember that there is God in every thing. Whatever you do will be for your own progress. I will come to you whenever I get time." But Sharat was not the one who would have got convinced so easily. At last Narendra was compelled to give him disciplehood. Sharat also became a sannyasi in every aspect i.e., mind, words and action and went to Rishikesh along with Narendra. Sharat who had all through his life led a life of comforts found the life of yogi to be uncomfortable. Aimless life, limited food, broader work area, many kinds of difficulties and discomforts on the route. It was in fact a hard endeavour. Walking along with Narendra he fell unconscious due to hunger, thirst and tiredness. But Narendra helped him a lot. On the way while going towards the jungle they saw the skeletal remaring of a human being, near which rags of saffron clothes covered with dust was also lying. A sense of pity came over in Narendra's eyes. He said, "See the king of jungle has killed and eaten the flesh of a sannyasi here. Are you afraid?"

"Swamiji, why should I fall in your company?" The disciple answered in a fearless manner.

Swami and the disciple reached Rishikesh. The whole atmosphere enveloped in the colour of spiritualism created a sense of magic over Narendra. The mountain ranges covered with snow, the playful waves of the Ganga flowing, the yogis living in small grass hutments engaged in meditation, the echoes of mantras being chanted by priests and saints and the fragrance of incense flowing in the air – everything had the magic of attraction. Navendra had reached a place of his heart's disk. But after some days Sharat had become very weak. Hence, he had to return back to Hathras along with Sharat. As soon as they reached Hathras, Narendra suffered from Malaria. The Guru brothers in Baranagar somehow came to know about it. They came to Hathras and forcibly took Narendra to Hathras. After some months of stay at Baranagar, he totally regained back his health.

Now Narendra also joined the activity of teaching and learning that had been going on there. In order to make the residents of the ashram well-versed in Vedopanishad, he got a copy of the Veda written by his friend at Benaras and a renowned Sanskrit scholar Pramda Babu. While learning the Veda whenever there arises some controversial passage and he feels unable to solve it, he instantly put up the doubt before Pramda Babu through letter. After staying at Bara Nagar along with his Guru brothers, in December 1889, he set off to Vaidyanath Dham once again. Then he went to Benaras again. He wanted to stay there for some time. But he could not do so. A few days after reaching Benaras he received the information that one of his Guru brother was ridden with chicken pox. Narendra reached Allahabad. There the Bengalis in the city intended a hearty welcome. After serving and looking after the Guru brother, Narendra entered into a discussion of spiritual and social issues with the people there. There he came into contact with a Muslim saint. Narendra soon got attracted towards him because he resembled Sri Krishna in form and figure. At Allahabad, he heard some surprising facts about a yogi staying in Ghazipur. He could not suppress his desire to meet that yogi and went towards Ghazipur.

The yogi at Ghazipur was popularly known as Pawhari Baba. He was born in a Brahmin family at Kashi and had left his home in his childhood itself and had come over to Ghazipur. At Ghazipur, he stayed with his uncle – a Brahmachari saint and learnt Law, Grammar, Vedanta and practiced Yog Sadhna. On the Gurnar mountain in Kathiawad, he did severe penance and tapasya. During his youth days, he travelled all over India, met different kinds of people and nurtured his life with different types of experiences and returned back to Ghazipur. At Ghazipur, near the river bank he dug the land and prepared a small room for himself and stayed there in meditation for many days. Sometimes he never came out of the place even after the lapse of a month. People used to doubt whether Pahwari Baba was either dead or alive. In the name of food, he partook just the leaves of Neem and red chillies, that too only after first offering it to God. Rarely ever, whenever he could grain food, he first offered it to God and after that made a poor fellow or a tired traveler eat it and he himself remained hungry. Hence, he came to be known as Pahwari Baba (one who survives on air) to have a glance of Pahwari Baba was a big problem for Narendra because he rarely came out from the den where he practised sadhna. Rarely he sits inside the den near its door when people used to see him and talk to him. Narendra also saw him in that situation. He was fortunate enough and both of them got attracted towards each other's personality. Later on in his writings Narendra had made a mention about Pahwari Babu stating that undoubtedly, he is a great saint. He is an example of a person possessing a surprising capacity to do yoga and meditation even during these days of atheistic tendencies. And it is indeed a Mutter of surprise. I have taken shelter with him and he has assured me which is not so easy to achieve for everyone."

Pahwari Baba had already met Sri Ramakrishna Paramhansa at an earlier occasion and was well aware of his greatness. He honoured Narendra, being the disciple of Ramakrishna. He was also greatly impressed. Slowly Narendra became very close to Pahwari Baba. One due to ill health he could not go and meet him and he himself sent a person to collect information regarding Narendra. When Narendra came he said – "Give me comfort, staying with me here for a few days." He imparted Narendra knowledge regarding yog and sadhna in a humble and loving manner. Whenever they both entered into a discussion on philosophy and ideals they reached such heights that others present were unable to understand the actual meaning.

Narendra's association with such an enigmatic person like Pahwari Baba had made him quite restive. Two entirely different powers were pulling his soul towards two different directions. Sometimes he bent towards one direction and somet mes towards the other. On the one hand, his wish to attain the joy of practicing yog sadhna in the company of Pahwari Baba and on the other to save Indian from the pit of darkness, the keenness to awake it from the deep pit of darkness. And most of the time he got fatally attracted towards the inexplicable ecstasy that he enjoyed while engaged in meditation. But whenever he desired to follow the ideals of Pahwari Baba, the invisible hands of Ramakrishna tried to obstruct him. Narednra felt as if Ramakrishna was standing in front of him and staring at him. At that moment, Ramakrishna's voice echoed in his ears

– "You have tasted the ultimate state of samadhi. At present, we have kept it locked and its key will remain with me. Now you have to do your work. When you complete the work then you can enter into a state of continuous samadhi. This way all his keenness to continue with his discipleship under Pahwari Baba disappeared. This happened many a time. At last, Narendra turned his mind away from Pahwari Baba. After these incidents, new revelations about the personality of Sri Ramakrishna that were till now unrevealed to Narendra, came to him. He came closer to Gurudev and understood him in a thorough manner.

At the same moment, Narendra felt that he should build a memorial in honour of Sri Ramakrishna in his birthland Bengal. When he returned back to Baranagar from Ghazipur he was busy for long in collecting things to fulfill his ambition. Most of Ramakrishna's devotees, who were leading a family life and had extended all sorts of help during Ramakrishna's illness and in setting up the Bara Nagar Mutt, had already left the earthly abode. Narendra communicated his intentions to Pramda Das Babu staying in Benaras through letters. It proved to be beneficial to a certain extent but not to the extent of building the memorial so easily. Narendra was not able to calm himself – it seemed as if he was searching for something he had lost. He felt restive at the precarious condition of Indian society bound with the shackles of illiteracy and superstition, the bad activities taking place at the pretext of Hindu religion, the lifeless eyes of people ridden with poverty, hunger and disease. Narendra's heart was in utter turmoil. He was not able to choose a proper direction to initiate his action. Once again he became fed up of his stay at Bara Nagar. The valleys of Himalayas beckoned him. He felt as if those mountain peaks were calling him – "Come, rest in my lap, then you will attain peace."

When Narendra embraced the life of a wanderer, he came to be known as 'Swamiji'. His Guru brothers and others whom he met during his journey used to address him as "Swamiji". Henceforth, it will be appropriate to refer to him as 'Swamiji'.

Swamiji was earnestly keen to journey the Himalayas. Life at Calcutta had become disinteresting to him. His condition was like the bird caged in a golden cage. He received honour, respect and every sort of happiness in Calcutta. But he did not want all that. He wanted a wide sky, with no corner of it untouched by him. He could not control the attraction of traveling with free mind, touring of the motherland and experiencing different and new thing. He began to forget his responsibilities with regard to Baranagar Mutt. It was very important for Guru brother to attain proficiency in organizing the activities of the Mutt. He called all of them and said – "I am going to the Himalayas. I won't return from there unless I attain the power of awakening the whole humanity with a mere touch and that power will be achieved only by gaining a first hand experience of truth."

Swamiji went to meet Mother Sharda, sought her blessings and set on his journey. He was also accompanied by Guru brother Akhandanand. Both of them first reached Bhagalpur and stayed there as guest of Nityanand Sinha and then stayed with Manmathnath Choudhary and Mathuranath Sinha for a few days. Earlier they did not give much attention to Swamiji considering him to be a common Swami. But after conversing with him they realized that a strange kind of talent was present in his personality. And soon the residents of Bhagalpur assembled to meet him. After Bhagalpur, their next destinations were Vaidyanath Dham, Benaras, Nainital and then Almora. Wherever they went and stayed, after sometimes their name and fame spread far and wide. There they met two other Guru brothers Sharadanand and Vaikunthnath. They had left the Mutt quite early with the wish to journey the Himalayas. Swamiji stayed at the residence of one Amba Dutt. Only a few days might have lapsed after Vivekanand's stay there that he received a quite unexpected and shocking news. One of Swamiji's sisters had committed suicide unable to bear the sufferings inflicted by the society. Such a miserable fall of the society! Swamiji was greatly perturbed at hearing this. This incident converted the hidden spark of social upliftment into a huge fire ball.

After this, he took along with him only Akhandanand first going to Garhwal and then to Srinagar. There also he continued with his daily routine of learning—teaching, prayer, worship, thinking-meditation, etc. They first partook whatever grains they received in alms and slept under a tree for almost a month. There Swamiji came across a teacher who originally belonged to the Vaishya caste but had converted himself into Christianity. But impressed and influenced by Swami Vivekanand he once again embraced Hinduism.

Swamiji stayed at Dehradun for a week and again returned back to Rishikesh. The solitary beauty of nature, the Ganga flowing as if dancing to some unknown tune, the small hutments roofed with grass spread all over the hills and valleys – how could Swamiji resist all these attractions. His ashram was near the Chandreswar Mahadev temple. There the conditions once again defeated him very badly. He was entrapped in a severe illness. The valley was extremely cold. Blanket was spread on the hard floor of the hutment and Swamiji was lying unconscious on it down with high fever. In such an unconscious state he was mumbling abnormal things when the residents there saw the miserable state of Swamiji. They provided him with medicines for treatment. Slowly Swamiji's condition improved. But to regain back his health completely he took some time. He stayed there for some more times even after gaining his health. During this period of illness Vivekanand felt that he was dependent on Akhandanand to a certain extent and was in the clutches of desire. A true yogi should lead a solitary life and should have trust in luck. Then only he will be able to fulfill his objectives. He discussed his longing for solitary life with Akhandanand. But Swami Akhandanand was not ready to leave Swami Vivekanand alone. Hence, one day in the early morning hours, when nobody was awake, Swami Vivekanand left the hutment in Rishikesh without telling anyone.

Swamiji wanted to remain in a self imposed exile without the knowledge of his relatives and acquaintances. Hence, he christened himself with a new name. He called himself Vividishanand. Now Delhi was the centre of attraction for him. Delhi was the symbol of ancient glory. The Hastinapur of Kauravas and Pandavas, the memories of Gulam, Khilji, Tughlak, Lodhi was still alive in the crumbled monuments. The worshipper of prosperity and luxury – Mughal Emperor Shahjahan had changed the very image of Delhi. To make his memoir permanent he built his fort near the banks of Yamuna which became famous as Lal Quila. This fort built with red sandstone still stands tall reflecting the glory of the Mughals. From the age of Kauravas and Pandavas, the ever youthful Delhi transitioned from bride to widow and then to bride a number of times. The process of beautification, decoration and destruction kept on happening. During the reign of Shahjahan, Mughal architecture was in its golden period. Swamiji experienced a sense of satisfaction and joy after inspecting the remains of the Mughal architecture.

In Delhi, he stayed at the house of Sh. Shyamal Das. The people there were greatly impressed by the scholastic teachings of Swamiji. Two Guru brothers from Baranagar who were at Meerut at that time heard the name and fame of Swami Vividishanand, and his deep knowledge of not only religious texts and scriptures but also holy books of every religion as well as contemporary western thoughts and philosophy. They also heard about the young Swami's grasp over English language both spoken and written. They were drawn to Delhi, out of curiosity to meet this young wizard of knowledge. But when they actually met Swami Vividishanand they were greatly surprised.

Both the guru brothers were thrilled at meeting Swamiji after so many days. They expressed their wish to stay with him. But Swamiji was not ready to accept their proposal. He said – "My dear brothers, I had already told you that I want to stay alone. I had also told you not to follow me. I repeat the same things again." After this the guru brothers started staying away from him. After a short stay in Delhi and leaving a long lasting impact on Delhites he went towards Rajasthan (Rajputana). During those days Swamiji was very keen and particular about staying away from people who knew him and he enjoyed it. He had taken a firm decision to keep on marching ahead even if there is a way or not. This feet will crush every thorn that will come his way and will create a new path. Now he should not stop any where. He wanted to embrace all the experiences in this world. The very thought made Swamiji's heart so firm that his heart became pure and devoid of worldly attachments and emotions.

At Rajasthan, he first stepped at Alwar. After alighting from the train as he walked on the main road, he reached in front of a royal ayurvedic medical shop. He met there a nice doctor, named Gurucharan Laskar who looked like a Bengali. Hence, Swamiji enquired him about a place of stay for saints. Gurucharan was greatly attracted by the humble behaviours, personality and sweet conversation of Swamiji. He arranged a room upstairs in the market itself for Swamiji and introduced him to one of his Muslim friends who was a teacher of Urdu and Parsi in the nearby school. He had a long discussion with them about the religion of Islam. Greatly impressed by Gandhiji's talks and knowledge, he called some more of his Muslim friends to meet Swamiji. In this way, at Alwar also people crowded at the place where Swamiji stayed to hear his discources on philosophy and other topics. The people of Alwar were spellbound after listening to the Urdu songs, Hindi devotional songs, Bengali songs and other quotations from Upanishads, Bible and Quran. The number of visitors who came to meet Swamiji increased day by day and his small room was no more sufficient to accommodate them all. Arrangement for a big room was made for Swamiji at the place of a retired engineer Pt. Shambhunath.

The room had ample space to accommodate more numbers of people. Hence, to have a glimpse of Swamiji and to hear his discourse more and more, different types of people came. Once Swamiji was describing about some secret topic. At that time one of his guest audiences put a question – "Swamiji, you belong to which caste?"

Swamiji answered in a serious tone – "Kayasth". Then came the next question – "Swamiji, why do you wear saffron outfit?"

Swamiji again answered in a calm tone – "Because this is the dress code of saints. If I wear bright dresses then people will seek alms from me also. Since I myself am a beggar I do not have even a single paise in my possession that I can give in alms. If somebody asks me something and I am not able to give that to him then I feel wretched and miserable. When other beggars see my saffron outfit they understand that I am also a beggar and do not think of seeking alms from me."

Swamiji never felt irritated at such kind of silly and unintellectual question in between his discussion on serious and important topics. He welcomed every question in an equally calm and patient manner whether asked by a scholar or an illiterate, a cunning or a stupid person, a good or a bad man, rich or poor and gave satisfactory reply to all of them. Manlavi was one of the greatest admirers of Swamiji and he was also Swamiji's beloved. He longed that Swamiji went to his home and have meals. But being a Muslim, he never expressed his desire directly. One day he presented his desire before Swamiji in a hesitant manner. He said that he will get the cooked food in clean utensils by a Brahmin and will get all the utensils cleaned by a Brahmin. Swamiji made him understand that he was a sannyasi and sannyasis do not differentiate between caste, creed or status of a person whosoever invites in a devoted manner, he accepts the invitation. Hearing this the Muslims were greatly thrilled and many of them invited Swamiji to their homes for meals.

During those days, Emperor of Alwar state Mangal Singh was greatly influenced by the culture and civilization of British. His minister discussed about Swamiji's with him. The king was also greatly impressed by Swamiji indepth knowledge of English. When he first met Swamiji he asked – "Swamiji, you are such a great scholar and if you wish you can earn wealth by the means of imparting your knowledge to those who are keen to earn knowledge. But instead you are involved in begging alms. Swamiji gave an appropriate and fitting reply to the question in a fearless manner.

"Maharaj, first you tell me why you like the company of westerners. Why are you overlooking your kingly responsibilities and involved in hunting and other luxurious endeavours?"

The king's ministers and other courtiers were taken aback by this question on the part of Swamiji. But the King replied in a calm and peaceful manner – "I cannot say properly why. But there is no doubt that I love such kind of life."

Swamiji replied – "Then I have also embraced this life style of a wandering sadhu."

The king was thoroughly against idol worship. He did not like that and had no faith in it. Once he sarcastically said how one can consider a stone idol to be God. The manner in which the king made this statement hurt Swamiji. Flames of anger were shown in his eyes. A huge portrait of the King was hung on the wall and he removed the portrait from the wall and kept it on the floor and ordered the king's minister in stern voice – "Spit on this. What is this, just a piece of paper. Why are you hesitant to spit on this paper?"

There was complete silence in the king's court. Swamiji's countenance made the minister and other courtiers shiver in fear. A duel was going on in the minister's mind. He felt as if his intellect and reasoning abilities have failed. On the one hand, the situation of the king where his honour was at stake and on the other the fear of Swamiji's anger. He sometimes looked towards the king and sometimes towards Swamiji in an intimidated manner.

Swamiji again roared – "Spit on this. I am asking you to spit."

The minister who was afraid and intimidated shouted like a mad man – "What Swamiji? What are you asking me to do. This is the picture of our King. How can I do so?"

Swamiji countenance was calm. He said – "This is what happens. In this the king is not present. This is a mere piece of paper. It does not contain his bones, flesh or blood. It does not move around, nor speaks nor even behave like the King. Still you all do no want to spit on it because you see his image on this paper. And by spitting on it you would undoubtedly feel that you are disregarding your King.

Turning towards the King, Swamiji said that thought the picture is not made of the actual ingredients with which the King's body is made but the picture is the alter image of King. Hence the minister was unable to spit on it. Similarly the true devotee of God sees the image of God in the idol. The image of some special God comes to the mind of the devotee when he sees the image of some special God. We have trust on the God and have full faith on the God. And one attains the God whom he trusts.

The King listened to Swamiji's words quite attentively and with deep gratitude. As soon as Swamiji ended his talk, the king said – "Swamiji, with your blessings I have been able to attain new knowledge regarding idol worship. In fact if I look through your perspective. I haven't seen even a single worshipper of wood or stone. Till now I was not aware of the actual secret behind idol worship and did not even try to understand that. But today you opened my eyes. Swamiji, kindly bless me."

With affection filled in his eyes, Swamiji said – "Who else other than God himself has the power to give blessings. Take shelter at his feet with simple and pure thoughts and he will surely bless you."

Swamiji's behaviour touched the king's heart. Seeing Swamiji off in a reverential manner, he called his minister and said to him that he had never met a great personality like Swamiji. Such splendour and personality would be rather rare.

The people of Alwar were greatly influenced by Swamiji. Many people came before him with a view to oppose his views but were unable to escape from his influence. Many young men who were impressed by his knowledge of Sanskrit came to learn Sanskrit from him. In addition to teaching them Sanskrit, Swamiji drew their attention towards developments in science taking place in the western world and convinced them that by merely learning Sanskrit, India cannot progress. The western world had made a pretty good progression on the path of science and technology. Hence we should gain more knowledge in the field of science so that we are able to tread our steps with them. Then only we will be able to survive and live with other countries and develop ourselves. Jaipur was Swamiji's next destination after Alwar.

At Jaipur he stayed for over two weeks. There he became acquainted with a renowned scholar of Sanskrit grammar. Swamiji went to him and considering his Guru expressed his wish to learn Sanskrit grammar from him and attain proficiency in it. The teacher started with teaching Ashtadhyayi written by Panini. Even after two three days of continuous efforts the scholar was not able to make Swamiji understand the first stanza. On the fourth day the scholar said to Swamiji – "Swamiji, you won't benefit much by studying at my place because for the past three days I have been trying hard to teach you one chapter and I have failed in my attempt."

Swamiji felt ashamed at this. He took the book from his Guru and took a firm decision in his mind that till the time he learns all the chapters in the book, he won't partake even a single grain of food or even water. Within two days he learned the whole book thoroughly and went before his teacher with all humility and respects. Guruji asked him the meanings of certain stanzas. After answering the questions being asked by Guruji, Swamiji explained the meaning of the whole book. The scholar was wonderstruck. He had never come across such a genius student who had become the teacher of the teacher in just two days.

Swamiji became a good friend of the chief of the army of the Jaipur state Sardar. Hari Singh. He also stayed at Hari Singh's home for a few days. Hari Singh who believed in the Vedanta philosophy did not have faith in idol worship. He always discussed about it with Swamiji but in spite of all this there occurred no change in his thoughts. One evening both Swamiji and Hari Singh were walking along the road side talking with each other. Suddenly they heard sweet and melodious song accompanied by music. Some devotees were taking out a chariot procession of Lord Krishna. All of them were very much engrossed in singing songs in praise of Lord Krishna. Swamiji and Hari Singh walked along with the procession. Swamiji himself was lost in devotion. But for Hari Singh all this was just a joke. At that moment Swamiji touched Hari Singh's hand and said → "Look at the lively form of God."

Hari Singh's eyes were resting on the idol. He kept on looking at the idol without blinking his eyes and tears of love came rolling down his eyes. What kind of magic it was, that was quite unknown. He regained back his consciousness after a long time. He was overwhelmed with love and said, Swamiji, the thing I had not been able to understand even after so much reasoning, I have understood with a mere touch from you."

From Jaipur, Swamiji went to Ajmer and from Ajmer to Mount Abu. Mount Abu was famous for its beauty and the architecture of Dilwara temple. The temple was built with white marbles. A very delicate sculptural etching was done on these white marbles like the one done on elephant tusk. Swamiji stood spellbound looking this wonderful piece of art. At Mount Abu also within a short span of time he became surrounded by many friends and devotees.

One evening, Swamiji along with his devotees strolled along the mountainous roads and reached near the stream and enthralled by the beautiful and peaceful envirous sat there and began to sing devotional songs. Slowly people strolling nearby gathered near him attracted by his emotive melodious voice. Within a few minutes, a good crowd gathered around him. Some western and European tourists also got attracted towards the melodious song and stood listening to him spellbound. All who assembled there became keen to have a glimpse of the singer. With great difficulty, they made a way to reach near Swamiji and all of them showered praises on him for his melodious rendition.

Swamiji had set up his camp inside a cave in one of the mountains. One day, a famous Muslim lawyer of the king of Khatri was passing through the mountains when his eyes fell on the young sannyasi sitting in deep meditation. The passerby was obviously attracted towards the gentle-loving personality of Swamiji. When the Muslim lawyer became acquainted with Swamiji, the former was greatly attracted by Swamiji's incomparable knowledge and loving nature. During rainy season Swamiji had to face great difficulties due to the absence of door. After much insistence on the part of the Muslim lawyer, Swamiji finally agreed to go to his house. The lawyer introduced Swamiji to many renowned people in the area. During those days the king of Khatri along with his ministers had come to spend the summer at Mount Abu. The lawyer invited the Diwan of King of Khatri, Munshi Jagmohan Lal to his house to introduce him to Swamiji. When Diwan Jagmohan Lal reached the lawyer's house, Swamiji was sleeping on a cot just wearing a loin dress. Diwan kept on looking at him and thought – "He is looking like a simple sadhu. Even thieves and robbers resemble them." Within few seconds Swamiji opened his eyes and got up seeing a stranger in front of him. Diwan gave his self-introduction and asked – "Swamiji, even after being a Hindu Sannyasi you are staying at a Muslim's house. You might be eating the food touched and prepared by Muslims."

Swamiji answered in a serious manner, "Sir, what do you mean by this? I am a sannyasi. I am above all social barriers. I can have my meals in the company of a sweeper even. This is the directions of God. Hence, I am not afraid. I am not afraid of any religious texts because even those religious texts support this. But yes, I am afraid of some people like you who are acquainted with English language. You people are not bothered about religious texts or God. I perceive the Almighty God in every thing around us and I do not believe in high or low birth."

Talking in this manner he became very aggressive. Swamiji's thoughts influenced Diwan very much. When he returned back to the king he discussed about Swamiji with the king. When the king of Khatri heard all this he was so impressed that he sent an invitation for Swamiji. The Diwan himself took Swamiji to the king's court. The king extended a hearty and honourable welcome to Swamiji, first made Swamiji to sit and then he himself took his seat. As soon as he sat, he shot the question – "Swamiji, what is life?"

"An inherent strength, which persistently makes effort to show its real self but the outside nature constantly tries to suppress it. This whole endeavour is life." Swamiji gave an instant reply.

After this the king asked so many questions and he was happy to receive an appropriate and scholastic reply to each of his questions. Swamiji narrated to him the story of Gurudev Sri Ramakrishna Paramhansa. He listened to the story of Gurudev quite intently and with full devotion. After a few days, the king compulsively took Swamiji to his state.

At Khatri, the king Ajit Singh and Diwan Jagmohan accepted the discipleship of Swamiji. After much request on their part he accepted their invitation to stay in the palace. The king indulged in conversation on western and Indian philosophy, religion, Sanskrit literature, music etc with Swamiji on daily basis.

Swamiji and the king had struck a chord of camaraderie which was based on simplicity, innocence and generosity. The faith and trust they had on each other had now transformed into a strong friendship. The king had great fascination for music. He himself was a very talented veena player. He was also well acquainted with playing harmonium. Swamiji also loved music very much. Hence, sometimes both of them used to get so much engrossed in musical endeavours that one used to sing song and the other played either veena or harmonium. Sometimes they rode on horses to tourist locations. They partook meals also together.

The king was well acquainted with both Sanskrit and English. He also had good knowledge of Shastras too. But he did not have any knowledge regarding science. He began learning the science of chemistry, physics and astrology from Swamiji for practical learning a science laboratory was set upon the first floor of the palace. To see the position and movement of stars a telescope was also set up. Many a times they went to the roof top of the palace at night and studied the movement and position of stars for hours together.

During Swamiji's stay at Khatri it was summer season. The hot dusty winds that blew during day time troubled Swamiji a lot. He became ill. When the king saw his conditions he suggested him to wear a headgear. In places having hot climate one should cover his head to save from loo. Swamiji followed the king's advise. The king himself taught Swamiji to tie the headgear. After this, Swamiji made the headgear a necessary part of costume for the rest of his life. It made Swamiji's personality even more attractive.

After becoming a sunnyasi, Swamiji changed many names. At the Baranagar Mutt, all the disciples of Sri Ramakrishna changed their names to snap all their relations with the past. At that time Narendranath changed his name to Swami Sachidanand. After a few days when he felt his increasing attachment towards the Guru brothers, he left the Mutt to undertake a journey of India and learn more about Indian. Then he changed his name to Swami Vividishanand, so that the other Guru brothers were not able to find him out easily. When he met the king of Khatri, then also he was known by the name of Vividishanand. One day, while Swamiji was sitting along side the king at his palace, the king said in a joking manner – "Swamiji, your name is very tough. For common people it would be quite difficult to understand its meaning without the help of a dictionary. Moreover, it is a bit difficult to pronounce too. Above all, the period of your 'Vividisha' is also over. ('Vividisha' means desire for knowledge)

"Which name do you like?" asked Swamiji.

The king thought for a while and replied, "In my opinion there is one name that best suits you – Vivekanand."

Swamiji revered the king very much and his wishes. Hence, from that day onwards he accepted his name and Vivekanand and he became world famous by that name.

One evening, Swamiji was sitting along with the king in the palace. They were discussing on topics pertaining to religion. A dance programme by danseuse was also organized in the palace. No. sooner than the singer entered the hall and Swamiji saw her, he got up to leave the place. His face was red with anger and hatred. But the king made him sit pulling his hand saying – "Swamiji, just listen to her song, it awakens the highest of emotions within us."

Swamiji was in a dilemma as to what to do. Then he thought that he will listen to one song and leave the place, and sat there. The singer also noticed Swamiji's first reaction, read the emotions on his face but being at a distance could not listen to what the king had said. She felt as if she was insulted and she was ashamed. She somehow controlled herself and rendered a song written by Surdas in a very touching manner.

Surdas, beautiful lyrics described the feelings of a fallen woman. The song touched Swamiji's heart and a feeling of pity arouse in him. He felt ashamed of his earlier behaviour.

Swami Vivekanand: A Biography

Self-condemnation poked him. He gained a unique lesson from a dancer – the lesson of humanity, the lesson of morality and above all the lesson of eternal truth. He had forgotten the universal truth that in all beings, the single Almighty Brahm was present. He later on wrote about the incident – "When I heard this song I thought, is this the life of sannyasa which I have been leading all through. Even after being a sannyasi I am differentiating myself with a woman."

Swamiji was only physically present in the palace of the king of theatre, but his thoughts were roaming elsewhere – along with a Tibetan family residing on the foothills of the Himalayas. They were six brothers but all of them shared a single wife. Swamiji whose social and cultural parameters were different from theirs, found this custom of Tibetans immoral and sinful. Swamiji tried his level best to convince the six men about the stigma associated with this custom. But the men condemned Swamiji's advise.

They considered it selfish and mean to have a desire for one wife for each. The curtain of ignorance that veiled his eyesight got unveiled suddenly. He got an insight into the advantages of this custom followed by Tibetans. That day Swamiji took a firm decision that in order to understand the custom or tradition of a particular caste or community, he will widen his own moral perspective.

In the company of the king of Khatris, many such experiences came to Swamiji's mind. Now Swamiji was a changed man. His fundamental, religious and social beliefs had freed themselves from every shackles. He was surprised to gain one novel experience or the other at every step of his life. Later on, when he analyzed those experiences at depth, he attained knowledge – knowledge that enlightened the path of others. By wandering the country and abroad, he received this very knowledge which cannot be found in any book.

During those days, a renowned Sanskrit grammarian, Pt. Narayan Das used to stay in the palace of the king of Khatri. Swamiji began to learn Panini's Sutras based on Patanjali's Mahabhashya from him. Within a few days Panditji taught everything to Swamiji. Now Swamiji also gained perfect control over Sanskrit grammar. But he always referred to Pt. Narayan Das as his Guru.

The king of Khatri had great trust on the godly powers of Swamiji. He did not have a son till that date. One day, he discussed his hidden agony of not having a son. He requested in a distressed manner – "Bless me in such a manner that I beget a son."

Resting his glance on the king's face, Swamiji said in a calm voice – "Okay, with the blessings of Sri Ramakrishna, your wish will get fulfilled."

And indeed the king's wish got fulfilled. It was not so that residing in the palace of the king of Khatri, Swamiji had snapped all his contracts with Swamiji. He went to the homes of miserable and poor devotees and partook food from them. The whole of Khatri state was impressed by the personality of Swamiji.

After his five months long stay in Khatri, Swamiji went to Ahmedabad. He journeyed on foot continuously for many days and survived on the alms given by people. Later on, he was given shelter at a judge's house. He stayed their visited the famous places in Ahmedabad. During those days, many scholars of Jain literature and religion stayed in Ahmedabad. Gradually, Swamiji became acquainted with those scholars and he gained knowledge regarding the religion of Jainism and the literatures pertaining to it.

Swamiji's next destination was Limbdi. At Limbdi also he had to wander a lot before setting down at a specific location. After much enquiry he gained knowledge about the location of a saints society. It was quite away from the city at a lonely place. The members of the society extended a hearty welcome to Swamiji. Later on, Swamiji realized that those saints were worshippers of 'Linga' sect and they had a group of woman accompanying them. One night, Swamiji tried to escape from there unnoticed but he found his room locked from outside. Two people were guarding his room from outside. Swamiji pretended as if he was unaware of the situation. One day, the leader of the saints called Swamiji and said, "There is the brightness of celibacy on your face. You have followed this difficult ritual till now and we are in search of a glorious person like you. By destroying your celibacy we will be able to fulfill a unique worship. Then we will be able to gain a strange and rare knowledge of Brahma. The fire of rebellion flared inside Swamiji's heart but outwardly he behaved in a calm manner. The saints were unable to understand Swamiji's actual state of mind. A young boy from Limbdi used to visit Swamiji at the said ashram. Swamiji slipped a letter to the king of Limbdi with a request to save him from the clutches of these saints. No sooner than the king received the letter, he sent his men to release Swamiji from the ashram and bring him to his palace. The king's men brought Swamiji to the palace of the king. This was a new experience that made Swamiji careful regarding the future. With the help of the king of Limbdi, Swamiji visited some famous nearby areas such as Bhavnagar, Junagarh, etc. Junagarh attracted Swamiji very much due to the overt presence of ruins of Hindu and Muslim civilizations. The fragrance of incense and the reverberation of the clear chanting of shlokas from the temples of Hindu, Buddhist and Jain religion was spread all over in the atmosphere there. Crowds visited beautiful mosques and monuments. Swamiji developed a great likeness for the place, especially the Girnaar mountain ranges which made Swamiji spell bound. Swamiji camped in one of the caves in these mountains. He was able to concentrate on his prayer and meditation. The Diwan of Junagarh state extended all necessary assistance to Swamiji.

Like in other places, Swamiji's fans, friends and devotees assembled there also. Swamiji's next destination was Bhoj where he reached with the help of the Diwan of Junagarh who gave him introduction letter addressed to big wigs in Bhoj. At Bhoj, Swamiji stayed in the house of the Diwan of the king of Bhoj. The Somnath temple, which possesses great significance in history, repeatedly attacked by Muslim kings and stripped off its prosperity decorated by the Hindus – Swamiji longed to see the temple of Somnath that endured persistent foreign attacks to uphold its glory. Soon he set out on his journey to see the ancient temple of Somnath, the sun temple and the newly constructed Somnath temple by Rani Ahilyabai. There Swamiji got acquainted with the king of Kutch. The king extended a warm welcome to Swamiji and had long discussions with him on religion, philosophy, literature, science, etc. After listening to Swamiji's deep scholarly talks, the king said that he felt the same state of dizziness that he experienced after reading books on tough subjects.

Swamiji was a person with such a royal personality that wherever he went the kings and emperors extended him a honourable and appropriate welcome quite befitting his personality. All of them wanted Swamiji to stay with them in their palace forever. He stayed in the palaces as long as he felt the need to do so. Some people questioned the legitimacy of his royal stay and slandered against him. Somebody even mustered up the courage to question him about the appropriateness of a saint's stay in royal courts. Swamiji made him understand his objective behind this in an extremely calm manner. He said that his area of responsibility was quite broad and by influencing the kings and heads of the state, he was in a way lightening his task. His motive was to instill true and permanent emotion of dependence in the minds of the kings. This sense of dependence and just rule will in turn bring out welfare of the subjects. The welfare of the citizens means not only the fulfillment of their physical needs of food, clothing and shelter but also their mental and moral development. Influenced and inspired by the objectives and feelings of Swamiji, all the kings who had become acquainted with him promised to bring about improvements that had wider social significance. "If I am able to win over their hearts, who had the power of money as well as domination once hundreds and thousands of people, then my objectives will get fulfilled at a much faster pace. By influencing just one king, I am indirectly improving the life of thousands of people." These words from Swamiji was an eye opener to the person who questioned him. Moreover it is wrong to presume that during the course of his journey of India Swamiji spent all his time with aristocratic and rich people.

In spite of his glorious and royal personality, Swamiji led all sorts of life – sometimes he stayed in royal palaces, sometimes he lived in caves and concentrated on worship and meditation and sometimes he wandered on foot partaking whatever people gave him as alms. Swamiji never tried to restrict himself in any specific or comfort – oriented lifestyle.

During his stay at Junagarh, Swamiji visited Kutch and Katiawar as well. At Porbander, the Diwan of the state of Porbander – Pt. Shankar Panduranga, who was also shouldering the responsibilities of administration as the king was a minor, honoured and welcomed Swamiji. Pt. Shankar Paduranga was a great Sanskrit scholar. During those days he was engaged in the translation of Vedas. When he became aware of Swamiji's in-depth knowledge of religious textures, he became attracted towards Swamiji. Swamiji helped Pandit translating some obscure shlokas from the Vedas. To accomplish the task of translation of the Vedas, Swamiji was compelled to stay at Porbander for almost a year. During this period, Swamiji's friendship with Pandit became all the more strong. The Pandit revered and honoured genius people. At Porbander, Swamiji began to study French also.

After visiting many places in and near Porbander, via Baroda and Khandva, Swamiji reached Bombay in the summer of year 1862. He spent some days in Bombay and then went to Pune. Some Gujarati devotees of Swamiji had come to the station to see Swamiji off. From Bombay in the train which he boarded for Pune, the great patriot Bal Gangadhar Tilak was also traveling. Swamiji's Gujarati acquaintances introduced him to Bal Gangadhar Tilak. After initial introduction and formalities both of them entered into discussion on varied topics. Tilak was spellbound by the knowledge inherent in the young Swamiji. Tilak somehow prevailed over him to stay at his house. Lokmanya Tilak later on had mentioned about his meeting with Swamiji in one of his writing – "We reached Pune and that sannyasi stayed with me for eight-ten days. Whenver I asked his name he just said that he was a sannyasi. Here he did not address any public meeting. At home, he almost always discussed about Vedanta or the Advaita philosophy. This Swami was not interested in meeting with people. He did not have money in his possession. His only wealth was an animal hide, one or two clothes and one kamandal (pot containing water). To undertake any journey, someone or the other used to sponsor the rail fare till the destination point where he desired to go."

Swamiji was also very much impressed by Lok Manya Tilak's sharp intellect and his command over Vedas and Vedantas. Both the great personalities exchanged in-depth views on various topics.

The next destination of Swamiji, after his brief stay at Pune's Tilak Bhawan, was Mahabaleshwar. The king of Limbdi, Thakur Sahab was on a vacation at Mahabaleshwar at that time, One day, he spotted Swamiji wandering on the Rajpath like a torn-worn beggar. He somehow took Swamiji to the place where he was putting off and pleaded him to accompany him to Limbdi and stay there permanently in his palace. At this Swamiji said, "Thakur Sahab, a strange power is making me wander. Lord Sri Ramakrishna has entrusted a big responsibility on my shoulders. Till the time

I do not accomplish that work, I do not hope to have any rest. If at all, in my life, I get an opportunity to take rest, I will definitely come to you and stay with you."

After this, Swamiji went to Kolhapur. The queen of Kolhapur soon became an ardent devotee of Swamiji. She gifted a set of saffron dress to Swamiji. Swamiji accepted the gift and blessed the queen. But after accepting the new dress he left the old clothes there itself. When asked the reason for this he replied that sannyasis do not need more than two sets of clothes. A high-ranking officer from Kolhapur wrote a letter to a benevolent Maratha in Belgaum mentioning about Swamiji. At Belgaum, Swamiji resided in the house of this Maratha. His son Prof. G. S. Bhate, had written about Swamiji in his memoirs –

"On the first day itself of Swamiji's arrival some incidents happened which changed our opinion regarding Swamiji. The first thing that we noticed was that though he wore saffron coloured clothes like other sannyasis his dressing style was entirely different. He used to wear a vest. Instead of the thick stick he used to carry a thin stick. His main belongings included a smallest edition of the Gita and two other books. During the course of conversation he made use of fluent English, expressed his knowledge on different topics and news. We had not come across such a sannyasi earlier. On the first day, after the intake of meals he asked for betel leaf or arcanut. After that, on the same day or on the next day he demanded tobacco. From his conversations, it was revealed to us that he was not a Brahmin, but still he was a sannyasi. Even though he was a sannyasi he showed his desire for all those things which a family man desired." With a view to erase the disinterestedness towards life, Swamiji gave an interesting interpretation and description of Gita to Haripad Babu. Haripad Babu was not aware of the significance and importance of Gita in making the daily familial life disciplined and firm. The knowledge regarding the duties of a family life as given in the Gita, that too by a celibate sannyasi. What an irony!

One day Haripad Babu expressed his desire to enter into sannyasa ashram to Swamiji. Swamiji gave him a firm explanation that it is very important for a human being, whether a student or a family man, to have control over his mind, then whatever he becomes whether a sadhu or whatever, he will be happy. Without a firm bent of mind, if one wears the attire of a sannyasi, he cannot become one. Haripad Babu again expressed his doubt that if he does not give place to pride and anger in his personality, then the society will not give him due respect and will not even let him live. Swamiji recounted the tale of the snake told to him by Sri Ramakrishna. The venomous snake, the sight of which made the villagers shiver, one day met the sadhu. The sadhu advised the snake that why he was accumulating the sin of killing innocent people on his head. From that day the snake promised to remain calm. When the villagers found the snake lying calm and unaggressive under the tree, they began pelting stones on it. The wounded snake laid there without any kind of reaction. The sadhu who was passing through the village went to meet the snake. The snake recounted his plight to the sadhu. The sadhu said, there is no sin or harm on the part of the snake in frightening his enemies by making hissing sound and keeping them at bay. In this manner he can safeguard himself without harming others. From that day onwards, by following the advise of sadhu, the snake led a happy and peaceful life.

With his conversation on various topics, Swamiji convinced the Maratha that the desire to have betel or tobacco by a successful sannyasi will in no way cause any harm to the Swamiji's devotion and penance.

Swamiji's acquaintance with a Bengali forest officer Haripad Mitra in the forest of Belgaum also later on developed into a strong friendship. At that time Swamiji was staying as guest at the Maratha's house. One day Haripad Mitra invited Swamiji for lunch at his home, but when Swamiji did not reach his house at the stipulated time as promised by him, after waiting for a long time, Haripad Mitra headed towards the house of the Maratha where Swamiji had been staying. When Haripad Mitra reached there, he to his consternation found that Swamiji was sitting encircled by people belonging to different professions – scholar, literature, scientist, lawyer, doctor, Sanskrit and all of them were shooting obscure and incomprehensible questions at him and Swamiji was answering and clarifying the doubts of each one in a calm and unirritant manner. Swamiji was using the medium of English, Hindi, Bangla and Sanskrit in expressing himself. After seeing the situation, Haripad Babu could not say anything and he himself sat down amidst the crowd. After sometimes when the crowd thinned Swamiji sought forgivance from Haripad Babu for not reaching his house at the stipulated time. He said that how could he have come for dinner, leaving such a huge number of curious audience. Haripad Babu requested the Maratha with whom Swamiji had been staying to let Swamiji stay in his house. After much compulsion he gave his consent and Swamiji collected his two-three possessions – kamandal, stick, one pair of dress and the three books (one was the Gita and the other two were on French music) and accompanied Haripad Babu to his home. Haripad Babu was a person with weak bent of mind. He used to get nervous even at normal circumstances. Swamiji expressed his opinion was that as long as there is no provision of employment for the poor and handicapped, there is no harm in giving alms to them. Rather that would be advantageous. In a situation when they are unable to fulfill their basic necessities they will resort to theft and robbery to fulfill their basic requirements, which will be disadvantageous for the society. A spiritual bond was established between Haripad Babu's family and Swamiji. Haripad's wife was also an ardent devotee of Swamiji. Both the husband and wife sought discipleship under Swamiji.

In the end of the year 1862 Swamiji proceeded towards Banglore from Belgaum. For two to three days, he stayed there among the people disclosing his actual identity. But slowly and gradually, the number of Swamiji's acquaintances kept on increasing as it happened in other places. During this period, Swamiji got acquainted with the Diwan of Mysore. The Diwan was greatly impressed with Swamiji just after a short conversation. He had come across a Swamiji with such a wonderful personality for the first time in his life. Swamiji stayed at the Diwan's place for around three-four weeks. In the meantime, Swamiji exchanged his views on various topics with various high ranking officers and scholars of different subjects, Diwan introduced Swamiji to the king of Mysore. The king was also attracted by the brilliance and charm of Swamiji. Swamiji stayed in the palace of the king of Mysore as the state guest. The king consulted Swamiji to resolve various problems pertaining to administration. Swamiji also drew the king's attention towards the weak points of his administration and the ways and means of rectifying them. A basic tenet of Swamiji's nature was that he always referred to the negativities of his acquaintances on their face itself thinking that the person will make improvements but he always praised them on their back.

One day, a meeting of scholars was held in the palace. Great masters and scholars were invited from far and wide. The topic of discussion was Vedanta. After the turn of all the scholars, it was the turn of Swamiji to interpret it. People sat attentively to listen to what the young and gentle personality was about to speak. When Swamiji made the analysis of Vedanta in a simple and easy manner and that too in a sweet voice, the people present in the meeting were totally spellbound. All those present there were impressed and gave a huge round of applause. The pride of experienced and vainglorious scholars got crumbled into pieces. There Swamiji met an Austrian music composer. When Swamiji began to discuss the concept of European music with the Austrian composer, the people present these were taken aback by his knowledge. One day the Diwan handed over one thousand rupees to his secretary and asked him to accompany Swamiji wherever he went to visit important places and purchase anything that Swmiji liked, on his behalf. In the evening Swamiji set on his visit to the nearby market place. Different kinds of articles were displayed in the lined-up shops. Swamiji looked at them attentively, curiosity of a young child was evident in his eyes, an element of surprise and excitement was reflecting in his sight. But when the secretary requested Swamiji to choose something he liked from those articles Swamiji just ignored his request as if he was more interested in looking at them than possessing them. He kept on loitering and doing window shopping and at last they reached a shop selling cigarettes and other items of smoking. There Swamiji said to the Diwan's secretary. "Friend, if the Diwan desires to gift me something which I like, then purchase for me a good quality cigar." Thus a cigar was purchased from the shop and Swamiji walked back, enjoying the puff.

Swamiji had already spent a long time in Mysore. He wanted to extend his journey down south. When he was taking leave from the king of Mysore, the king tried to shower him with many expensive gifts, but Swamiji did not accept any of them. With a view not to hurt the sentiments of the king, Swamiji said – "If you want to gift me something, then give me a non-metallic hukka, which will be of some use to me." Eventually the king gifted him a beautiful hukka made of wood artistically carved and etched. The Diwan of the king of Mysore tried to hand over some money to Swamiji, but Swamiji did not accept that. When he saw that the Diwan felt bad about it Swamiji asked him to get him a second class train ticket to Trichur. As such Swamiji wanted to go to Rameshwaram but thought of visiting Trichur for one or two days also. The Diwan got him a ticket to Trichur and handed Swamiji a letter addressed to the Diwan of Cochin.

Swamiji stayed at Cochin for two days and from there went to Prof. Sundaram Aiyer, the teacher of the first king of Travancore and stayed there for over 9 days. In his memoirs, Sundaram Aiyer has written about his meeting with Swamiji – "I first met Swamiji at Trivandrum in December 1962. I was fortunate to get the opportunity to see and know more about him. He came here with a Muslim travel guide. My twelve year old son led him to me and called him too a Muslim. The kind of dress he wore was a strange costume to the Hindu sannyasis belonging to South India. I took him upstairs and began talking to him. As soon as I came to know what kind of person he was I extended him due welcome and regard. The very first request he made to me was to provide food for the Muslim guide who had accompanied him. He was the sentry from the state of Cochin and was entrusted with the task of leading Swamiji to Trivandrum. For the first few days, Swamiji did not partake anything other than a small quantity of milk. Till the time his Muslim guard did not take leave of him after having proper meals, he paid little or no attention to his own needs. During my short conversation with Swamiji itself I realized the greatness of this person. When I asked him what kind of food he liked, he replied, 'Whatever you give me. We sannyasis are not particular about any specific taste.'

"The presence of Swamiji, his voice, the brightness of his eyes, his thoughts and the flow of words were so effective and inspiring that on the day I could not go to Martand Verma, the first king of Travancore ruling the state during those days who was also preparing for his M. A. studies and I was his teacher." Sundaram introduced Swamiji to many scholars in the state. With his knowledge and personality Swamiji attracted all of them towards him and made them his ardent devotee. As long as Swamiji stayed in Trivandrum, this schedule continued. As a result of his stay at Sundaram's residence and interaction with his children Swamiji learned Tamil language. He conversed with the Brahmin cook of the household and children in Tamil language itself. Sundaram had written – "When Swamiji took leave from our house, for a few days we felt as if the lights in our home had been switched off."

From Trivandrum, Swamiji went to Rameshwaram. Enroute he took a break at Madurai and there he met the king of Ramnad, Bhaskar Satpute. The king made Swamiji stay there for a few more days. The king had become an admirer and ardent devotee of Swamiji. To spread education among the public and to improve agricultural returns Swamiji gave some suggestions to the king. The king was surprised to hear such developmental thoughts in the minds of a sannyasi who was leading a life of detachment from the material world. Swamiji, able to read the emotions in the king's eyes said – "The actual aim of a sannyasi is of course to attain salvation but I have received directions from my Gurudev that my actual salvation lies in the progress of the people of my country – India."

After completing the journey of Madurai, Swamiji set off to the greatest land of pilgrimage of South India – Rameshwaram. After defeating Ravana, the king of Lanka when Ram along with his wife stepped in India, he first of all offered worship to Lord Shiva in the holy land of Rameshwaram. In the memory of that historic incident, a temple was constructed at Rameshwaram. The main gate of the temple is situated at the height of about 100 ft. from the ground. The entry to the temple is possible only after climbing many stairs. Swamiji dreamt of visiting the Shiv temple at Rameshwaram from his childhood days. The day when he fulfilled his dream he felt very excited and satisfied. As he walked on the soil of this pure land, images of various episodes from the epic of Ramayana flashed before his eye. Lord Rama and demonic Ravana all had been lost in tumultuous time. But the memories of this epic was still fresh in the minds of people as if everything happened a few days ago. Therein belies the greatness of our culture.

The next destination after Rameshwaram was Kanyakumari – the last track of India's land – the mere imagination of which sent shudders within Swamiji's heart.

When he reached there and witnessed the beauty of the place, Swamiji was overwhelmed with delight. There was a temple dedicated to Goddess Kali at Kanyakumari. Swamiji was crazy for getting a sight of Goddess Kali, as if a long separated child was excited at the thought of returning back to his mother's affectionate lap. As soon as he reached in front of the temple he laid on the ground in reverence and remained in the position with closed eyes totally concentrating his mind with the thoughts of the goddess. When he was over with his worship, he got up and walked towards the sea as if the sea was inviting him. The footsteps of Swamiji got imprinted on the sand spreading over the vast area.

The memories of various experiences he had during his journey without break from Kashmir to Kanyakumari agitated Swamiji. Sometimes he enjoyed a comfortable stay in the palaces of kings, relished tasty and different kinds of foods and sometimes for four-five days together he wandered thirsty and hungry resting under tree shades when he got tired. He took alms from low caste sweepers and cleaners. Sometimes he enjoyed homelike affection and love in the homes of family men and sometimes he stayed in the group of sadhus engaged in worship and penance and the systems of worship followed by them. He visited the doors of every kind of people – a king and a commoner, a person belonging to high class as well as low class, a scholar and a foolish. He got an opportunity to study closely every kind of personality. He saw and assessed the customs and rituals followed by people belonging to various communities and provinces. He was able to compare and contrast the lifestyles of people hailing from different provinces. Amidst all those similarities and dissimilarities he saw the glimpse of a singular culture – the glimpse of a soul. But above all he saw the deep rooted poverty, evil mental impression, superstitious beliefs and rituals and heartless rules and regulation of Hindu religion. What pinched him most was the illiteracy in India. From one corner to the other India was in a state of slumber. How to awaken it and how to set it on the path of progress? This question kept on haunting Swamiji. By thinking a solution for this question, he not only gave a new direction to his own life but for the whole of India – a new turning point.

On the Path of Winning the World

·As Swamiji stood on the Kanyakumari beach, it seemed as if Swamiji's feet got affixed there and his body had turned immobile. He stood unperturbed by the noise and movement on the seashore. The experiences he had during the two years of his journey throughout India whizzed past his eyes. Different kinds of sound reverberated his ears. A storm of thoughts had enveloped his mind. He felt disturbed as if he was getting crumbled into pieces. He wanted to run away, get his self detached from himself. A strange kind of dilemma, and impatience. Where to go to attain peace of mind for a while.

A few meters ahead of the shore a big rock surrounded by water was there. Yes, there in the loneliness some peace could be attained. But how to reach there. Row boats were present there but Swamiji had no money with him. Swamiji began to think of a way and at that moment a playful wave came and touched his feet and returned back. Soon Swamiji's footsteps began to move along the waves. But his bid to compete with the waves disbalanced his footsteps and he lags behind. But he had never learnt to return back halfway in his life. He threw himself on the waves and within second swimmed across to reach his destination.

Swamiji sat in the posture of meditation on the rock piece. His wet clothes stuck on to his body. His closed eyelashes contained the complete image of India. At the distant north the peak of the Himalayan ranges enveloped by diamond like snow and here in the south this water source was touching the feet of Mother India. The nature had left no store unturned in decorating the mother. But make up is not complete. How can it be complete—eyes filled with tears, silent shivering lips, dry hair devoid of any love, weak body, untidy dress. Thousands of her child half naked, undernourished, exploited, dumb and illiterate. After all what are the reasons behind this?

On the one hand, the rich and powerful class indulged in luxury sucking the blood of poor and the weak. On the other hand, the so called educated Brahmins were misbehaving with low class poor people and exploiting them. People were losing faith in the Hindu religion and more and more people were embracing Christianity. They were getting enough food to fill their stomach, sympathy, education and above all human behavior. After all why they won't accept another religion. The Hindu religion was becoming a butt of criticism and condemnation. We were getting degraded in our own eyes. We were pulling our own legs. Then who will honour us? Who will help us?

Swamiji felt miserable and sorrowful. His closed eyes had unending suffering within it. The shadow of this suffering enveloped his whole face. He contemplated—the main objective behind my stay at the palaces of these kings was to draw their attention to the miserable condition of their subjects so that they make improvements in their administration. If they wished they can bring about drastic improvements in the lives of people because they have both wealth and power with them. But how much of wealth and power can they devote to erase poverty, illiteracy and evil beliefs? Will they be able to bring about a revolutionary will change of joy and prosperity in the Indian society by wiping the tears of those Indians who had been subject to exploitation and repression since ages together? With they be able to uproot the complex feelings within them and grow self-confidence in its place? All these are far from possible for them. These native kings are not competent enough to find any solutions to the problems our country is facing. For that I will have to do something special, I will have to develop a sense of confidence in their mind. It will be possible only when Indians become spiritually strong. But no, all these are false excuses. Gurudev used to say that a hungry stomach cannot sing with devotion. Yes, it is true. First of all, I will have to fight a battle with India's poor economic condition and the only way to fight poverty is to achieve literacy of every Indian. An educated mind can find out solution for its every problem.

The person clad in saffron outfit, who sat in a meditative posture on the rock was not a sannyasi but was an ambitious person inspired by the will to bring about drastic changes and complete transformation of our society. His heart was a sea of emotions and an actual sea raged outside. The innumerable waves hit the bottom of the rock and got crushed into pieces but the rock stood firm and unchanged. He thought, in the way of fulfillment of objectives many such waves will create hindrances but his heart will remain even firmer than that piece of rock. The end was quite clear before his eyes but the means to that end was not to be found anywhere. He experiences a sense of dejection which is quite clear on his face. He thinks—how can a mere sannyasi without any material possessions bear this huge responsibility. Money was the main requirement for the fulfillment of his requirement. Where to go to collect this money and what to do and from where to raise funds? If at all somebody gives the money, why and how much? There is no public support behind.

Amidst the darkness of despair there arose a ray of hope. At the moment the richest country is America. That is the only place to arrange money. But how? Will I beg for funds there? Then I will not only not get money but I will lose my self-respect even. No, there is only an asset left with this poor country and that is the philosophy of Vedanta—the boundless treasure. Why should not I spread its teachings in America and Europe and accumulate wealth? What else do I have in my possession which I can give to these countries in exchange of money? Without giving anything if I accept something that will be against my honour. Give and take is a permanent law of nature. If I have to go to America, I should go there as a spiritual Guru not as a beggar. If I am successful in my attempt, the country will gain honour and the countrymen will attain self-confidence. Then innumerous youths will come forward to extend a helping hand.

Swamiji's countenance brightened up with determination. That brightness was all prepared to fight against worries, despair and inertia that pervaded all over India. The halo of this brightness faded even the brightness of uninterrupted Samadhi. These centres give happiness to the individual who undergo the Samadhi. It is of no good to the society. Today the society as well as the nation needs Vivekanand. The country is calling him. Gurudev also wished so. "If I am able to worship only that God whom I believe is present in every being, then I will take another birth for that and suffer all kinds of difficulties. My God is cruel people. My God is sad and miserable people. My God is the poor people from all castes." Gurudev Ramakrishna had sowed this kind of sentiment and feeling in the mind of his favourite disciple. And this very sentiment has manifested in Swamiji's heart.

That day only after midnight Swamiji's trance broke. When he opened his eyes, his sight got affixed on the horizon. The night shimmered with the presence of moon and twinkling stars. The huge ocean in its deep and serious form is in front of him. Hanuman, the son of wind god leapt this very ocean at a go to reach Lanka and search for Mother Sita. "If I also had possessed that magical power in my body," thought Swamiji. But no, human beings are not incapable. If they have got strong will power, then nothing is impossible. He can even go up and pluck stars from the sky. Many images of his past journeys came before his eyes in a lively form. Many kinds of sounds reverberated in his ears.

"Swamiji, I am afraid, you will not be able to do much in this country. Here very few people will be able to judge your true qualities. You should go to the west. The people there will easily identify you and will be able to make a true judgement of your real worth. With your advise pertaining to Hinduism, you will undoubtedly be able to influence and impress the people of the western world. "These were the words of the Diwan of Porbander. He himself was a great Sanskrit Scholar and during the days of Swamiji's visit at Porbander, engaged in the translation of the Vedas. During Swamiji's eleven months long stay, they had developed strong friendship. He was the first person to encourage Swamiji to go abroad. He believed that the talent of a true talented personalities is identified abroad not in their own countries. They get honour from other countries first before gaining recognition in their own country.

During his stay at Porbander Swamiji had been quite restive. The suggestion to go abroad reminded Swamiji the words by Gurudev who always used to say—"Naren, you have the strength to shake the world." Is it true that some great power is inherent in me? Swamiji contemplated. One day Guruji had transferred all his powers, all the godly powers to me and said with tears rolling down his eyes that—"Naren— now I am a pauper."

Drowning in the flow of these memories Swamiji halted at one point for a second. That place was Khandwa where he heard about the World Religion Conference to be held at Chicago in the next year and his heart fluttered at the prospect of attending the same. If somebody sponsored his tour to America—he thought. Suddenly the image of Mysore Palace came to his mind. The king of Mysore had asked him as to how he could help Swamiji. During his Bharat Darshan, describing the contemporary situation of the country Swamiji had said—"Our present necessity is to set our society and economy on a progressive path with the help of western education. Our mission will not be fulfilled by merely standing at the doors of Europeans and crying and wailing for alms. As they educate us on the lines of new techniques in the field of agriculture and other aspects, we should also give them something in exchange other than the only spiritual knowledge. What else India has in its possession to give to European countries? Hence, sometimes I wish to go to western countries to spread the Vedanta philosophy. Every Indian, for the welfare of his own community and country, should make such initiative so that relationship based on such exchanges are established with other countries. If royal and powerful kings like you, take initiative in this regard then this work shall begin. My sole desire is that you make your contribution in this significant task. The king of Mysore had considered Swamiji's suggestions seriously and was ready to sponsor Swamiji's journey to America. But at that time Swamiji declined the offer thinking it to be unnecessary at that time as the date of Chicago World Conference was far away. Swamiji was satisfied with the promise made by the king. He had then thought that at the right time he will think about it. How can a wandering sannyasi like him carry such a huge amount of money? That day, he became reaffirmed in his belief that Indian philosophy and the philosophy of the Hindu religion (Sanatan Dharma) the unity of all religions was the basic mantra of India. It was the mother of all religions. It was the source from where the rivers of all other religions originated. With this, the whole world can be won.

:Swamiji felt as his Gurudev Ramakrishna was helping in choosing the appropriate path in an invisible manner. Now his way lay ahead quite clear without any hindrances. His countenance was shining with confidence and a sense of decisiveness. He finally arrived at a decision—of going abroad. "With my mental strength, I will earn money and come back to my motherland and will devote my mind, body and money for the service of my country."

Swamiji began walking towards the city leaving the waves of the sea behind. Before giving a form to his imagination, he wanted to complete his journey of India. Some places—Madras, Hyderabad etc. were yet to be seen and understood. Swamiji now began his journey on foot-from Kanyakumari to Madras. He had to take a break and stay at Pondicherry for some rest. The manner in which butterflies get attracted with the fragrance of flowers, in the same manner, after reaching Madras, within a few days Swamiji's personality, talent and intellect attracted the educated society towards him. Swamiji discussed science, literature and philosophy with both the teaching community as well as the students from the university. Many youths debated on western philosophical thoughts with Swamiji. Swamiji was well aware of the psychology of those youngsters. Few years ago, he also used to visit Gurudev with such curious mind and Gurudev used to win over their curious minds and thoughts with simplicity and without much efforts. Swamiji saw his own reflection in these young students' hungry of knowledge and always ready to come up with some rationale or the other. Like his Gurudev, Swamiji also solved the doubts that enveloped these young students in a simple and natural manner. Many educated young students became Swamiji's disciples and devotees. Swamiji confided with them the objective behind his foreign trip. He discussed with them his plans for the welfare of the country and drew their attention to their duties and responsibilities towards the nation. Some old devotees and disciples came to know about his journey and presence in Madras and they also reached them. All these old and new disciples and devotees of Swamiji were very sincere and dedicated when Swamiji was on his visit to abroad, all of them carried out his directions in a dedicated manner and communicated with Swamiji the latest developments and changing circumstances in India.

Madras was the main centre of Hindu religion and its activities. To listen to Swamiji's philosophical discourses, normal educated people gathered at the place Swamiji had been staying. But when the scholars and philosophers in Madras came to know about Swamiji's name and fame, they also took part in his meetings and seminars. The main

Swami Vivekanand: A Biography

attraction of his personality was an appropriate blend of humility and ego. A simple scholar out of ignorance insulted Swamiji and the latter sought apology from him. On some occasion when his audience, intentionally and without any rationale refuted his thoughts, he exploded like a cloud and there emerged a stroke on lightning. in his eyes. Swamiji believed in God's monistic form. In a meeting attended by great scholars, he strongly interpreted this thought. Those present expressed their doubt that if they do not differentiate between self and the God then their whole responsibility will be over in a single go. "Even if we are on the wrong path or right path, there will remain no control over us." Hearing this rationale, Swamiji expressed his view point which silenced all of them. He said—"If we whole heartedly believe that the Surpeme Being and we are one, then the sin will distance itself from us and we need not require nay kind of control." In the same way, one day as Swamiji was addressing a gathering of students and teachers at the Christian college, one lecturer from the science department who was also an atheist namely Singaravelu Mudaliyar could not resist himself from laughing in a sarcastic manner and make some critical remarks about Hinduism and Christianity. He was very sure that Swamiji will not be able to repudiate his arguments. But Swamiji, with great patience and perseverance not only refuted his arguments one by one but also won over him to make him his follower. Swamiji used to call him "Kiddy' lovingly. Swamiji joked about him—had said, "I came, saw and conquered" but "Kiddy came, saw and was conquered over." Mudaliar transformed himself into a sannyasi and led the rest of his life as per the directions of Swamiji. He put forth the suggestion to publish the magazine named 'Prabuddha Bharat' which came out with Swamiji's views, teachings for the people to imbibe and follow. Mudaliar was the unsalaried manager of the said magazine.

The date of the World Religion Conference to be held in Chicago was nearing. Swamiji put forth his intention to participate in the conference before his followers in Madras. They were very enthusiastic about the prospect of Swamiji taking part in the conference. They began to collect funds for Swamiji's expenses for the journey. Within a few minutes, about five hundred rupees got collected. But Swamiji did not find it appropriate to accept the money at that point of time. In such situations he experienced a kind of dilemma. He had already made up his mind to go to America and attend the conference. He was also aware that the whole exercise of going to America as well as his stay there involved a huge expenditure and he himself discussed it with his disciples. But being a sannyasi, he was hesitant to safekeep such a huge amount of money with himself. His thinking was on the lines that if God is really willing to send him abroad to unfurl the flag of Hindu religion then why should he be worried. "It is not good for me to accumulate wealth and keep it with me. I am not a family man to save wealth for securing future. As a sannyasi, I never worry for my next day's survival or living, I need not worry about my travel expenses. I am just a puppet at the hands of Mother Kali. I should work according to Her wishes. He called his disciples and instructed them to obey the wishes of Mother Kali. If the goddess desires so, at the ripe moment, the money for his journey to America will get arranged with the blessings of the Mother. He ordered his disciples to spend the five hundred rupees raised by them for the welfare of poor people.

A strange facet of Swamiji's personality was that on the one hand overwhelmed by a feeling of patriotism, with a scholarly mind believes in the union of soul with the supreme. On the other hand like an ignorant child he is waiting for the orders of Mother Kali that one day or the other she will express her desire. For this wish fulfilment, Swamiji left no stone unturned in terms of prayers, worship and penance.

In the meantime, the people of Hyderabad began to express their desire to meet and listen to the discourses of Swamiji. The people of Hyderabad had heard about Swamiji from their counterparts in Madras. At Hyderabad, arrangements for Swamiji's stay was made at the house of Madhusudan Chatterjee, working as Engineer at the house of Hyderabad. Swamiji accepted the invitation from the people of Hyderabad.

A day prior to Swamiji's arrival at Hyderabad, the Hindus organized a huge meeting and charted out the programme to extend a warm welcome to Swamiji. The next day when the train in which Swamiji was travelling arrived at station a crowd of more than 500 people was gathered at the station to receive Swamiji.

Swamiji stayed in Hyderabad for over a week. One day, Swamiji went to meet the Nizam of Hyderabad Sir Khurshid

Jung Bahadur. The Nizam had visited all the Hindu places of pilgrimage from the Himalayas to Kanyakumari. Even after being a staunch believer and follower of Islam religion he revered every Hindu philosopher and scholar. At the palace of the Nizam, Swamiji explained and discussed various theories and principles of different religions. The Nizam was greatly attracted towards Swamiji's humility, intellect and above all his oratorial skills. He tried to donate one thousand rupees to Swamiji to carry out his religious works but Swamiji declined the offer and said—"Nawab Bahadur, before this, my good friend the king of Mysore and my disciple king of Ramnad wanted to extend financial help to me for my foreign trips. But I think that time is not ripe. If at some time I get the orders of God to undertake a journey to the western world, then I will inform you."

At the Mehboot College in Sikandrabad Swamiji gave a powerful speech on the topic—"Objectives of my foreign trip." Many renowned personalities and people from Europe were present their. After this speech, Swamiji became all the more confident about his intellect and power of expression in influencing and impressing the people of Europe. Wherever he went in the city he received honour and respect from every one and at the same time people assured their support and cooperation for his foreign trip. But Swamiji's coffin was empty. He kept on evading to accept any financial help.

In mid February, Swami once again departed for Madras from Hyderabad. A huge crowd gathered at the Railway Station to see him off. At the Madras Railway station a huge crowd had assembled to welcome Swamiji. A few days after he reached Madras, Swamiji saw Gurudev Ramakrishna in his dream. Gurudev was walking on the ocean on foot and was indicating Naren with his hands to follow him. The next day when he woke up his heart was calm and peaceful. He felt as if he had been granted permission to go abroad.

Swamiji wrote a letter to mother Sharda to seek her blessings. Before beginning his life of a nomad also he had sought the blessings of Mother Sharda. Now he felt like seeking Mother Sharda's blessings before beginning this auspicious work. Mother Sharda sent a reply letter which was filled with love and affection and all good wishes. Swamiji called his disciples and said, "It is the will of the Mother that I go abroad. Hence, let me collect money from the common men here because I am going abroad for the sake of Indians—poverty ridden and miserable."

During this period a strange thing happened. Swamiji had made a brief stay with the king of Khatri during his tour of India. The king of khatri was an ardent devotee and friend of Swamiji. He firmly believed that he was blessed with a son due to the blessings of Swamiji. On the auspicious day, the son was born to the king of Khatri, grand' festival was organized in the state. The king of Khatri, with great difficulties, gained information about Swamiji's presence in Madras and that he was making preparations to go to America. Instantly, he sent his Diwan Jagmohan Lal to Swamiji to bring him and secure blessings for the new born baby.

Diwan Jagmohan Lal reached Madras and conveyed the king's message to Swamiji and requested him to accompany him to the state of Khatri. But Swamiji expressed his inability to join the celebrations taking place in Khatri saying that he was getting ready to set on his journey to America just a month after he had to make so many arrangements for it. But Jagmohan was persistent with his request—"Swamiji, just come to Khatri for at least a day. If you do not pay a visit, the king will be in a state of despair. You need not worry about any arrangement for your journey to America. Leave it on the king, you just accompany me to Khatri. Finally, Jagmohan Lal emerged victorious and Swamiji got ready to accompany him to Khatri.

Once the celebrations at Khatri were over, when Swamiji got ready to leave for Bombay. The king of Khatri asked his Diwan Jagmohan to accompany Swamiji and make arrangements for ticket for his journey to America, necessary clothings and other articles required for his journey and stay abroad. On his way at the Abu Road Station he spent one night at the house of a common railway employee. That poor fellow extended all possible help on his part to Swamiji. At Mount Abu, Swamiji coincidentally happened to meet two of his favourite Guru brothers Swami Turiyanand and Swami Brahmanand. Swamiji was happy with that unexpected meeting.

After reaching Bombay, preparations for his journey to America began in full swing. Diwan Jag Mohan got stitched shirt, headgear, etc. for Swamiji with expensive saffron cloth. In addition, all necessary articles required during a journey kept in a box. This was the first time in Swamiji's life when he had become the owner of so many articles. The very thought of keeping all those things in his possession caused a kind of duel in his mind. One who had taken the vow to seek only cooked food as alms, for such a person all these were a kind of burden. But on the path he had chosen, he could not have spared all these possessions. He pacified himself and felt happy at that mere consideration. But when Diwan Jagmohan reserved first class ticket for Swamiji's journey, he opposed it and demanded general ticket. But the Diwan was firm in his decision and argued that the sentiments of king of Khatri will be hurt if Swamiji travelled in general compartmen. Thus Swamiji was prepared over to travel in first class category.

Swamiji was compelled to fulfil one more demand of the Diwan and his disciples that was to wear the new silk saffron outfit as he set off on his journey to America. When Samiji boarded the ship to America from the Bombay port on May 31, 1893 he looked like a handsome prince: healthy body, bright countenance, big and calm eyes, resembling lotus petals and above all his well fitting expensive apparel. The Diwan and two of his disciples accompanied Swamiji up to the entry gate of the ship. As they returned back they kissed the soil where Swamiji's footsteps had got imprinted. Tears filled the eyes of all those who were present there to see Swamiji off. Swamiji who always remained calm and unperturbed and never betrayed any subtle emotions also could not hide his emotions. His eyes were also filled with tears.

The first bell rung when the entry gates of the ship opened. All the passengers hurried inside the ship. Swamiji's glance rests on his disciples' face for a second and then he also hurriedly went inside the ship merging along with the passengers entering inside. Once inside the ship, he straightway made his way to the upper deck. From there he was able to see his near and dear ones properly. There was a strange kind of commotion all over. Some of the passengers were happy at the prospects of meeting their loved ones and some of them sad because they were leaving their loved ones behind. Swamiji stood holding on to the railings of the deck. The last siren blew, the bridge attached to the ship to enable the passengers board the ship was pulled towards the shore. Slowly and gradually, the ship began to distance itself from the port. The noise of the wheels rolling over the water was audible—each moment Swamiji also got distanced from his motherland, the bank of his mother and the people of his motherland. Swamiji rested his sight on those who had come to see him off till the time they became invisible behind the horizons. The ship was picking up its speed. The shore, the people everything were left behind. The birds who were indulged in flying on the seashore till now have also lost somewhere. Swamiji was unable to spot even a single one. Now the only thing that remained was the small ship swimming over the very heart of the water in the ocean. The blue sky above and the blue water below, the blueness of Mother Kali was spread over everywhere. The sea waves took high tides and disappeared into nowhere. Various thoughts and emotions took tides within Swamiji's heart too. Snippets of various incidents connected with Gurudev, mother Sharda, Guru brothers, his near ones began to swim before his mind's eye. A kind of pain lingered in his mind. He had not informed about his journey to America to any of his Guru brothers in Baranagar nor his mother and siblings. In fact, he was not able to inform them. Was it essential on his part to inform them? No, he did not find it necessary. With the blessings of Mother Kali, the renown he will achieve at America will spread to them on its own. He had guessed so. He knew that the impact of such information would have been deeper.

Swamiji strolled on the deck for some time crossing his arms and resting them on his chest. Then he sat on a chair. His brain had become a haunt of many thoughts. The glorious history of India emerged before his eyes in a celluloid form. Its past, its religion and culture. He got a strange kind of inspiration from all of them. Not a single thought of worldly materialistic comforts came to his heart. He merely wanted to continue working harder and harder on the tough work area being allotted to him. As his mind assessed the hardships he was likely to force in the future he became all the more firm and strong. The idols of his Gurudev Sri Ramakrishna and that of Mother Kali was permanently present in his heart. Whenever he stumbled on his way during the struggle of existence, both the idols lent him equal support.

In the ship, for the first few days, Swamiji stayed aloof from other passengers, lost in his own thoughts. Perhaps the patriot emperors of Indian history and the characteristic

Swami Vivekanand: A Biography

features of Indian literature and religious texts were his only soul mates during that period. In the first half of his long voyage on ship he peeped into the past, present and future of India changing from time to time. In all these forms there existed one similarity and that was the similarity of its soul. Swamiji wanted to spread this unique image and laurels for the motherland. Through the medium of Sanatan Dharma (Hinduism) the world will be able to view the image of India and identify it. The thought of the World Religion Conference to be held in the city of Chicago and the prospect of his participating in it on behalf of his motherland for its welfare gave him a unique sense of satisfaction and peace. His face brightened up at the thought.

Swamiji easily got mingled with the new circumstances he was in while in the ship. He did not feel a bit uncomfortable about the new recipes and strange people. Within a few days, he became the centre of attraction among many of his co-passengers. The main Captain of the ship became Swamiji's partner of loneliness when he used to be free from his duties. He took along Swamiji to different parts of the ship, showed him the ship's mechanical parts and explained about their working. The Captain enjoyed Swamiji's company.

After approximately one week, the ship reached Srilanka. The ship was stationed at the Colombo port for almost a day. Swamiji along with other passengers deboarded the ship and spent the whole day in visiting famous Buddhist temples. Travelling via Penang, the ship's next halting point was Singapore. At the Singapore port also Swamiji alighted from the ship to visit some famous places like the museum, the botanical garden etc. After Singapore, the next half was Hongkong where the ship remained stationed for three days. There he visited many Buddhist temples and monasteries situated in Southern China. He compared and contrasted the two heirs of ancient Buddhist civilizations—India and China. He found a glimpse of influence of India over Chinese civilization and culture, especially in the field of religion he found the significance of Buddhist religion. In many Buddhist temples, the Sanskrit mantras were embedded in Bengali style. In most of the handwritten books in Sanskrit there was an impression of Bangla on it. Swamiji had already read much about Buddhism as followed in China. When he saw Buddhist temples and monasteries in person, he became sure that some time back there existed a cordial relationship between Bengalis and Chinese. That is why, many Bengali saints were able to gain entry into China. He also noticed that the poverty experienced in China was also similar to that in India. In their day to day lives, there was abundance of scarcity and shortage of small things.

As the ship halted at Japan, Swamiji got an opportunity to visit many famous cities such as Yukohoma, Osaka, Kyoto and Tokyo. After seeing the poverty-ridden miserable India and China, when Swamiji saw the beautiful and refined Japan, he felt very happy. There was such a huge difference between India and China on the one hand and Japan on the other. The Japanese were well off and were not deprived of necessities and comforts of modern living. They were not rich in terms of wealth, but cleanliness, artistic creativity and humility was spread in every field of life. Clean and tidy cities, wide roads, light-weight houses decorated with flowers and plants, colourful and delicate looking gardens, artificial fountains and lakes— everything inspired a sense of joy from within. There also he visited many Buddhist temples and monasteries with Sanskrit Mantras etched on their walls. Japanese were courageous, brave and hard working and more importantly educated also. Their face glittered with optimism and excitement. Though money was not in abundance the people there were happy and healthy. Perhaps the soil was unique which gave birth to such kind of people. From Japan, Swamiji wrote a letter to one of his disciples in Madras—"So many things are coming to my mind in relation to Japanese. I am unable to express every thing in such a brief letter. But I want to tell that youths from our country should visit China and Japan in groups, especially Japan. In Japanese view, India is a dreamland of high standard and great things....and what are you people doing? You are wasting your whole life in unnecessary talks. Come and see these people and go back and hide your face in embarrassment. It looks as if, the destructions meted out to India have destroyed its intellect and power of thinking. If you go out of your country, you think that you will lose your piety and uprightness. You are still carrying on your head the burden of false beliefs and superstitions. For thousands of years you have been wasting your time and energy in thinking of the purity and impurity of the edible and inedible foods. You are spending your time in the whirlpool of foolish advice of priests. The social exploitation and torture you have been experiencing for thousands of years have snatched away your very humaneness. I want to ask whether there is scarcity of water in the ocean. Why don't you drown your books, gown, university degrees, diplomas in the ocean. Come and become a human being. First of all, keep these cruel priests at bay, because they are devoid of any brains and won't listen to good things. Their hearts are vacant and they are not going to progress anymore. They are born amidst the evil culture and tormentations taking place since ages together. First of all, break away from them and become a human being. Get out from the narrow dark and dingy well and go out and see how other countries are marching ahead on the path of progression."

From Yakohama the ship traversed the ocean to reach Vancouver (Canada). Now Swamiji had completed his journey from East to West, from the old world to the new world. By the time he reached there in the month of June the severity of cold had increased. Although Swamiji experienced cold waves quite some days ago and had born it on board of the ship. But as the ship reached Canada, Swamiji could not reduce the severe cold that pierced into his body and chilled his bones. The Diwan of the king of Khatri had kept all necessary articles required during a journey in the box which he himself got for Swamiji's comfort. But there were no woolen clothes in the box to fight the cold. Neither the king of khetri nor his Diwan was aware of the severity of cold in Europe and America. Neither Swamiji nor his disciples and devotees thought of it. Hence, he had to become a victim of cold waves. He travelled from Vancouver to Chicago by train. The train kept on moving day and night. It crossed rivers, streams, forests, hills, fields, wastelands, cities etc. On the third day, he stepped on the land of Chicago city thus fulfilling his ambition that he had been nursing since long.

The city of comfort and luxury—Chicago had been specially decorated during those days. A world fair was organized there a few days ago. As a result, people from different countries were walking in crowds wearing their native outfits. The atmosphere was very jovial and colourful. It was mid July. The climate was very nice. But Swamiji did not have the patience to see or enjoy the scenic beauty around. The main question in front of him was where to go from the station. Because of his attire people were staring at him. Children out of surprise ran around him and broke out into laughter. The situation was such that people considered him an object from the museum. He made enquiries about a commonplace hotel. When the coolie transferred his luggage to the hotel room and went away Swamiji felt somewhat relaxed.

The next day, Vivekanand set off to visit the world fire. Almost all the major countries of the world had put up there stalls displaying that indigenous handicrafts and machine made articles. In addition, there was also a science exhibition, Vivekanand watched everything very minutely. He inspected every article on display. He got a first hand knowledge of the progress made by Europe and America in the field of science. He was very much impressed by the power, prosperity and the inventional talent of the western world. He felt awed and at the same time wonderstruck by the articles of science he saw there. By that time, he became used to the noisy atmosphere of the Chicago city. He no more felt any kind of fear or boredom with the atmosphere their. Four-five days after his arrival at Chicago, he went to the enquiry office to seek more information about the World Religious Conference. The information he gained was quite shocking. The conference was planned to held in the second half of September. The names of all the participants had already been registered and even in some unusual case, registration of a new name was possible even if recommended by a high ranking officer.

Vivekanand became greatly worried. He had come to America due to his own will. He was not being sent to represent India by any social or religious body in India. At that time, the Ramakrishna Mission was not even established. In the Baranagar Mutt near Calcutta many of Ramakrishna's disciples were practicing yoga, meditation, prayers and involved in various social services. They were not even aware that when their "Naren" got transformed into Vivekanand and reached America. When he departed to America from Khatri, at that time no particular organization was there to see him off. In the same manner, when he reached America, he did not have any certificate in his possession. This hindrance stood before him like a big problem. He felt it next to impossible to gain a membership in the 'Religious Representative Conference.'

That day, Swamiji straightaway returned back to the hotel from the enquiry office. He was totally despaired and worried. In an expensive city like Chicago, Swamiji had almost run out of his pocket money. The winter season was also just one-and-a-half months away. He did not have in his possession any thing to protect himself from cold. His mind got gripped in tension. After much contemplation, a ray of hope became evident. What if he seeks help from his friends and devotees in Madras. He wrote a letter to his friends in Madras to send some money to him through some religious institutions. But no religious organization was charitable enough to help a person without prior acquaintance especially a person who had reached a distant country like America without the help of any religious organization. The main officer of a religious organization replied to one of Vivekanand's friend's request in this manner—"Let the scoundrel die of cold."

But the 'scoundrel' did not die. He kept holding on to the extreme end of fate and kept a close watch on its irony. He was a person with indomitable spirit and self-confidence. He handed himself to the hands of fate and kept on doing his duties without any desire or ambition.

The hotel expenses in Chicago were too much for Swamiji to bear. He had almost run out of money. Whatever meagre amount was left with him was not enough to support his stay in Chicago till September. Somebody told him that Boston was a cheap city as compared to Boston. Hence, after about ten-twelve days Swamiji shifted his base to Boston who knows the changes in fate. His luck helped him and resulted in a turn of events. While Swamiji was travelling by train to Boston, a rich old lady saw Swamiji. Swamiji was talking to the passenger sitting next to him. They were talking on various topics pertaining to mind and soul and the essence of existence. The lady overheard their conversation and felt it to be very interesting and enjoyed it. The lady was so impressed by Swamiji's thoughts and personality that she compelled him to accompany her to her house in a village named Bridge Meadow situated in the province of Massachussets. The lady named Kate Sunbourne was unmarried and had great respect for scholars and artists. She was very famous for her generosity and social service. She introduced this remarkable person to her female acquaintances. The ladies continued to look at his strange attire with a sense of surprise and enjoyed his speech and discourses. Sunbourne took Swamiji along with her in car and showed her the small town and villages around. Wherever they paid a visit, Swamiji became the main topic of discussion there. People mistook this young sannyasi who wore a saffron-coloured silk headgear and shirt to be of a king of some Indian province. His queer outfit made him a object of surprise. At last he was compelled to purchase for himself a western outfit from Boston. In one of his letters, he had mentioned about it—"If I have to stay here for more days then I cannot make do with my strange dress. People specially crowded along at roadsides to get a glimpse of mine. Hence, I want to wear a black coloured long coat and only for giving discourses I will avoid my saffron shirt and headgear. Sunbourne kept on introducing the Indian king to all her acquaintances in Massachussets. It was this generous lady herself who introduced her guest to the famous Principal of Harvard University, John Henry Wright. Soon, a strong bond developed between Swamiji and Wright's family, Swamiji's personality had a deep impact on Wright's family. In a letter addressed to her mother Prof. Wright's wife had written—"At this moment we are spending our time in a strange manner. Kate Sunbourne has a Hindu sannyasi as a guest at her home about whom I had mention in my previous letter. John went to meet him at Boston and when he returned back, he nursed him a lot and called him here itself. He arrived here on Friday wearing a long saffron robe, which made people behold him surprised. That image was very attractive. He had tied around his head a very good looking thing, he looked very handsome, his age seemed to be around 30 years but if one takes into consideration the level of his knowledge, it seemed as if he belonged to an ancient age. He stayed here at our house till Monday and I found that he is the most interesting person I have met among all our acquaintances. We kept on talking for the whole day and the whole night and again the next day we talked on an altogether new topic. Everybody in the town is keen to meet him. Those residing in the Kumari Lane are also very curious to meet him. They kept on sitting inside and outside their houses to have a glimpse of Swamiji and out of excitement their cheeks had turned red. The main topic of our discussion is religion. It seems to be a kind of revival or restoration. I myself have not experienced the kind of excitement I am experiencing now in the past. On Sunday John invited him to give a speech in the church.

He is an educated fellow and possesses knowledge equivalent to any scholar. He became a saint at the age of 18 years. He is strangely shrewd and expresses his argument or thought in a clear manner. You can neither mislead him or confuse him nor beat him in debates.

They mainly discussed topics relating to religion, but in addition they touched on topics relating to Indian history, politics, society, etc. Generally, Vivekanand remained calm and serious but whenever the discussion turned to British rule over India, his brows straightened, his voice pitched high and face turned red with anger. This very image drew the real miserable condition of Indians. But India was waking up from its slumbers, its days were in the process of change. He firmly believed it and expressed it very openly."

Prof. Wright soon became aware of Vivekanand's talent and encouraged him to participate in the Chicago Religion Conference and solved the difficulties he had been facing in gaining a membership for it. Wright said—"This is the only way to introduce you to the world on a large scale." But there were two hindrances in Swamiji's way—First, he didn't have any certificate or Identity card. Second, his pocket was empty. Vivekanand put forth the problems before Prof. Wright. Prof. Wright said, "As far as your certificate concerned, I would rather say that it is like somebody questioning the sun's right to shine." Then he assured Vivekanand that he will gain him membership to the World Religion Conference as a representative who will explicate Hinduism. Prof. Wright had close friendship with many officials associated with the World Religion Conference. At that very moment he wrote a letter to one of his friends who was the Chairman of the committee to choose the members—"The knowledge of this person is more than the knowledge of all the professors here put together." He purchased a ticket for Swamiji's journey to Chicago and wrote an introduction letter regarding his food and accommodation to the special committee of the Conference. Swamiji's joy knew no bounds. He felt as if God himself has taken the form of Prof. Wright to help him. On a path filled with thorns and darkness, brightness spread and thousands of lamps of hope lit up.

Swamiji took leave from the Wright family and set off towards Chicago from Boston with a new enthusiasm in his mind. On his way, he met a trader. He said him to guide Swamiji to his destination after reaching Chicago. But no sooner both Swamiji and the trader alighted at the Chicago Railway Station than the latter got lost in the crowd. Perhaps he was busy with his business and in a hurry forgot to guide Swamiji to the office of Dr. John Henry Baroj (Member—President of the Electoral Committee). Vivekanand searched his pockets for the address slip of Dr. Baroj given to him by Prof. Wright but unfortunately it was also missing. He was in a big fix. He made enquiries about Dr. Baroj's office but none of them from whom he enquired could direct him properly because Vivekanand was at the North-Eastern part of Chicago where mainly German's resided. Hence, neither they were able to understand what Swamiji was saying nor was Swamiji able to understand them. This way, in the process of enquiry day gave way to night. Vivekanand could not arrive at a decision as to where to go and what to do. He was unable to enquire about any nominal hotel where he could spend the night. He kept on wandering and at last he reached back towards the station itself. On the backside of the station there was the goods yard. Huge vacant bores made of wood were lying there. Vivekanand's body and mind were really tired by them. He handed over himself to the lord Almighty and laid down on the box to take some rest and withen a few minutes sleep freed him from the worries and difficulties of the world. He was in a deep and sound sleep. The next day the rays of the new sun awakened him from his slumber. The early morning breeze carried it with an amazing fragrance which brought about an altogether new energy in his body. He got up, picked up his cloth bag which contained a few clothes and books. Following the footsteps of the enchanting breeze, soon Vivekanand reached a beautiful part of the city. That part displayed a unique grandeur with palatial buildings and houses, beautifully landscaped gardens having colourful flowers and plantsa and wide and roads. Vivekanand felt as if he had reached the town where

Swami Vivekanand: A Biography

Lord Kubera, the god of wealth and prosperity, resided. That was the area where high class businessmen and rich people stayed. Vivekanand's condition at that time was totally opposite to the circumstances there. Tough journey, strange mode of sleeping at the previous night which resulted in shoddy and wrinkled appearance of his dress, hunger had stolen away the sheen of his face and in such a situation he went door to door with the hope of getting something to quench his hunger and some guidance towards his destination. But to what he saw in this grand city of rich people. Many doors opened at his knock but before he could ask anything, they got shut even more vehemently. Neither did he get any sympathy nor any kind of assurance from any place. At many doors he was welcomed with abuses and at many doors he was subject to condemnation at the hands of servants. He was not among those who got burned in the fire of indignation but in turn became all the more bright and pure like gold. By that time he had become helpless and weak due to hunger and tiredness. Till that time he was not aware of the existence of name and address directory of the city or the phone numbers and because of that he felt all the more helpless. He was unable to decide about the course of action he should take. At last like a defeated warrior he sat on the road side without making any kind of efforts. After some time the door of the palatial house on the other side of the road opened and a very well educated and civilized woman came out, she came near Swamiji and in a soft and humble tone asked "Sir, are you a member of the religious conference?" Swamiji felt relaxed and he described 'his problems to the lady. The lady took Swamiji to her house with great respect and ordered her servants to take him to the guest room ad take care of his needs. She assured Swamiji that once he got free after taking bath and having his meals, she herself will take him to the office of the Religious Conference. Swamiji's heart filled with gratitude for the woman and thought God is gracious, at one moment you are in difficult situation and in the other it is extremely opposite. Indomitable courage and unlimited confidence filled Swamiji's heart. He felt as if the invisible blissful hand of his Gurudev Shri Ramakrishna was on him and no power in the world can stop him from achieving his objective.

After taking bath and having meals Swamiji got ready to accompany that lady Smt. George W. Hail to the office of the Religious Conference and handed over the introduction letter given to him by Prof. Wright. The office happily gave validity of his membership and made arrangements for his food and accommodation along with other members from eastern countries who had come to take part in the conference. That was 10th of September. The first meeting of the World Religious Conference was to begin on the next day. All members were busy getting prepared for this important day. After meeting the people present there Swamiji became busy in his meditation and silent prayers. The problem relating to his membership to the Conference got resolved but the main test was slated to take place on the next day. He wanted to achieve victory, the victory of his Hindu religion, the victory of his India. Swamiji was lost in all these thoughts. At that very moment, memories of Guruji came before him, his last words reverberated in his ears—"Today I have handed over to you, now I am a mere poor beggar who has nothing in his possession. With this power you will bring about welfare of this world."

■■

Swami Vivekanand: A Biography

On the Stage of
Religious Conference

The morning of September 11, 1893. The newly constructed Art Institute building in Chicago was decorated with lights and other articles. There was much turmoil and turbulence inside and outside the venue. The inner room and the gallery on four sides on the upper storey was filled with around six-seven thousand educated men and women. In addition to the main hall people crowded in the nearby rooms. The spacious stage was in the hall. On the middle of the stage, large human size idols of two great philosophers were there .Onto the southern side was the brass idol of the goddess of knowledge. But the most strange and unseen thing on the stage was the throne like chair. On both its sides and on its back, wooden chairs were arranged in half circular manner. The national flag of all the participant countries were hoisted on the stage. After some time the huge echoing sound of bell was heard-tun....tun. First, second and the third.....it went on ten times. The peaceful atmosphere in the hall had now become almost breathless. With the echo of the last ring of the bell which almost got merged with the atmosphere inside the hall, groups of participating members lined up in a disciplined manner emerged from a room on the backside of the main hall and walked towards the pre-arranged stage with measured steps. The group was led by the Chairman Charles Carol Bauni and the main priest of the American Catholic Church, Cardinal Gibben holding each others hands. They were followed by the main officials of the Conference, followed by the representatives. The sight was rather wondrous. The strange and colourful dress of the representatives, the varying cloth length of different members from the knee portion to the head, different shirts, caps, styles, headgears and the symbolic cross of Christians, half moon of Muslims, some having long hair and some having clean shaven heads.

On the throne like seat on the stage sat Cardinal Gibbens wearing a bright coloured dress and the Chairman Bauni wearing long black coat side by side. Towards the right side sat the reverent old priests of the ancient Roman Church. They wore loose black coloured clothes and had a strange shaped black hats. They held in their hands sticks made of elephant tusks with beautiful art works. The members from China being sent by their emperor who were to explain the theories of Confucious were wearing heavy dresses more than there height. In the manner, representatives from Japan, Africa, Greece and from different religions in India sat on the stage in there best outfits. There were many people from India—Pratap Chandra Majumdar representing Brahmo Samaj, Virchandra Gandhi representing Jain religion, Smt. Annie Besant representing Theosophcal Society, Nagarkar was there from Bombay. Among all these great personalities sitting in a particular order, Swamiji was also seated wearing his saffron coloured long shirt and headgear exactly resembling a saint surviving on alms. His eyes reflected his indifference towards materialistic comforts. The curious eyes of the audience slipped from the faces of the people sitting on the stage to rest on the face of this young saint.

It was the actual and formal beginning of the World Religious Conference. Many meetings pertaining to two three religions used to be held in other parts of the world. But truly such kind of conference on a large scale had never been held before wherein so many representatives from the entire world had ever participated. In the history of the world, this world religion conference undoubtedly enjoys a special place. In the history of religion, especially in the history of Hindu religion, the World Religion Conference held at Chicago was a milestone. Representatives from every nook and corner of the world participated in the conference representing different religions of the world. The words spoken by these reflected the faith and belief of crores of people all over the world. The followers of different religions of the world were granting strength to their representatives in an invisible manner.

The objective of the World Religion Conference was to enable people assess the view points of different religions in the proper perspective, people develop a sense of respect and equality towards different religions of the world and people came closer towards one another and form together in a bond of love. There were many members who were not associated with any particular religion. They believed in the religion of humanity. They were of the opinion that this conference will help in establishing a sense of understanding and unity in the minds of seekers of truth. The Chairman Bauni was also one among those who believed in the religion of humanity. Swami Vivekanand wrote about Bauni in one of his letters— "What a wonderful person Shri Bauni is! Just think about his brains which thought about organization of such a unique event and accomplished it successfully. It is worth mentioning here that he was not a priest but a common lawyer who in spite of his profession led the representatives of different religions. His behaviour is very sweet and nice and he is a thorough scholar possessing a high level of patience. The serious and touching emotions of his heart is quite evident in his bright eyes."

But among the organizers of this Conference, there were some people who thought that this conference will establish the unparalleled supremacy of Christianity. Even though Swamiji maintained a free minded and reverential attitude towards Sh Bauni, deep in his heart Swamiji also had the same opinion. In one of his letters, Swamiji wrote— "In order to display the supremacy of Christianity over all other religions of the world, this World Religion Conference was organized in America." This kind of opinion about the religious Conference, which earned Swamiji name and fame as well as a place in the pages of history, may seem to be inappropriate and unbecoming on the part of Swamiji. But if you put the whole conference and its proceedings in a deeper perspective then the idour of partiality towards Christianity becomes clearly evident. Behind the mask of universal brotherhood, Christianity was reiterating its importance.

But if one thinks, keeping away all these complexities, then emerges another image of the whole exercise. The nineteenth century was giving way to the twentieth century when the world was speeding up its pace towards acquisition of worldly comforts and materialistic possession and in such a situation, the very fact that such a religious conference was being organized in America was quite heartening and something unimaginable. It seemed as if some invisible hand was working on it. Swami Vivekanand also felt this kind of premonition. While departing to Chicago from India, Swamiji had confided in his Guru brother Swami Turiyanand that— "This World Religion Conference is being organized for this fellow (pointed towards himself), my heart says so. After some days you yourself will come to know about it."

Though these words on the part of Swamiji looks too egoistic but to a certain extent he was true. This conference spread a new school of thought in the mindset of the western world—the Indian Hindu Philosophical thought. The Western World was unaware of, in fact a stranger to the purity, the flowing sound and above all the enormity of its form.

Horible Mervin Merry Suel, who was then the Chairman of the Science Division of the Religion Conference had said— "The greatest advantage of this conference for the Christian society, especially the people of America is that, it has made it clear cut that there are other religions even more reverential than Christianity which with its ethical beauty and competence, without harming even the smallest of creations is uite ahead in terms of philosophical depth, spiritual strength, liberal thinking power and humaneness."

Swamiji attended the world conference with a view to represent this kind of religion. The conference was formally inaugurated with a rendition of sweet instrumental music. After this all the members stood up and prayed to the God almighty in a singular voice. After each stanza, Cardinal held up his hand and within of second the music ceased. After the prayer, the Chairman called the names of the representatives turn by turn and each one stood up and gave brief introduction of themselves. The morning session of the conference ended with the introduction of the participants and short speeches on the part of organizing committee members. First of all, the chief of a Greek Church gave a speech. It was very long but emotional. The audience gave him a huge round of applause. Then some more people addressed the audience talking on different topics. The audience also encouraged them with applause.

In between the Chairman called the name of Vivekanand to present his point of view but every time he replied—'No, not now.' He was a bit nervous because of the gandeur of the conference. But the nervousness was not a bit evident on his face. He had not witnessed such a scene or heard about it let alone participating in it. His nervousness remained imprisoned within his heart. He mentioned about his feelings at the time of the conference in a letter which he wrote to one of his disciples in India—"Undoubtedly, my heart was beating and my mouth almost dry. I was so nervous that I could not muster up courage to present my views in the morning session." He was unable to make up his mind as to what to say and how to begin his address in such a big meeting. Almost everyone present there had made prior preparation, after in depth study, research and analysis and were reading out from the note prepared by them. But Swamiji had not made any preparation nor any pre-written speech with him to read out to the audience. Still he was not without any kind of support. He possessed great powers— invisible strength that he received from Ramakrishna and Mother Goddess Kali. It was not that he was unaware of this power inherent in him. Hence, inside the hall he was lost in a continuous and silent prayer. After noon also when Swami Vivekanand did not show any initiative to present his views, the Chairman of the Conference became a bit dilemmatic as to whether this sannyasi will be able to speak something or not. Finally, during the afternoon session, after four representatives read out their speech, after much insistence on the part of the main head he stood up to speak.

On Swamiji's countenance there was the brightness of fire. His big shining eyes journeyed from one corner of the hall to the other, looking at each one present there. There existed a calmness filled with curiosity all over. Swamiji worshipping the goddess of knowledge Goddess Saraswati silently, began his speech in English.

The first line—"Sisters and Brothers of America" had just come out from his lips, that the electrification that it caused to the audience became clearly evident on their face. The sound of applause echoed inside the hall for a while. Later on, Swamiji had written in this connection—"The sound made me deaf for two minutes."

Another reference that is available in this context is from Smt. S.K. Blowget, who was Swamiji's hostess during his stay in Los Angeles. She had written, "I was also present at the World Religion Conference that was held in 1863. When this young man stood up and said "Sisters and brothers of America," around seven thousand people who were present there, got up in reverence due to some reason which she herself could not understand, giving him a standing ovation. When it was over I saw that around twenty ladies where jumping over the benches to reach near him. I told to myself—"Oh dear son, if you are able to withstand this attack then surely you are the God Almighty." It seemed as if the whole audience had crossed the limit of excitement due to happiness.

The manner in which Swamiji was extended a hearty welcome by the audience by a huge round of applause, made Swamiji give a befitting reply. He resumed his speech—"As I stand on this stage to express my gratitude to you for welcoming us with so much love and affection, I am experiencing the kind of joy which is inexplicable. I thank you on behalf of the ancient traditions of sannyasa in the world, on behalf of mothers of all religions and on behalf of the thousands of Hindus belonging to different castes and creeds. The sound of applause and encouragement continued for a while even after Swamiji began with his thanking address. But when he began to explain about the large heartedness of Hindu religion the hall turned into a silence zone—there was pin drop silence. He continued, "I am proud to be the follower of one such religion which had taught the lesson of perseverance and acceptance of every religion to the world." To reiterate the large heartedness of Hindu religion he quoted and explained two shlokas from religious texts on the occasion.

Ruchinam Vaichitryadhriyu Kutilananapath Josham
Nrinameko Gamyastvamasi Paysamanav iva.

In the manner different rivers originate from different sources to join the ocean, people having different interests and chosing straight and complicated ways finally end up conjoining with you. Oh Lord.

Yeyatha Mam Prapadyanthe Tanstathaiv.
Bhayamyaham
Mam Vartmanuvarta te manushya parth.
Sarvasha

Whosoever comes to attain me, whatever they are like, I am attainable to all of them. People choose different ways but in the end takes shelter in me only.

The World Religion Conference, which had brought with it the message of hope for the world was making people of the world listen to the song of the golden day break. Swamiji expressed about its objective at the end of his speech.

"Communalism, sectarianism, obstinacy and the more heinous religious fanatism have been ruling over our beautiful earth for the past so many years. It will be filling the earth with acts of violence, causing human bloodshed, destroying the very civilizations and pushing every countries into the dark pit of despair. If those rikeful demonic powers were not present then the condition of human society would have been in a much more progressed state. But all those demonic forces are on the verge of collapse and from deep within my heart. I wish that in the morning the sounds that emerged from the ringing of bells in the morning to formally inaugurate this conference may prove to be the death fell for all those forces."

By the evening of 11 September, Swamiji ended this first brief lecture. After the meeting, at night when Swamiji entered the rest room being allotted to him, he started crying like a child who cries when he loses his toy or breaks his toy. The image of the broken soul of people of India, their scattered courage and honour, their disdainful poverty and sufferings everything was haunting his heart and making him weep. In a happy, prosperous and materialistically luxurious country like America, he received so much of honour, applause and cheering—Will it be helpful in weeping away the sufferings of Mother India? Will the people away in his motherland be happy? The image of thousands of Indian living in the darkness of despair with illiterate minds hungry stomachs and naked bodies emerged before his eyes. The moment the sufferings of his countrymen came to his minds the comforts he had been enjoying there as one of the members of the conference began to pinch him. For sometime he was in a state of bewilderment. He was thinking that if he was not capable of redeeming his countrymen from their sorrows and sufferings, then his life there and the renown that he had achieved there, everything was futile-worthless.

The meetings of the conference took place in three sessions—morning, afternoon and evening for continuously seventeen days. Thousands of essays were read out and debates were conducted on these topics. Day-by-day the number of audiences kept on increasing. On the fourth day the crowd became uncontrollable to be restrained within the 'Art Institute.' Arrangements for accommodating the audiences were made at the Washington Hall adjacent to it.

Arrangement for word to word telecast of the proceedings here was made there also. The first lecture delivered by Swami Vivekanand was very short but still it touched the hearts of, those present there. The perseverance, universality, inherent truth and large heartedness of the Hindu religion impressed and influenced the audience at large.

On 15 September Swami Vivekanand delivered his second lecture on the topic—"Reasons of our difference of opinions." On the afternoon sessions before Swamiji's speech, representatives of different religions were all but on proving the supremacy of their respective religions over others. Heated arguments and counter arguments were going on. When Swamiji's turn came, he did not present any statement in support of his religion but in order to make them understand the cause of indifference between different religions narrated an interesting story of a frog. A frog was born and brought up in a well, the narrow well was his whole world. One day a frog living in the ocean fell into the well. The first frog asked the second one—"From where have you come?" The second one replied—"from the ocean." Then the frog from the ocean began to explain to the frog living in the well about the vastness of ocean. But the frog in the well had never experienced the leap in the ocean so he did not believe what the frog from the ocean was telling and was thinking his well as the whole world itself. He asked—"nothing can be vaster than the well. You are a liar. Oh somebody kick him out from here." Swamiji said, "We all religious believers, setting in our narrow wells in this manner, are fighting with each other over the supremacy of our respective religions. I consider you Americans to be the bless ones, because you have taken the initiative, made efforts to break the small boundaries around us."

Eventually on 16 September Swami Vivekanand gave his major speech on Hinduism. It was a pre-written essay. In this he explained about the origin, enormity, psychology and the scientific basis of various philosophical principles associated with it. About the origin and expanse of Hindu religion Swami Vivekanand's opinion was that "The Hindu community achieved their religion from the Vedas and that he considers the Veda to be eternal—which has no beginning or end. The audience present here might find this to be a laughing Mutter that how can any book be without beginning or end. Vedas means a dictionary compiled of the spiritual truths invented and experienced by different men. In the manner the law of gravity was very much existent and working before it was actually invented and even if the whole humanity forgets about it, it will continue working. The same principle is applicable for the laws governing the spiritual world. Principle of spiritual and ethical relationship between the soul and the supreme soul had been in existence even before we knew it and will continue to be inexistence even if we forget it. From the heights of spiritual experience of Vedanta philosophy to the new and latest inventions of science, the lowest level of idol worship to the ancient stories, the principles and philosophies of Buddhists and Jains all these have adequate place in the Hindu religion.

Explaining about the Vedanta philosophy of the Hindu religion he said that Hindu religion conjoins every religious thought and every kind of worship. According to Hindus, the soul is totally the part of the supreme being. This supreme being is pure and formless. He is eternal. With his orders the wind blows, fire burns, clouds rain and death dances on the earth. Because of this the soul is also eternal, pure and free. It is also devoid of any birth or death. No laws can break it, fire cannot burn it, water can not drench it and air cannot dry it. Swamiji said, "Soul is such a circle which has no limits but it is centred around the body. Death means the transfer of this center from one body to another." The Hindu religion believes in prior birth. The present birth status of an individual is based on his fast life's course of action (Karma) and the future life is based on the present life's karma. While explaining about salvation, Swamiji presented a quotation from the Veda—"Soul is a divine form which is bound within the prison of the five senses and when it breaks the shackles it will attain wholeness or completeness." This condition is called salvation or emancipation, which in layman's language is known as freedom—freedom from the shackles of incompleteness, freedom from the cycle of birth and death." It is possible to break this shackle with the blessings of the God and this grace is attainable only to pure souls. Hence, the purity of soul is the only condition to attain the blessings of the God.

He further said that "in order to witness God or to become one with God, human beings should free themselves from the trap of egoistic thoughts. To attain that highest level of salvation, destruction of this prison like body and this miserable and lowly personality is very necessary. When I become one with the Almighty then only will I be freed from the cycles of birth and death. When my identity becomes one with God then only will my sorrows and sufferings end; when I become aware of God then only will my ignorance end. This is an essential scientific truth too. Science has also proved that my physical personality is just an illusion. In actuality, my body is just a temporal peace of flesh which is subject to changes and my other part—the soul that is permanent as proved by the Advaita philosophy."

Swamiji in the last paragraphs of his essay, explains the importance of worshippinhg the different attributes of God. In his opinion, "People of India did not believe in multiple Gods. Though devotees having faith in different qualities of God worship different Gods and Goddesses each possessing each quality, still if one listens carefully to the prayers made by them at the temple dedicated to a particular God or Goddess—one will find that the devotee is seeking all kinds of blessings from that one God. This can neither be called faith in multiple Gods nor can this condition be set off against faith in single God. For example, even if you give another name to 'rose' flower, its qualities and fragrance will remain the same and sweet respectively. A name cannot be defined."

In support of idol worship he said—"With the image of any idol in mind it is as much impossible to pray or concentrate as it is impossible to stay alive without breathing. That is why, during Hindu worship physical symbols are put to use. In reality without the symbol of any image in mind it is very difficult to concentrate on your prayers. Almost all devotees who worship the various attributes or qualities of different Gods are well aware that the idol of their favourite God is just a symbol of the omnipresent, eternal and formless God Almighty.

Swamiji quoted a shloka from the 'Dharma Shastra' to emphasise and drive home in point, "Idol worship or worship of physical symbols is the lowest situation, the next step or the next higher level of worship is meditation where only the mind is involved and the highest situation is when one witnesses God and becomes face to face with him."

He also quoted another shloka from 'Upanishad'. An idol worshipper had reached the last level of his worship and is saying—'Sun, moon or the stars cannot give light to that Supreme Being, the power of electricity can also not brighten up that Surpeme Being, then there is no need to mention about this common fire. All these have light in them because He the Supreme Being has granted them this quality." But that idol worshipper will never denounce or dishonor any other idol of other gods or goddeses and will not consider worshipping other idols to be a sin. He will not only accept this to be a necessary situation of life but also will bow before it. Many worshippers in India have attained the divine form of God by means of idol worship. Even after attaining the divine form they do not call it illusory because in that extreme emotional stage they were able to witness the enormous divine form of God in that very idol of God. Swamiji made it clear that—"In the opinion of Hindus, human beings are not reaching out to truth from the state of illusion, but from truth to truth, from a lower category of truth towards that of a higher one."

Thus, after presenting a brief outline of the religious thoughts of Hindus, in the end, Swamiji presented a discourse on an all embracing religion—"One which will not be bound by any country or borders—it will be limitless like the limitless almighty God." Who will disperse light on every creature belonging to every class all over the world in an equal manner. This World Religion Conference will absorb the positive attributes of all religions in its clutches and will give the message of love and good action to the society. In the end, addressing America he said—"Oh! Motherland of freedom, Columbia! You are blessed. It is your good fortune that you never stained your hands with the blood of your neighbor, you never tried to steal your neighbours' belongings to make yourself rich. Hence, you are the chosen one, the lucky one to lead the civilization hoisting the flag of harmony."

It was but obvious that Americans were glad to receive so much of praise.But above all there was one more thing that cast a magical spell on the audience and that was Swami Vivekanand himself. His safffon outfit, his healthy and youthful appearance, his big and piercing eyes, pointed nostrils, his lips, and the words of truth that originated from his lips—all thus gave a magnet-like attraction to his personality. His oratorial skills were emotive and language poetic. He had in front of him the whole American public both curious and aware. He also recited an English poem which all the more charmed the audience especially the Americans. His soul was fragrant with the feeling of harmony.

Sister Nivedita had made mention about Swamiji's speech in one of her writings—"When he began his speech the topic was 'the religious thoughts of Hindus', but by the time he concluded his speech the Hindu religion had already been created." The vast audience that Swamiji was facing at the conference were all supporters of western philosophy and thoughts and were representing the same. But after listening to the speech by Swami Vivekanand, direction of their thoughts changed. They became aware that other than western philosophy there are some other streams which possess the qualities of purity and clarity that can attract others.

On 20th December, Swamiji gave a brief speech on the topic "Religion is not a major necessity for India." In this, he was highly critical about the Christian missionaries being sent to India to propagate Christianity. He had never learnt to hide any bitter truths. In the Christian country itself he denounced the activities of Christian Missionaries in India. He said—"You Christians who with a view to uplift the souls of idol worshippers are keen to send propagaters of your religion, why don't you do something to save themselves from hunger and poverty? When India was in the grip of the most dreadful famine, thousands and lakhs of Hindus were dying of hunger, but you Christians did not do anything to help them or save them from such a disastrous situation. You people go to India and construct a lot of churches, but religion is not in scarcity in the east. There religion is in abundance—Lacs of Indians are crying out for bread. They are asking us bread and we are giving them stone. Imparting religious preaching to a hungry person is like disgracing him. In India, if a priest indulges in preaching to earn money, then such a priest will be castigated and people will spit on them. I have come here to seek help for my poor brothers, but I have clearly understood the difficulties of attaining help for idol worshippers from believers of Christianity.

On 26 September, Swamiji gave a lecture on the 'Consummation of Buddhism and Hinduism.' He said that there exists no much difference between Buddhism and

Hinduism. Buddhism has also emerged from Hinduism or the vedic religion. He further stated that Hindu religion is divided into two parts—ritual (karmakand) and intellect (Gyankand). Sannyasis indulge in special studies of Gyankand. Buddhism is mainly associated with it. Gyankand does not believe in caste difference, hence, there is no casteism in Buddhist religion. Hinduism and Buddhism are closely connected in the same manner as Jewish and Christian religions. Jesus Christ was a Christian and Shakya Muni a Hindu. Jews did not understand or recognize Jesus Christ and nailed him on to the cross but the Hindus worshipped Shakya Muni (Lord Buddha). It is a different issue that Hindus accepted the Hindu religion and Buddhist religion in different versions. The main reason for this was that during that period in the Karmakand form of Hinduism many impurities had creeped in. The Sanskrit language in which Hindu religious texts were written was not a common man's language. It was the language of the higher class Brahmins. Hence, the actual philosophy governing the Hindu religion was not known to common men. But Lord Buddha through the medium of common men's language, giving equal status to every caste—whether high or low—imparted knowledge and awareness to every one. The birth of Lord Buddha was instrumental not in destroying Hindu religion but to bring improvements in it. The Buddhist religion enjoyed only a short stay in its birthland India because 'it erased the presence of the Amighty Supreme Being from the public with whom every man and woman took shelter.' But at the same time the Hindu religion turned a blind eye towards interest taken by the Buddhist religion in social service and caring attitude for the poor, weak and the ignorant.

In his speech, while depicting Hinduism as the mother of Buddhism, Swamiji did not forget to emphasise on some of the characteristic features fundamental to Buddhism. While concluding he said—"The Hindu religion cannot survive without Buddhist religion and Buddhism cannot survive without Hinduism as such. As long as the scholarly philosophy of Hinduism and the large heartedness remain separated from each other, the downfall of India is essential. With the union of the two religions only welfare of India is possible."

During the conference, Swamiji gave speech n one topic or the other daily. Sometimes even when he was not well enough to speak, he was requested to speak for at least 10-15 minutes at the end of the conference. The main reason for this was that the audience who took there seats at 10 in the morning slowly left the hall by the evening. But when am announcement was made that Swamiji will present a lecture before the dispersal of the meeting for the day, the audience glued to their seats for hours together to gain the enjoyment of Swamiji's speech even for ten minutes.

The last day of the World Religion Congress, that was 27 September. During the last session of the meeting Swamiji stood up to speak. He thanked everyone present there for organizing the conference successfully. "I have all gratitude for all those great men, whose large heartedness and love for truth first dreamt the wonderful thing and later on executed it, my thanks to all those who presented their views on this stage, my thanks to this enlightened audience who supported me and welcome all those thoughts that lightened up the difference of opinions. Amidst this equivocal missed tone, some unmusical tones were also heard, my special thanks to them because they with their strange tones added more sweetness to the equivocal tone. After this thanks giving, he explained to the audience the real meaning of religious unity—"If someone is hoping that this religious unity will prove to be the triumph of one particular religion and the destruction of all others, then I would like to say to such brothers of mine that such a hope on his part is impossible. Do I wish that Christians get converted into Hindus? Never, God never let such a thing happen. Do I wish that Hindus and Buddhists get converted into Christians? But yes, every individual should get through with the crux of other religions and should safeguard its speciality and make progression."

In fact, the Religion Conference reiterated the very thoughts stated by Swamiji. If it has exhibited something to world, it has proved that purity, piousness and generosity are not the personal possession of any particular faith and that every religion had given birth to great men and women who were great and possessed wonderful moral character. In spite of clear evidences if one thinks that unjust religion will get destroyed and only his religion will survive, then I express heartfelt sympathy to him and make him quite clear that in the presence of all kinds of opposition it wil be written on the flag of every religion—"Help others, do not indulge in fights. Give due respect to others feelings, do not destroy them—unity and peace not differences of opinion or ill feeling."

In this manner, only this Indian saint, expressed the truth about the significance of each religion and proved them to be related to each other. But at the same time he explained the philosophy of Hinduism in such an impressive manner that he was able to win over the heart of innumerable foreigners. His attractive personality, intellect, humility, oratorial skills and sweet conversational skills made Swami Vivekanand an object of discussion in the city of Chicago. At every root and corner of streets and at various places Swami Vivekanand's portrait size posters were displayed with 'Swami Vivekanda' written in big letters. Thousands of passers by belonging to different religious affinities showed honour and respect, and bowed before the posters before leaving the place. Many major newspapers and magazines in America published about Swami Vivekanand showering praises on him. 'New York Herald' wrote—"Undoubtedly, he was the shining star of the World Religion Conference. After listening to him, it is felt that what idiotic thing we are doing by sending religious propagation to his country."

'Boston Evening Transport' said—"He was the most favourite among the audience throughout the conference because of his personality and lofty ideals. Even when he passed before the stage people applauded and cheered for him. He accepted this special attention and individual praise with child like gratitude and he displayed no sign of ego. To make people wait till the end of the session, they kept Vivekanand's speech at the end."

'The Press of America' wrote about Swamiji—"Among the scholars of Hindu philosophy and science present in the conference as members, Swami Vivekanand, with his oratorial skills kept the audience spellbound. In spite of the preservor of fathers of modern Church and propagators of Christianity Swamiji's flow of language swayed away their opinions and presentation, like a storm. Some newspapers like 'The Interior Chicago', 'The Sutherford America' and 'The New York Critic' published articles in praise of Swami Vivekanand. Some newspapers published Swami Vivekanand's complete speech.

Sh. Merwin Snel, the chairman of the Science Department of the Chicago Religious Conference in an article published in the famous magazine 'Pioneer' had written—

"The kind of enormity with which the Hindu religion had been able to create an impact on this conference and the public at large, no other religion had been able to achieve. The only ideal representative of the Hindu religion Swami Vivekanand is undoubtedly the most popular and impressive member of the conference. He gave a number of speech during the Religious Conference addressing the people who attended the conference as well in the meetings of the Science Department. No other orator representing any other religion-even Christianity received such kind of encouragement. Wherever he went, crowds of people gathered there and people were curious to listen to every word that came from his mouth. People who heard his speech, especially people who got an opportunity to closely interact with him, everyone showered praises about him. Even Christian fanatics said about him— "Swami is a super human among human beings! India has sent the Swamiji—hence, America is expressing gratitude. But those who have not learnt the lesson of world fraternity and generosity of heart and mind, to give an insight into those ideals to the children of America and to teach them those ideals, if possible, send more such morally upright men. This is humble prayer from America."

The chief of Theosophical Society, Dr. Annie Besant was also present in the conference. Some rooms at the 'Art Institute' were kept apart for the accommodation of the members. Annie Besant first met Swami Vivekanand in one of the rooms. After many days, referring to this memorable meeting, she wrote in the 'Brahmavadin' magazine—"A unique personality, wearing saffron outfit, in the dust-polluted environs of Chicago city bright like the Indian sun, brave like a lion, piercing eyes, vibrating lips, sharp and clearly defined bodily features—in the room meant for the members of the conference, thus was the first image of Swami Vivekanda that was captured by my eyes. He was famously known as a sannyasi, but it was not an appropriate title because at the first sight other than a saint his looks closely resembled to that of a warrior and he was in fact a warrior saint. That man who painted the glory of India, who upheld the shining face of his country, the representative of the most ancient religion, in spite of being the youngest among the representatives of the conference was in no way inferior to others. He was the epitome of the most ancient and the greatest of the truths. Even mother India would have felt honoured by nominating her most eligible child as the messenger to the egoistic and all powerful western world."

Even after the lapse of many months after the conference, discussion about this wonderfully talented and prodigious Swamiji shared space in American newspapers along with other news articles. Representatives of newspaper organizations, scholarly teachers from schools and colleges, renowned theosophists, some philosophers and seekers of truth, every one came to meet Swamiji. Among those, numbers of women folk were also not less. Such a surprising impact of the spirituality of an Indian saint on the worldly materialistic western world. This much of name and fame. If it had been someone else in palce of Swami Vivekanand, he would have been puffed up with pride. But Swamiji was above all these mean emotions. He considered himself to be a machinery, by means, of which the message of Gurudev Ramakrishna had to be spread throughout the world, who with the philosophy cf monism wanted to light up the dark paths of the western people. The heart of the nation of America was unhappy and disturbed due to prosperity and overt luxury and it was hankering for spirituality. Swamiji gave them the nectar of Indian philosophy which appeased the soul of America.

Swamiji presented even the harshest of truths before an individual or the society. This dauntless nature, many a time, put him in difficult situations. But he never endeavoured to present truth in an attractive manner. In the country belonging to Christians, the respect and devotion with which he praised Jesus Christ and his messages, he deeply condemned and criticized the propagators of Christianity. On the stage of World Religious Conference, he condemned the activities undertaken by Christian Missionaries in India to spread their religion. He said that the under-educated Christian missionaries are indulged in spreading education, building churches, first converting the hapless poor people into Christians and giving them food and clothing. Was this the kind of sympathy and generosity they nursed for Indians when scarcity, like a huge cobra had taken a monstrous form and swallowed lakhs of men, women and children, then what had these missionaries done to save their lives. This fearless and staunch criticism on the part of Swamiji had indeed made the fanatic Christian missionaries irritant. They began to spread false propaganda against Swamiji. They even tried to indulge in his character assassination. They tried to make him go astray from his path with the help of some beautiful women. But Swamiji had in his possession the shield of 'Brahmacharya' which was unsurpassable and strong like a diamond. Every word of defamation against Swamiji crumbled into pieces after hitting that iron-like shield. He continued with his work unperturbed about things happening around him.

This kind of public slandering against Swamiji became a cause of worry and sorrow for his well-wishers. They gave different kinds of advice to Swamiji asking him to appease everyone with sweet words and not to criticize and unveil the harsh truths in such an open manner. An American woman who was a well-wisher of Swamiji wrote to him about this. But Swamiji gave a reply to her stating that a sannyasi is never affected by any kind of criticism. He quoted an old adage in support of his claim.

Hathi Chale Bazar, Kutta Bhawnka Hazar, Sadhu ka Durbhav Nahin, jab Ninde Sansar.

When elephant passes through the market thousands of dogs follow it and bark at it, but the elephant never turns to look back. He keeps on walking ahead with a calm mind. In the same way worldly men always criticize the selfless work of saints, but the saints are least affected by them all.

The hearts of pious yogis, on the one hand are softer than flower but on the other harder than rock. But the heart that gets melted by the sorrow of the others, that heart endures the criticism of others. He is not at all perturbed by any amount of praises or condemnations.

Not only the Christian priests and missionaries laid thorns on Swamiji's path. They had with them the support of one Pratapchandra Majumdar, who had come from Calcutta to represent Brahmo Samaj. Majumdar felt jealous of the enormity of fame enjoyed by Swamiji and he began to spread rumours about him. In a letter to his favourite disciple Shahi, Swamiji discussed about it—"With God's will, I was able to meet Majumdar Sir here. At first he showed much love and affection but when the men and women of complete

Chicago city gathered around me in crowds, he became jealous. When I heard about it I was rather taken aback. And Majumdar condemned me at the conference and with the Chrisitian priests to a great extent. He tried to create misunderstanding about me by saying that "He is nobody. He is a fraud, he is misleading you by presenting himself as saint, etc."

In a letter to another disciple Alasinga Perumal, he again discussed it.

"Undoubtedly, these fanatic Christian priests are against me. And knowing very well that it is difficult to defeat me in any other way they have taken up the weapon of slander to condemn me and defame me. In all these attempts on their part, Majumdar is helping them out. He is gone mad with jealousy. He has told them that I am swindler and a crooked fellow. And in Calcutta he has spread the rumours that in America I am leading a sinful and wanton life. May God help him and save him! My brother, without opposition no good work can be accomplished. The one who tries hard till the end, he only becomes successful and emerges victorious."

The Christian missionaries also indulged in a lot of false and negative campaign against Swamiji in India. In a state of, emotional frenzy. Swamiji used to criticize Americans proximity with physical and material comforts. The missionaries used to quote such excerpts from different speech and got them published in leaflet form and distributed among pubic to provoke the public sentiments. During those days, a magazine on Hindu religion named 'Bangavasi' used to get published and circulated. The magazine carried defamatory articles related to Swamiji. They sent the copies of such magazines to religious priests in America. They began to be highly critical about Swamiji's eating habits and lifestyle. They spread the news that this fraudulent saint was not practising vegetarianism in America. This was true to a certain extent. He used to be so engrossed in accomplishing his mission that he never used to worry about hunger or thrust. Whatever people gave to him, he partook to fill his stomach. He used to eat to live. He was not interested to live in order to eat. He did not want to trouble his host to make vegetarian dishes specially for him and he didn't have time to prepare food for himself. One whose mind was busy with thought processes and meditation, who was so lost in analyzing the minutest of philosophical thoughts, how could he waste his time in giving heed to such a commonplace thing like food. Some well-wishers from India wrote letters to Swamiji in this regard and advised him to remain on vegetarian diet. In reply, he wrote:

"I am surprised to know that you people are becoming perturbed by the foolish and false rumours spread by the missionaries. If any Hindu is giving me advise to remain on a strict Hindu diet then ask him to send a Brahmin cook and some money for the same. I am unable to control my laughter—Those who do not have the capacity to extend financial aid of even a single paise, how can they consider themselves eligible of giving free advise. On the other hand, if these missionaries are saying that I have broken the vow of sannyasa, then tell them that they are mendacious and untruthful. Remember, I am not ready to be guided by others. I am very well aware of the objectives of my life. I am least bothered or affected by any kind of slanders. Am I a slave to any particular person or caste?"

The missionaries of America and some Hindus influenced by Majumdar tried their level best to create problems for Swamiji. Sometimes it so happened that when Swamiji got invitation for a speech from some organisations and whenever his opponents came to know about that, they indulged in slandering against Swamiji and achieved success in getting the same cancelled. Many a time it so happened that whenever Swamiji arrived at the house where he had been invited he found the premises locked. But later on when they realized the actual situation they sought forgivance from him.

Majumdar and the Chrisitian Missionaries together sent many anonymous letters to Swamiji's close friends with a view to bring dishonor to him. One such letter was received by Mr. Hale. Bewaring him, he was advised not to let Swamiji meet his two daughters and nieces. Mr Aale read the letter and tore the letter into pieces and put them into fire. Those who were in contact with Swamiji, those who knew him well, they were not at all affected by these rumours. Swamiji was also very well aware of that. Hence, he remained pacified in spite of all such incidents. His only worry was about his country, from where he was absent. Sometimes he became perturbed thinking about the impact of all this negative propaganda on people, especially during his absence from his motherland. He was especially worried about his mother as to what she would think. This made him sorrowful. He wrote a letter to Isabell Mr. Cidell discussing about this—"I am not bothered about what my own people are saying about me, except for one thing. I have an old mother. She suffered a lot of chardship during her life and in spite of, I being her beloved and favourite child she spared me to serve God and men. What will happen to her hopes? Majumdar, who is spreading all sort of false rumours about me in Calcutta that I am leading a sinful and unethical life, will be enough, to take my mother's life away."

Even the members of Theosophical Society tried their level best to create hindrance in Swamiji's work, but in face of such a versatile personality like that of Swamiji all their attempts failed. They were not able to reign the pious impact of this Hindu saint. Later on perhaps to save their face and redeem themselves from the act of slandering they had committed, Smt. Annie Besant wrote an article in praise of Swami Vivekanda in the magazine 'Brahmanadin'.

Later on when the American public came to know about Swamiji's words and action, they ignored all the rumours about him. They were well aware that Swamiji's character was like pure gold which had undergone the fire test. There was not even a speck of impurity present. He never hid anything about himself nor nursed any secret. He used to say that "I am a seeker of truth and worshipper of truth. Truth will never, in any situation strike a friendship with falsehood." Swami Vivekanand was not at all egoistic. He used to speak the words from Vedas, words of truth and that of God."

In this manner, the storm of slander unleashed by a group of American missionaries, Christian priests and jealous Hindus against Swamiji, gradually got subsided and became calm. Vivekanand was a person whose personality, character and workstyle reflected a kind of grandeur and glory. Its brightness faded the darkness of all the rumous. Victory of truth over falsehood was very essential. Within a short span of time Swamiji's opponents became his friends. Swamiji's joy knew no bounds when he realized that in a country that believed in materialistic comforts, there was no dearth to worshippers of truth. He felt as if majority of American population was keen to attain spiritual progress.

Experiences in America

Even after the conclusion of World Religious Conference, Swamiji stayed back in Chicago city and gave discourses at various places. The most revered thinker of Chicago Mr. John B. Lean and his scholarly wife invited Swamiji to stay at their place. Soon Swamiji got mingled with this family and became an inseparable member of the family. Mrs. Lean's personality resembled greatly with his mother's. Perhaps because of this he had a feeling of affection towards her. Mrs. Lean also pampered him with love and affection as towards a son. One day, a friend of Mrs. Lean gave her a little and spicy chutney. At.meal time, the hostess kept the bottle of chutney on the dining table. When everyone began with their meals, Mrs. Lean told Swamiji that the chutney was so spicy that mere drops of it will make the food delicious. At once Swamiji took the bottle and helped himself with the chutney. He spread it all over the food served in his place in large quantity. People sitting there felt surprised at this act on the part of Swamiji. But Swamiji smilingly partook his food relishing every bite. Swamiji liked the chutney so much that Mrs. Lean placed special orders for the bulk purchase of that spicy chutney.

Swamiji stayed with Lean couple as guest almost for a month. People came there to invite him for presenting his views within Chicago and nearby cities. He began to get good remuneration for his speeches and discourses. Some generous people used to give him donations for carrying out welfare activities in India. Swamiji used to tie the cash or money he got in a handkerchief, brought it home and handed them over to Mrs. Lean with a conquering smile like that of a child. Mrs. Lean used to keep the account of his income and expenditure.

Swamiji's personality was so strong that especially women used to get attracted towards him and they indulged in displaying all sorts of body languages to attract his attention towards them. Mrs. Lean did not like all this. She was afraid that this simple straight forward young saint does not go astray. Hence, she warned Swamiji to be careful and cautious in this regard. Swamiji was greatly touched by Mrs. Lean's concern for him. Patting her hands as if in an assuring manner he said—"Mrs. Lean, you are my mother. My dear American mother. Please do not worry about me. It is true that most of the times I have spent the night under a banyan tree after partaking whatever I received in alms from a generous farmer. But at the same time, it is also true that sometimes I have stayed in the palaces of kings as guest and there the maids have fanned me with the fan made of peacock-feather throughout the night and I am well experienced with such kinds of temptations. Please do not worry about me."

After staying for almost a month with the Lean couple, Swami Vivekanand stayed with some rich devotees in Chicago for over one and a half months. He mentioned about this period in one of his letters—"The doors of most beautiful houses have been open for me. I am always staying as guest at one place or the other. The house of Mr and Mrs. George Hale like that of the Lean couple enjoys special significance among all others. Swamiji had much attachment towards the house of George W. Hale. Mrs. Hale was the one who lit the lamp of hope and confidence on the despaired path of Swamiji. In that vast city, she was the one who gave food to quench his hunger, gave proper direction to help him reach his destination. If that Goddess like Mrs. Hale had not made appearance before Swamiji and not helped him to reach the venue where the religious conference was stated to be held a day before the conference, then God only knows if Swami Vivekanda's name would have inscribed in the pages of history.

Swamiji commanded great respect and love from the members of Hale family. Out of reverence, Swamiji called Mr. Hale 'Father Pope' and Mrs. Hale 'Mother Church'. Till the end of 1864, when he visited different big and small cities of America for giving speech and discourses, his permanent address was the residence of the Hale family. The letters from his disciples, friends and well-wishers in India were received at the address of Hales who in turn sent them to Swamiji's present temporary address. The Hale couple had two daughters—Mary and Hariett. Mr. Hale's two nieces

Harett Mc Cidelle and Isabel Mc Cidelle also stayed there. All four of them were of the same age group. Swamiji was very close to the four sisters. All of them got brotherly affection from Swamiji and they on their part showered sisterly concern and love on Swamiji.

Even when Swamiji used to be away from the city of Chicago, he carried out correspondence with these sisters especially Mary Hale and Isabel Mecidelle. Swamiji liked these sisters more because their mental inclination was towards spiritualism. Sometimes Swamiji used to be so overwhelmed with emotion that he wrote letters in poetic language. Being younger to him, Swamiji imparted knowledge to them in poetic language, expressed his love and care and when necessary even scolded them.

Swamiji was not a poet. In view of art of poetry, his poems were not very substantial. But during emotional situations, poetry emanated automatically from his soft tender heart.

Swamiji was a yogi, a saint. But his saintliness was not the one that made people cut off from the world. He was not in need of such a kind of sannyasa which diverted one away from the world and one who with the sole desire of attaining redemption indulged in lonely endeavours. The purpose of his saintliness was to enlighten people. His saintliness endeavoured to divert the path of mankind from selfishness to attaining the supreme truth. He was a social worker in spirit. His life was flowing in between the parallel lines of attachment towards life and detachment towards life. The person who does not have a feeling of love towards society and the inhabitants of society, how can one expect him to serve the universe. Swamiji adored life in any form whether it was the tiny or minutest of creature or the very nature itself.

Swamiji had complete control over his emotions and feelings but in spite of that he relished new recipes, enjoyed smoking and dressing up in a stylish way. Hence, sometimes in spite of being detached and calm and possessing a personality beyond any comparison, he sometimes displayed a commonality and seemed to be a very simple person, one amongst the common people, possessing all those weaknesses. But an indepth analysis of his life will help us in distinctly understand how he was different from the commonplace—the weaknesses of life destroys us but such kind of men play with weaknesses and destroys them when necessary.

Swami Vivekanand: A Biography

One of the letters that he wrote to Isabell Mc Cidelle reflects one of the facets of his personality.

"Dear sister, I am helpless, right now instantly I cannot send you the booklet. I am sending you some newspaper clipping which I received from India. I am sending them to you. After reading them please send them to Mrs. Baigley. She is related to the editor of this newspaper Sh. Majumdar. I feel sorry for poor Majumdar.

Here I did not get the lemon coloured cloth material for my coat. Hence, I had to be satisfied with the colour almost similar. The coat will be ready in few days.

That day for my discourse at Waldorph I got a remuneration of 60 dollars. It is hoped that I will get some more for tomorrow's discourse.

A programme is being organized from 7th to 16th at Boston, but they will pay me considerably less. Yesterday, I bought a pipe for 13 dollars—Please do not discuss this with 'Father Pope'. The stitching charges of coat will be 30 dollars. I am getting proper food over here and sufficient amount of money as well. After the forthcoming lecture I will be able to deposit some amount in bank. I am going to speak at a vegetarian dinner party in the evening.

Yes, I am a vegetarian...., hence whenever I get such food I like that more. Day after tomorrow, I have been invited for a lunch at the place of Leaman Evaunt. I will spend my time in an enjoyable manner except for those boring lectures. No sooner than 16th will be over, a leap from Boston to Chicago and then only rest...a deep breath of rest taking for two, three weeks. I will just sit and talking, just talking and smoking.

Yes, your counterparts in New York are simpletons. They possess more wealth in comparison to intellect. I am going to deliver a lecture to the students of Harvard university. Mr. Breed has organized three lectures each at Boston and Harvard. People are organizing some lectures here also. On my route to Chicago, I will halt at New York and give them some strong puches and drain their pockets and will fly back to Chicago.

If you want to get something from New York or Boston which is not available at Chicago, do write quickly. Right now I have with me a good amount of dollars. I will get whatever you want within seconds. Do not think that it will look odd. There is nothing false about me. If I am your brother then I indeed am. If I hate something in the world that is falsehood." –*Your loving brother Vivekanand.*

Many people came across Swami Vivekanand during his life towards whom he had deep devotion and love. His emotions and sentiments towards them took the form of poetry. Swamiji had unfaltering love for Prof. Wright of Harvard University, who helped Swamiji to attend the World Parliament of Religions by giving him a reference letter. Whenever Swamiji wrote letter to him by addressing him as "Dear Teacher." Once while writing to his 'Dear Teacher', he was so overwhelmed with emotions that the words he wrote took the form of poetry. In this poem, he was given a beautiful description of the search of omnipresent Almighty and His grace. Prof. Wright was not aware of the poet within Swamiji. When Prof. Wright came to know about this hidden talent of Swamiji he was very happy. Later on also in face of such emotional circumstances, he expressed his emotions by the medium of poetry.

After the conclusion of World Parliament of Religion, for two months, Swamiji's stay with the all families in the city of Chicago is quite unclear. His maximum period of stay was with the Lean family and the Hale family. His letters were ample proof for it in which he has also mentioned about them in great detail. This shows the strong bonding, he had with them.

During the period of two long months of his stay after the World Religion Congress, Swamiji gave discourses on various topics like Indian religion, society and culture at various places. His fame had spread far and wide. He was at his prime of youth which instilled in him new vigour and energy. His countenance displayed a unique kind of splendor. He not only gave lectures about his own country but during those two months he undertook an in-depth study of Western culture and civilization. He used to spend his time thinking of ways and means of Indianisation of western society and civilization, how can India gain benefit from such a transformation. He wanted to add strength and vitality like that of westerners to the handicapped and weakened parts of India. In the infertile gardens, which had been rendered day due to the age long trampling it had been suffering at the hands of foreign invaders, Swamiji wanted to instill the fragrance of the west. In many of the letters that he sent from America to his friends, followers and well-wishers, he had drawn attention to the structure of the western society, the positive aspects of their behaviour and culture expressing his keenness that Indians also imbibe those values. He wanted that Indians receive the things that are pure and leave the residual part. During his stay with George W. Hale, Swamiji wrote a letter to one of his disciples in India—"I have not come to this country out of curiosity, nor name and fame but to find out a means to put the poor Indians on the path of progress. If the God Almighty helps me in this endeavour, then you will come to know about it slowly and gradually. There are many negativities inherent in Americans. They are at a lower realm in Mutters of spirituality but their social status is much higher. We will teach them spirituality and will imbibe their positive social values."

Swamiji had high opinion about American women. In his life, American women enjoyed a special and important position. When Swamiji reached a materialistic country like America empty handed, like a wandering monk, with no identity, fame or any help or backing, American women helped him and arranged for his accommodation and food. They took him to their homes, behaved with him like a brother or a son. When the priests of the church and missionaries declared him as a grave opponent of religions and compelled people to boycott him accusing him of fallacy, at that moment also American women supported him and remained his friends and well-wishers. Those women were a source of hope and optimism when he was in a state of despair and dejection. All these were ample reasons for Swamiji's soft corner towards American women in his heart. He was never tired of praising them. In a letter to the King of Khatri, Swamiji wrote about American women—"I got to hear some baseless stories about the familial life of Americans. I heard that the limit of absurdity in the lives of people was to such an extent that the females led an amoral life and intoxicated by the liberalism 'they indulged in all sorts of immoral acts, keeping the peace and prosperity of familial life at stake. I heard more of such rumours. But with my experiences here for a year, it has become clear to me that those rumours were just false and baseless. American women! I will not be able to repay you back for all your help and cooperation even after taking birth for hundred times. I do not have words to express my gratitude towards you. 'If only the ocean were the ink pots, Himalayas the ink itself, branch of the Parijata tree the pen and the earth the page and Goddess Saraswati herself the writer who keep on writing for eternity, then also I won't be capable to express my gratitude towards you.

I have seen end number of beautiful familial lives over here. I have seen innumerable mothers whose purity of character and selfless love for their children is beyond expression. I have got opportunities to meet so many unmarried girls and women who are as pure as the dewdrops at the temple dedicated to Goddess Dyna, who are highly educated and who possess great mental and spiritual thoughts. Does that mean that all American women are goddess like? No, it is not so, good and evil exist everywhere.

In another letter, to his disciple Haripad, he wrote—"I have seen thousands of women here, whose hearts are as pure and clear as snowy Himalayas. Oh! They are so liberal minded. They are in-charge of controlling activities of the society and the city. Schools and colleges are full of women and in our country it is not safe and secure for our women folk to travel on roads alone. And see how kind are women here. From the day I arrived here, they have given me the shelter of their homes, given food for me, arranged lectures and discourses for me, accompanied me for shopping and have done everything for my comfort. I have no words to describe what all they have done for me. Women here are so pure. They hardly get married before the age of 25-30. They are free like birds in the sky. They are engaged in all sorts of professions—shopkeeper, teacher, professor, business, everything. Those who are rich, are always ready to help the poor. And what are we doing? As a rule, we marry off girls at the young age of eleven. What orders have our Manu given for us? "Daughters should be brought up and educated with the same care and caution as sons." In the same manner, our sons have to undergo education and practice *Brahmacharya* till the age of 30 years, daughters should also be educated and compelled to practice *Brahmacharya*. But what are we doing? Are we in a position to improve the condition of women of our country?

All this does not at all mean that Swamiji had no respect for Indian women. In fact, he was of the opinion as long as the condition of women does not improve our society cannot progress. Only an educated woman can make his children successful citizens. And successful citizens are the strong body parts of a society. In America, Swamiji gave a lecture on 'Indian women'. A true patriot and a person full of patriotic fervour, Swamiji did not get tired praising the qualities of Indian women. He explicated the status and position enjoyed by women in a family, and the tradition and rituals followed by them. Through his lectures he drew a picture of the four roles played by women—as mother, wife, daughter and sister. Depicting the picture of mothers of India. He said—"In India, the ideal beginning and end of the life of a woman is motherhood." He made the westerness understand that in India a woman is first a mother then a wife. But in America the situation was totally opposite. There a woman is first a wife, then a mother.

After two-and-a-half months after the conclusion of World Parliament of Religions, Swamiji got an invitation from a major Institute of Discourse to tour different cities of America and deliver lectures on Vedanta philosophy and Indian culture. Considering it to be an order on the part of Almighty God, he accepted the invitation. This invitation fulfilled an innate desire that Swamiji had in his life. He earnestly desired reveal the myth that the westerners had in their minds about Indian culture and civilization. This according to Swamiji was essential, because otherwise they would never have been able to attain an insight into the reality about India and its people. And without making them aware of the real situation, it was difficult to expect any kind of help from them for improvisation of the condition of India. The second reason for his happiness was that by giving lectures he could have earned a pretty good amount of remuneration. He was in dire need of money with which he wanted to undertake welfare activities in India.

In the mid of November 1863, the programme of Swamiji's tour-cum-lecture began. His first trip was to Madison, Minneapolis and Iowa cities. Wherever he went people extended a warm welcome. He was given accommodation facilities at the residence of renowned people of the city where his lecture was organized. In addition to general meetings, small personal seminars and meetings were also organized in those cities where Swamiji was given an opportunity to express his thoughts. Swamiji's next destinations were St. Louis, Hartford, Buffalo, Boston, Cambridge and Baltimore.

The Institute of Discourse did not give Swamiji any kind of peace or rest—continuous speech and travel—tonight at one location and at the next night at another location. The Institute in its advertisements released in newspapers referred to Swamiji as 'the future maker of new India.' It seemed as if American people were gathered together to show a strange thing from India. People belonging to small towns and villages, whose mental level never looked beyond mundane day-to-day living, who was never aware of spirituality—after listening to Swamiji's speech sat like stone statues. It was like reading Bible before an illiterate. How Swamiji tolerated such a situation God only knows. Perhaps he wanted to accumulate wealth for India, hence, he bore such mental trauma. But behind the darkness of despair, rays of hope are hidden. During his tour, he encountered such situations very rarely. Most of the time he was acquainted with scholars and intellectuals. In the end of February 1864, Swamiji went to Detroit. There he stayed as guest at the residence of Tomes W. Palmer, the chairman of the Chicago World Parliament of Religions, for two weeks. He was extended a warm welcome here. In a letter to the Hale sisters he wrote—"I am quite happy with old Palmer. He is a very jovial and kind hearted old man. For my last discourse, I earned 126 dollars. On Monday, I am again going to give a lecture at Detroit. A daily newspaper here has written a strange thing about me that 'a stormy Hindu' has made his entry here and he is a guest of Mr. Palmer. Mr. Palmer has converted himself into a Hindu and he is going to India." In reality, I am not at all a stormy kind of person. What I actually want is not available here and I cannot bear this 'stormy' environment for long. The path to completeness is to make oneself complete. To help others, according to me, is to develop the capabilities of people having uncommon calibre. It does not mean reading out a Bible in front of a buffalo and wasting my time, energy and health for it."

After this, Swamiji stayed as guest at the residence of the scholarly wife of ex-governor of Michigan Mrs. John. Mrs. Baigle held a position of high profile among the leading ladies in Detroit. She took Swamiji from Mr. Palmer's house and in his honour organized a dinner in which she invited renowned people from the city. The very next day, a big article appeared in the *'Detroit Tribune'* in which it was written—"In the huge bungalow of Mrs. Baigle, anybody could have easily spotted Swamiji donning saffron headgear and long robe, sitting in the middle of men and women."This kind of welcome ceremony had happened in Detroit after a long gap. Mr. Baigle was also present at the World Parliament of Religions organized in the city of Chicago. From that day onwards she was longing to have Swamiji as her guest at her home. At the Unitarian Church, Swamiji's lecture was organized for three consecutive nights. In addition to the Vedanta philosophy, Swamiji had to deliver lecture on the topic 'Rituals of India'. In the newspapers, beautiful descriptions of Swami Vivekanand were also published. Mrs. Baigle's wealth, fortune and love had a great influence on the people of Detroit. Due to Mrs. Baigle's initiative, the people of Detroit got a chance to meet and understand Swamiji quite intimately.

Swamiji had written a letter to Ms. Isabel Mecidelle from Detroit which depicts his feelings explicitly.

"I received parcel sent by you, yesterday. You sent the socks unnecessarily, I would have purchased them here itself. But innately I feel very happy because this gesture on your part expresses your love, care and concern. My bag has already become inflated like a bag. I don't understand how I will carry it now.

Today I returned back to Mrs. Bagle's house. She was offended because I stayed at Mr. Palmer for more days. Of course, I spent my days at Mr. Palmer's house in an interesting manner. He is a social and carefree person, more than necessary and then his 'hot scotch'. But he is totally innocent and simple like children.

He was unhappy when I left him but I was helpless. Here there is a very beautiful girl. I met her twice. I am forgetting her name. But she is so bright, pretty, spiritual and unworldly, God shower his blessings on her. Today in the morning, she came along with Mrs. Mac Dwell and presented her thoughts in such a beautiful and spiritually serious manner that I was taken aback. She knows everything about yoga and has gone quite ahead in meditation.

'Your style is beyond discovery.' May God keep such an innocent, pure and pious girl like her always happy. Amidst my harsh and miserable life, it is a great gain for me to meet such pious and joyous people from time to time. There is a major prayer among Buddhsits—"I bow in reverence before all the

pious people on this earth." I understand the actual meaning of that prayer when I see such image over whom the God almighty has clearly written 'Mine'. May God always keep you pious and pure. The dirt and dust of this frightening world may not touch you. The only prayer on the part of your brother is that you always live like a flower, as you are born."

Whether man or woman, if their life was enveloped with piety and spiritualism, they used to attract Swamiji naturally. In the months of March, April and May, Swamiji travelled Chicago, New York and Boston and kept on giving discourses without break. In the month of June, he received an invitation from Ms. Sarah Farmer to give lecture at Green Acre in New England. Ms. Sarah had met Swamiji during the World Parliament of Religions and at the same time had planned to organized a religious meeting at Green Acre and invite Swamiji over to present a discourse. Green Acre was a beautiful place in terms of natural beauty which was located near a small river. Hence, it was but natural that the climate was not that as was in New York. There was a big inn as well as a farm house in Green Acre. The rich and famous who had come to participate in the conference were made to stay in the inn or the farm house and common people were made to stay in the tents set up near the river bank.

In his letter to Hale brothers, Swamiji had written about the life at Green Acre—"This place is extremely beautiful and landscaped. Bathing is very comfortable here. Mr. Kora Stockhum has got a swim suit made for me and I am enjoying water like a duck." Arrangement for Swamiji's accommodation was made at the beautiful inn. At the Green Acre Conference, Swamiji gave a series of lectures on the Advaita philosophy of Vedanta. In this meeting, both—rich and poor people from Green Acre attended in equal numbers. All those who attended the conference had a strange kind of devotion and a keen desire to enhance their knowledge. Swamiji defined the meaning of 'Shivom' to them. At the instructions of Swamiji, all the assembled audience repeated the word many times with pure thought in their mind. Swamiji experienced great joy and a sense of pride in imparting knowledge to such people.

Here some students curious to learn the Vedanta philosophy got assembled to learn it from Swamiji. They formed the class underneath a shady tree expressing reverence and

Swami Vivekanand: A Biography

devotion to their teacher as was the ritual in India. Swamiji was made to sit in the middle and the students sat around him in half circular form on the ground and listened to what the Guru taught. Once those who were accommodated in the tents expressed their desire to sleep under the open sky. Swamiji also came out to sleep in the open along with others. Underneath the sky donned with stars and constellations, in the lap of mother earth, all of them spent the night with a calm and sound sleep. This was the first opportunity that Swamiji got abroad to spend the night under open sky. This programme of sleeping under the open sky was organized later also many a time. Swamiji got many joyous opportunities to be in close contact with nature like sleeping in the lap of earth, sitting underneath the tree and indulge in deep meditation, during his stay at Green Acre. Swamiji who used to be in deep thoughts and meditation remained serious most of the time. But sometimes used to display a jovial mood. People enjoyed his company when he was in a lighter mood and indulged in talks less serious in nature.

Ms. Sarah Farmer, who had invited Swamiji over to Green Acre continued with Swamiji's teachings and religious preachings even after he left the place. She made all possible efforts to inculcate his teachings in practice among the common folks. From Green Acre, Swamiji went to the cities of Boston, Washington, etc. and when he returned back to New York, he received an invitation from Charles Higgings. He was the member of 'Brooklyn Ethical Society' based in New York. Higgings distributed a ten page booklet among the members of the society to widely publicise about Swamiji's discourse even before his arrival at New York. In the booklet, a compilation of articles published in praise of Swamiji in all leading newspapers was made so as to give people a prior information about his calibre and qualifications. The Chairman of the Brooklyn Ethical Society, Mr. Louis G. James had heard swamiji's lectures earlier also. The Brooklyn Ethical Society had organized Swamiji's speech at 'Panch Mansion', a very big auditorium. In the evening of the last day of the year 1864, Swamiji gave a discourse on Hindu religion at the large hall inside the Panch Mansion. The hall was completely full with audience setting at every corner of the hall. Swamiji's speech left a deep impact on the audience. People were so spellbound by Swamiji's oratorical skill that Dr. Louis James, Chairman of the Brooklyn Ethical Society requested Swamiji to deliver lectures for the society for more days and Swamiji accepted the request. In addition to presenting a critical appreciation of ancient religions, Swamiji presented lectures on Indian society and culture. When he discussed about the role of women in the society, the men folk didn't show much interest. In this regard, Swamiji later wrote a letter to Ms. Isabel Mc Cidelle—"Menfolk did not praise my last discourse much. But women appreciated it beyond expectation. You know it very well that Brooklyn is a centre which hold an opposing view in respect of women's rights. And when I said that women are more capable and talented in all sorts of work, it is obvious that people here would not have liked it and approved of it. But never mind, women were totally overwhelmed and engrossed. After the series of lectures that he gave at Brooklyn, Swamiji became sure that propagation of Vedanta will continue in America with any sort of interruption or hindrance. There he met many believers and devotees of Vedanta philosophy who were keen to attain a thorough knowledge on the subject and later on spread the teachings among others.

The tour and lecture programme organized by the discourse company proved to be a blessing for Swamiji. It gave him an opportunity to closely perceive and make assessment about the people of America. In addition, Swamiji was able to accumulate a good amount of money for undertaking welfare activities in India. The new daily experiences, honour and respect, name and fame instilled a new sense of vigour and vitality within Swamiji. But non-stop touring and lecturing had taken a toll on his health. He was becoming tired and weak physically. But still when he put his glance to the future he was able to envision hell a lot of work to be accomplished. How could he have even thought of taking rest? He was able to accumulate huge amount of money by way of giving discourses at different places which took away most of his time. He hardly got any time to do anything else and Swamiji didn't like this. Swamiji was very well aware of the expenditure involved in any endeavour he wished to begin in India. And as the time for his leaving America neared, he had his worries about continuation of his efforts even in his absence. For this, it was extremely necessary to train some people in a proper and systematic manner. He had been developing a feeling of disinterestedness towards giving speeches in return of money. He felt it inappropriate to impart knowledge in return for remuneration. Hence, he got himself detached from the Discourse Society and set up a permanent school in New York to impart knowledge regarding Vedanta totally free of cost. Swamiji charted out the syllabus for the class in his mind. When such a free class room was set up at New York many of his disciples from Green Acre and Brooklyn came over there to gain knowledge. In addition to his disciples, other people also came in the class to hear his lecture regularly. Many American people were puzzled at this act on the part of Swamiji—Why he dropped the idea of accumulating wealth by means of giving discourses. They considered it to be a wrong decision on the part of Swamiji. But Swamiji was firm in his decision.

In the class room of Vedanta in New York, usually lectures pertaining to Gyan Yog and Raj Yog were held. The manner in which the Guru and disciples sat in the class room was also purely in the Indian style. Both girls and boys sat on the ground. In addition to the tenets of Vedanta, Swamiji taught the students the art of living·life spiritually. *Brahmacharya* (practicing celibacy) and mild food were the first step towards character formation, according to the tenets laid down by Yog Shastra. Swamiji kept a strict vigil on the day-to-day activities of the students, the way they carried themselves, their behaviour and talking manner, their style of argument and their nature. Whenever they failed to comply with the spiritual criteria, Swamiji used to warm them. In the words of Swamiji, 'Rajyog learning first of all shows man the way to maneuvere internal conditions. Mind is the machine for this maneuver. The only way to attain proficiency in this is concentration. The power of mind is like the scattered rays of life. When all those rays of right are concentrated at a central point, then it lights up everything. This is the first step towards attaining any kind of knowledge.

Swamiji gave many discourses explicating Rajayoga. The fame of all these discourses spread far and wide. Famous philosophers, scientists and teachers of the city attended these discourses. Question answer rounds were also held in the class room. Swamiji devoted most of his time in organizing the activities of this class room. He used to feel that whatever America gave to him till then—name, fame, wealth, etc. everything was futile, and the actual thing of significance was what he was doing them. This was the only way to fulfil Shri Ramakrishna's dreams and spread his message. While demonstrating the art of practicing meditation, Swamiji's sight got fixed on any one particular thing, body turned stone like and his breathing became slow suddenly stopping. He used to be so lost that it seems that he was cut off from physical world. He lost his consciousness. After sometime when he regained back his sense and consciousness after breaking the trance, he became sad, because he was supposed to teach others the art of meditation not to enter into meditation himself. To save himself from such a situation he gave a solution to overcome it. From their onwards whenever he entered into a deep trance and lost his consciousness, one of his disciples chanted some mantra in his ears. No sooner than the melodious Sanskrit shloka reached his ears, his trance began to break slowly and gradually.

In this manner, Swamiji carried on with his yogic and meditational practices while teaching his disciples Swamiji compiled all his lectures in a serial order and published it in the form of a book titled 'Raj Yog'. At the last page of the book, he published a quotation from Patanjal philosophy. The book attained great popularity in America and served as an answer to many of the doubts and questions that remained in the minds of readers, researchers and scholars. Prof. James, America's renowned Professor of Psychiatry, after reading the book published by Swamiji was so impressed by his talent that he went to meet Swamiji at the place where he was residing at that time and became an inseparable friend of Swamiji.

After continuous lectures and analysis of various philosophies and practice and teachings of yogic mythologies in the classroom he had founded in New York, Swamiji was greatly tired. The renown of the class had spread far and wide. As a result, in addition to the permanent students. Other people also used to assemble in the class room. With the onset of summer season, many people, afraid of the heat, went to cold places. Swamiji also made up his mind to get far away from New York and take some rest.

One of his disciples, Ms. Ducher, finding it to be an opportune time invited Swamiji to her house. Considering his busy schedule and declining health, Swamiji readily gave his consent. Some ten-twelve disciples, who were his favourites, were not ready to part with him. Hence, Ms. Ducher invited them also to her house.

Ms. Ducher's house was situated about 300 miles away from New York at an Island called Thousand Island Park. The small island was located on the heart of St. Lawrence river. The length of the island was around 9 miles and its breadth was not more than three miles. The forest, gardens and mountains there were enveloped with natural beauty. Ms. Duche's house was situated on the slope of a mountain, which faced towards St. Lawrence river and thick forest at its background. On the ground floor there was a big hall and the kitchen. On the first floor there were a number of small bedrooms. The room situated at the end was entirely appropriate and safe for Swamiji so it was given to Swamiji. The entry to that room had a personal stairase other than the general one and a big verandah was attached to it. From there, the beauty of the nature looked irresistible. Since the house was at a height the sight of branches swaying in the wind from top seemed like a green ocean with tides. The population in this beautiful island was almost nothing. On the plains, the small houses built at distance apart looked hidden behind huge tree trunks. There was an empire of peace all around. The peace of the place got disrupted only with the chirping of birds and the sound of crickets. Any other human sound was scarce to hear other than from the inhabitants of this house. At one end, the small boats tossing over the waves of the water in the river added to the beauty of nature.

The place definitely offered peace of mind and relaxation to Swamiji as if a caged bird had been freed. How different was life there from that of the busy life of New York? How one felt at his own? Swamiji's heart brightened up with spirituality. On the very first day, Swamiji reached there, i.e., 11 June; Swamiji began his routine work of giving lectures and teaching his disciples. In the huge hall downstairs, Swamiji's disciples sat around him in half circular form on the ground and Swamiji sat in the middle. Swamiji was holding the Bible in his hand. Opening the Bible he said that "Since all those who are present here are Christians, today I begin my lecture with teachings from the Bible. From that day till 6 August, every day in the early hours of morning, for two hours, Swamiji discussed Vedanta philosophy, the Gita, New Testament etc. But his teaching was not limited within the four walls of the class room.

After class room lecture, the group of teachers and disciples set off to wander around the island. That was the time of day break when the new rays of sun peeped and soft breeze coming from St. Lawrence river gave fresh energy to all of them. They walked up and down amidst the trees and mountains and returned back home walking along the river bank.

Even as they walked, Swamiji continued with his discourse. He gave instant examples from nature to clarify his point. He explained big spiritual truths with common things from nature like river, stream, forest, mountains, trees, plants, birds and animals.

During his stay at the Thousand Island Park, Swamiji strolled towards the river bank and in the extremely peaceful environment near the river bank sat engrossed in meditation. He had already given necessary instructions to his disciples as to how to bring him back to his normal self in a situation of severe Samadhi when he lost his consciousness. Hence, whenever there occurred a delay in Swamiji's regaining his consciousness, his disciples managed the situation.

All the guests who had come over to Ms. Ducher's house helped her in the daily chores of the household. Swamiji also extended a helping hand in preparing food. According to the Indian art of cookery, he prepared oily and spicy food and served it to everyone so lovingly. The spicy dishes did not suit some of them. Their tongue and throat became hot, later came from their nose and eyes but still they ate everything because they were not willing to show disrespect towards Swamiji by leaving the food he so lovingly prepared for them.

After partaking food, in the afternoon, Swamiji sat with his disciples in the balcony upstairs and talked with them about ancient Indian civilizations. He also explained medieval history of India to them and the way Muslim invaders came to conquer Indians and got conquered by Indians and stayed back in India. He used to address Muslims as 'my muslim brothers.' In his view, India was not only a country of Hindus but also of Muslims.

Sometimes a voice came from his inner self and he became a future teller. Once in such a state of mind he foretold about an impending doom that would happen in the world that would give way to the rise of a new world order. Strangely, Swamiji had said that this turbulence would happen because of China and Russia. He also made a prediction that Europe was set on the brink of a volcano. And if the fire is not quenched with the help of spiritualism then a total holocaust will be the result. He said thus in 1865. Within twenty years in 1914 the volcano erupted in the form of First World War and in 1917 the Great Russian revolution happened and the world was witnessing turbulent times.

One of Swamiji's female disciples, S.I. Baldaw, who had accompanied him from New York had given a beautiful description or life as Thousand Acre Island—"Though Swami was a sportive kind of fellow who loved to wander around and indulge in humorous and witty conversations, still he never loitered away from his life's basic percepts or deviate from his principles. From every thing, he got a topic to talk about or show an example and within a fraction of second he drew us to serious philosophy from attractive ancient Hindu tales. Swamiji was a storehouse of ancient tales. In fact, no other people knew more stories than the ancient Aryans. He used to be very much pleased to tell us all those stories and we also listened them very happily because he showed us the truth behind the story and never forgot to discover invaluable religious advise from them.

In addition to story telling, Swamiji was also well versed in writing. Once while discussing about the sacrifices made by saints, with his disciples, he was so overwhelmed with emotion that he suddenly left his seat and got up and began to stroll. Then after a few seconds he took his seat again and began to write a poem titled 'Song of saint'. Stanzas and stanzas kept on adding to the song and in this manner many pages got filled. When he wrote the concluding stanza, then only did he breathe a sigh of relief. An inexplicable tenderness and a sense of satisfaction reflected on his face. He held the pages in his right hand and began to sing the song in a melodious manner.

. When the recitation ended, he kept the pages on the ground and stood up in hurry as if he had remembered something urgent which he had forgotten. Then in a sweet tone he said—'Now I am going to prepare food for you people and began to prepare some Indian recipes in the kitchen and as he did so a sense of peace and calmness was evident on his face.'

Swamiji considered it his duty to fulfil even the minutest of needs of his disciples and whenever he accomplished it he felt extremely happy. Some of his disciples were elder to him in age but still he endowed fatherly love and devotion to all of them. Whenever he felt that he is ignorant or not competent enough to respond or react to any situation in accordance with western mannerisms, he used to seek suggestions or inputs from his western disciples in childish curiosity as to how he should behave in such a situation or how he should talk in such a situation. Even after being a saint, different from the common people, he did not want to break social rules or mannerisms. But after all he was also a human being and sometimes things went wrong also. In the words of Swamiji's favourite disciple Sister Christine, "In those days when men never used to smoke in front of women, he used to smoke the cigarette and exhale the smoke on other's face intentionally. If that had been done by somebody else, I would have sat turning my back towards him and would have never talked to him again. But the very next moment, I regained back my self and thought of the reason why I was there I have come to that person in whom I have found spirituality and about which I had never been able to imagine even in my dreams.

Swamiji stayed at Thousand Island Park for about two months. There whatever preachings he made among ten-twelve students, was scripted into notes by one of his disciples. Later on, it was published with the title 'Inspired Talks'. 'Devvani' is the translated version of that very book. There Swamiji initiated two disciples into sannyasa. In accordance with the rules of sannyasashram their names were changed to Swami Kripananda and Swami Abhayananda. Five more disciples took oath to embrace Brahmacharya. The rest of them were initiated as disciples by chanting vedic mantra. Swamiji wished to propagate Vedanta philosophy in America through these confidante disciples. He chose sister Christina to supervise the welfare activities that he was planning to organize in India. But another disciple felt dejected and were unable to fulfil her wish to travel to India. When she expressed her desire before

Swamiji, he said: "You have got a family and household. Go back to Detroit. See and experience God in serving your husband, children and other family members. For the present, that is the only path for you to tread."

Though, at Thousand Island Park, Swamiji was mostly engaged in thinking-meditation, studying-teaching, religion and philosophy, still he got sufficient time to take rest. Sufficient rest, good weather condition and the peaceful environ brought about improvement in his health slowly and gradually. After two months, he returned back to New York along with his disciples and became engrossed in propagation of Vedanta philosophy with renewed energy and vigour.

In America, Swamiji's life was very busy. Even then he never diverted his attention from India. He was curious to know whether or not the taste of success that he enjoyed at the World Parliament of Religions reverberated in his motherland also.

The episode of Chicago World Parliament of Religion got published in all the major newspapers and magazines in India with complete fanfare. Articles published in praise of Swamiji, in foreign newspapers were quoted in Indian newspapers and magazines. Indians back home were puffed up with pride when they got the news about how Swamiji enhanced the honour of Hindu religion and hoisted the flag of Vedanta. But when during the course of World Parliament of Religion, when Swamiji condemned the propagational activities of Christian Missionaries in India, in harsh terms, Christian Missionaries in India also turned hostile towards Swamiji along with the Christian missionaries in America and began to spread rumours against Swamiji. Sh. Pratap Chandra Majumdar of Brahma Samaj, who was overwhelmed with a sense of jealousy over the unlimited name and fame enjoyed by Swami Vivekanand added fuel to the fire of Christian Missionaries. The purity of Swamiji's name and renown was slowly and gradually giving way to ill-fame. The stink of the polluted atmosphere in his motherland, spread to America also though people in America who closely knew Swamiji were unaffected by its impact. Swamiji knew that an invisible force was working behind him and hence, he was confident that all these rumours, won't have any effect on American people.

But he was not the kind of saint who would sit idle without making any efforts. He was a hard working saint. He had the talent of a capable administrator. He was well aware of the truthful way to attain success in any endeavour. In order to free himself from the controversies spreading like wildfire in America against him, on April 6, 1864 he wrote a letter to Alasinga—one of his disciples in India asking him to organize a meeting presided over by some powerful people and applauded Swami Vivekanand for representing India at the World Parliament of Religions and earning laurels for the country. He further asked him to pass an unanimous memorandum in this regard and send the copies of the same to the offices of different Newspapers and magazines in America. He also sent to Alasinga the names and addresses of the chairperson and other important members of the World Parliament of Religions and asked him to send the copies of the proposal to them also. He gave instruction to give wider publicity to the meeting and ensure participation of maximum number of renowned people in it. He further gave instruction to procure letters from King of Mysore, Khatri, etc. and the Diwans thereof certifying support to such a meeting and thereby publicizing Swamiji's achievement at Chicago and making the meeting a grand event. "The theme of the proposal should be that the Hindus in Madras are all happy with my activities in America, etc. The sooner thus task is accomplished it will have its impact. My dear brother, the members of Brahmo Samaj are spreading all kinds of false rumours against me here. We should seal their mouths as soon as possible.

But this work could not be accomplished as quickly as desired. April, May and June lapsed but no news as expected reached to Swamiji. There in America he was faring all the rumours. In such a situation, it was obvious for Swamiji to be despaired and angry. On 28 June again he wrote a letter to one of his disciples at Madras—"I have already tried Hindus a lot. Now whatever God wishes will happen. I am ready to accept any outcome. Do not consider me thankless. Whatever the people of Madras have done to me, I did not deserve thus much from them. They helped me more than their capacity. It is my foolishness that I forgot that we Hindus have not achieved humanity and I have lost my self-dependence and have become too much dependent on them. And because of this I am undergoing this much of sufferings. I spent each second waiting for some good' news but I have not received

Swami Vivekanand: A Biography

even a single newspaper from India. My friends waited for months together and when no voice was heard, then most of them became disinterested in me and left me. I have got the punishment for depending upon human beings who are animal worshippers, because till now a sense of humanity has not been developed in human beings. They are always ready to listen to their praises but when it is their turn to say something to help somebody else then nobody is there in the scene."

Swamiji's followers did not sit idle for more days. The name and fame of Swamiji had already spread across the major cities in India. Meetings were held at many places and Swami Vivekanand's works and achievements were appreciated. In Madras, a huge meeting was organized under the leadership of Sir Ramaswami Madaliyar, the king of Madras, Sir Subramanya Iyer, the Diwan and C.I.E. Renowned Scholars and famous people from the city attended the meeting and appreciated Swamiji's efforts in spreading the fame of Vedanta philosophy and Hindu religion across the world. They sent a letter of encouragement to Swamiji giving details of the agenda of the meeting. Along with that they sent the unanimously passed proposal approving and endorsing Swami Vivekanand for representing India and the Hindu religion at the World Parliament of Religions. King of Ramnad Bhaskar Setupati and king of Khatri Sh. Ajit Singh Bahadur, both the royal disciples of Swami Vivekanand, called a special meeting of their subjects, praised Swami Vivekanand for his work towards enhancing the glory of Hindu religion. They wrote a beautiful commendation letter acknowledging Swamiji's role in spreading the fame of Hinduism far and wide

The biggest of all the events took place in Calcutta. After all it was Swamiji's native land. Many people in Calcutta knew him personally, especially his Guru brothers who were feeling joyous and jubilant at Swamiji's achievements. Earlier when they read about Swami Vivekanand's success and fame in America from newspapers, they were not able to believe that this Swami Vivekanand was their own 'Naren'. But they could hear the voice from within which was calling out in a voice that Swami Vivekanand was none else but their own 'Naren'. He had such kind of powers which could shake the whole earth. Then they received a letter from Vivekanand, six months after the Chicago World Parliament of Religions which proved their doubt. The grand success of the meeting in Calcutta was due to the efforts of Swami Vivekanand's Guru brothers, and this was quite obvious. On September 5, 1864 a huge meeting was organized at Town Hall which was presided over by the king Pyare Mohan Mukherjee. Thousands of people gathered at the Town Hall to attend the meeting. The meeting was organized by many famous and powerful representatives of Hindu religion. Many renowned scholars, landlords, rich businessmen, judges from High court, social workers, Principals and teachers from university, lawyers, politicians etc. from Calcutta participated in the meeting. All those present there were so excited by the glory and honour that Swami Vivekanand had been able to achieve for the country, that they gave impressive speeches to acknowledge Swamiji's efforts and endeavours. The whole meeting unanimously supported the thanks giving motion presented during the meeting. The Chairman of the meeting sent an acknowledgement letter to the Chairman of Chicago World Praliament of Religions. In reply to this letter, the Chairman of Chicago World Parliament of Religions wrote a letter to King Pyare Mohan Mukherjee—Your friend Swami Vivekanand was granted membership to participate in the World Parliament of Religions with much honour. With his oratorical skills, he attracted a huge number of followers during this grand event. He was able to spread his personal charm on everyone who came into contact with him. With his efforts people in America have been initiated into following religious rituals. In renowned universities and colleges, arrangements are being made to introduce his lectures and teachings in the curriculum. The people of America take this opportunity to express our deep gratitude and love towards India. We believe that we will have to learn many topics from your pious literature."

Swamiji also received the news of the appreciation he received for his work in India. He got the complete details of meetings organized at various places to felicitate him. Now his mental tension calmed down. Swamiji felt happy that even after some delay his countrymen have recongised his work. In November 1864, Swamiji wrote a loving letter in reply to the commendation letter from Sri Raja Pyara Mukherjee. "I have received the proposal unanimously approved in the pubic meeting held at Calcutta Town Hall. I express my heart felt gratitude for the loving appreciation and commendation from my countrymen." He also wrote a letter to his disciple in Madras, Alasinga—"Till now you have accomplished a wonderful job. My son, sometimes I write incoherent things out of fear, don't bother about it. It is but natural for a person staying fifteen thousand miles away from his own country and fighting a battle with fundamentalist Christians to be overwhelmed with fear. My brave child, you should continue with your work, keeping all this in mind."

Swamiji's Indian friends, disciples and followers desired to have Swamiji back in India soon and be their guiding force for the construction of the new India. But Swamiji was not prepared to return back to India that soon. In reply to those letters he wrote—"My plans regarding returning back to India is like this. As you all know very well I am very firm in my decision. In this country I had sown some seeds, now they have grown up into plants and I hope that soon they will grow up into big trees. I have about two-four hundred followers. I will make many saints over here and entrust the task to them and then only return back to India. As long as Christian priests will oppose me, to that extent I have decided firmly that I will leave a permanent sign of mine there." Swamiji desired to establish many centres to propagate Vedanta at different places in America. He had a feeling that America was the most appropriate place to spread any particular thought. Once he wrote to his disciples in India— "These foreign people respect me to such an extent that I have not even received thus much of honour and respect from my countrymen even. If I want I can lead a comfortable and luxurious life here. But I am a sannyasi, and Oh India, in spite of all your demerits I love you so much. Hence, I will return back to India within a few months."

He was not able to accomplish his works and plans totally in America that he received an invitation from England. Swamiji had been nursing a desire to go to England and propagate Hindu religion there since so many days. Ms. Henrietta Muller who had great love for Indian philosophy, called Swamiji to England many a time. But Swamiji was unable to fulfil her wishes. When Swamiji returned back to New York from Thousand Island Park, he received many letters from Mr. E.T. Sturdy inviting him to London. He was an ardent devotee of Swamiji. He gave assurance to Swamiji through letters that he will extend all possible help in his campaigns. At that very juncture a rich friend of Swamiji in New York offered to take Swamiji to France and England. Swamiji readily agreed to accompany him.

Two years of continuous efforts in America had left Swamiji quite tired. As such he enjoyed a great deal of rest during his stay at Thousand Island Park. But he was not able to totally relieve himself from classes, lectures, seminars, meditation, Samadhi, etc. He thought that undertaking a journey by sea would give him complete rest both mentally and physically. Then he will be totally energetic to spread the message of Hindu religion in England after reaching there.

In the middle of April, Swamiji departed for England along with his friend. There he stayed for almost three-and-a-half months. His stay in England was quite significant in many respects. Swamiji was well aware of the importance of his stay and work in England, but he had not been able to complete his work in America. Hence on December 6, 1865 he again returned back to New York. He along with his disciple Swami Kripanand took two huge rooms on rent where he could take classes for at least 150 persons. Swamiji held regular classes on Karma yog at that place. The series of lectures delivered by Swamiji on Karmayog later on got published as a book titled 'Karmayog'. The book earned great fame. In addition to giving lecture on the topic of 'Karma Yog', for 15 days Swamiji gave lecture on other important topics. The main topics were—religion and its assurances, its rituals and use, the ideal world of all encompassing religion, etc. It was essential to script these invaluable discourses made by Swamiji. For this purpose, two people were deputed. But both of them could accomplish the task properly as they were unable to keep pace with Swamiji's flow. At that appropriate juncture, an acquaintance of Swamiji in England who was a stenographer came over to London. His name was Mr. J.J. Godwin and at the request of Swamiji's disciples, he began to typeset the lectures given by Swamiji. Godwin had to remain in the company of Swamiji always to properly accomplish this task. Hence, he became acquainted with Swamiji's thought process very soon. The self-restrained life and work of Swamiji had a deep impact on him. He assisted Swamiji in his personal work also and became his closest disciples in words and deeds. Swamiji also showered love on him. He used to address him as 'My trusted Goodwin'. He accompanied Swamiji wherever he went and left the earthly abode when he was in India. At that juncture, Swamiji said— "My right hand has lost." Most of Swamiji's lectures bound in book form except for 'Rajyog' was the result of Goodwin's untiring efforts.

By the time Swamiji returned back from England, the snow enveloped America was spriucing up for the festivities of Christmas. At that time Swamiji received an invitation to Boston from Mrs. Anti. Swamiji readily accepted the invitation and soon reached Boston. There women at the Cambridge university expressed their desire to listen to Swamiji's speech. Swamiji gave a very interesting speech on the topic—'The ideal of Indian women.' The scholarly women \ ' o were present there over greatly influenced by this. They were so spellbound by what Swamiji had said during his speech that they decided to write a thanks giving letter to Swamiji's mother. On the occasion of the festival of Christmas they dispatched a letter along with the picture of Virgin Mary holding Baby Jesus to Swamiji's mother. The contents of the letter stated—"Today we are celebrating the day of the appearance of Jesus Christ on the earth as a result of the charity done by Mother Mary. At this moment, we are reminded of something. The presence of your son in our midst make us low before you in reverence. With your blessings, a few days ago, by giving a speech on the topic "The ideal of Motherhood in India", he has done a great deal of good for all of us-men, women and children. His worship of mother will prove to be a source of inspiration for the audience and will help him in his progression. We are grateful to your dear mother whose life and work's influence on your dear son is clearly evident to all of us. The blessings of motherhood and unity may spread the whole world. With the deep desire in our heart that your lively ideals may set him on to the path of his action, we once again express our gratitude.

After returning back from New York, Swamiji gave daily public discourse at the Hardiman Hall in New York from 5 January, 1896 onwards. Huge crowd assembled to hear Swamiji's speech that he gave at Brooklyn Metaphysical Society and New York People's Church. It seemed as if Swamiji had been endowed with some supernatural power and energy that in addition to delivering lectures on daily basis, he saved time to hold question-answer session twice a day and gave satisfactory replies to the queries of curious audience. In addition, he imparted training in 'sadhna' to some devotees. The number of audiences that gathered at the venues where Swamiji gave discourses increased day by day. The number of audience kept on increasing to such an extent that it became impossible to accommodate all of them. People were even ready to stand and listen to Swamiji. At last, to solve this problem of space crunch, in the month of February the authorities renovated the Madison Square Garden which had the seating capacity of 1500 people, to organize Swamiji's speeches. But the situation was such that, there also people didn't get seats. Still people listened to Swamiji's speeches in a spellbound manner standing for almost two hours. In the same, Swamiji gave a speech on 'Soul and the God' at Hartford Metaphysical Society and on various other topics at Brooklyn Ethical Society. Everyone who heard these lectures were so influenced by Swamiji's views and thoughts that encouraging articles appeared in major newspapers like *'Hartford Daily Times'* and *'New York Herald'*. A renowned scholar in Brooklyn Helen Huntington wrote in an article in 'Brahmanadin' magazine:

"It is indeed a blessing on the part of God that he sent a spiritual guide for us from India. The beautiful philosophical view points of this great teacher is slowly but definitely entering the moral life of this country. This person who has in his possession strange powers and pious character has given us a system with the help of which a high quality spiritual life can be led and has explained to us the emotions required to respect every religion, generosity, self-sacrifice, etc. Swami Vivekanand has spread before us such a religion which is totally devoid of communalism or sectarianism and which has the capacity to lead us to the way of spiritual progression, purity and enjoyment of heavenly bliss and which is totally innocent....Swami Vivekanand has created a circle of many friends outside the boundaries of his disciples and followers. He has, with this feeling of friendship and brotherhood entered into every level of the society. To listen to his speeches and interactions inside classroom many thinkers and scholars attended. His influence in spiritual awakening spread all over like a strong flow of water current. No amount of praise or condemnation, no approval or disapproval caused any kind of excitement or aggression in him. Wealth and honour also could not leave any impact on him nor made him to behave partially towards anyone or any Mutter."

On 28 February, Swamiji concluded the series of lectures he had been giving at Madison Square Garden. In the same month, he organized celebrations and functions in connection with Sri Ramakrishna's birth anniversary. On the occasion, he gave a poetic rendition on the topic 'My teacher' (Mere Gurudev) for which he received much appreciation. Swamiji enunciated three persons into sannyasa on the occasion. In addition to these sannyasas, many family people also became Swamiji's disciples—the Wilcox couples were the most prominent among them who deserves special mention. Mrs. Wilcox along with her husband had gone to listen to Swamiji's speech out of curiosity. After many years in 1907, she recounted her experience at that time in a magazine named 'New York American'..."After a lapse of ten minutes I felt that we have been carried towards a minute, lively and secretive world. When the speech ended we returned back to our homes with renewed courage, hope, energy and faith. My husband said—This is the science of philosophy, this is the actual belief in God. The one which I had been searching for all these days—this is that religion."

After accomplishing his task at New York, Swamiji went to Detroit for 15 days. He was accompanied by his typist the 'trusted Godwin'. They booked two rooms in a small family hotel named 'Rishlu'. In the spacious meeting hall of the hotel he organized meetings and interactive classes. But the meeting hall was not that spacious to accommodate so much of people. Many had to return back in despair. The meeting hall, verandah, stairs and the library room used to be full to the extent that no place used to be left to accommodate even an extra person. In spite of being in the midst of so many people and interacting with so many people, Swamiji was away from the materialistic world in the world of imagination. In Detroit, his last interaction and presence among public took place at the Bethel temple. It was a Sunday and on that day in the evening a crowded numbering about thousands had gathered there to hear Swamiji. But due to scarcity of space many had to return back disappointed. Swamiji with his oratorical skills fascinated the huge crowd of audience.

The topic of his speech was—"The message from India to the Western World" and "The Ideal of World Religion." The natural brightness on his countenance was being reflected in all its luminosity as he spoke. But some of the audience saw another image of Swamiji belying that luminosity. Mrs. Fun ki who was one among the audience described that the image of Swamiji that she saw that night she never witnessed again. There was something innate in his beauty which was not belonging to the earth. It seemed as if the soul was trying to break free from the shackles of the body and run away. And that moment she had a premonition of his impending death. His continuous efforts and hardwork for so many years had left him fatigued. This very fact hinted at his short life on this earth. She tried to pacify her soul but her soul had the power to recognize the truth. He needed rest. But he was thinking that she should continue with his work.

While in Detroit he used to tell his disciples—"Oh, this body is a big boundation." Sometimes words as this came out from his mouth—"If, I was able to hide myself for ever."

In all probability Swamiji might have looked tired while in Detroit but in actuality two personalities lived within him— one who was totally engaged in his area of work and the other totally engrossed in thinking and meditation. And almost every day both his personalities came to the fore at one time or the other. On the one hand, he remained busy with lectures and classrooms, on the other, whenever he got lime he entered into deep thinking and meditation and in such situations it seemed as if he yearned to leave everything to get totally merged with eternal peace.

After returning to New York from Detroit, Swamiji again went to Harvard. There on March 25, 1896 he gave a substantial speech on the Vedanta philosophy. It had a deep impact on the teachers and students of Harvard alike. The series of lectures that Swamiji gave at Harvard was later on published in book form. The Principal of the university Mr. C.C. Evret wrote a detailed preface to the book wherein at one place he had written—Swami Vivekanand has evoked great interest in public with regard to his personality as well as his works. In fact, there is no subject above Hindu thought." Swamiji was offered the post of Head of the Department of Ancient Science of Philosophy but he declined the offer stating himself to be a sannyasi.

Before leaving America, Swamiji wanted to lay the foundation of our such institute which would continue with his work of spreading the Vedanta philosophy. His return to Harward fulfilled that wish of Swamiji. The American sannyasis enunciated by Swamiji shouldered this responsibility, the main among them were—Swami Kripananda, Swami Abhayanand, Swami Yogananda and Sister Hari Das. The institute was christened as 'Vedanta Society'. In addition to these sannyasis many of Swamiji's rich friends, devotees, followers and disciples assured their contribution in spreading the Vedanta philosophy. Mr. H. Ligate, a rich and renowned person was appointed the Chairman of the Vedanta Society. The society began its work in an organized manner. Swamiji had great faith on his friends, devotees and disciples. Hence, on April 15, 1896 when he was bidding good bye to America his heart and mind was experiencing unusual peace and joy.

As it was but natural, while taking leave from America, Swamiji made an analysis of the life that he led there. He was totally tired of his constant travel and discourse and was longing for a bit of peace and rest. But he was completely happy and satisfied with his work in America. Sometimes before leaving America, on January 25, 1896 in a letter addressed to Mrs. Auli Bull he wrote—"I have worked according to my strength. If it has any seed of truth init, it will soon sprout out into a seedling. Hence, I am not worried. Now I am totally tired of my hectic schedules of giving lectures and teaching disciples. Now I am increasingly into the belief that the objective of ones action is to make one's mind pure so that he becomes entitled to attain more and more knowledge. This world works in many forms including good and evil. Righteousness and sinfulness will just take a new name and will make a new place. My soul is longing for incessant and immortal peace and rest.....Oh I am longing for the worn out clothes, my clean shaven head, sleeping under the tree and the food given in alms. In spite of all evils inherent in it, India is the only place where the soul finds its freedom and God. The luminosity that we witness in the Western World is but trivial, just a shackle for the soul. I had never experienced the triviality of the world in its true sense before."

Before bidding good bye to America the most sentimental letter that Swamiji wrote was to Ms. Mary Hale. The letter written by the 'ever loving brother' to his 'beloved sister' not only displays the pure relationship between the two but also reflects Swami Vivekanand's state of mind during his last days of stay in America.

"Because of continuous work, this year my health has almost crumbled. I am experiencing a sense of fear. During this winter season I could not get a sound sleep even at one night. I feel that I am doing a lot of work still so much of work is left to be done in America.

I will have to suffer this, but I feel that I will be able to take sufficient rest after reaching India. Throughout my life, I have been making efforts in accordance with my capacity to do good to the world. The result is in the hands of God.

Now I want to take rest. I hope that I will get rest and the people of India will give me leave. I am longing to become dumb for many years and not speak a word.

I am not born to face all these problems and conflicts of this world. In reality I am a dream and a seeker of rest. The mere touch of reality makes my vision blurred and makes me sad. May God fulfil your wishes.

I am ever grateful towards all four of you, dear sisters. Whatever possession I have in this country is all yours. May God always do good to you and keep you happy. Wherever I will spend the rest of my lie, I will remember you with love and gratitude. Our whole life is a garland of dream. My desire is to dream while awake. Now only this much! My love to Jospphine also."

What an irony! Vivekanand kept on thinking. Enough of hectic activities. Now peace can be gained only after reaching India. But he was well aware that he had to accomplish more work and even more significant work after reaching India.

In fact, even while travelling in America he was charting a course of action for the work to be done in India within his mind, slowly and gradually a plan outlay was getting constructed in his mind. He gave an insight into his plans to the letters he wrote to disciples and friends in India. He considered it very essential that his followers understood the real form of religion. His God was not only limited to religious scriptures and temples. In a letter to his disciple Alasinga, Swami Vivekanand wrote—"I do not believe in that God or religion which cannot wipe the tears in the eyes of widows and cannot put a piece of bread into the mouth of an orphan or a hungry person. Howsoever kind or binding the principle or philosophy of a religion might be, but as long as it is limited to religious texts and sects, I do not believe it or follow it. Our eyes are in one front not at the back hence, keep on moving ahead. The religion which you follow and which makes you proud should be converted into an action oriented one. If you really want to do some good then surrender the conch and bell into the Ganges and worship the real image of the God i.e. mankind. This world itself is the huge form of the Almighty God and serving it is the real service to God. In this reality, is the real 'Karma' or action, not meaningless rituals or worship. After chanting mantras or ringing bells, offering a plate of delicacies to God and waiting for 10 minutes or half-an-hour is not Karma but madness. The doors of temples in Kashi and Vrindavan gets opened or closed by spending lakhs of rupees. At some places, God is changing dress and at others God is partaking food but we are ignorant as to what is really happening. But on the other hand, Gods in flesh and blood are dying of hunger and ignorance. The traders in Bombay are constructing hospital for bed bags but they have no feeling towards human beings even if they are dying. You people do not even have the common sense to understand all these things. All these activities undertaken by our people are like a plague for our nation and our country is like land of insane people."

According to Mrs. Annie Besant, Swami Vivekanand was a 'saint soldier'. She gave this name to Swamiji taking into consideration the task that he accomplished during his stay in America. In the same context some people addressed him as 'Hindu Napoleon'. But his soldier-like qualities came to fore during the course of his work in India. While in America he kept on encouraging his followers to march ahead and totally get involved in establishing an altogether new religion in form and identity. The innumerous letters that he wrote from America to his friends, disciples and followers in India gives an insight into his commander like qualities that inspires the fellow soldiers. "Do not look towards me, just look at yourselves, March ahead. You have a vast field of action in front of you. Just move ahead and everything will be fine. If you all are my children in true spirit then will not be intimated by anything or stop at any cost. You will become as a brave and courageous as a lion.'

In Swamiji's view, the major task in front of him was to fight a battle against poverty and ignorance. What he wished was that the innumerable saints and sannyasis who with the ambition to attain redemption are wasting their time wandering here and there or sitting somewhere should get involved in social work. In a letter to one of his Guru brothers he wrote—"Brother....I am unable to sleep properly in face of our country's poverty and illiteracy. I have a plan in my mind which I will definitely turn into reality. In the temple of Mata Kumari in Kanya Kumari, sitting on the last rock of our country I had arrived at a conclusion that we all saintes had indulged in the most insane of activities be imparting knowledge on Indian philosophy to people. Our Guru used to say that no religion can survive with empty stomach. Those poor people who are leading the life of animals are living such a life due to ignorance and illiteracy. Rich and privileged class have sucked their blood for years together and have tranipled them under their feet.

Just think how many saints are wandering in villages. What are they doing? If some selfless generous saint wonder from village to village imparting knowledge to every individual irrespective of caste, religion or creed, then will it not be beneficial to all and for the country as a whole. (I cannot describe all these plans in such a short letter). The crux of the Mutter is that if the mountain cannot go to Mohammed, then Mohammed will go to the mountain. It means, if poor children cannot attend school, then somebody should visit their homes and teach them. The condition of poverty ridden people is so precarious and miserable that they cannot afford to attend schools or colleges. And teaching them poetry, etc. would do no good. In comparison to the honour of our country we have almost lost our personality and this is the reason for all demerits. We should regain back our nation's lost glory and its actual identity and upgrade its people. Hindus, Muslims, Christians all have trampled the country under their feet alike. But the power to uplift the country will come from within i.e., from the Hindus.

After witnessing the high social status of people in America, Swamiji's heart longed for the upliftment and progression of the poor and ignorant countrymen back in India. The only way to improve the condition of his poor and miserable countrymen, in view of Swamiji, was education. In every letter addressed to his friends and disciples he kept on drawing their attention to this very fact. In one such letter he wrote: "My greatest ambition in life is to set that wheel in motion which would carry the highest of thought and ideals on to the doorstep of every individual. So every man and woman could decide his or her own fate. Let every commoner understand what our forefathers have thoughts on significant questions pertaining to life. Let them see what others are doing and then let them decide on their own. Collect chemical components and they will take any shape on their own according to the law of nature. Do hard work, be consistent and have faith in God. Begin the work. Early or late I will soon join you. 'Without harming religion, progress of public'— Make this your motto."

"Remember the major chunk of the nation is settled in hutments. But tragically nothing has ever been done for them. Our modern revolutionaries are too busy in conducting widow re-marriages. Of course, I endorse all sorts of improvement. The future of nation does not depend on widows getting more and more husbands but in the improvement of the condition of general public. Can you do anything for the progress of public? Can you help them regain back their lost identity without harming their natural spiritual tendency? Can you reign supreme in the Western world in terms of equality, freedom, capability, capacity and manliness?"

The most significant knowledge that Swamiji gained from the world was that of unity and organization. During his stay with the Lean family in Debroit, Swamiji once told Mrs. Lean that in America he had found the biggest of temptations in his life. With an intention to tease Swamiji Mrs. Lean asked that who was that lucky lady towards whom he had got so fatally attracted. Swamiji broke into a peal of laughter and said—"It is not a lady but unity and organization." Whatever he saw in America, he became sure that with the strength and power of unity many welfare activities can be accomplished for the society. Back in India, many of his Guru brothers were engaged in social work at different villages. But without proper organization they were not able to gain the desired outcome. If they all worked together in union how much could they have achieved. Though he was not clear as to the form of the organization, he was totally convinced about the importance of unity. This very thought later on took the form of Rama Krishna Mission.

■■

In Britain and Other Countries

In August 1895, when Swamiji went to Britain via Paris along with one of his American friends he had many doubts in his mind. A mixed kind of feeling merged in his mind when he stepped on that land which was pining in the pride of supremacy and imperialism—the country which had snatched the honour of India, had shackled its freedom and treating his countrymen as slaves. It was but natural on the part of Swamiji to have doubts in his hearts when he first stepped into the country which had been exercising its domination upon his own motherland. He had his doubts as to how that imperialistic country would treat a common saint and religious propagator from the country which it has been dominating for years together. But soon all the clouds of doubt that he had in his mind were steered clear. At the London Station, along with Mr. Sturdy and Ms. Henrietta Muller whom he had already met in America, there were many other English friends gathered at the station to welcome Swamiji. Many of them expressed their desire to have him as their guest. Swamiji fulfilled their wishes by staying at each one's place turn by turn. For the first two-three days, he visited the historical places and other places of architectural significance in London during day time and gave lectures in seminars and meetings during morning and evening time. Soon his fame spread far and wide. Britishers belonging to all classes—High, Middle and Lower—came to meet him and hear his discourses.

Within about three months Swamiji was totally entrapped in his work. Journalists of many newspapers took his interview. Daities like 'The West Minister Gazette' and 'The Standard' praised Swamiji a lot. In the evening of 22 October, at Princess Hall, in Piccadelly, London Swamiji gave a speech on Indian philosophy to an audience of more than thousand people. The topic was—'Knowledge of the Self'. People belonging to every walk of life in London turned up at Princess Hall. The crowd even bursted out of the hall. The very next day all the major newspapers published articles critically analyzing his speech. 'The London Daily Chronicle' wrote— "The famous Hindu sannyasi Vivekanand whose countenance has close resemblance to that of Buddha has stated our business prosperity, blood shedding battles, religious intolerance to be an evil and has said that Hindus who are soft in nature, will not at any cost, ever accept this highly appreciable civilization of ours. The editor of the magazine 'The West Minister Gazette' interviewed Swamiji and published a descriptive article about Swami Vivekanand. The magazine expressed its opinion that Swami Vivekanand is a human being with his calm and compassionate personality attracts people towards him. His countenance, bright and innocent like a young boy, is simple and clear. During his conversation with the editor of that magazine, Swamiji expressed his desire to spread the message of his teacher Sri Ramakrishna Paramahansa throughout the world. His mission was neither to establish a new creed nor to spread any particular religious belief. He just wanted to spread the knowledge of Vedanta, which would prove to be beneficial for the whole world. People having any religious affinity can imbibe it within their religious freedom.

'The Standard' wrote about Swami Vivekanand—"Except for Keshav Chandra Sen, after Ram Mohan Roy, no other Hindu orator had appeared in London's Princess Hall to give such an interesting discourse as given by him. In his discourse he presented a dozen of words by Buddha and Christ in comparison to our factories, engines, scientific inventions and books for human kind and criticized them. While presenting his discourse he never had any points written down on pieces of papers. Whatever he said came straight out from his mind. His voice was clear and tone straightforward without any predicament.

Within almost a month, Swamiji attained fame in London. Wherever he went people encircled around him with a huge round of applause. People nicknamed him as 'the stormy Indian'. In addition to public discourse at the Princess Hall, Swamiji spent most of his time in organizing Vedanta class and seminars. People expressed their desire to organize public meetings but Swamiji with his experience in America had understood that no amount of oratorical skills or show of scholarly talent would be of any good. Hence, he gave more stress on classroom teaching. Whosoever had interest in Vedanta philosophy and wanted to learn the same, was imparted training in a proper manner. The magazine 'Indian Mirror' referring to this work on the part of Swamiji wrote— "We are happy that Swami Vivekanand has been able to attract the attention of various high profile ladies and gentlemen. In his classes pertaining to Hindu philosophy and Yog many interested devotees are participating. The editor of a leading newspaper in London who attended many of Swamiji's classes wrote—"Many fashionable ladies in London belonging to the higher strata of society, due to lack of chairs are sitting crosslegged on the ground with total devotion like any Indian student and listening to Swamiji's advise. This is of course a scarce scene."

In November, Swamiji wrote a letter to one of his disciples in Madras regarding his work—"In England, my work has received success beyond imagination. Groups of people are coming to me and I do not have sufficient space to accommodate them. Hence, both men and women adjust themselves and sit on the floor. When they heard that I will leave London next week, many people became sad. Many people think that if I leave Britain, all the work done by me will be undone. But I do not think so. I am not dependent on human beings or any other thing. God is my support. He is making me do all these karma in a mechanical manner."

Like in America, in Britain also many people in the audience, unable to bear the critical remarks made by Swamiji on them stood up and raised voice against it or left the place in protest to such remarks and statements by Swamiji. In such situations, Swamiji's image got totally transformed. His eyes flared with lightening and his voice resembled like thunder. The image of a humble sannyasi devoid of any ego got lost somewhere. One day, in a pubic meeting Swamiji was describing about the glory of India, when a person questioned—"What have the Hindus in India done? Till date they have not been able to reign over any other religions." Instantly came the reply—"Do not say they have not been able to but say they did not. And herein lies the glory of the Hindu religion that they never shed the blood of people belonging to other religions or nation. Why should they exercise power of others' countries? For mere greed for money? God has always honoured India like a giver. Indians have been the religious teacher for the whole world. They are not the blood sucking demons longing to steal others' money. And hence, I am proud of the honour of my forefathers." Another person from the audience shot another question—"If your forefathers were so keen to give religious teachings in charity, then why did they not come to our country for religious propagation?" A smile came over Swamiji's face. He replied—"During those ages your forefathers were barbarous people inhabiting in jungles. They used to cover their bodies with leaves and lived in caves. In such a situation, would my forefathers have come to jungles to preach religion to them? When Swamiji expressed his views about Jesus Christ and Christianity, many people considered his gesture to be unauthorized and questioned his audacity—"Swami, since you are not a Christian how can you understand the ideals of Christianity?" Swamiji replied—"He was a renouncer, recluse from the Eastern world and I too am a saint from the East. I understand that the Western world has not been able to understand him properly. Didn't he say—'You go and distribute all your belongings and then follow me. How many of your comfort-loving countrymen have understood the truth of this command and sacrificed all their belongings." In this manner Swamiji silenced all his critics. A huge number of people in England which included large number of educated people were attracted towards the Indian saint with complete devotion. He was given respect and renown according to his stature. Swamiji made an investigation into this unlikely and new behaviour on the part of Britishers. His views about Englishmen underwent a rapid transformation. On one occasion, he made a confession about this—"No other person had ever stepped on to the British land with as much hatred I had....But today there is no other person here who loves Britishers more than I do."

In England also, like in America, Swamiji received a good amount of help in propagating his thoughts. He had not at all expected this much of support and success in the first visit itself. He had just made a visit to make an assessment as to what steps he should take for spreading the Vedanta philosophy in Britain within two months, the disparity in the mental perspectives between Americans and Britishers had become clear to Swamiji. The people of America were spellbound by the novelty of his oratorical skills. On the other hand, the conservative Britishers were quite thrifty in praising any new thought or ideal. In such a situation, it was difficult for them to imbibe or accept any such thought. But in such a complex situation, after much argument and counterargument, questioning and answering with Swamiji those who became convinced with his view points, later on, not only became his fast friends but also his most serious and trusted disciples.

Among such English disciples that Swamiji had, Ms. Margaret Nobel was the most prominent. Before meeting Swami Vivekanand, this strange scholarly woman was the Principal of a school. She enjoyed a place of honour in the intellectual community. She was an honourable member of the renowned seasame club. She had special interest in analyzing the impact of modern thinking in education. She had heard about Swamiji from many educationists and scholars. She also became curious to see and meet the Indian saint, whom people kept on praising without getting tired.

The winter season in the month of November when London city was reeling under severe ice cold winds and chilling cold. During one such Sunday, in the afternoon, Ms. Nobel set off to meet Swami Vivekanand. The house of Lady Isabel Margesan. That day Swami Vivekanand had to deliver a speech there. In the sitting room decorated in a purely western manner, Swamiji was sitting wearing his saffron outfit according to pure Indian tradition, on the floor. Around fifteen-sixteen people were sitting in front of him facing him in a half circular form. Behind them, at the fire place, fire was burning giving warmth to them. Swamiji was giving the message to the audience. As he talked, he chanted 'Shivam-Shivam' in the middle. The audience were putting up one question after the other.

Swami listened to each and every question and gave reply to each of them patiently. He supported his answers quoting Sanskrit Shlokas and other texts. That day the topic of his speech was 'The three means to spiritual development i.e. Karma (action), Devotion and Knowledge. When noontime gave way to evening and evening to night, no body got to know the spark at the first place shone all the more in the night. That meeting in London resembled the imagery of a village scene in India—as if in the cold winter season to save themselves from shivering cold, they had lit up fire nearby, where under a tree near the river bank some saint was giving preaching to his disciples. After some time, a light bulb was lit in the meeting hall. That dim light totally dissolved the Indian imagery. Then there remained only that Indian saint and his eternal words. Rest of the things regained their western identity. The union of the ancient east and the modern west was worth witnessing.

Ms. Nobel entered the meeting with soft steps and sat among the audience in a quiet manner. She listened to what Swamiji was saying in a patient manner. There reflected a sense of humility in her eyes but her countenance shone with self respect. When the discussion of the topic ended, Ms. Nobel also got up to go as others did. Lady Margesan heard her saying to many of the audiences that there was no substance, anything new in his talks. It seemed as if he had made a pre-formed opinion that whatever Swamiji said she would not accept that. Ms. Nobel did not give any special weightage to the topic discussed by Swamiji and his view point. After reaching back to her home she became busy with her work but could not forget Swamiji's talks simply and easily. Again and again she could hear the voice of her inner self. It is not proper to oppose the strange features of a strange culture. The worshipper of truth should have an open mind and heart. Any kind of bias or prejudice is just inappropriate. As she analysed the views presented by Swamiji in depth, the more she felt the reflection of truth in it. At the end of November Ms. Nobel heard two more speeches presented by Swamiji. She had gone to hear them assuring herself that she would try to thoroughly understand whatever Swamiji said. She will detach herself from the limitations of her country, caste, religion etc. But her doubtful heart did not get detached from her. As a result, during Swamiji's question answer sessions 'buts', 'hows' and 'whys' remained persistent on her lips. Patriotism and self-confidence were inseparable aspects of her personality and were present in her flesh and blood more than required level. How could she have so easily accepted the words that were spoken by Swamiji? She measured all that he said with her own yardstick and then argued with them. When Swamiji convinced her properly with

Swami Vivekanand: A Biography

his counter arguments and rationale then she accepted those views, making them thorough in her heart.

As Ms. Nobel shot questions at him, his own past flashed alive in front of his mind's eye—the atheist, stubborn young 'Naren' sitting in front of Gurudev Shri Ramakrishna Paramahansa with self-respect and confidence brimming. It seems as if he were sitting in front of Swamiji with the sole mission of dissecting the views presented by Gurudev. But Gurudev's two confident eyes and his innocence had some magic inherent within them that conquered the rebel 'Naren' and made him its worshipper. During those days, 'Buts', 'Whys' and 'How's' flowed too frequently from Narendra's lips. The same incidents were getting repeated again. The second 'Naren' was present in front of him in the image of Ms. Margaret Nobel. Swamiji had to toil a lot to instill any of his thoughts in Ms. Nobel's mind. But he knew that once those thoughts got instilled in her mind, that will remain there forever. He knew that there was no other appropriate person in whom his thoughts could be so thoroughly imprinted. Once during the course of delivering lecture Swamiji overheard one lady telling Ms. Nobel that she was able to understand what Swamiji meant to say and totally endorsed his views. At that moment, Swamiji did not say anything but later on said to Ms. Nobel—"One should not be guilty of not able to understand what I teach. I had a verbal duel with my Gurudev for over 6 years—argued with him, the result is that now I am totally aware of my path. Everything is on my tips." Before Swamiji left London, Ms. Nobel began to address Swamiji as 'Gurudev'. Later on, in her book titled *The Master as I saw Him*' she wrote about her decision—"I had identified his generous nature and became desirous of becoming a slave to his love for his countrymen." That very Ms. Margaret Nobel later on became the renowned disciple of Swami Vivekanand in the name of Sister Nivedita.

* * *

Swamiji had just begun the ground work of propagation of Vedanta in Britain that he began to receive call after call from America. As he had some more work to accomplish there, Swamiji decided to return back to America.

After winding up his work in America, on April 15, 1896 Swami Vivekanand stepped on to the British land for the second time. When he reached the house of Mr. Sturdy in

London, who was both his friend and disciple, his joy knew no bounds. Swami Shardanant had already arrived there from Calcutta as guest. The scene of union between the two guru brothers after a gap of so many years was indeed a heart rending scene. Both of them were overwhelmed with emotion and tears came rolling down her eyes. Swami Sharadanand had in his possession the magic box of news from Calcutta. He informed each and every development that took place in Calcutta to his Guru brother after he had left for America. He also talked about the Alam Bazar Mutt and about the Guru brothers. The news of Swamiji's arrival at London for the second time spread like wildfire. As a result, many men and women gathered their to get a glimpse of Swamiji and to hear his teachings. Swamiji's daily schedule in London had become very busy. In addition to teach some select, people at home, he was engaged in giving public speeches and discourses and also to clear the doubts and queries regarding Vedanta philosophy. He gave interesting lectures on serious topics such as 'Indian philosophy and their significance in modern living' and 'Role of Yogi in Modern Living'. In the beginning of May, he started regular classes on 'Gyan Yog.' By the end of May, he presented speeches of high standard on topics—'Necessity of religion', "All encompassing religion" and "The Real form of human being" at the Royal Institute of Painter's Auditorium situated in Picaddel London. This made him all the more popular. People became all the more eager and excited to meet him and listen to his discourses. Some of them organized more of his discourses at Princess Hall. There he spoke about 'devotion' and 'Karma Yog'. Other than this, people invited him for conversations at clubs and drawing rooms. At the bungalow of Mrs. Annie Besant and Mrs. Martin, where he was invited, Swamiji gave speech on 'Devotion' and 'Hindu thoughts regarding soul' respectively. He also organized daily classes in which he taught topics relating to philosophy, Veda and the history of Aryans. Where Swamiji travelled, his 'trusted Gudwin' also accompanied him and scripted his speech.

Sharadanand in the 6th June edition of 'Brahmaradin magazine wrote about Swamiji's activities—"Swami Vivekanand has begun his work in a very beautiful manner. Every day large number of people attended his class. His discourses are really interesting. On the previous day, the leader of the Anglican Church Mr. Cannon Harris listened to his speech and was totally spellbound. He had met Swamiji at the Chicago Parliament of World Religions and from then onwards he had great love towards him. Last Tuesday, Swamiji gave a speech on education at the Seasame Club. For the advancement of women education, the women there have established this significant club. In the speech, Swamiji compared ancient and modern educational system in India and made it clear that the objective of education should be to make a human being a human being not to stack different subjects into the brain."

'The London American' magazine published a beautiful and critical essay on Swamiji's speech on the topic "Hindu views relating to soul" that he had given at the bungalow of Mrs. Martin. In such an environment when he was burdened with praises, appreciation and honour from all quarters, the memory of Ramakrishna came to his mind again and again. On many occasions, he very humbly attributed the success of himself and his work to Gurudev. He used to be overwhelmed with emotions as he discussed about his Guru.

During that period Swamiji's life was very busy. It seemed as if he wanted to end his work as early as possible. He had no desire to take any rest during the course of his life. On his second visit to England he got an opportunity to meet the renowned Sanskrit scholar Prof. Max Muller. Swamiji had already heard about this renowned personality who loved ancient philosophy and was nursing a keen desire to meet him. Later on, in a magazine named 'Nineteenth Century' Swamiji read an article in praise of Sri Ramakrishna. The article was written by Prof. Max Muller. After reading the article Swamiji could not resist his curiosity of meeting Max Muller. At that very juncture, Max Muller invited Swamiji to his residence. Max Muller's residence was a beautiful small house with flowers, trees and plants surrounded on all four sides. The seventy year old who had with him both happy and sorrowful experiences stored in his memories looked a philosopher in the true sense. White hair and innocent face. But eyes? Eyes were like a mirror. It reflected the life time devotion and deep spirituality.

He welcomed Swamiji with great love. During the course of conversation, Swamiji got a glimpse of his in-depth knowledge about India and he was very surprise at this,

Swamiji was greatly impressed by the old Max Muller's deep love for India. A citizen of the country that was proud of overruling his country, having much of love for his country. Such people are rare. Max Muller kept on talking about Sri Ramakrishna with Swami Vivekanand. He said, "After coming into contact with Sri Ramakrishna, the sudden change of religious affinity by Keshav Chandra Sen attracted my attention towards him for the first time. From that time onwards whatever I received in the form of his life and teachings, have been teaching others with great devotion." Prof. further said to Swamiji—"If you collect necessary things for me, I am ready to write a biography of Ramakrishna." Swamiji was happy to hear Prof. Max Muller's thought. Swami Vivekanand entrusted the task of collecting all necessary facts and information pertaining to Sri Ramakrishna from India and hand them over to Prof. Max Muller to Swami Sharadanand. Later on, after somedays, with the help of the information made available by Swami Sharadananda, Max Muller wrote the famous book titled "Life and Messages of Sri Ramakrishna." This book helped a lot in propagating Indian philosophy. Swami Vivekanand informed the professor that still Ramakrishna is worshipped and adored by lakhs of people in India. At this Prof. Max Muller said that such great personalities deserve-worship. He enquired Swamiji as to what he had been doing to spread Sri Ramakrishna's message throughout the world." Swami made him understand about the efforts he had been taking in spreading Vedanta. Professor appreciated Swamiji's efforts and works. Swamiji kept on asking Prof. Max Muller as to when he will visit India. He said that every individual of the country will be longing to welcome a person like him who has discussed the thoughts and philosophies of their forefathers with so much of devotion and truth. The old intellectual's face brightened up when he heard such words of gratitude from Swamiji, tear filled up his eyes. Shaking his head in an affirmative manner he said. "Then I will not return back from their. You will have perform my last rites their." That day Prof. Max Muller talked with him and took him on a round of Oxford University. At night, Prof. Max Muller enjoyed a tea with Swamiji and his disciples and accompanied them on a visit to the industrial fair being organized in the city. In the brightness of electric lights, Swamiji witnessed the various facets of scientific progression that had taken place in Germany.

Swami Vivekanand: A Biography

The next day the Professor took Swamiji and his disciples to nearby famous places. Dyson wanted Swamiji to stay with them for a few more days so that he could exchange views on philosophy and spirituality in a complete manner. But already he had spent almost one-and-a half months there and wanted to resume his propagational activities after returning back to London. Professor understood Swamiji's limitations. Hence, he decided to make a trip to London himself and gain more knowledge, remaining in the company of Swamiji. He promised to join Swamiji at Hamburg and saw off Swamiji and his disciples.

In the end of June, Swamiji sent Sharadanand to America and for assistance in his work in London called another Guru brother from India Swami Abhedananda. He imparted all sorts of training to Swami Abhedananda so that he could later on entrust the task of spreading Vedanta with him. Within few days, Swami Abhedananda also became proficient in teaching Vedanta and imparting training in Yog Sadhna.

After visiting various European countries, in London Swamiji gave public lectures on 'Gyan Yog'. Seeing the increasing number of audience day by day, his disciple Sturdy arranged a huge room appropriate to organize meetings at Victoria Street. The Xavier couples arranged for a rented accommodation for Swami Vivekanand and Abhedananda adjacent to that room. Prof. Dyson had also accompanied Swamiji from Germany to London. He met Swamiji daily and discussed the different philosophies related to Vedanta with Swamiji, he was able to easily understand even the minutest of arguments. Dyson said to Swamiji that among the discoveries made by human mind to search the truth, Upanishad, Vedanta philosophy and Shankar Bhaskya were the most significant. Dyson had such a deep interest in the science of philosophy that it seemed as if discussion on Vedanta was the sole aim of his life.

In the months of October and November, Swamiji was busy delivering lectures on many important topics at various public places. The first topic of the series of discourses was 'illusion' (Maya). After that he gave lectures on 'material and illusion', 'material and thoughts about God', 'material and redemption', 'unity in diversity', 'vision of God in everything', 'redemption of soul' and 'practical vedanta'. The ability of Swamiji lied in the fact that he presented every complex topic in a most simple manner before the general public. He gave examples from people's lives and from nature to drive home his point. The series of lecture on 'Gyan Yog' helped him achieve great success. In his speech on the topic "Utility of Vedanta in practical life', Swamiji presented a detailed analysis of the philosophies of Vedanta and Advaita. "The only unlimited power of this whole universe is what we call 'sat-chit-anand.' It is the truth, it is the knowledge and it is the supreme happiness. It is the internal nature of human being, it is the soul of human being and it is the meaning of human being. It is totally free and divine. Every thing around the universe represents the soul." After describing about Advaita, he described about its utility of life. Swamiji emphasized again and again that the western world who are worshippers of science, if they donot embrace the Vedanta philosophy, then they will fall victim to the holocaust caused by science itself. It was quite clear to the visionary within Swamiji that at that juncture the western world was on the brink of unquenchable volcano of desire and dissatisfaction.

Swamiji received invitation for discourses from different clubs and scholarly people in the months of October and November. Swamiji had very limited time available with him so he accepted some of them and declined some. Swamiji was then keen to return back to his homeland. But still he was keen on getting a book published on Hindu philosophy before returning back to India. But he did not get even a few seconds to sit and write. At last, a compilation based on the series of public lectures that he gave on 'Rajyog' was got published in the form of a beautiful book in October, which got sold off like hot cakes. In the November, when its second edition was getting ready, more than 100 people had already placed orders for the same.

By then Swami Abhedanand had emerged quite capable in carrying out the propagational activities. The students who attended his Vedanta classes honoured him a lot. One day, Swami Vivekanand was supposed to deliver a lecture at Bloomsbury Square but due to some unavoidable reasons Swamiji could not attend the same. At last in place of Swami Vivekanand, Swami Abhedananda delivered a lecture on Vedanta philosophy. People were present in huge numbers. All of them listened to him in a calm manner and later on praised his oratorical skills. The increasing popularity of Swami Abhedanand was a cause of both happiness and satisfaction for Swami Vivekanand. Now he was fully assured that in his absence Swami Abhedanand will take charge of his work of propagation of Vedanta. In the same way, he had entrusted the task of spreading Vedanta in America with Swami Sharadananda. After reaching New York, he had been totally engaged in his work. People of America gave him the same love and respect as they had given to Swami Vivekanand.

When the news about Swami Vivekanand's departure for India reached to the ears of Ms. Alobull she informed Swamiji that she was ready to give as much money as he wanted for undertaking public welfare activities in India. She was also taking initiative for establishing a 'Ramakrishna Sannyasi Mutt' for Swamiji. Swamiji was very happy with the initiatives taken by Mrs. Bull. Swamiji wished to establish Mutts for sannyasis in the memory of Sri Ramakrishna at Calcutta, Madras and the Himalayas. But he was not prepared to take a hurried decision in this regard. His basic nature was to do things patiently and in a planned out manner. Hence, he informed Ms. Bull through a letter that he will write to her about this after reaching India. At that moment, he did not want to carry money along with him during the journey.

Swamiji decided to return back to India in the month of December. The Xavier couples arranged for his journey tickets. Swamiji had planned to make his return journey to India via Italy. Hence, a ticket on ship was reserved from Naples. Mr. and Mrs. Xavier had vouchsafed the rest of their life for rendering their services in India, so they were also accompanying Swamiji during his return journey.

When the people of London came to know about Swamiji's return to India, they became sad and distressed. His friends and disciples in London organized a farewell meeting for Swamiji under the presidentship of Mr. Sturdy at the huge auditorium of 'Royal Society of Painters' at Picadelly. That was Sunday 13th December. All the shops and business establishments in the city were closed for the day. Everything had come to a stand still. Roads were devoid of traffic. London enveloped with fog was resembling a wasteland. On the roads and streets there were only the movement of people going to church. That was the only sign of life in the city. That very evening, Swamiji's friends, disciples and well wishers were giving him a farewell. The huge hall was made beautiful with floral decorations. The stage was also made very attractive. The orchestra troupe were already ready with musical instruments. That was the last lecture that Swamiji was about to deliver in the land of England. The hall was jampacked with men and women. They expressed their sorrow by taking part in the farewell ceremony with heavy hearts. Many people wanted to say something to Swamiji but could not utter a word. Overwhelmed with emotions, they just stood silent with tears in their eyes. Tender hearted Swamiji also could not witness the scene for long. He also turned emotional. He expressed his heartfelt gratitude to the people of Britain and reiterated the love bond between the two nations. In the end, he said, "It is possible that for the well-being of people I may renounce this body, I may renounce this body considering it to be a torn dress. But tell the day, every individual in this world does not attain the supreme truth, I will continue with my propagational activities for the welfare of humanity." Yes, even after he left this earthly abode, his work continued. The seed of religious propagation and human service that he had sown in the hearts and minds of his Indian disciples in America, England and India grew up into trees with extended branches and bore the desired fruit. Even today, the followers of Swami Vivekanand are carrying forward his legacy of spreading the actual philosophy of Hindu religion.

There is no doubt that Swami Vivekanand's speech had a deep impact on the people of Britain. The renowned political leader, Sh. Vipin Chandra Pal in an article published in the Indian Mission on 15 February 1898 wrote—'Some people in India think that the speeches made by Swami Vivekanand in England were worthless and that his friends and well wishers displayed it beyond proportions. But here I am able to assess the strange impact he had made on people here. I talked with many people at different places in England. I have found that these people are having a deep devotion and respect towards Vivekanand. Even though I do not belong to his society and my views are different from his school of thought, still I am compelled to say that

Vivekanand has opened the eyes of the people here and have widened their perspective. His advise made people has believe that the ancient Hindu scriptures have many spiritual truths inherent in them. He had not only awakened those lofty emotions within them but have also achieved success in establishing cordial relationship between India and England."

Swamiji was fully ready and prepared to leave London. He was regular in his correspondence with his disciples in Madras informing them about each and every developments taking place in England and America. Before departing from London he wrote about his future plans to his disciple Alasinga.

"I will depart to Italy from London on December 16 and board the ship named 'North German Lloyd S S Prince Regent Leopold' from Naples. I will be accompanied by three English friends— Captain, Mrs. Xavier and Gudwin. Mr. and Mrs. Xavier are planning to set up an ashram at Almora near the Himalayas. I am planning to make that my centre at Himalayas wherein I will teach western Brahmachari disciples. Gudwin is an unmarried young man. He will accompany me on my tours and will stay with me. He is almost like a sannyasi.

I am indeed longing to reach Calcutta before the birth anniversary celebrations of Sri Ramakrishna. My present plan is to establish two centres of training for young prapagators in Calcutta and Madras. I have in my possession sufficient funds for setting up the Calcutta centre. Calcutta is the field of Sri Ramakrishna's activities hence, it attracts my first attention. I am hopeful that I will be able to accumulate funds for the Madras centre also.

We will begin our work in these three cenres. After that we will establish centres at Bombay and Allahabad. With the will and blessings of God, not only at the three centres, but throughout India and all over the world we would be able to send our propagators. You should not forget that my work is of the international level, not limited to India alone."

On December 16, 1896 Swamiji bade good bye to London along with the Xavier couple. Mr. Gudwin was to board the ship from Southampton and Swamiji from the port of Naples.

After almost four years of continuous work in America and England, Swamiji was returning back to his homeland. He felt as if suddenly he had been bereft of responsibilities and he had become carefree. He had complete faith on Swami Sharadananda and Swami Abhedananda that they will continue with the work of spreading Vedanta education in America and England. He in a joyful tone said to Mr and Mrs. Xavier—"Now only one thought is left in my mind and that is about India. I am seeing India in front of my eyes."

At the time of bidding good bye to London one of his English friends asked him, "After spending four years in this powerful, luxurious western land, how would you feel in your motherland?" Instantly came the reply. "Before coming here I loved India. At this moment each and every speech of dust is pure for me. Its air is pious. Now it is a blessed land for me, a place of pilgrimage.

After crossing the land of France and the Alps mountain ranges Swamiji's train reached the city of Milan. There he stayed at a hotel with his disciples. There he was greatly inspired by the painting of Leonardo da vinu's—"The Last supper". He visited the bending forts at Pizza Nagar and other famous historical places. Swamiji's next destination was Phirage. Swamiji was spellbound by the various tourist places there.

While taking a round of garden, coincidentally. he met · the Hale couple. Swamiji was greatly attached to them. They also had showered son-like love on Swamiji. When Swamiji went to Chicago while in America, he stayed with them. This unexpected meeting made Swamiji very happy. They were on a tour to Italy and they were unaware of Swamiji's visit to Italy. Swamiji spent a lot of time with them. Swamiji went to Rome alongwith by Xavies couple. There they stayed for a week and visited places of historical importance. During their visit Rome was in a state of fervour and excitement for the city was sprucing up for the Christmas festival and was decorated like a new bride. Roads, streets and shops were crowded by innumerable people. Churches were decorated. Swamiji wandered the place for six to seven days and remained very happy.

At last on 30 December they boarded the ship from Naples which had begun its journey from South Hampton in which Gudwin had already been present. Swamiji was extremely joyous of having Gudwin on board of the ship. After some days the ship reached Adan. The ship was to halt there for some hours. Many passengers alighted from the ship to have a glimpse of Adan. Swamiji also along with his companions alighted from the ship to visit the city. In between the hilly ways, the shops on both sides were a blessing for the visitors.

Swamiji was taking a stroll of the place along with his companions while talking to them. Suddenly, his eyes got fixed over a person sitting far away at a betel shop. The Indian looking person was enjoying the puff of hukka. Swamiji took fast pace leaving beyond his companions, going straight towards him. After reaching near the person, Swamiji like an innocent child asked for the hukka. The stranger finding a saffron clad sannyasi begging for his used hukka was both confused and amazed for a while but then handed over the hukka to him. Swamiji took a few puffs with joyous satisfaction. His companions were also in a state of amazement and surprise. When they reached near Swamiji, Mr. Xavier said—"Now we understood. You left all of us behind in a hurry for this thing." Swamiji smiled and returned back the hukka and walked ahead. When the person came to know that the sannyasi was Swami Vivekanand he ran towards him and fell on his feet. This incident left a deep impact on Xavier couple and Gudwin. After wandering through the street of Adan for few hours, they returned back to their ship. When the ship resumed its journey the 'Chap-Chap' sound began to be heard. The ship was steering through the water at high speed as it had to reach Sri Lanka port on 15 January.

Days kept on passing at its usual place. In the morning of January 15, 1897 as Swamiji stood on the roof of the ship, he could see the port of Lanka nearing. Lanka seemed to be a part of India. The people there had the looks resembling to that of Indians. Oh, the land of Sri Lanka. The beauty of the land is so attractive. Near the sea beach, these was a row of coconut trees. The pretty day break covered with a golden coloured shawl, with the red sun decorated on its forehead had come to behold the beauty of earth. The ship had neared the port.With the sound of the ships the ocean got subdued. Swamiji's happiness knew no bounds. From the rooftop itself Swamiji recognized—the Guru brother and disciples from Madras who were present there to welcome him. Many people were also present there. As Swamiji alighted the ship a huge round of applause reverberated at the sea bank. His disciples and devotees welcomed Swamiji with floral garlands. Arrangement for Swamiji's stay was made at a bungalow at Cinnamen Garden. Swamiji was made to sit on a decorated chariot drawn by horses. Roads were specially cleaned and made up. The chariot in which Swamiji was travelling moved at a slow pace and was accompanied with musicians playing Indian classical music on the instruments. Huge crowd of people stood as onlookers on both sides of the road to have a glimpse of Swamiji. The chariot reached its destination in front of a big stage in front of Cinnamon Garden. No sooner than Swamiji stepped down from the chariot people began to collect the dust where his footsteps got imperiled.

In the evening, Swamiji came on to the stage. The Hindu community in Colombo presented him with a commendation certificate. After the ceremony, Swamiji stood upto speak and the people assembled there began to applaud him in excitement. Swamiji in reply to the welcome and appreciation extended to him said—"I am not a great politician, nor a brave soldier, or a rich man but a sannyasi surviving on alms. Now that people have extended a royal welcome to me, it has become evident that spirituality is still present in the Hindus. During the course of his speech, Swamiji emphasized on the fact that spirituality is the characteristic feature of Hindus. It should not be allowed to be destroyed. In spite of all kinds of oppositions, Hindus should stick to the ideals of their religion.

The next day, on 16 January he gave a speech on the topic—"The pious land of India." In the evening, he went to the local temple dedicated to Lord Shiva. On the way, many people presented him with floral garlands and fruits. Women folk stood on both sides of the road showering flowers and sprinkling rose water. At the temple entrance crowds of people shouted 'Jai Mahadev' as a mark of support to Swamiji. After offering worship to Lord Shiva, Swamiji had a brief exchange of views with the priests of the temple. Then he returned back to the place where his accommodation was arranged. There till 2'oclock in the night he discussed religion and various other topics pertaining to religion with them. The next day he gave a discourse on Vedanta philosophy at the Public Hall in Colombo. A group of youths were also present among the audience who betrayed

Swami Vivekanand: A Biography

westernism in their behaviour and dressing sense. Swamiji was deeply hurt by the western touch in their mannerisms. During the course of the speech he said that it is a lead habit to blindly imitate others. It should be the duty and responsibility of every countryman to safeguard its culture and religious identity. It would be better to imbibe the good qualities of other nations and countries for the benefit of our own nation.

On 19 January, Swamiji went to Kandy by a special train and later on went to the ancient Buddhist city of Anuradhapuram. He was extended a warm and hearty welcome at both the places. Thousands of Buddhists and Hindus had gathered there to get a glimpse of Swamiji. After accepting the commendation certificate he gave a discourse on the topic 'worship'. From there Swamiji went to Jaffna where he was to address a public gathering at the Hindu College. The excitement of public knew no bounds. After a brief thanks giving, Swamiji gave a speech on Vedanta. Once the speech was over people kept on coming to seek his blessings.

Swamiji's Lanka tour ended with Jaffna. From there he boarded on a small ship to India. He was curious to reach his motherland at the earliest. He felt as if the sad and miserable, mother-India was calling her long separated son and the son hearing her beckon was getting impatient on meeting her.

■■

Awakening

The news of Swamiji's return back to India spreaded like wildfire. The people of India were busy in the preparation for his welcome. In Madras, Bengal and many other provinces articles recounting his personality and work were published in the newspapers. Welcome committees were formed in major cities like Madras and Bengal. Two of Swamiji's Guru brothers had gone to Lanka for his welcome. Rest of them stayed back in Madras for the arrangement of his welcome. But Swamiji, unaware of all these arrangements were planning and imagining about the construction of a new India.

After a long stay of four years abroad Swamiji stepped onto the soil of India for the first time at Pamban. King of Ramnad, Bhaskar Verma was waiting impatiently along with a huge gathering to welcome Swamiji. After alighting from the ship Swamiji preceeded towards the boat of the king of Ramnad which was ready to take him. As soon as the boat neared the bank people began to cheer Swamiji with excitement. The king of Ramnad and many others laid down on the earth to touch the soil where his footprints got imprinted. The people of Pamban read out the welcome letter and Swamiji in turn expressed his gratitude. He gave special acknowledgement to the king of Ramnad. Swamiji said that he was the first one to give Swamiji the idea of going to Chicago and attending the World Parliament of Religions. After the meeting he was taken to a beautifully decorated chariot drawn by horses. The King ordered to untie the horses from the chariot. The King himself and the other devotees began to draw the chariot. The next day Swamiji went to the Rameswaram temple. At the entrance of the temple a huge crowd had gathered, cheering around him and orchestra and music was also being played to welcome him. At Ramnad also he received the same kind of welcome. The king of Ramnad present him certificate in a beautifully carved box made of gold.

The welcome ceremony at Madras was the most glorious. The welcome committee was formed under the leadership of Sh. Subramaniam Iyer. The buildings on both sides of the road were decorated with flowers and colourful papers, flags were hoisted on. The processions, playing of musical instruments were going on as a mark of welcome. The name of Vivekanand was on the lips of children, youths and elderly. Swami Vivekanand was the main topic of discussion everywhere. A week before Swamiji's arrival at Madras people began to shout slogans cheering Swamiji. The whole province looked as if sprucing up for a big ceremony. It looked like a new bride.

On route from Ramnad to Madras, welcome ceremonies were organized at many major cities. Whenever he undertook his journey by train, the sight at the station was worth witnessing with crowds of people shouting slogans to hail the great spiritual leader, presenting him with garlands. At one station people compelled the train to stop. The train by which Swamiji was going to Madras did not have at a small village station. The people of that village was keen to have a glimpse of Swamiji. They made a request to stop the train for a while at the station so that it could be possible for them to meet Swamiji but the station master did not listen to them the crowd became agitated. Thousands of people laid on the railway track on which the train was supposed to come. Seeing such a scene the station master was shocked. He became intimidated. The train was nearing the station at high speed. But the guard on board of the train saw the situation from a distance and ordered the train to stop at once. As soon as the train came to a halt people went near the bogey in which Swamiji was travelling. They felicitated Swamiji by loud cheers and floral garlands. Swamiji stood on the door of the train and blessed the people with both his hands. His heart was overwhelmed with the love and warmth expressed by the people.

The platform at the Madras Station was decorated with flowers, colourful flags and banners. Around ten thousand people were present there. To avoid crowd inside the station premises, the welcome committee had fixed entry tickets for entry inside the station. But inspite of that a huge number of people had gathered there. The train was to arrive at Madras station at 7:30 in the morning. People were waiting impatiently for the arrival of the train with their sight affixed towards the southern direction. Finally the train whistle prior to the arrival of the train blew and the train reached the platform at a slow pace. As the train came to a halt the sound of cheer reverberated the atmosphere. Swamiji was accompanied by two of his Guru brothers, Swami Niranyanand and Swami Shivanand and his European disciple Gudwin. The members of the welcome committee made them alight from the train with full honours and led them out amidst the crowd with great difficulty. They were made to sit on a decorated chariot drawn by horses. The scene on the route was worth watching. Thousands of people crowded both sides of the roads. People sat on the branches, stood on rooftops and balconies of houses and buildings to catch a glimpse of the great man. The soft music of Shehnai that merged with the slow movement of the Chariot and the slogan cheering their beloved spiritual leader who had earned laurels for the nation was a soothing melody for the ears.

That much of excitement and emotional overflow was not found earlier in the people of Madras. For them Swami Vivekanand was like a winner of the universe. He had not won any battle. He had won over the heart of the people of the West and the East. Swamiji waved his hands and blessed the crowd sometimes sitting and sometimes standing. After some distance the excited youngsters detached the horses from the chariot and began to draw the chariot on their own. Many women offered gifts of fruits and flowers to Swamiji and worshipped him like a God. One incident took place during the course of Swamiji's journey from station to his home. An old woman braving the crowd came towards Swamiji's chariot holding a plate containing coconut, fruits and flowers. Her eyes were welled up with tears of love. She believed that Swamiji was the incarnation of Lord Shiva and a mere sight of him will redeem her of all her sins. All the people who witnessed this sight were wonderstruck by the gesture of the old woman.

The welcome committee had planned out the itinerary for Swamiji according to which he had to stay in Madras for nine days. During those nine days the city of Madras was as if in a festive spirit. The very next day of Swamiji's arrival in Madras the welcome committee presented him with the felicitation certificate. After that they read out the

Swami Vivekanand: A Biography

congratulatory note sent by the King of Khetri. Felicitation notes from different regions which were in different language were read out to him. Swamiji's public speaking was organized at the Victoria Hall. The Hall was crowded with an audience numbering over five thousand. Outside this huge hall till the main road people were waiting for an opportunity to gain entry but to no avail. Inside the hall Swamiji was expressing his thanks. The people outside were excited and keen to listen to Swamiji's speech on philosophy. The crowd became uncontrollable and they made a forced entry at the main gate. Because of such jeopardy it had become impossible to hear even a single word of Swamiji. Swamiji came out of the hall. The horse chariot was stationed outside the hall. He got into the coach box of the chariot and standing there began to address the public who were in an aggressive and excited mood—"My dear friends. I am really happy to see your excitement. It is indeed commendable. Yes this kind of spirit and excitement and energy is what is required. The only thing is that it should be retained permanently. Let it remain and don't quench this fire. We have to accomplish many big tasks for India. I will give a detailed discourse on some other occasion. I am really thankful for your hearty welcome.

The scene of Swamiji's addressing the public in such a manner was indeed attractive. The picture of Lord Krishna giving the message of Bhagvad Gita to Arjun got enlivened in the eyes of thousands of people. Though Swamiji gave a brief speech but it was full of energy. Thousands of year before, Lord Sri Krishna had awakened the slumbering emotions within Arjun. He had shown light to the truth lying deep in the darkness of Arjun's heart. In contrast, Swamiji with the help of the philosophy of Advaita had brewed life into the weak, hopeless people of India who were almost on the brink of death. "I do not give much emphasis on 'Dwaita' but I propogate 'Advaita'. I very well know that love, devotion and worship is inherent in the Dwaita philosophy. But dear brothers, we are not in a situation to be in a blissful state and shedding the tears of love. We have already shed a lot of tears. It is not the time for us to be in a soft emotion. By being soft and worshipping softness we have become tender and almost on the brink of death lke a pile of cotton. At this juncture our country needs people with strong muscles and well built body. We are in dire need of people with strong will power whom no body even dare to oppose. This is of prime importance to us and its beginning, establishment and affirmation is possible only if we understand the philosophy of 'Advaita' or 'the importance of our soul' in its real spirit and also experience the same.

A person who believes in the principle of Advaita does not make any difference between God and the soul. He is what the Almighty is—one with him. Hence a believer of Advaita is all powerful, full of inner energy, strength and devotion." Swami continued speaking, overwhelmed with emotion: "Devotion, devotion, on oneself and on the God Almighty— this is the sole secret of greatness. If you have faith in the 33 crore Gods as mentioned in the Puranas and the Gods of the foreigners but not on yourself, then you have no right to attain redemption. First learn to believe in yourself. On the strength of this very belief and devotion on self, stand on your own feet. This is the secret become powerful. This is the need of the hour. Why are these 33 crore of Indians under the domination of a few handful of foreigners? The reason for this is that those who ruled over us had trust on themselves but we could not achieve that. We have lost trust and devotion on ourselves. Hence the need of spreading Advaita philosophy has arisen so that people should be awakened to the truth of the importance of soul."

People were truly awakened by Swamiji's words and understood the importance of soul. India which had been in a deep slumber, suddenly arose from it as if they have heard the blow of a counchshell. India opened its eyes rubbing them for a while, glanced at its own body and recognized its strength. It realized that the strength was inherent in its heart more than its arms. The encouraging call made by Swamiji caused excitement in it. "Just remember that every soul has eternal strength in it. Then only you will be able to reawaken the whole of India. Get up, awake and achieve your objective, tell our countrymen to keep on progressing towards it. Be courageous, do not fear. One should be without any fear so as to fulfil our aim. Young men of Madras, my hopes are pinned on you. Will you be able to hear the call of your country? If you people have faith in me then I would tell you that each one of you have a bright future ahead of you. Keep as deep and unbreakable faith on yourself the same kind of trust which I used to have on myself during my childhood days. I am converting that into reality now. I am applying the same into practice. Each individual among you should have faith in yourself. Just believe that the soul of each one of you have endless power inherent in it. Then only you will be able to reawaken and instill a new life into the whole of India. In Vedas it has been said that—'Youthful, strong, sharp intellectuals, God like and men with a sense of excitement can achieve closeness to God.' This is the right time to be decisive about your future. Hence I am asking you to work in this youthful age when your spirit is still young. When you turn old and tired nothing could be done. Do work because this is the time to do work. Fresh, untouched and unsmelled flowers are offered at the feet of the God and He also accepts the same. Life span is short but the soul is devoid of death and eternal, death is imminent. Hence come on, let us built a great ideal before us and sacrifice our life for that."

Swami Vivekanand stayed at Madras for nine days. There he gave five major discourses. The topics of his speech were—My Revolutionary Plan, Utility of Vedanta in Indian contest, Great men of India, Our Present Task and Future of India. His invigorating and exciting force created a storm like turbulence among the people and transmitted unlimited energy into the weak bodies and minds of people. In his speech titled 'Future of India', first of all he recounted the glorious past of India—"This is the very same ancient land where before going to any other country, wisdom had made its residence. This is the very same India wherein the current of spirituality is reflected in its rivers with sea-like size, wherein eternal Himalayas have line up and the peaks of these mountain ranges seem like enjoying the secret sights in the heaven. This is the very India where greatest of saints traversed and got their footprints imprinted on its land. This is the land where the secrets of inner world and human nature took shape. The concept of eternity of soul, existence of omnipresent God Almighty in every being of the universe took birth in this land. And it is on this land that Philosophies and ideals of religion attained ultimate progress. This is that very land, wherein religions and philosophies took birth like frequent floods and irrigated the whole world. This is the very same land where again such tidal waves will emerge that will transmit energy and lividness into the body of inert people. This is that very India which in spite of suffering from centuries of shocks, foreign attacks and transforming through thousands of systems and rituals stood upright enduring everything. It is the very same India which is still standing straight and firm like a mountain with its indestructible courage.

The memories of our past is the foundation of our self respect and Swami Vivekanand wanted to build the future on this very foundation. Many people think that by glancing at the past the mind and heart of a person gets degraded. It will not in any way help in human progression. Hence one should forget his past and move ahead in accordance with the need of the time and build the future on a new note. But Swamiji did not believed this. Criticising this point of view Swamiji said—"The future is constructed on the past foundation. Hence as far as possible look at your past and get inspiration from it and try to make India brighter, better and higher than the past. Our forefathers were great. First of all we should remember that. We should understand what we are made up of and what blood is running in our veins. We should have faith in that blood and our past actions as well. With faith on our past and knowledge about the glory of our past we will be able to lay the foundation of India which would be better than the earlier. It is true that sometimes India has passed through a state of degradation and miserable condition, but I do not give much significance to them. We all know about them. It is necessary to have such phases. A huge tree gave birth to a beautiful ripe fruit, the fruit fell on the ground, got withered and damaged. The seedling grown from this destruction could be possibly bigger than the earlier tree. The age of degradation that we passed through was extremely essential. From that state of degradation future India is going to originate. It has already sprouted, new leaves have already come out and the basis of an all powerful tree has already been laid."

Keeping in view the needs of contemporary India he stated a new thing about religion, Gods and Goddesses, worship and prayers—"For the forth coming 50 years, our mother land, Mother India should be worshipped. For the period if we erase out the thoughts and images of other deities, it would do not harm. Divert our complete attention on the very God. Our country is our universal God. Its hands are spread all overs, its legs are spread all over and its ears are spread all over. Just believe that other Gods and Goddesses are in a state of slumber. We are unnecessarily running behind the Gods and Goddesses whom we are unable to see and the huge Goddess who is spread all over us, we are unable to see it worshipping it. When we will worship this visible God then only we will be capable of worshipping other Gods and Goddesses otherwise not. _

"*Janani Janmabhumishcha Swargadapi Gariyasi*" – Mother and the motherland are greater than heaven—many greatmen said thus and honoured the motherland like their own mother. But till now no body had the courage to say that our motherland India is our only deity whose worship in every possible way is our first duty. No other God enjoys significance in comparison to this God. In this context Swami Vivekanand do not fit into any category—not of a Sannyasi, not a Yogi, not a religious propagator, not a social reformer. He was a true patriot in the real sense of the term. The focus of his religion and worship was to serve his motherland which had been experiencing subjugation, domination, weakness and poverty for hundreds of years.

Swami Vivekanand believe that every nation has a heart and its thousands of arms have singular strength in it. In a letter to one of his devoted friends, Swamiji had written from America, "The difference between East and West lies in the fact that they are one nation and we are not. Education and civilization are widely spread over there but in India it is not so. Both the countries have a wide gulf in the condition of the lower strata of society. How was it possible for the English to win over India so easily? Because they were united as a nation and we are not." Swamiji wanted to see India as a unified nation. He wanted that we should consider ourselves to be Indian—not as Bengali, Bihari, Punjabi, Marathi, Gujarati or Madrasi. "If we think of any good it should be for the whole nation—our thought, action and sight everything should be devoted to the nation as a whole." In another letter from America to a friend in India, Swamiji wrote—"My sole ambition in life is to cause a change in the wheel of time so that lofty ideals and supreme thoughts reach the doorstep of every individual and every man and woman is able to take his or her own decision. By collecting the chemical compound (education) they can attain any shape according to nature. What he meant by chemical compound was education." In his view the only solution to remove country's poverty was education. An educated person can think of his own good or bad, the society's good or bad and the country's good or bad and can work accordingly.

Youths of Madras showed great interest in assisting Swamiji in his work. Some renowned people of Madras gave him a request letter to stay in Madras for some more days so as to set up a centre for propogation of his thoughts. Swamiji appreciated this proposal but he did not want to prolong his stay there. Hence he promised them to provide all sorts of help in their endeavour by calling a Guru brother from Calcutta. Within a few days Swami Ramakrishnanand took the responsibilities of campaigns in Madras on his shoulders. During his nine days stay in Madras, innumerable invitations came to Swamiji from Calcutta. The birth anniversary of Guru Sri Ramakrishna was also getting nearer. It was impossible for Swamiji to leave the opportunity to participate in the birth anniversary celebrations of his Guru after such a long gap. At last with heavy heart and tears in their eyes, people of Madras bade goodbye to their beloved Swamiji on 15 February. Swamiji's next destination was of course Calcutta.

Swami Vivekanand was greatly tired by his travels, welcome meetings, delivering discourses, conversations and interviews. Hence, he decided to undertake his journey to Calcutta by plane. In the meantime Lokmanya Bal Gangadhar Tilak invited Swamiji to Pune. Swamiji was very much keen to meet him but his physical condition made him helpless and he could not go to Pune.

Grand preparations were on in Calcutta for the welcome of Swamiji. Like in Madras, roads and streets were decorated with flowers, leaves, colourful papers, flap, etc. Welcome gates were made at many places. Swamiji alighted from the plane at Khidirpur. From there a special train was ready to take him to Sealdah. At 7:30 in the morning his train reached Sealdah station. There thousands of people were waiting anxiously to welcome him. As soon as the train came to a halt the crowd hailed 'Swami Vivekanand ki Jai'. It reverberated through the station premises. Swamiji was standing at the gate of the bogey itself with his hands folded.

The crowd competed with each other to attain the blessings of Swamiji. The members of the welcome committee under the leadership of Sh. Narendranath Sen (Editor of the newspaper Indian Mirror) helped Swamiji, Mr and Mrs. Xavier and Gudwin. A specially decorated chariot to be drawn by four horses was kept ready at the station entrance. Swamiji and the guests accompanying him were made to sit on the same. The chariot began to move towards Ripen College. A long procession of people accompanied it. The chariot had only moved a few steps ahead that some youngsters detached the horses from the chariot and they themselves began to draw it.

A group of musicians playing Indian instrumental music was going ahead of the chariot. The chariot reached the premises of Ripen College amidst the melody of musical instruments and the loud slogans hailing Swamiji. The members of Welcome Committee ensured proper refreshment and rest for Swamiji and his European disciples. But Swamiji was not the person interested in any kind of rest. He conversed with some scholars during the period stipulated for his rest. Innumerable people came with complete devotion to have a glimpse of Swamiji. After this Swamiji along with some of his Guru brothers were invited for a welcome function at the residence of Rai Pasupathinath at Baag Bazar. Day gave to way to evening. The members of the Welcome Committee had made arrangements for the temporary accommodation of Swamiji and his western disciples at the farm house of Sh. Gopallal at Kasipur. The place used to be crowded daily by visitors. Some scholarly people who came to visit Swamiji entered into a conversation on Vedanta philosophy with him. Almost every night, Swamiji went to Alam Bazar Mutt and discussed his future plans and proposals with Guru brothers. He received invitation from every nook and corner of India requesting him to oblige people by a personal visit and lecture.

After almost a week's rest, on 28 February Swamiji was given a grand welcome at the palatial residence of Sh. Raja Radhakant Dev at Shobha Bazar. It was a huge public meeting. Almost 5000 people were present there which included renowned scholars, politicians, renowned advocates, doctors, writers, educationists, saints, kings and high ranking European officers of Calcutta. The meeting was chaired by King Vinay Krishna Dev. As soon as Swamiji approached the stage sound of cheers and applause deafened the atmosphere. The chairman read out the appreciation and handed over the certificate to Swamiji on a special plate made of silver.

The commendation certificate appreciated his efforts in spreading Hindu religion and Indian civilization and culture abroad. Swamiji was born in the city of Calcutta and he grew up playing in that very soil. His return back to the place and the appreciation that he received at the land where he was born made him overwhelmed with emotions. Words heavy with emotions flowed from his lips: "Human beings want to merge its personal existence with that of the existence of Almighty, he wants to get detached from the familial relations. He wants to detach himself from all worldly attachments and run away from the world. He tries to renounce all physical aactivities. He tries to forget that he is a human being in flesh and blood. But a soft voice speaks within him which he hears constantly, whether in East or West, your motherland is like heaven. I have come before you not as a sannyasi for religious propogation but has come to you to talk like a child as before. I wish even today to sit on the dusty road of this city and talk to you like a child and disclosing every thought in my mind to you. You people have addressed me as a 'unique brother' and for this I am grateful to you. Yes I am your brother and you all are my brothers."

Swamiji was not tired explaining the meaning of 'Janani Janmabhumischa Swargadapi Gariyasi.' Every son of a mother looks after his own mother and all her comforts, but there are rare sons who looks after the motherland. Swamiji called the youngsters for this very service. He wanted to muster public power for that. And that was possible only when public had confidence on self. Hence he discussed Vedanta at every place wherever he addressed a public gathering. During his Calcutta speech Swamiji said—"Every individual category have different systems of accomplishing their mission. Some makes politics, some social improvement and some others take some other issue as basis for their working system. British would perhaps understand religion through the medium of politics. American would understand religion through the medium of social service. But Hindus will understand politics, social science and every other topic only

Swami Vivekanand: A Biography

through the means of religion. It is here that huge gulf becomes evident between other philosophies and that of Indian philosophy. Every one whether having faith in any school of thought has a firm belief that the whole power is concentrated in the soul. Our soul is an eternal power house. The only thing is to spread its power all over. It is the basis of indestructible power. Nobody can destroy it. It is waiting for the clarion call to display its never ending power. Devotion within us is what helps in echoing the call. Devotion creates melody in the string of the heart and brings out the sound of this call. The person who has devotion towards his country, his country's Vedanta philosophy, he can turn impossible into possibilities."

Swamiji challenged the youths of Bengal by cautioning them towards their duties: "We have to win over the whole universe. Yes we should do that. India has to win over the whole world or will get itself destroyed. There is no other alternative. The sign of life is very much expansive. We should come out of our narrow borders, spread our heart outwards and show that we are alive. Otherwise, we will have to die in this very degraded condition."

Here victory does not mean materialistic win but moral victory. According to Vivekanand, our ancestors have left with us invaluable gems in the form of religion and the western nations are keen to achieve benefit from them. During his speech he kept on reiterating that we should not exist like a frog within a narrow well but go to western countries and make the people there aware of our spiritual knowledge, our Vedanta philosophy and in place of it learn science from them. By the process of give and take only the feeling of self respect remains. Otherwise the way we stand subdued in front of developed countries, we will remain so forever. In the words of Swamiji: "Will we continue the process of taking or borrowing from others? Are we going to sit with westerners and learn religion also along with other things? Yes we can learn the work of factory and production from them and even more but we should also teach them something and that is our religion, our spirituality. In our own country, our ancestors have left this heavenly nectar and lakhs of people outside India are begging to get a mere drop of this nectar. How can we know about it? For this we have to go outside India. In exchange of our spirituality, in exchange of our strange philosophies we should attain the wonderful facts from western countries. By remaining as student forever, our objective cannot be fulfilled, we should become teachers for others. Without equality it is impossible to achieve friendship."

The people of Bengal were considered to be more emotional, imaginative and worshippers of art. On one hand they received much fame and renown and on the other some people were made the butt of humour considering them to be of the weaker section. Discussing about this, Swamiji addressed his highly emotive Bengali brothers and said—*"Uttishtatha Jagrat Prapya Varanibodhith'*—Get up, awaken and keep on marching ahead till you fulfill your ambition. Youths of Calcutta, get up, the auspicious time has arrived. Everything is getting opened before you on its own. Be brave, don't be afraid.....awake. Your motherland needs the supreme sacrifice. And this work will be accomplished by youngsters only. This work is for those who are firm in their decision, have leadership qualities and strong. In other parts of India people have intellect as well as money, but the fire of spirit is present only in our land. We should bring that out. Therefore, Oh youths of Calcutta instil excitement in your blood. Don't think that you people are poor and you do not have any friend. Have you ever seen that money makes human being? But it is the human being that makes money. This whole universe is inherent with the power, strength and trust of human beings."

It will not be much difficult to imagine what impact these words had had on those who heard them. Of course they people would have received an information about the onset of a new dawn in India. Swamiji's vision pierced through their innocent eyes as he said: "Don't be afraid because if you look back to the history of mankind, it will be found that whatever strengths have been developed till now have emerged from within a common place fellow. The most influential persons in this universe have all emerged from the common men. And history repeats itself. Don't be afraid of anything. You can do wonders. The moment you get intimidated you will lose all your strength. The main cause of sorrow in the world is fear itself. It is the most important sin. This fear is the cause of our sorrows and fearlessness can help us attain heaven within a second."

The students of Calcutta were greatly impressed by

Swamiji's talks. Swami Vivekanand was well versed in the art of attracting students. With them he used to discuss not only spirituality but physical and mental health, sports, education and many other topics. At the same time he dexterously instilled within them a feeling of love and confidence towards the ideals of our ancient civilization and culture. According to him, the reason of mental and physical weakness among youths was child marriage. It destroys human strength. He wanted to organize some unmarried youths who would wholly sacrifice their lives for pubic welfare activities. But Swamiji did not achieve much success in his endeavour. Only a few handful of people could become his confidante in social service. But whosoever came to him, they became his for ever.

Once, a young man affiliated to the Theosophical Society came to him. His mind was in great turbulence. He in an unhappy state said that he had been in search of truth for quite some days. He sat in front of the deity with closed eyes for hours together, worshipped, prayed and indulged in yoga and meditation but still he could not attain peace of mind. He could not concentrate on anything. At last he resorted to spend time in mediation in an isolated room. But was still unsuccessful. He was unable to find a way to discover truth. Swamiji listened to the youth in a calm manner. With loving and sympathetic tone in his voice Swamiji said: "My dear, if you would listen and follow my advise you will have to open the doors of your room. Instead of remaining with closed eyes you will have to glance all over. There are hundreds of poor and helpless people in the vicinity of your house. With your power of understanding you should help them and serve them. Whosoever is ill and does not have anyone to look after them, for them you should bring medicines, and provide other necessities and take care of them. Those who do not have anything to eat, you should provide them meals. Those who are ignorant, you should provide them with education." Swamiji considered service to public as the most important duty of a human being. This is more important and valuable than every other endeavour such as prayer, meditation and worship. He always used to tell his Guru brothers that it is not appropriate for today's sannyasis to sit inside hutments and try to achieve self-realisation. Today's sannyasis are social servants. They should stand in his full of action and help the whole mankind. He should wipe away the miseries of poor and helpless. Giving food to hungry, clothes to those who do not have it and medicine for the ill are the tasks he should do. He should continue fighting against the evils of poverty and ignorance in India till they are totally rooted out. The only and effective medicine for the ailment is education. Swamiji always used to tell his Guru brothers that if in accomplishing this good work, the sannyasi community have to go to hell instead of attaining redemption then they should happily accept lit. *'Bahujan Hitaya, Sukhai'* was the teaching of Sri Ramakrishna. If his disciples cannot sacrifice them for the welfare of public then what is the difference between them and common people. This comment on the part of Swamiji had a deep impact on his disciples and Guru brothers. Swami Ramakrishnanand had been engaged in prayer, worship and meditation at the Alam Bazar Mutt for the past 12 years and at the request of Swamiji he went to the south for the propagation of Vedanta and other social services. Swami Akhandanand went to Murshidabad to serve people suffering from famine.

Swami Vivekanand's name and fame had spread far and wide. But he was untouched with any kind of pride. His humility won so many hearts. Once as he was conversing with some honourable men from the city, nephew of Sri Ramakrishna, Sh. Ram Lal Chattopadyay came to meet him. Swamiji and other Guru brothers used to call him Ram Lal Dada. As soon as Swami saw Ram Lal Dada, he got up from his seat, said obeisance to the guest and asked him to take seat. Swami Vivekanand strolling across the room said— 'Guruvat Guruputreshu!' Guru's son or any of his relatives is equally honourable as Guru.

According to Swamiji, without devotion towards ancient culture no country can make progress. But he was not ready to accept everything in the name of tradition and culture blindly. Whether ancient, medieval or modern thoughts, he applied his rationale before accepting any of them.

Once, a committee engaged in safeguarding cows approached Swamiji for funds. They said that they purchased cows from butchers. In addition they looked after ailing and old cows. Swamiji in turn asked them what their committee had been doing for the thousands of people dying of famine in central India. The reply of the committee was that those people were suffering the sins of their previous life and the committee cannot do anything for them as their work was only to look after and safeguard the interest of cows. Hearing this Swamiji turned red with anger. Controlling his fury, in clear words he stated that he had no sympathy towards such institutes which is least bothered about human beings dying of hunger and concerned for animals and spending thousands of rupees on them. He clearly, stated that after providing food for the hungry, clothes for the naked and medicines for the ill, if something is left then he will give it to birds and animals. Hearing Swamiji's words the representatives of the committee felt embarrassed and returned back.

A few days after reaching Calcutta, the birth anniversary celebrations of Sri Ramakrishna was held at Dakshineswar in a grand manner. On that day, Swamiji reached Dakshineswar along with his western disciples. At Dakshineswar memories of the past came alive in Swamiji's mind. The days that he spent with Guru dev and other Guru brothers enlivened in his mind. Those who came to meet him requested him to speak a few words. He himself wanted to present a discourse. But the noisy environment was not congenial for that.

After the celebrations Swamiji gave a powerful speech at the Star Theater. The topic was 'Vedanta everywhere'. By explaining the origin and development of Vedanta, he tried to make people understand as to how the upper caste Brahmins utilized it according to their whims. He criticized this act on the part of Brahmins. First of all he stated how the teachers of Vedanta philosophy made interpretations of the topic from time to time in different ways. As a result of this, many opponents sprang up, and slowly and gradually people distanced themselves from spiritual meditation, the most difficult but loftiest of thoughts of Vedanta.

People owned and followed the practices as mentioned in Puranas and other ancient scriptures because according to Brahmin Pandits those practices were much easier to be followed by common men to help them redeem themselves from every sins and secure them a place in heaven. Swamiji said—"Today kitchen is our temple, the utensils are our gods and our religious is 'do not touch me, I am pious'." In the light of Vedanta philosophy, Swamiji gave an insight into the contemporary rituals and tradition. Later on Swamiji was highly critical of the 'Kul Guru' tradition being practiced in Bengal. He said—"The Kul Guru (teacher of the clan), even though he is a fool devoid of any knowledge regarding the various shastras, why are we supposed to attain knowledge from them. The custom of 'Kul Guru' is a kind of religious business. In front of thousands of audiences Swamiji declared that it is the duty of every individual to detach every existing social and religious beliefs and superstitions. After this he did not give any pubic discourses anywhere in Calcutta. Continuous speech and crowd made Swamiji sick. Now he wanted to take some rest so that he could plan out his future endeavours.

But in Calcutta how he could have enjoyed peace of mind. As long as he stayed there, people came to him to discuss Vedanta philosophy. Once some Gujaratis who were great scholars of Vedas and theologies came to Swamiji for discussing Shastras. They gathered around Swamiji and one by one shot one question after another in Sanskrit. They were speaking incessantly. Swami listened to there questions in a calm manner and answered their questions. Once Swamiji made a grammatical error. At once the team of scholar made fun of Swamiji and began to laugh. Swamiji understood that he was being made the butt of humour. Instantly Swamiji rectified his mistake and said—"I am slaves to scholars, I seek forgivance for this mistake on my part. The scholars were quite happy with Swamiji's humility. Arguments and counter arguments went on for some time. At last they felt satisfied with Swamiji's knowledge. After the debate they indulged in happy conversation before taking leave of Swamiji. As those scholars rose to leave, some other guests who were present there asked them about their interaction with Swamiji. The chief among the scholars who was an old fellow answered that even though Swamiji do not have good command over Sanskrit grammer there is no doubt regarding his grasp over the obscure facts of Shastras. His command over Shastras is undoubtedly beyond comparison.

Continuous hard work, made Swamiji ill. Doctors advised him complete rest. But even then he ignored his ill health conditions and was accomplishing various plans that he had in his mind. His first plan was to establish a mutt in the lap of Himalayas. He wanted to lay the foundation of religious and social work in the name of Ramakrishna Mission. But the doctors put strict restrictions on his physical and mental stress. As a result, he was compelled to leave Calcutta at the earliest and his tours to other parts of the country were also cancelled. Swamiji went to Darjeeling along with the Xavier couple. The king of Burdwan Nagar gave a portion of his Rose Bank residency to them for stay. When Swamiji reached there Swami Brahmanand, Gudwin, Dr.Turnbull, Girish Chandra Ghosh, Swami Turiyanand, Swami Gyananand and three disciples from Madras joined him at Darjeeling. There Swamiji got complete mental and physical rest. In the morning and evening he strolled around the mountain ranges in Himalayas, visited the Buddhist monasteries in the neighbourhood and conversed with people who loved him. Swamiji stayed at Darjeeling for about two months but there was no much improvement in his health. Swamiji found it difficult to spend time in such a manner. Hence he returned back to Calcutta after two months. He also got an excuse to return back to Calcutta soon. The king of Khetri. Ajit Singh had returned back to his residency after his foreign trip. When he came to know about Swamiji's ill health condition, he had come to Calcutta to meet Swamiji. This gave Swamiji an opportunity to return back to Calcutta. The king of Khetri along with his major ministers went to Alam Bazar Mutt. The residents of the Mutt and other Guru brothers extended a hearty welcome to the King and his ministers. The King of Khetri, was not satisfied with his meeting with Swamiji. He wanted to take Swamiji along with him to Khetri. But the doctors had kept Swamiji under strict observation. He wanted him to take complete bed rest. Hence Swamiji assured him that he will visit him in the near future and bid farewell to him.

Swamiji did not return back to Darjeeling. The life at Alam Bazaar Mutt along with other Guru brothers had special attraction for him. Memories of the past came across his eyes. Imaginative Vivekanand got lost in those images frequently. The Kali Mandir at Dakshineswar was only a short distance from Alam Bazar Mutt. Swamiji felt the presence of Gurudev at that place. He got renewed strength and inspiration from that very feeling. At Alam Bazar Mutt many educated youths approached Swamiji to get initiated into sannyasa. Swamiji took daily classes on Vedanta and Bhagwat Gita also. During that period the other Guru brothers raised a question regarding the integrity of one of the disciples accusing him of immoral past. Hence they did not want that person to stay in the Mutt. They were of the opinion that if he would stay there it would have a negative impact on others too. Swamiji did not endorse this view on the part of his Guru Brothers. He said: "What is this? If we stay away from sinner then who will safeguard them. Moreover, the very fact that he has come to this ashram to attain sannyasa reinforces his pure intentions. In such a situation we should surely help him. Even if some one is bad, impious, you should try to reform his character. If you cannot do so what good is it to wear this saffron? Then why did you took the form of a teacher?"

This issue was raised earlier also. In the year 1896 when Swamiji was in Switzerland, the birth anniversary celebrations of Gurudev Sri Ramakrishna was being organized at Dakshineswar. On the occasion many prostitutes visited the temple to offer worship and prayers. Many people objected to it and wrote letter to Swamiji opposing this. Swamiji, in reply, wrote to one of his Guru brothers Ramakrishnanand: "If prostitutes do not have permission to go to such a great place of pilgrimage as Dakshineswar, then where will they go? God appears specially for the sinners and not for the pious ones. The one who thinks that they are prostitutes are the lowest among men. The number of such people should be as less as possible for the benefit of society. Is it possible for such people who consider the caste, sex and trade of others to understand God in the real sense? My prayer to the lord is that thousands of prostitutes should come there and bow their heads on the feet of the Lord and if not a single upright man come here, there is no harm in that. Let prostitutes come, drunkards come, robbers come, all come—the doors of the Lord are always wide open."

Continuous efforts without rest had made Swamiji physically weak, but his unlimited self-confidence kept on drawing him. His physical condition was a cause of concern and worry for the other Guru brothers and disciples. Doctors who were treating him advised him to take rest at some place with cold climatic conditions. In the meantime,

Swamiji had received invitation from various renowned and wealthy residents from Almora. Not for himself, but for India his physical well-being was essential. Hence he decided to take rest for a few days in the laps of Himalayas to regain his health. Though he was not wishing to leave his responsibilities, considering the gravity of his ill-health he proceeded to Almora for the sake of his health.

On 6th May 1896, Swamiji departed for Almora from Calcutta. Some of Swamiji's Guru brothers and disciples accompanied him till Calcutta to see him off. Swamiji was extended a hearty welcome by the Hindu residents of Almora. They came to receive Swamiji at a place called Lodia. People made Swamiji sit on a decorated horse and accompanied him along in a huge procession. Women folks rained flowers and rice on him from rooftops as a mark of honour. The procession hailed Swamiji and they reached the place where the meeting was to be held. The excited public of Almora were not aware of the physical and mental condition of ailing Swamiji. Two commendation certificates were read out at the meeting. Swamji had been longing to spend the rest of his life in the laps of the Himalayas. He counted to establish an ashram there to educate and propogate the tenets of Hinduism. During his speech he paid tributes to the power of endurance of the Himalayas. He said that the Himalayas was the dreamland of our ancestors where Goddess Parvati took birth. It is that pious place where the truth seekers would like to spend the rest of their lives. On the peaks of these divine mountains, inside these caves and on the banks of these rivers the great saints have invented the most secretive thoughts and emotions. And today we are able to see how even a part of these thoughts have gained so much of significance among the westerners and the most renowned of scholars have called it beyond comparison. Swamiji, declaring the Himalayas to be the epitome of detachment and sacrifice, expressed his hope that in the future when the fights among different religions will come to an end, then people from all corners of the world will take shelter under the Himalayan ranges for the sake of peace. In the same manner as our forefathers took shelter under these mountains at the end of their lives, all the powerful souls on this earth will get attracted towards the Himalayas. It will happen when the differences between different religions will become a thing of the past and people will become aware that there is only one religion and that is the realization of the Supreme Being. According to him, the most supreme memories of the Hindu religion are connected with the Himalayan ranges, hence he was keen on setting up an ashram in the laps of these mountain ranges. "If the Himalayas were to be detached from the religious history of India, then the left over will be something very less. Hence a centre should be set up here itself."

Swamiji's attention got drawn towards peace and meditation, time and again but his life was action oriented and he was keen on doing action. For some days, of course, he stayed inert without doing anything. A renowned businessman of Almora town, Lala Badrisahai was very insistent on making Swamiji, his Guru brothers and disciples as his guest. He made them stay at his farm house almost 20 miles away from Almora and looked after their every comforts. Swamiji's health began to recover slowly and gradually. He went for strolls in the morning and the evening and his daily chores also included prayer, meditation and religious discussion with Guru brothers and disciples. But this routine could continue for only a few days. Even though he was away in the remote jungles of Himalayas, Swamiji was not cut off from the outside world. The felicitation ceremonies after his return from foreign trips still continued. The day by day increasing fame of Swamiji, the unity among Hindus, awareness regarding their religion—all this made the American missionaries jealous. After Swamiji's success in the World Parliament of Religions, there arose a wave of religious awakening among Indians. The American missionaries were unable to put a curb on it. They began to make false propaganda against Swamiji. But nobody in India could be entrapped in their words. Hence they diverted all their strength in spreading false propaganda against Swamiji in America so that in the absence of Swamiji there, his endeavours of spreading Vedanta could be thoroughly uprooted.

The president of the World Parliament of Religions at Chicago, Dr. Barouge also had his due share in spreading such a false propaganda. Dr. Barouge had come to India with a view to tour India before Swamiji had returned back from his foreign trip. Swamiji had written from London a letter to one of his Guru brothers to extend an appropriate welcome. Hence he was given a hearty welcome in Calcutta. But he was unable to win over the hearts of the people with his speech and behaviour. In this regard Swamiji wrote a letter to one of his friends in Chicago—"I wrote a letter to my country man to extend an appropriate welcome to Dr. Barouge. They gave a hearty welcome to him but he could not instil any sort of inspiration in the hearts of the people. I am responsible for this." Amidst the waves of Swamiji's name and fame, the personality of Dr. Barouge got lost. He was not able to come to terms with it. Hence, the heart that showed unending love and consideration to Swamiji in Chicago, the very same heart burned in jealousy and in a bid to assassinate Swamiji's character made false accusations against him. After returning back to his own country he gave assistance to the missionaries against Swamiji. In America, he gave critical remarks about Swamiji to the press and made false accusations against him. He said that Swamiji made derogatory remarks against American women. As a result of all these, a mass movement against Swamiji took birth in America. Many newspapers and magazines published spicy gossips about Swamiji. In India also certain newspapers published critical comments about Swamiji. The news reached Swamiji's ears too, which eroded the peaceful spiritual atmosphere of the Himalayas. But Swamiji remained calm and unaffected just like the stoic Himalayas. He was well aware of the truth that propagators of new ethics have to face many obstructions and oppositions and at many a times have to put even their life at stake. This was not a new thing for Swamiji.

In a letter to a friendly disciple Swamiji wrote about Dr. Barouge's unsuccessful visit to India on 28th April, 1897—"I hope that Dr. Barouge might have reached America by now. Poor thing, he had come here to spread fundamental Christianity but nobody paid any attention to him. The only thing was that they welcomed him heartily and that too on my directions. Moreover he is a person with strange character. I have heard that the warmth and joy extended by the people of my motherland on my return to India made him mad with jealousy. Nevertheless, you should have send someone who is more intelligent than him. Because of Dr. Barouge, the World Parliament of Religions, has become a sort of drama in the eyes of Indians. No nation on this earth can ever guide Hindus in spiritual education. And the strangest of things is that so many people from the Western World come to this country and foolishly argue that Christians are rich and powerful but not the Hindus, hence Christianity is superior as compared to Hinduism. In my opinion Western countries are superior in terms of scientific culture but as far as spiritual education is concerned, they are mere kids. Physical knowledge can give materialistic prosperity but spiritual knowledge is permanent for life."

On 9th July Swamiji wrote a letter from Almora to Mary Hale, in which he wrote about the false propaganda being organized against him and accepted the fact that once he had made discussion about gossip mongering and rumour spreading qualities inherent in some American women. He thought that the missionaries were utilising this one lapse on his part in mustering support against him. "What happened was that, during one of my discourses I said something about the Christian priests. In that context I made reference about the extremely religious American women and their gossip mongering nature. To spoil my work in America, the priests are making noise that I have made derogatory remarks about entire Americans, because they know that whatever is said against me will be a cause of happiness for the entire Americans." By saying so Swamiji not only made his stance clear but also emphasised on the fact that America should not be scared by any sort of criticism especially when they themselves are always keen on criticising others. He further wrote:—

"My dear, even if I have made some remarks about Americans, will that be able to purify even a small portion of what these people have told about Indian mothers and sisters. American Christians, both men and women call us barbaric and look down on us with a feeling of hatred, will the water from seven oceans be able to wash off that behaviour? What harm have we done to them? Americans should first develop patience to bear critical comments about them, then only should they dare to criticize others."

Swami Vivekanand make it very clear that he was least bothers about the opinion that the Americans formed about him. He wrote—"I am not indebted to them in any manner. Other than your family, Mrs. Bull and the Legate family and two three other well wishers, who else have done any good to me? In order to convert my thoughts into practice who have given a helping hand to me? Many a times I was face to face with death during the course of my efforts. I had to spend all my strength in America so that people there became more generous and spiritual. In England I worked for just six months. There nobody condemned me, except for one person and that too due to an act on the part of an American woman and my English friends were satisfied to hear that." Making assurances about himself he wrote to Mary Hale—"My dear, don't be bothered about me. People of America are quite big. And even if the Americans behave harshly with me, it will be to my good. Whatever be the case, I am quite happy and satisfied with my work. I am least bothered by what people say. Those people are like ignorant children. Their perspective is very narrow. Why should I, who have attained self realization of the soul and have understood the meaninglessness of the entire materialistic world, get deviated by these childish talks? Do you think that I am the kind of person who will back out?"

Vivekanand was totally confident that in spite of whatever the missionaries did, a wave of awakening had spread across India and that nobody can put a curb on it. In the same letter he further wrote: "I know that my work has been accomplished and that a maximum of three or four years of my life are left. I do not have any wishes regarding my redemption and I have never wished of any worldly comforts. My only desire is that my machinery be useful and strong. The very thought that I have established a machinery for the welfare of human beings that no power can ever destroy, will let me have sound sleep without any anxiety regarding the future. My sole ambition is to take birth again and again and suffer thousands of sorrows and worship that singular entity which dominates all the souls, whose rule is truly dominant and on whom I have my complete faith."

Swami Vivekanand had by then began to believe that only three-four years of his life were left. Hence his mental condition remained somewhat detached. He had the feeling that his work was almost complete. His major task was to awaken his countrymen who were in deep slumber. He was confident that this work will continue at the desired speed and his presence was not essential for it. To a letter to one of his favourite disciples, Sister Nivedita (Ms. Nobel), he wrote—"It is true. We are got entangled in a web and the sooner we get out of it, the better. I have already witnessed the truth and even if the body gets destroyed I am least bothered."

During the period, Murshidabad was under the grip of a severe famine. Swami Akhandananda was both mentally and physically involved in relieving the sorrows of people affected by the famine. He sent more disciples to Almora for providing relief to the victims of the famine. Swami Vivekanand was becoming impatient to go there and help the people. But his doctors did not allow him to go there. Vedanta education was going on in full swing in Calcutta and Madras. Swamiji was satisfied with its popularity. The propogational works being organized by Swami Abhedananda in England and by Swami Sharadanand in America in spite of all kinds of obstructions on the part of the missionaries, gave a sense of peace of mind to Swamiji. A new kind of energy and vigour vibrated in his ailing body. He felt as if some invisible force was providing him strength to accomplish his tasks. Still he experienced the shadow of death hovering around him. He became overwhelmed with the feeling that only a few days were left and within that short time span he was left with so many tasks to be accomplished. He told his disciples that in spite of being not totally well, he cannot stay inert. He was keen on touring North India and make people aware of the Vedanta philosophy. He wanted to attain both mental and physical energy to accomplish his task and attain fulfillment. His doctors wanted him to stay at Almora and take rest for some more days, but in face of his decision the advise of doctors proved futile. His sudden decision to tour North India made his disciples and Guru brothers worried. Swamiji's decision was final and nobody had the courage to bring any change in it.

The news about Swamiji's departure from Almora spread all over. The people of Almora were longing to listen to Swamiji's discourses but his ill-health conditions restrained them from putting pressure on him. When people came to know that Swamiji was about to leave Almora, they put forth a request before him. Swamiji gave his consent and gave speech on Vedanta philosophy in simple Hindi language at a programme organized at the local District school. People were overwhelmed at hearing his speech and his name and fame spread all the more. The Englishmen staying there also heard about Swamiji and became curious to hear him. As a result, a programme was organized under the chairmanship of Gurkha Army Corps' Col. Puli at the 'English Club'. The meeting place was crowded with local Englishmen and high ranking Indian officials. The topic of Swamiji's speech was— "Vedic teachings: Theory & Practice." Swamiji began his speech with the origin of Modes of Worship, then the forms of Vedas and their characteristic features and in the end put a light on the relationship between soul and the Almighty. By the end of the speech, Swamiji was so overwhelmed with emotions that the whole atmosphere turned spiritual. His disciple, Ms. Muller, who was present there, later on wrote— "For some times it was felt as if the audience all have got unified into a single entity. All those who were present there, as if merged with the light of spirituality that emanated with great force from the body of Swamiji. They stood as if they were spellbound and lost."

After spending about two-and-a-half months in Almora, on 7th August, 1897, in spite of ill health, Swamiji resumed his journey. He had received many invitations from Punjab and Kashmir. He reached Bareilly on 9th August, accompanied by his Guru brothers and disciples. No sooner he reached Bareilly, he was again gripped with severe fever. The Welcome Committee of Bareilly had made good arrangements for his stay and food at the Bareilly Club House. Swamiji stayed there for four days. He was not totally relieved from fever. In spite of physical weakness he continued his work with total devotion. In addition to the morning and evening session of religious talks, he encouraged the followers of Arya Samaj to continue their social reform movements to materialize their ideals and principles. He expressed his desire to form a committee of students. On 12th August, he made up his mind to leave Bareilly. But in the afternoon, after he had his lunch, again Swamiji contracted fever. But he did not drop his journey. The same night he departed for Ambala. There, he stayed for a week. At the station, he met Mr. and Mrs. Xavier. The people of Ambala also extended a hearty welcome to Swamiji. After reaching Ambala, Swamiji was totally cured of his fever and he accomplished his work in a speedy manner and held meetings and interactive sessions with

Muslims, Brahmo Samajis, Arya Samajis and members of other communities.

Swamiji's next destination was Amritsar and from there he went to Rawalpindi. Everywhere, he was extended a hearty welcome. Because of his ill health, he could not address any huge gatherings in spite of his keen desire to do so. From Rawalpindi he departed to Mari. His next destination was Kashmir via Baramula. Xavier was accompanying along with him. At Mari, Xavier became ill. He was unable to endure the tough journey. Hence, he stayed with his wife at Mari. One day before Swamiji's stipulated Kashmir tour, he send Swamiji an envelope containing 800 rupees as part of his Kashmir expenses and sought excuse for his unability to accompany Swamiji to Kashmir. Swamiji was greatly surprised to find such a big amount of money. He made mental calculations that the amount was more than what he required to undertake his journey. Hence he himself went to Xavier and requested him to take back half the amount. The next day Swamiji and others who accompanied him departed to Baramullah on a horse cart (tonga). From Baramulla they reached Srinagar on a boat. At Srinagar arrangement for Swamiji's stay was made at the house of the Chief Judge of Srinagar, Rishivar Mukhopadhyay. On the third day, after reaching there, Swamiji was honoured at the palace of the King of Kashmir, Amar Singh. One of King Amar Singh's officials requested Swamiji to visit the palace of the king's younger brother, King Ram Singh as he was very curious to meet Swamiji. The very next day Swamiji appeared in the court of King Ram Singh along with his co-travellers. The King gave due honour to Swamiji. He got up from his throne and made Swamiji sit there. The religious discussion continued for over two hours. They made discussions about how to improve the condition of Indian Citizens. The minister of King Amar Singh made arrangement of house boats for the comfortable stay of Swamiji and recovery from ill health. On these house boats he toured Kashmir and enjoyed the natural beauty of Kashmir. Swamiji also visited places of historical importance in Kashmir. The highly educated public of Srinagar, organized a grand ceremony and presented him with the commendation certificate. In reply Swamiji gave a small speech. But people were not happy with it. On their request,

Swami Vivekanand: A Biography

Swamiji gave a 2-hour long continuous speech in English on Hindu religion. The king of Kashmir was on a tour to Jammu. He invited Swamiji to Jammu. Hence after 20 days stay in Kashmir, he departed for Jammu.

At Jammu Station, the employees of the province were present to welcome him. He was extended the kind of welcome equivalent to that of a state guest. He was provided with a grand accommodation. After lunch, Swamiji was taken to the royal palace. There he discussed about religion in general and emphasized on the constantly degrading condition of the society. Swamiji emphasised that by following the meaningless traditions, and superstitions beliefs the country can never be on the path of progress. All these meaningless rituals and traditions lead the society to a more sinful state. The king took up the issue of sea transportation. Swamiji emphasized on the meaningfulness of foreign trips and reiterated his belief that without a visit to the Western World one could not understand the real importance of education. Only by going abroad we will be able to make an assessment of our actual condition. We can imbibe their good aspects in one own way according to our requirements and can make them aware them about their bad aspects. At the request of the King, Swamiji also addressed a public meeting. After eight days stay there, Swamiji took leave from the King of Jammu.

On 5th November, travelling via Sialhot, Swamiji along with his cotravellers reached Lahore. There the members of 'Sanatan Dharma Sabha' and a huge public had gathered to welcome him. The members of Sanatan Dharma were entrusted with the task of Swamiji's care. From the station, Swamiji was taken to the palace of King Dhyan Singh. The editor of Lahore Tribune, Narendranath Gupta interviewed Swamiji. The very next day, a meeting was organized at the open space in front of the palace. The venue was jampacked with four thousand people. Many people were still waiting at the main gate to gain entry and after waiting for a long time outside and finding it futile they had to return back in despair. The topic of Swamiji's speech was 'Our Problems'. In addition, during his short stay at Lahore, Swamiji gave three more significant speeches—'The general basis of Hindu religion', 'Devotion' and 'Vedanta'. In every speech, Swamiji expressed his concern over, how India can achieve back its past glory and position at international level. He desired that each countryman should forget every kind of differences—caste, creed, religion, etc. and unite together to serve Mother India. He reminded the people of India again and again that, inspite of religious and caste differences, they can take India to great heights by upholding their individuality. He said—"I have not come here to find out what kind of differences exist between us but I have come here to find out the land which is likely to unite us. I am making efforts to find out the basis on which all of us can remain as brothers forever. On which foundation stone will that voice, which we have been hearing from time immemorial, achieve more strength and vigour. I have come here to put before you some creative endeavours not destructive ones. Because the days of criticism have gone by, now it is time for creative endeavours. The time has become ripe for reconstruction and unification. It is time to accumulate all the scattered strength and with 'that unified strength pave the path of progression for the country, which had been a state of standstill for the past so many years. The sons of Aryans, march ahead!'

At Lahore, Swamiji got an opportunity to establish close relations with the leaders of Arya Samaj and better understand them. They people were also greatly impressed by Swamiji's thoughts and view points. Swami Vivekanand always had a cordial kind of argument about idol worship with Arya Samaj as they opposed idol worship. He was all praise and reverence for the strength of character, sacrificing nature, social welfare activities of Arya Samajis. But Swamiji openly criticized their fundamentalist views regarding caste and religion. Swamiji was never afraid of opposing anything which was against his rationale beliefs. But his style of expressing his opinion against them was so sweet that others never got offended or became angry with Swamiji. Rather, their respect for Swamiji increased all the more. Swamiji's generosity and sense of equality towards every one irrespective of their religious or caste affinity attracted Hindus and Arya Samajis alike. A former member of Arya Samaj and Swami Vivekanand's special devotee, Swami Achyudananta had written in his diary: "Once Swamiji was praising some one. At that one of his followers said: 'Swamiji, but that person does not follow you.'

Swamiji instantly replied—'To become a man, is it necessary to follow me'?"

During Swamiji's stay at Lahore, among the people who met him there was one Mathematics Professor Sh. Tirathram Goswami. He was very much impressed with the personality and oratory of Swamiji. He left his job and devoted the rest of his life in propogating Vedanta philosophy. Later on Sh. Tirathram became famous in the name of Swami Ram Tiratha. In addition to India he went to England and America and also teach Vedanta philosophy. At the time when Swamiji was leaving Lahore, Sh. Ramtiratha gifted him his golden watch which Swamiji accepted too gladly. Then the very next moment, Swamiji put back the watch into Sh. Ramtirtha's pocket and said—"I will operate this watch from here itself," Sh. Ramtirtha understood the meaning inherent in Swamiji's words.

In respect of health, the ten days that Swamiji spent at Lahore was extremely painful for him. Day and night he was busy meeting people, discussing the meaning of Shastras and giving speeches. Whatever strength he had mustered during his stay in the Himalayas had drained to a great extent. But he was satisfied with his Lahore trip as he felt he had achieved some success in his work at Lahore. It was not an easy task to win over the hearts of Arya Samajis in Punjab. But Swamiji achieved success in his attempt beyond expectations. But he was still not satisfied. He felt that the people of Punjab had no inclination towards spirituality. Once he said that the land irrigated by the five rivers were arid in terms of spirituality. He wanted to instil the flow of devotion in the soul of the people in Punjab. Devoted worship of God has the capacity to make human beings more sensitive. As long as people are insensitive, social welfare is impossible. Swamiji could not prolong his stay at Lahore due to ill-health. He had to leave for Dehradun hurriedly for rest. But he was not destined to take any rest. Soon after reaching Dehradun, he received invitation from the King of Khetri. The King was very much keen that people of Khetri also gain benefit from Swamiji's presence and discourses.

Swamiji could not evade the king's invitation for long. He came to Delhi from Dehradun. At Delhi, he stayed with the Xavier couple and other Guru brothers for five days and toured the entire Delhi. Swamiji felt as if the ancient monuments, structures at Red Fort, Old Fort, Qutub Minar and other monuments were relating the story of India's glorious past standing in a silent manner. Delhi in its prosperous and degraded form whizzed past in front of Swamiji's inner eyes. Swamiji's emotional heart went back to the past. Wherever he went, he gave an insight into the history of the place to his fellow travellers. He explained everything in such a rivid manner that his co-travellers felt as if actually drawn to that period of history. The five days that he spent in Delhi was totally utilized for travelling. He was totally free from giving speeches and discourses.

After Delhi, Swamiji's next destination was Alwar. A good gathering was present at Alwar Station to welcome Swamiji. Local rich, renowned and educated people extended a hearty welcome to Swamiji. He had earlier also visited Alwar during his days of youth as a wandering saint. There was a huge difference between then and now. Arrangement for Swamiji's and his co-traveller's lodging was made at the Raj Bhawan itself. As Swamiji was being taken to Raj Bhawan, suddenly his eyes fell on a person standing far away in the crowd. Without giving a second thought on considering the circumstances, Swamiji began to call out the name of the person—'Ram Snehi! Ram Snehi!' The person clad in the most common and faded cloth heard the call and a shine came to his eyes as if he had attained wealth from Lord Kuber (the God of wealth). During his first visit, when Swamiji was not as renowned as now, it was Ram Snehi who extended a warm welcome to Swamiji at his home and had played perfect host to him and later he had also become Swamiji's disciple also. Ram Snehi came to Swamiji overwhelmed with emotion. Swamiji talked with him lovingly for quite some time. Swamiji experienced a strange kind of happiness as he talked about this past meetings.

That day Swamiji went to stay at the Alwar Raj Bhawan. But even during his short stay at Alwar, he did not forget to stay at his poor disciple's home and have meal at his place. During his earlier tour to Alwar, he had partook meal at the home of a poor old widow. He still remembered it and send a message to the old woman that he was longing to eat the rotis made by her. When Swamiji went to her home and ate the meal prepared by her, tears came rolling her eyes. She

Swami Vivekanand: A Biography

said—"I am so poor that even though I am desirous of preparing more good and delicious food to you, I am unable to do so, my son." As he ate the food in a relishing manner, Swamiji replied—"Mother, I never got such delicious food as the rotis prepared by you anywhere." The poverty faced by the old woman was quite evident. While taking leave, Swamiji handed over a 100-rupee note to the caretaker at the woman's house.

From Alwar Swamiji went to Jaipur and then to Khetri. The distance to Khetri from Jaipur was about 30 miles. The king of Khetri had made arrangements for chariots, horses and camels for Swamiji and his co-travellers. The king himself had arrived 12 miles ahead to extend a hearty welcome to Swamiji. The whole Khetri city was decorated with flowers, flags, lamps, etc. in honour of Swamiji's arrival. People were happy and excited. At night, crackers and fireworks were burned. Meals were given to poor people. When Swamiji arrived at the meeting place, people touched his feet and sought his blessings and each gave two rupees as gift. The King himself gave Rupees 3000 kept in a plate as gift. After gift-giving, the commendation certificate was read out. In reply to the commendation, Swamiji gave a short speech on Child Education.

Swamiji was staying at Raj Bhawan along with his disciples. On 20th December, he gave a speech on Vedanta for over one-and-a-half hour at Raj Bhawan. Local educated high class Indians and many Europeans ladies were present in the meeting. The King himself chaired the meeting. He introduced Swamiji to all those present there. During the course of his speech, first of all he drew an outline on the ancient culture and civilization of Greeks and the Aryans, then he described how Indian thoughts impacted the different ages in the Western World. Then he discussed about the ancient Veda. He stated that Veda is not the teaching of any particular person. With the gradual development of one thought after other, there arose the need of computing them into book form and such books became testimony to them. Many religions got compiled into book form. Their impact on human beings is limitless. The religious book of Hindus is the Veda and they have to rely on it for thousand of years. But they should change their views on them and should establish them on solid rock. He explained the two parts of Veda—Karmakhand and Gyankhand and also gave an analytical explanation of Advaita philosophy.

The days the Swamiji spend at Khetri proved to be really joyful for him. He was experiencing honour, welcome, speech, discourses on day-to-day basis. During such a hectic schedule, he turned a blind ear to his tired body. Before he satisfied one host, invitations and requests poured in from other places. How could have he avoided any one? It was against his nature to avoid a person or ignore an invitation. From Khetri he went to Kishangarh, then Ajmer, then Jodhpur then Indore and finally reached Khandwa. While in Khandwa he got invitation from Baroda, Gujarat, etc. But by then his body had become utterly weak. His doctors advised him to proceed on complete bed rest. Hence in mid January 1898, he along with his disciples returned back to Calcutta.

Swamiji's all India tour took almost a year. Wherever Swamiji went he blew the conch of national awakening and called upon the youths to plunge into action. Whenever, due to acute ill-health conditions, he was compelled to take rest at Darjeeling, Almora or Srinagar, then Swamiji instead of speeches continued his work through letters. It was impossible for him to sit idle and take rest. He had the feeling that the illness (diabetes) that he had protracted was not recoverable, hence he should complete the work he had in mind hurriedly, for he believed that death may snatch his body anytime. On 20th May, 1897, Swamiji wrote a letter to Swami Brahmanand from Almora—"Why are you afraid? Is it possible for a human being to die so early? Now only the evening lamp has been lit, we will have to continue with songs and dance for the whole night. Get engaged with your action. We have to create a storm for once."

Swamiji always bent upon accomplishing his task. He himself was not desirous of taking any rest and did not allow his disciples and other Guru brothers to sit inert. Whenever he wrote letter to his disciples he gave them the clarion call to plunge into action. During that time, one of Swamiji's disciples, Swami Akhandanand was engaged in relief work for famine hit people at Murshidabad. Swamiji gained information about his work there, while he was in Almora and in a letter to Swami Akhandanand wrote—"I am getting detailed information about the work undertaken by you and

I am experiencing extreme sense of joy and satisfaction. You can win over the world with this kind of work. What meaning can be achieved by differentiating between castes and religions? Congrats! Accept my hugs and blessings. Action, Action, Action—I am not concerned about any other thing. Engage yourself in some type of action or the other till the end of your life. Those who are weak should equip themselves to become a great social worker, a great leader. Do not worry about money, it will rain from the sky."

In Swamiji's point of view, the most noble work was to help the weak and the poor. At famine hit areas his disciples were doing this very work. Hence, he was extremely pleased and felt honoured.

On 4th July 1897, in a letter to sister Nivedita, he wrote:

—"After Lord Buddha, we are once again able to witness Brahmin sons taking care and serving poor and miserable people dying of Cholera. India is not going to gain much with good oratorical skills or education. At present the need of the home is charity." On 9th July in a letter to Swami Brahmanand he wrote—"The going is good at Burhumpur. Only these kinds of work will achieve success. Is it possible for some thought or philosophy to touch the heart and soul of other? Only Action can do so. Lead a life based on ideals. What value does philosophies and thoughts have? Philosophy, yoga and penance, places of worship, flowers, rice and other offerings—all these are personal choices for religious following. But helping others or doing good to others is the noblest of all services. Every being can embrace this religion of service to others. Stone never does anything unethical, trees never indulge in robbery but of what use it is? We believe that you do not indulge in robbery or never lies nor lead an immoral life and spend four hours in meditation and spend double the time in worshipping. But of what benefit these activities are?

Enumerating the significance of social work Swami Vivekanand further wrote—"What can mere discourse do without work? Is it possible to fill stomach with sweet words? If you can serve at least 10 distressed, then you will be able to gain control over all the ten of them. Hence, like an intelligent fellow give as much emphasis as you can on the action front. Organise some boys to go door to door and collect whatever they are able to gain as charity—money, old clothes, rice, eatables, anything. Then distribute those things among the needy. In fact that is what true service means. This will develop devotion in the minds of people and they in turn will do whatever you say. Vivekanand did not forget to say that in the times of scarcity, they should minimize their expenditure on worship so that money could be saved for other purposes. The sons of the Lord are dying of hunger. Worship the lord almighty by offering prayers along with water and basil leaves. Spend the money kept aside for offering food for the Lord to quench the hunger of the living Lords dying of hunger. Then only the Lord will be satisfied and shower blessings. In addition to distributing food for the poor, Swamiji's main emphasis was on spreading education. He strongly believed that such kind of education should be spread among the countrymen that would make themselves self dependent as well as help them develop their self esteem. At the time of scarcity, it is essential to distribute food but at they same time people should be taught about the importance of self-dependence, otherwise whose purpose of social service would prove futile. In a letter written from Almora on 11th July, 1894 he wrote: "Akhandananda is doing a splendid job at Mahula but his working system does not seem to be correct. It seems that he is indulged in wasting away his strength in a small village and that too in merely distributing rice. I didn't hear of any propogational activities other than this being carried out. If people are not sensitized about the importance of becoming self sufficient, then even the whole wealth of the world would not be enough to help even an small Indian village. Our first priority should be to impart education—both ethical and spiritual."

In 1897, Swami Vivekanand got an opportunity to make it clear that while serving the society one should not keep any prejudices on the basis of caste, creed, religion or any such things. When Swami Akhandananda planned to open an orphanage at famine struck areas and raised the question as to whether Muslim children should also be admitted to the orphanage, then Vivekanand wrote a letter to him from Mari on 10th October—"You should take Muslim boys also, but you should never pollute their religion. You should only make arrangement for their food separately and teach them the importance of exercising pure living, mainly behaviour and serving others. And that is religion in the true sense. He further wrote—Let the Vedas, the Quran, the Puranas and the Shastras rest for some times. Let the country worship the Lord who is the epitome of love and generosity. Every feeling of difference is a shackle and every feeling of oneness is freedom. Accept boys of every religion— Hindu, Muslim, Christian or any other, but begin gradually. Be careful of their eating habits and advise them about the unity of religions."

Vivekanand was well aware that the unity and organization was very essential for the work he had begun. He was quite serious about this that just after his return from foreign trip he gave special attention to it and in 1897, in spite of ill-health conditions, he laid the foundation for such an organization. As a first step towards this he called the meeting of all the disciples of Sri Ramakrishna. Addressing everybody, Swamiji said—"After travelling many countries, I have come to the conclusion that without creating a proper union no large scale or permanent work can be undertaken. But in a country like India, in accordance with its democratic set up it is not so comfortable to work as a union with the consent of people. In the west the situation is different. In our country. With the spread of education when we will learn to bear sacrifices for the sake of the society or the nation, then only with the country be considered democratic in its true sense. Keeping all these in mind, we require a chief coordinator for our organization. Whose orders will be obeyed by everyone. Then, at an opportune time, work will be accomplished with the consent of all the members of the union." Swamiji named the union after the name of his beloved Guruji—'Ramakrishna Mission.'

The proposal received the support of all members. They discussed about the objectives of the Mission and its policies and programmes. It was decided that whatever Ramakrishna taught them for the welfare of humanity and the ideals he established with his life, would be propogated by the union. In Sri Ramakrishna's opinion every religion of the world was a slight variation of the Hindu religion. Hence the main objective of the union would be to establish peace and brotherhood between people having different religious faiths.

The union made plans to accomplish their objectives which were as under:

a) For the worldly and spiritual progress of human beings, those who are capable of teaching others will be educated.

b) Encourage art, craft and other industrial professions.

c) Vedanta and the teachings of other religions as entangled in the life of Sri Ramakrishna to be spread in the society.

Two groups were formed to accomplish this work. One was entrusted the task of carrying out work in India and the other was to carry out activities abroad. The group meant to work in India was supposed to establish Mutts and Ashrams in India which would impart education to both sannyasis and disciples who were leading a familial life, who in turn would educate others. They were supposed to find out ways and means to educate people from different provinces. The group in-charge of carrying out activities abroad were supposed to send enlightened sannyasis abroad. They were under oath to establish Ramakrishna Mutt abroad at various places and impart Vedanta education to people there. In doing so they wanted to establish friendly ties and draw sympathy for the Indian cause from other countries.

The union had no political alliances or orientation. Swamiji made it categorically clear to all members present in the meeting that those who have faith in the principles of the union and are ready to devote themselves wholly for the fulfillment of the objectives of the union should understand themselves as members. All those present in the meeting unanimously accepted the conditions. When all the members accepted the proposals put forth by Swami Vivekanand, then the President of the union was elected and Swami Vivekanand became the Chief President. It was also decided that the union will hold a meeting every Sunday in the evening at the house of Late Balram Babu. In the meeting, there will be a reading session of the Gita, the Upanishad and other Vedantic texts and also Buddhist scriptures. The President will prepare the agenda for each meeting. After the first meeting, the members of the 'Ramakrishna Mission' met at Balram Babu's house every Sunday without fail continuously for three years. Whenever Swami Vivekanand was present at Calcutta, he made it sure to attend the meeting and speak on some topic or the other or read some vedic texts or sing some devotional songs.

It was quite evident to everyone that Swami Vivekanand considered social service to be the major objective of Ramakrishna Mission. Some of his Guru brothers were extremely surprised to find that he gave more significance to social work than worship and prayers. After the setting up of the Mission, many Guru brothers and disciples felt that the working of the Mission was largely influenced by Western thoughts than the thoughts and teachings of Sri Rama Krishna. According to them, Sri Ramakrishna followed isolated devotion, thinking and meditation and believed in attainment of God. But Swami Vivekanand due to his foreign influence kept on calling his disciples to keep aside worship and prayer of God and asked them to work for the world by helping the poor and the miserable lots, progress and development in the field of education, propogation of Vedanta, etc. Some Guru brothers and disciples considered them to be worldly activities causing hindrance in their prayers and worships.

One evening, Swami Vivekanand was engaged in talking with Guru brothers and other disciples at the residence of Balram Babu. At that moment, one of the Guru brother put forth before Vivekanand about his doubts and openly opposed the social welfare activities being carried out by Ramakrishna Mission. Suddenly Swamiji became serious, his countenance overhwhelmed with emotion and eyes shining as he shot back—"How can you say that these works are not in accordance with his (Sri Rama Krishna's) thoughts? Can you bound Sri Ramakrishna, who was the epitome of eternal thoughts, within your boundary? I will break all boundaries and spread his thoughts all over, all over the world. We should of course remember his teachings and the systems that he followed for practice of spirituality, meditation, worship or religion and should hand it over to the human race as a whole so that they follow them for the good of mankind. His thoughts were unlimited and there are many ways of following it and fulfilling those objectives. I have not born in this world to establish a new religion— this world is already full of different religious thoughts and ideologies. We are very lucky to get a place at the pious feet of Gurudev and our first responsibility is to necessarily spread his teachings all over the world."

Swami Vivekanand kept on saying that whatever work he had undertaken was as per the wishes of Gurudev, he felt as if Gurudev accompanied him at every step and he was making him do whatever he had been doing. Swamiji looked towards the Guru brothers and laughingly said: 'Do you mean to say reading-writing, propogation of religion among common people, serving the poor, ill and orphans or trying to relieve people from misery will get you entangled in worldly Mutters? Yes, once Sri Ramakrishna had said to some one that "Search for God, doing favour to the world is an unnecessary endeavour." If on the basis of this very statement you consider this work as bad, then you have not understood the real objective of Sri Ramakrishna.'

As he said this, Swamiji's countenance once again became serious and he roared—"Do you think that you have understood Gurudev more than me? Do you think that knowledge can be attained by mere intellect, killing the soft emotions on an infertile path? Your devotion is just foolish emotion, which makes man fearful. You talk about Sri Ramakrishna teachings as if you are well versed with what he has said. But the truth is that your understanding is very less. Leave all these things. Who is concerned about your Sri Ramakrishna? Who is bothered about your devotion and redemption? Who listens to or follows what the Shastras say? If I am able to make my countrymen who are inert at this moment, to stand on their own feet then I would be too ready to go to hell a thousand time. I am not going to follow your Ramakrishna or any other one. I am following the person who helps me accomplish my plans. I am the followers of those who serve others leaving aside the desire for their own redemption."

At this time, Swami Vivekanand was overwhelmed with emotion and words stuck in his throat. His countenance turned red. Tears came rolling down and his whole body began to shiver. He was unable to calm himself. It seemed as if the sorrow of manknd was breaking himself. Suddenly he stood up, went to his room in a hurry and closed the door. The Guru brothers who had criticized him a while ago felt agonized. The others who were present there were wonderstruck and at the same time overcome by fear and began to look at each other. Two Guru brothers slowly went ahead towards Swamiji's room. The window was open and through the window they·saw Swamiji sitting in meditation—his countenance serious, body immobile and eyes half open but fixed with tears roling down incessantly. The two of them returned back. All were silent, no one dared to talk.

Almost an hour had passed. They saw the door of Swamiji's room had opened. He came out. He washed his face with cold water and proceeded towards the meeting hall. The atmosphere inside the hall was serious as before. After a second's silence he said—"One whose heart is filled with devotion, his thoughts become so soft that he cannot bear even a slight floral blow. As you know, these days I cannot even read topics related to love or devotion. I can neither think nor talk without being emotionally overwhelmed by Sri Ramakrishna, for long. I am always trying to keep a control of this overt flow of devotion. I have kept myself bound within the shackles of knowledge still now because I have not yet finished with my service to my motherlands, and the message I wanted to give to the universe is still pending. Hence, whenever the emotion of devotion try to overwhelm me, I with my inherent knowledge subdue it. I have to do so many things. I am the servant of Ramakrishna. He was left the burden of his responsibilities on my shoulder. Till the time I am not able to complete it, he won't let me have peace."

As he talked about Gurudev, Swamiji was in the grip of emotion. His disciples and other Guru brothers controlled the situation. By then, evening had given way to darkness of night. The room gave a dim look. No wind was blowing and the heat accompanied by humidity made all of them restless. To relieve Swamiji from his worries, the Guru brothers put forth the proposal of strolling on the roof top. Swamiji accompanied them to the roof top and strolled along with them. But Swamiji's mind was haunted by different kinds of thoughts. By dinner time, Swamiji had attained control over his thoughts and mind.

Many such situations arose later also but Swami Vivekanand remained firm in his decision. The Guru brothers realized that the work done by Swamiji was indeed the work entrusted to him by Sri Ramakrishna. Now everyone was clear about the objective of Rama Krishna Mission and each one contributed to it whole heartedly.

Swamiji was greatly pleased by the outcome of his efforts. Now his only worry was to establish one Mutt in Calcutta which would function as the central office for all the volunteers of Rama Krishna Mission working all over India and from there instructions will be given to them from time to time. His deteriorating health made him worry about this all the more.

■■

Organisation and Training

The Belur village is on the western bank of the river Ganga, adjacent to Calcutta. The major population lived four miles away from the sandy banks of the Ganga. The land lying in between was peaceful and clean. On the banks, big-small, new-old boats were tied around waiting for their turn. It seemed as if the boatmen had monopoly over the place. Slightly away from the banks their dilapidated tents were situated as if failed in their attempt to hide their poverty.

In January 1898, with the financial assistance of Swamiji's English disciple Ms. Henrietta Muller, about 7 acreas of land were acquired in the village for construction of the Mutt. A dilapidated building on that land also automatically became the part of the Mutt. After accomplishing his tour to North India, Swamiji completely devoted himself to the construction of the Mutt. The farm house of Nilamber Mukhopadhyay of Belur was temporarily taken on rent for the stay of Guru brothers and disciples. Swamiji's Guru brothers and disciples came over to Belur village from Alam Bazar Mutt. A wealthy American devotee and disciple of Swamiji Mrs. Aulibull shouldered the construction expenditure and rent for the premises where Swamiji and his disciples stayed. In this manner Swamiji was able to breathe a sigh of relief as the work of construction speeded up.

Mrs. Aulibull, wife of a renowned musician was a scholarly lady and she enjoyed a place of honour in the society. She spent a lot of money for social causes and welfare of people. Swamiji stayed as guest at her place in Boston. She organized many meetings in honour of Swamiji where he gave speeches and discourses on various topics pertaining to Hindu religion and philosophy.

To give shape to Swamiji's imagination, Mrs. Aulibull got assistance from Ms.Henrietta Muller too. Swamiji had met this good hearted girl in both America and England. She was the one who introduced Swami Vivekanand to the Xavier couple and E.T. Sturdy. She was a very religious girl. She was able to see total spirituality in Swamiji's personality and views. She desired to lead the life of a saint breaking the shackles of worldly life. But Swamiji discouraged her from doing so saying that by leading a worldly life also one can contribute selflessly and whole-heartedly for the society. He made her understand that the duty of a human being is to serve others and reconstruct a new society. Ms. Muller, though was too much pinclined towards spiritualism, possessed a rebellious character, which was a sort of obstruction for her to completely transform her into a saintess. She was proud about her wealth. She was of the opinion that to become a renowned leader of the world, nothing but money is necessary. Swamiji had understood her nature quite well within a few days of his interaction with her. Hence, he made her apprise of the practicality of the situation and showed her the other side of life. Ms. Muller also considered Swamiji to be her guiding light and accepted his orders without fail.

During the course of construction of Belur Mutt and Sri Ramakrishna temple, many incidents took place. As fate would have it, as soon as Swamiji reached the farm house of Shri Nilambar Mukherjee at Belur to stay there and oversee the progress of the constructional work, all his Guru brothers who were engaged in propagational work and social work in various parts of India and abroad assembled there. Swami Shardanand and Swami Shivananda had returned back from their propagational work at America and Sri Lanka respectively in a successful manner. Swami Turiyananda was engaged in serving the famine affected people at Dinojpur. His work was also complete there and he had also returned back. In the absence of Swami Vivekanand, Swami Brahmananand was supervising the work of Sri Ramakrishna Mission. Swami Turiyanand was carrying out the task of educating and training new sannyasis and Brahmacharis at the Alam Bazar Mutt. Now they both also reached Belur to get terrified about the future course of action from Swami Vivekanand. The atmosphere at farm house of Shri Nilamber Mukherjee had got transformed into a spiritual one. The whole building echoed with the chanting of vedic hymns and mantras. The selfless work undertaken by the Guru brothers touched the heart of Swamiji. A new ray of hope shined in his eyes. He became sure that these supporters and friends will fulfil his dreams. Now he believed that they can take on any hardships in life. Swamiji felt the necessity to thank them and acknowledge their selfless efforts. In the evening of Shivratri, he called the meeting of his Guru brothers and disciples, praised their efforts and discussed the future course of action to be undertaken.

The ancient building adjacent to the land acquired at Belur village was made the place of residence for the newly arrived European women devotees. First of all, Ms. Muller with whose financial help the seven acre land was purchased, arrived at Belur. After this came Mrs. Bull and Ms. Mc Leod from America and Ms. Margaret Nobel from England. All these ladies had made contributions in some form or other for Swamiji's various social service works in India and abroad. They were totally devoted towards Swamiji. They were keen to see Swamiji's birth place, meet the people there, understand them and help them. They were curious to witness the situation in India. Swamiji had given them the warning that the climate there would be intolerable for them and they will not be able to come to terms with the social rituals of India. Still unable to resist their curiosity they came to India. Ms. Leod had left her own country for ever and had taken an oath to fully devote the rest of her life to serve Indians. Swamiji tried to discourage her too by asking her to reconsider her decision. On his first meeting with Ms. Nobel, Swamiji had understood her very well and knew that she was not the one to get discouraged inspite of her repeated warnings. On 29 July, 1897 Swamiji wrote a letter to Ms. Nobel.

"I want to make it clear to you that your future is bright as far as your work in India is concerned. The need of the hour is a woman, not a man—a true lioness who will work for the Indians especially the women.

As long as India does not give birth to great women, it will have to borrow powerful women from other countries. Your education, true feelings, pious nature; great love, decisiveness and above all the Caltic blood running in your veins have made you such kind of a woman, who is required at the moment.

But there are numerous difficulties too. You cannot even imagine the sorrow, fanaticism, slavery prevalent in India and you will have to stay with group of half naked men and women who have strange veins about caste and divisiveness, who want to stay away from the white people due to fear and anger and towards whom the white they also bear a feeling of grudge and hatred. On the other hand, your fellow white people will consider you mad and will watch your activities with suspicion.

Moreover, the heat here is unbearable. In most of the places the winter season is equivalent to your summers and in the South it is always hot. Outside cities, no foreign gadgets or comfort are available. In spite of all these, if you take the courage to work in India, then we extend you a whole hearted welcome. As far as I am concerned, I am nothing here as elsewhere but still I will try to serve you according to my capabilities.

Before entering into this work, you should think about it properly and if you fail in your work or feel unhappy about your work, I promise you from my side that whether you work for India or not, you renounce Vedanta or not, I will be with you till my death. "The tusk of an elephant grows outwards, not inwards, in the same manner a true man never breaks his promise. I make this promise to you but still I caution you."

This letter from Swami, instead of discouraging Ms. Nobel made her decision all the more firm. Why should she worry even if every grain hate or reject her? One person would be there in her support. With that sole source of inspiration she will follow the restrictions of this life. The words written by Swamiji in another letter came before his eyes—"In case of any danger, I will be near you. In India if I get a piece of bread, I assure you of an equal half from it—this you can be sure of."

Ms. Nobel remained firm on her decision. On 28th January, he broke every shackles of the western society and reached India. At the Belur village, she was made to stay at the ancient building along with other western disciples. It became very difficult for so many people to stay in a small space. Hence, small hutments were constructed adjacent to the building. Swami Vivekanand entrusted the task of educating Ms. Nobel with Swami Swarupananda. But Ms. Nobel wanted to contribute whole heartedly to the mission. She knew that in order to follow the footprints of Swamiji she will have to toally renounce herself. She was well aware of the responsibilities that accompanied with her duties. When Swamiji found that his disciple was truly bent on practising celibacy (Brahmacharya Vrat), then he gave permission for her enunciation. Four days after she arrived there, on a Friday she was enunciated into Brahmacharya and was given a new name. Ms. Margaret Nobel disappeared into nowhere with her western outfits and behaviour. In her place, appeared a new saintess Anglican in form but in Indian edition, dressed in saffron outfit, calm, peaceful and glorious with her new name— Nivedita. Swamiji blessed his newly enunciated disciple saying—"Go dear, follow those who before attaining enlightenment took birth for about 500 times and sacrificed their lives for serving the public. This incident has a significant place in the history of the life at Mutt because before sister Nivedita no other woman had been enunciated as a sannyasini.

A few days after this incident Sri Ramakrishna Paramahansa's birthday celebrations were organized with much enthusiasm and gaiety. Swamiji himself shouldered the responsibility for making arrangements for the celebrations. That holyday became memorable for many because around 50 non-Brahmin persons were made to wear the holy thread that used to be worn by Brahmins only. Some of them were devotees of Sri Ramakrishna and some of Swami Vivekanand. Swamiji entrusted the task of performing this ceremony and initiation of 'Gayatri Mantra' with his favourite disciple Shri Sharat Chandra Chakravarti. On the occasion, Swamiji gave a small but invigorating speech to those who were present there.

"All the devotees of our Gurudev is in fact a Brahmin. According to the Vedas, other than Brahmins two other castes—Kshatriyas and Vaishyas—have the right to undergo the sacred thread ceremony (Upanayan). There is, of course, no doubt that without undergoing this ceremony they are devoid of this. But today they will regain back their warriorship (Kshatriya) and tradesmanship (Vaishya). Today is the birthday of Sri Ramakrishna. Every individual can set himself on the path of piety by taking his name. Hence, today is a holy day quite appropriate for this ceremony. Give all those present here the holy Gayatri Mantra. When the time is ripe all of them will have to become Brahmins. All Hindus are tied in the thread of motherhood. We Hindus ourselves have been degrading some of our brothers saying that 'we cannot touch you.' This is the reason for our poverty, cowardice, stagnance and foolishness. You should upgrade their status by giving them hope and excitement.Tell those people that "you are also human beings like us and you also enjoy equal rights with us."

During those days, two more disciples got added to Swamiji's group. They were Swami Swarupanand and Swami Sureswaranand. Both of them got enunciated into sannyasa at the hands of Swamiji. They had met Swamiji earlier twice and were greatly impressed by his personality. Later on, one day both of them along with their friends came to meet Swamiji and did not return back.Their friends went back to their families and informed them about their decision. Their families were taken aback but did not resort to bring them back to the materialistic world. Swami Swarupanand was an humble, scholarly, renowned and revered person in the society. About Swarupanand, Swamiji said—"To gain a capable worker like Swarupanand is more valuable gaining thousands of gold coins." Swamiji trusted him a lot and just after a few days of becoming a sannyasi, he became the editor of the monthly magazine of Ramakrishna Mission—"Prabuddha Bharat". The very next year when Swamiji set up the Advaita Ashram in Almora, he appointed Swami Swarupananda as its chief.

Swami Vivekanand's responsibilities increased day by day. With more and more foreign disciples coming to the Belur village, the responsibility of imparting knowledge and training to them fell on Swamiji's shoulders. Outside India, Swami Vivekanand had made his appearance like a religious leader. There he had been propagating Vedanta for world peace and unity. But in his own motherland his western disciples witnessed an altogether different image of Swamiji. Here he was more a patriot than a religious leader. He believed in the necessity of patriotism and his main objective was to develop a feeling of devotion towards India in the hearts of his foreign disciples so that, they extend true support and service to India. For this purpose, first of all they had to be briefed about the lifestyle of people in India. Then only they could have worked for the people of India.

To fulfil this mission was not an easy job for Swamiji. It was a difficult task to bring about drastic changes in a wholly developed personality. But Swamiji was a reservoir of

Swami Vivekanand: A Biography

patience. From the house of Nilamber Mukherjee where he had been staying, he got up early in the morning and walked towards the old building where the foreign students were staying. There under the shadow of some huge tree he would untie the hidden secrets of Indian culture before them. He would present the ancient stories in the history, different customs and traditions, costumes and jewellery in a very simple manner. All his topics ended with the eternal God Almighty. Swamiji left no stone unturned in removing any false or wrong notion about India's culture and tradition in the minds of westerners. He also gave a detailed description about the ideals of Hindu religion, method of offering prayers and worshipping different Hindu Gods and Goddesses as well as the views of Hindus about life and death.

Among the female disciples, Sister Nivedita had renounced everything and completely devoted herself for the cause of India. Hence, Swamiji had special love for her. He knew that even after his death she will stick to the path as shown by him Swami Vivekanand presented before her the ideal of a religious Hindu widow. Sister Nivedita also owned the ideal—simple food and simpe living. A widowed Brahmin was expected to serve her family selflessly. Sister Nivedita had a large family. The whole of India was to get encompassed in it. Swamiji's effort was to convert her into a Hindu physically and mentally. He told Nivedita—"You will have to forget your past, even the memories of your past."

In the year 1898, Swamiji made a scarce appearance before the people of Calcutta for speeches and discources. He spent most of the time in imparting knowledge and training to his disciples. To bring about unity among his Indian and foreign disciples he intentionally took a very courageous step. To help the western disciples, mingle totallywith the Indian environment, Swamiji, according to their work, used to address them as a true Brahmin or a true Kshatriya (warrior), partook food prepared by them sitting in their company and he gave instructions to the Indian disciples to do the same. Swamiji never compelled his Indian or western disciples or Guru brothers to work against their wishes and never interfered with their freedom. He just briefed them about the reasons behind his thoughts and actions and the rest he left for them to decide. His disciples worked according to his wishes. Once during a meeting, Mother Sharda, wife of Sri Ramakrishna addressed the western disciples as 'my dear children'. Those who were present there at the occasion were overwhelmed to hear this. After some time, when they began to return back to their hutments, an old Brahmin widow was also taken there by Mother Sharda. The old widow known as 'Gopal ki Maa' belonged to a respectable high class family. Gurudev Sri Ramakrishna used to call her mother with complete devotion. That day the old Brahmin widow had food in their company and after a week again visited Belur village and spent a week with the western disciples in the hutment. During those days, when religious fanaticism was at its height such incidents were very rare and a Mutter of surprise.

After many days, in the month of March, the people of Calcutta saw Swamiji at the Star Theatre. There a meeting was being organized wherein Sister Nivedita was going to present a speech on the topic—'Impact of Indian spiritual thinking on England.' Swamiji chaired the meeting and from there he introduced Sister Nivedita to be a gift from England to India. After sister Nivedita's speech, Mrs. Aulibull and Ms. Heneriatta Muller also said a few words which enchanted the public. The speech had a good-impact on the public. People got introduced to Sister Nivedita and other disciples of Swami Vivekanand and people looked upon them with respect and reverence.

This was the first opportunity for Swamiji to secure a place for his western disciples in the hearts of the people of Calcutta. As long as the pubic do not accept them, how could they accept the services provided by them. During those days, Swamiji was totally concentrating on organizing his male and female disciples as well as the activities of the Mutt. But his illness sometimes proved to be a cause of obstruction for his endeavours. His doctors advised him to go to some cold place. On March 30, Swamiji went to Darjeeling and stayed as guest at the house of an old acquaintance. There he was on complete rest which helped him to regain his health for a certain extent. But he was not lucky to continue taking rest for long. A few days after he left Calcutta, the city was hit with plague.

Innocent children, youths and elderly were dying under its clutches and those who were unaffected by plague ran away from Calcutta. In such a miserable situation, Govt. tried to bind people under the law of Plague Regulation which was more dangerous than the plague itself. The city turned riotiuns. To subdue the riots and to enforce Plague Regulation, Govt. took the help of the army. The public became furious with the activities of the army. When Swamiji got the news about all these at Darjeeling, how could he have sat inert. He rushed to Calcutta and reached their on 3rd May. He began to advise people to exercise caution against the diseased. He made the volunteers distribute pamphlets having guidelines both in Hindi and Bangla to protect against the disease. Swamiji along with his Indian and foreign disciples plunged into action to serve the plague ridden people. At that moment, he made it clear that he had no other mission at that moment other than serving the plague victims of Calcutta. When the disciples became worried about the lack of funds and asked Swamiji about it, Swamiji instantly replied—"Why? If necessary we well sell off the land purchased for the Mutt. When thousands of men and women will die of plague and suffer hardships how can we stay in Mutt? We are sannyasis. If necessary, we will stay underneath a tree and whatever eatables or clothes that we get as alms will be sufficient for our survival."

By God's grace, they did not have to sell the land. Monetary help poured in from all corners seeing the fearless and untiring efforts of Swami Vivekanand and his team. A sprawling open ground away from the popular city of Calcutta was procured on rent. Small hutments were set up on the ground and every one without differences of religion, caste, creed, colour or status of birth were brought there and they all were subject to treatment. At places where plague was rampant those places were thoroughly cleaned and disinfected by Swamiji's team. Those who were considered untouchables and belonged to the lower strata of society were cared and looked after under the supervision of Swamiji. Those people who were looked down by the society with a feeling of hatred, were given generous treatment and love by Swamiji and his team. Swamiji addressed them as 'My brother, my blood.' People realized that Swamiji was not a Vedantic in principle but also in practice. Those who were once his opponents became his own after seeing Swamiji's selfless service. After some days the epidemic came under control and the Plague Regultaion enacted by the Govt. was also removed.

When the situation in Calcutta some under control, Swamiji along with some disciples went to Almora at the invitation of Xavier couple. Those who accompanied Swamiji included his disciples; Swami Turiyanand, Swami

Nirajanand, Swami Sadanand and Swami Swarupananda. Mrs. Patterson, wife of American Council General in Calcutta also went along with them whom Swamiji had met in America earlier. Swamiji had stayed as her guest in America. She did not bother a bit about the reaction of European-American society in Calcutta those days and set off on a journey to the Himalayas along with Swami Vivekanand and his other disciples. Mrs. Bull, Ms. Josephine Mcleodand, Sister Nivedita also joined them. Their programme was to go to Almora via Nainital. The journey proved to be extremely enjoyable. As the train crossed different cities, Swamiji related the ancient and historical, stories relating to those cities to his disciples. The train sometime passed through infertile marshy lands and sometimes through green fields. Seeing them, Swamiji sometimes discussed agriculture and sometimes about the life of farmers. During the journey, they saw many things— sometimes herds of elephants, sometimes that of camels. Swamiji gave a vivid picture of how these animals were utilized by the kings for battles and how traders used them for their business purposes. Everything from river, stream, forest, hills, mountains, valleys were like open pages of a book to Swamiji. He explained Indian culture and civilization in relation to them in a simple but elaborated manner.

In this manner, Swamiji kept on educating his disciples in an invisible manner and they finally reached Nainital on 13 May. The ing of Khatri was already present there. Hence, Swamiji stayed along with his companions. The king of Khatri was happy to get acquainted with Swamiji's disciples especially the foreign disciples. At Nainital Swamiji got acquainted with even more people there. One day, one of Swamiji's childhood friends—Yogesh Chandra Dutt came to meet him. He had once met him at Mari also. He put forth the proposal of sending educated youths to England to attempt civil services so that those youths can be helpful I the progress and service of the country in the future. But those youths would require money to meet their travel and educational expenses at England. Hence, Yogesh Babu put forth the proposal of collecting funds for the purpose. But Swamiji was not greatly impressed by the proposal. He said in a serious tone—"Things won't happen in that manner. All those youths after returning back will try to mingle with the European Society, be sure of that.They will imitate the style of Europeans in every thing that they do—whether eating or dressing. They won't think of their motherland or society even in the wildest of their dreams. After this, he continued saying about the callous and careless attitude of Indian youths towards their motherland and Swamiji turned emotional with tears rolling down his eyes and throat becoming heavy.

Later on, Yogesh Babu described the incident in a very touching manner as he wrote—"I will not forget that scene throughout my life. He (Swamiji) was a renouncer. He had renounced the whole world. Still the whole of India was spread over in his heart. His love was totally devoted towards India. He experienced both the happiness and sorro.. of India in his heart. He drained his tears for the sake of India and he renounced his body for the sake of India. India was his heart beat and each vein in his body pulsated for India. 'In fact, India had become one with his life."

From Nainital, Swamiji and his team went to Almora. There he stayed as guests at the Xavier couple. At a distance, a house was arranged for the stay of his disciples on rent. Early in the morning Swamiji along with his companion went for long walks. On his return, he went to the place where his disciples stayed and had breakfast with them and they began discussion on various topics. The major part of sister Nivedita's education whom people considered Swamiji's foster daughter took place here. The strong hearted Nivedita was still not able to crumble her personal freedom to be one with Swamiji's thoughts. In her eyes, Swamiji's knowledge, his personality, his objectives everything was great. But how could she have forgotten her country, her culture and her past. She found herself unsuccessful in her attempts to forget her past. The depth with which Swamiji loved his nation, the same depth he wanted to develop within the heart of Sister Nivedita. It was unbearable for Swamiji if he found any kind of indifference or inertness of attitude towards what he taught her. Matching of view points of two strong personalities was a difficult task. As much as Sister Nivedita thought of it after coming to India, she felt all the more sorrowful. She was undergoing a litmus test at that time. She felt as if she were once again undergoing her school life. Going to school unwillingly, blindly believing the lessons taught by teachers, all these were the stories of childhood. While at Almora, Sister Nivedita experienced severe mental conflict. One day, one of Swamiji's disciples told him about Nivedita's mental state. She was afraid that Swamiji would be perturbed by this. But he listened to that disciple very patiently and went away without giving any reply.

In the evening, all the disciples were sitting outside in the verandah. The second day crescent moon was shining. The disciples saw Swamiji walking towards them. When he reached near the verandah he turned towards that disciple and said in a simple child like manner—"What you said was correct, we will have to change this situation. I am going to the forest for solitary living. When I will be back, I will bring along peace with me. After that, after a brief pause he turned towards Sister Nivedita and said, "Muslims respect the new moon to a great extent. Come let us begin a new life with this new moon." Swamiji touched the forehood of Nivedita who was sitting on her knees near his feet, in a blessing manner. This divine touch brought out a great transformation in Nivedita. All her cultural affinities related to birth and caste disappeared into nowhere. Mentioning about the incident Nivedita later on wrote—"Few days ago, Sri Ramakrishna had told his disciples that a day will come when with a mere touch Narendra will transmit knowledge into others. On that evening, in Almora, Gurudev's future farecast became true."

During the first half of Swamiji's stay at Almora he met many people and gave them religious advise. During this period, he met Mrs. Annie Besant twice. Mrs. Annie Besant was staying there as guest at Sh. G.N. Chakravarti. Sh. Chakravarti invited Swamiji both the times to his hosue to meet Mrs. Annie Besant. There he talked with Mrs.Annie Besant for quite a long time. Life at Almora was not very peaceful. People always gathered around him in crowds. After some days, Swamiji developed an indifferent attitude towards his Guru brothers, disciples, friends and acquaintances. He began to love isolation. He began to spend at least ten to twelve hours from morning till evening in thinking and meditation. But when he returned back home in the evening, thne he found many people waiting for him. Swamiji wanted to avoid this also for some time.

Hence, he along with the Xavier couple went out from Almora for some time.

Swamiji who had been playing the role of a social worker and religious propagator all these years, now seemed to be fed up of that. Swamiji expressed his keenness to spend at least some trime as a solitary saint away from the world.

After almost a week, on 5th June, Swamiji again came back to Almora. When he returned, two sad news were awaiting him. Palwari Baba whom he revered next to Gurudev Sri Ramakrishna.had self-immolated himself. In addition, Mr. Gudwin who noted down Swamiji's speeches and discourse had also left the earthly abode after protracting severe fever.Swamiji was greatly aggrieved by the two news. He sat in the middle of his disciples discussing devotion and singing devotional songs. Swamiji's tender heart was deeply aggrieved at the death of his favourite disciple Gudwin. It was very difficult for him to forget Gudwin's devotion and service towards him. Swamiji became pathetic. It felt as if he was just like any common man embroiled in worldly living. His knowledge, his philosophy have got lost somewhere. It took some time for him to control himself. When he was able to reign in his overwhelming emotion he wrote a beautiful poem as a memoir to Gudwin and sent it to Gudwin's old mother. Swamiji felt disinterested towards that house in Almora where Gudwin stayed as he felt that the memories related to Gudwin were attached to that house which he was unable to forget that easily. Gudwin had went to Madras after staying at Almora for few days. From Madras, he communicated with Swamiji through letters on a regular basis. All those memories enhanced Swamiji's sorrow. During this time, another shocking incident gave Swamiji a setback—the untimely death of the editor of the magazine Sh. Aiyyar—*Prabuddha Bharat*—which was published from Chennai. The young Aiyyar was a person of great calibre. He was a propagator of Vedanta and an ordent devotee of Swamiji. Swamiji had a deep attachment towards the magazine. Now he made arrangements for getting the same published from Almora itself and the entire responsibility of its publishing was entrusted to Ramakrishna Mission. Swami Swarupananda was appointed its editor and Sh. Xavier its coordinator. '

Swamiji had become greatly perturbed after so many incidents. The Xavier couple advised him to go on a tour to

Kashmir for the change of his mind and attainment of mental stability. Mrs. Bull was in Kashmir during those days. Hence, Swamiji decided to become guest at Mrs. Bull's place along with the Xavier couple and his western disciples. During those days, a Bengali patriot was on his visit to Almora. He was a disciple of Sri Ramakrishna Paramahansa. At Almora, he got a news from his cook that in the town of Almora a strange Bengali saint was staying who indulged in horse riding, spoke fluent English and was staying at the bungalow of an English man. Sh. Ashwini Kumar did not take much time in grussing that it might be the 'Hindu warrior saint' Swami Vivekanand because he had read in the newspaper that Swamiji was in Almora during those days. He felt that almost an age has passed since he met Swamiji. He could not quench his desire to meet Swamiji and set off to meet him. On his way, when he enquired one person about the exact place of stay of Swami Vivekanand, the person asked—"Are you asking about the saint who rides a horse?" He pointed hig finger towards one house and said—"That is his house and look there he is coming towards us riding his horse."

Ashwani Babu saw him from a distance. The saffron clad saint riding a horse and as soon as he reached the gate he slowed down. A middle aged man took the reigns of the horse and took him inside the bungalow. The saint alighted from the horse and entered inside the bungalow. After witnessing all these scenes, Ashwani reached the bungalow after sometimes and asked another young sannyasi—"Is Narendra Dutt inside? The young sannyasi replied—"No, there is no Narendra Dutt here. His end occurred many years ago. Here, there is only Swami Vivekanand." But Ashwani Babu expressed his desire to meet the 'Narendra' of Sri Ramakrishna Paramhansa. Swamiji sitting inside was listening attentively to the conversation going on outside. As soon as Ashwani Kumar stopped saying what he had been saying, Swami Vivekanand called his disciple. When his disciple appeared before him he said—"Oh, what have you done? Bring that person inside quickly."

Ashwani Babu came inside. Swamiji stood up in his honour and wished him reverentially. Both the Guru brothers had met each other after a long gap of 14 years. Sweet-sour memories of the past whizzed past across their minds. Ashwani Babu said—"Gurudev had once asked me to talk to dear Narendra. But then he did not talk to me. Today after fourteen years I am meeting him. Gurudev's words never go futile." Remembering that incident Swamiji was overwhelmed with the feeling of guilt and he sought forgiveness from Ashwani for his behaviour then.

After this, both of them talked for hours about the present and future course of action. In the end, the conversation turned towards politics.Ashwani desired to know Swamiji's thoughts about Indian National Congress which was established in the year 1885 for the political upliftment of India. He asked—"Do you not have faith in the work being done by Congress?' Swamiji had been closely monitoring the developments taking place in the Congress and found that it was limited to a handful of educated and rich class people of the society. It had no relation with the common people of the society. Swamiji replied earnestly—"No, I do not have trust in it. But undoubtedly, where there is nothing, something has its value. The country lying in slumber should be awakened from all corners. Ok, can you say what the Congress is doing for common people? Do you think that by enacting such a handful of proposals, you can achieve freedom? I do not believe that. First of all, we will have to awaken the common people. Give them food to fill their stomach, then they will work for their freedom. If the Congress is doing something for them, I have full sympathy for it. They should include the good qualities of English too."

Ashwani Babu discussed about religion and sought Swamiji's views about it. Swamiji said—"According to me, religion means strength. The religion that does not give strength to the heart is no religion to me. The Upanishad and the Gita both say this. Strength is religion and nothing is above strength." Ashwani Babu could feel the beautiful dreams that Swamiji stored in his heart for the new India. In the fields of religion, politics, social improvement, service, education, his views likened invaluable jewels. In that light if somebody works with complete devotion, then not only India but all the slave nations of the word suffering sorrow and dishonor at the hands of powerful countries will see a new dawn. They talked on and on without knowing how much time they spent. After a lapse of so many hours. Ashwani Babu stood up and lovingly locked Swamiji in his arms. Then he said—"In my heart, your position has become all the more great. Now I understand that how you emerged victorious over the world and why Gurudev loved you the most?"

As decided earlier in the second week of June Swamiji along with his small group set off on a tour of Kashmir. The journey from Almora to Kashmir was extremely interesting, enjoyable and knowledgeable. First of all, from Rawalpindi they took a Tonga (horse drawn carriage) to Mari. There, after a stay of three days, they went to Baramullah by water route through the Jhelum river. On 22nd June, they reached Srinagar. During the course of the journey Swamiji related the stories of his sannyasa life and other tales relating the historical past of Srinagar. Swamiji took care of the food, accommodation and all other comforts of his fellow travelers during the course of the journey. He used to experience a sense of joy and satisfaction in doing so. In Kashmir, they travelled and discussed philosophy and God for a week.

After that, suddenly Swamiji felt a sense of detachment towards this life. Suddenly, Swamiji turned serious without informing his co-travellers. Swamiji set off on long and distant jourey to isolated places on boat alone. He spent the whole day in meditation. The western horizon turned red in the evening. The sun setting behind the mountains made Swamiji aware of the time with the help of its feeble rays. Then he regained back his sense and returned to his home. Sometimes by the time Swamiji reached back home it was dark. He enjoyed a spiritual kind of pleasure as he sailed back on the small boat with only the blue sky and the river water sparkling under the moonlight with lotus on them. He experienced a unique kind of peace. If it had been possible, Swamiji would have stayed there alone for days and nights together. But he was also worried about his disciples who would have got worried if he had not returned back.

To accomplish a unique plan successfully, Swamiji postponed this plan. On 4th July, at the National festival of America, Swamiji wanted to give his western disciples a surprise by specially inviting them. On 3rd July, Swamiji with the help of an American disciple went to the tailor and got an American flag stitched. Then he decorated a boat with flowers and leaves. On 4th July early in the morning the American disciples and others were invited on the boat. The American flag was hoisted on the boat. The American disciples were surprised to see all this. Swami Vivekanand recited an English poem that he had written for the occasion.

After this celebration, Swamiji felt all the more attracted towards isolation. On 6th July, Mrs. Dutt went to Gulmarg along with Ms. Mcleod for some work. At that time Swamiji also set off on a pilgrimage to the Amarnath without informing anyone. When Mrs. Bull and Ms. Mcleod returned back to Srinagar they came to know about Swamiji's disappearance. Such a kind of thing had never happened before that. Swamiji's whereabouts was not known for so many days. His disciples were very much worried. They began searching for Swamiji. On 15th July, Swamiji appeared before them. When they asked where he had gone then he replied that he had set off to Amarnath via Sonmarg but due to extreme heat the glaciers melted and obstructed the route hence, he had to return back without fulfiling his pilgrimage.

On 18th July, Swamiji and his disciples began the journey of Kashmir. They visited some ancient temples at Islamabad and Swamiji related the history of those ancient temples and monuments to his disciples. They also visited Icchabel where they spent a good amount of time at the banks of the Jhleum river. He discussed the historical facts pertaining to different religions and compared each with the other. Almost everyday in the morning the whole group strolled along the banks of the Jhelum and became so engrossed in discussing religion that they forget every thing else. In the evening, they returned back to their house boats. Swamiji's news on Buddhist religion and Lord Buddha were entirely different. During the conversation he told his disciples— "Lord Buddha did not live a second for himself. He did not give recognition to prayers and worship. He was not a human being but a country. He became overwhelmed with emotion as he said—"I have seen the door of this country, now you all may enter inside it." As he discussed religion he began to imagine about the glorious future of India. His brains never remained inert. He took others along with himself with new thoughts and new imagination.

At Icchabal itself he made plans again to go to Amarnath and gave permission to Sister Nivedita to accompany him. It was decided that till the time he returned back from Amarnath, other disciples will stay at Pahalgaon itself. After this preparations began for the pilgrimage. Tents, etc. were purchased for night stay during the journey. A big group of sannyasis also joined them for the pilgrimage. In the company of saints they forgot their travel woes. When it was evening they all erected their tents at a plain area.

Swamiji and sister Nivedita also erected their tents along with that of the saints. When the saints saw that an English woman was also erecting her tent along with them, they turned violent and objected to this. Swamiji tried to pacify them and make them understand but they were not ready to pay heed to them. Swamiji turned furious. At this, a Naga saint came upto him and said—"It is true that you have got powers but it is not correct to display it." Swamiji realized his mistake and became calm. Sister Nivedita erected her tent at a distance from that of the saints. Swamiji also changed the position of his tent from the earlier place. But the next day there occurred a sea change in the behaviour of the saints. It seemed as if they had deeply thought about Swamiji's reasonings and found them to be correct. Now they began to extend all kinds of help to Sister Nivedita unlike before. In the evening, Swamiji also sat along with the saints around the bonfire and discussed religion with them. Within two-three days,not only the saints became aware of Swamiji's strength of character, personality and knowledge but were also greatly impressed by him. At the next stop for rest they erected the tents of Swamiji and Sister Nivedita in front of all the tents as their guide. Swamiji also made his itinerary according to the other saints. Eating only once in 24 hours and that too during the evening time, taking bath in the ice-cold stream water and discussing religion. After crossing 10,000 ft from the ground level, their next stoppage was at a place called Panchtarni. Here from the mountain ranges five rivers got originated within short distances. It was a rule for those who were on pilgrimage to Amarnath should take bath in those streams of rivers one after the other and then proceed towards Amarnath. Swamiji had been unwell for the past few days. The long tedious journey had made him weak. He was afraid that sister Nivedita and other saints would crate hindrance in his routine and hence, he sometimes got himself detached from others. He took bath in the five rivers and then only he rejoined the team.

At the night of 2nd August, they resumed their journey. The sight of moonlight in the Himalayas was inexplicable.

The cold winds capable of benumbing even the bones, transmitted a new vigour and energy in Swamiji. The difficult ascent on the Himalayas began. After climbing a height they had to descent to a valley. The mountain was so steep that a slight disbalance would have resulted in death. But the path turned out to be smooth in good company. All of them crossed over to the valley easily. They walked for the whole night and the day dawned but they did not stop. They continued with their journey. After walking for a distance again there was a steep ascent. Slowly and gradually, they covered the difficult route and they could see the pious cave temple of Amarnath. As the pilgrims got a glimpse of the temple the sound of *'Jai Mahadev'* reverberated the whole atmosphere. Due to tiredness, Swamiji lagged behind other pilgrims. He took bath in a river on the route and then slowly proceeded ahead lost in his own thoughts. His companions were waiting for him. When Swamiji saw them, he signaled them to keep on walking and he walked slowly engrossed in Lord Shiva's prayers.

As Swamiji reached near the temple of Amarnath, he was so overwhelmed with emotion that his body began to Shiver. Sister Nivedita became worried at the condition of Swamiji. She was afraid that such an adventurous journey would take a toll on Swamiji's health. Swamiji saw his disciple and said to her that he was going to take bath and she should follow him. After taking bath, he like the Naga saints covered his body with ash and by wearing a single loin cloth entered the cave temple with utter devotion. The huge snowhite shivlinga made of ice was scattering its divine rays every where inside the tunnel. Swamiji felt as if his life long wish of visiting the Lord has been fulfilled. Hymns in praise of Lord Shiva emanated from thousands of throats. Swamiji became overwhelmed with emotion. At first, he bent down on his knees praising the Lord, then he lied on the land and touched the ice ling of Lord Shiva. He experienced a strange feeling at that moment which he described later on. He felt as if Lord Shiva was standing in front of him actually and blessing him with death as per his wish. Swamiji stayed inside the cave for some time in meditative pose. When he came out of the cave, luckily he got the opportunity to see the white pigeons. It was considered a blessing to be able to have a glimpse of the pair of white pigeons after visiting the temple. Very few people get an opportunity to have a glimpse of the pigeons.

Sister Nivedita also entered the temple and offered prayers and worship to Lord Shiva. Nobody made an objection to it. After offering prayers to the Lord at Amarnath, Swamiji, Sister Nivedita and other saints sat on a rock near the river bank to partake food. He said; "Actual Lord was standing there at the huge linga. Here there is only prayers and worship. There is no business of religion. In my whole life, till now I have not witnessed this much of beauty, excitement and inspiration."

The strange experience at Amarnath and the hardship involved in the journey left Swamiji totally broken and shattered. Due to extreme cold, blood had clotted at one place in his left eye. As decided earlier, Swamiji along with others first reached Pahalgam. Other disciples were waiting for him there. All of them reached Srinagar on 8th August. On the way, Swamiji described about their journey to Amarnath and the experiences that he had at the cave temple. He had become totally merged with Lord Shiva. For some time, he discussed only Lord Shiva as if he had no interest in other things.

At Srinagar from 8th to 30th August, their life in the houseboats continued as before. After returning back to Srinagar, once again Swami turned an introvert. He loved loneliness. Most of the time he took his small boat away from that of others and while enjoying the beauty of nature lost in some thoughts or the other. Sometimes, in the morning, when he became extrovert he talked to everyone. During the conversation, in addition to the disciples, high ranking officers of the State of Kashmir and other commonness also used to be present. In those meetings, they mostly discussed religions and social issues. Swamiji put forth his views on the country's condition and the ways to fight them. He strongly supported for removal of untouchability, casteism, etc. from the Hindu religion. He used to say that by following the life and ideals of Sri Ramakrishna India can only reach the peak of progression.

One person asked Swamiji that what one should do if one witnesses a powerful person ill-treating a weak one? Instant came Swamiji's reply—"Undoubtedly you should defeat the powerful person with your strength." During one such question answer session, Swamiji had said, "Where there is weakness and inertness, there is no value of forgivance. Their battle is the only honourable thing. When you are sue that you can achieve victory with the help of simplicity then forgive others. The world is a battle field. Clear your path by fighting a battle."

Another person put forth the question—'To uphold and safeguard one's rights he should sacrifice his life or should he not respond at all?' After a second's silence Swamiji replied, "In my opinion, saints should not put up any resistance or response but self-defence is the duty of a family man."

He upheld the non-violent and non-reactive attitude of Buddhism and Jainsim but he specified that such type of reaction are good for saints who renounced wordliness to follow. For family men such kinds of ideals are of no good even though non-violence is a good principle. But according to the Shastras, if somebody slaps a family man he should in return give ten slaps. If he does not do so then he is sinning. A person who endures physical torture and insult always get hell. It is the duty of a family man to suppress injustice and torture with courage and boldness. In support of his view, Swamiji gave the example of what Manu had said in the shastras that even killing the Brahmin who has come to kill you is not a sin. 'Veer Bhogya Vasundhara'— Only a courageous person can enjoy the goodness of earth. But undoubtedly these brave men should keep themselves away from injustice, suppression, etc.

The king of Kashmir also used to attend Swamiji's discourses. He extended all sorts of comforts to Swamiji and his group during their stay in Kashmir. Swamiji desired to establish a Sanskrit college and an Ashram in Kashmir. Swamiji discussed his wish with the king and the former chose the land near the Jhelum river to fulfil his dreams and the king promised to give Swamiji the land of his choice. Swamiji's disciples erected tents on the banks of the Jhelum river and settled there. On almost everyday in the morning Swamiji strolled from his house boats to the tents where his disciples were staying, talked with them for a while and then came back. He looked at the land and made plans regarding the construction of the Mutt and Sanskrit College. In the middle of September. Swamiji was informed by the Government of India that he won't get the land promised by the king of Kashmir.

Swamiji was very much hurt as he felt that his dreams have got shattered. As such after his pilgrimage to Amarnath, Swamiji had become more of a cloisterer and there were only scarce occasions when he entered into conversation with others in a jovial mood. He spent most of the time in prayer and worship. And whenever somebody asked him about the cause of his introvert behaviour, he would say that these days 'Goddess Kali' is appearing before him both inside and outside. He did not experience hunger or thirst. He behaved as if his body belonged not' to himself but to Goddess Kali. The qualities of leadership, social service, religious teacher, etc. which were the characteristic features of his personality had become totally invisible. He behaved like an all renouncer yogi indulged in deep meditation in a forest. He kept on wandering in the thick deep forests of Kashmir till midnight, lost in his own thoughts. In his house boat, people found him totally engrossed in Samadhi. In such a mental condition, one day, he wrote a poem titled 'Maa Kali'.

He cried 'Mother-Mother' as he hummed the poem: It seemed as if at an unknown place a small child has got separated form his mother and was calling his mother. In this condition, suddenly Swamiji set off to Kshir Bhawani from Srinagar on 30th August. He strictly ordered others not to follow him. On the pious river bank of Kshir Bhawani, Swamiji sat in Samadhi. The monumental remains of an ancient temple was there in front of the river. The Goddess was offered worship with 'Kheer' made of milk. Swamiji became engaged in organizing the same. As a special kind of worship, considering the small daughter of a local Brahmin as the representative of the Goddess, he offered prayers and worship to the girl as per the shastras. Many years ago, Gurudev Sri Ramakrishna had also done Shodashi Puja. Probably, Swamiji's state of mind had become like that of Sri Ramakrishna and perhaps he saw the image of Goddess Kshir Bhawani in that little girl.

The temple of Kshir Bhawani had got destroyed due to foreign invasion. Swamiji was deeply hurt to see the architectural remains of the plundered temple. He thought that if he had been present there at the time of the invasion he would have laid down his life to save the temple. As he was thinking so, he felt as if he heard the voice of the Goddess in his ear—"If the invaders destroyed my temple or caused impurity to my idol, why you are so concerned? Are you the one who safeguards me or is that I who safeguard you?"

The voice left Swamiji wonderstruck. Had he actually heard the voice of the goddess or was it a myth? He felt as if he was about to faint. Still being firm at heart, Swamiji was well aware of the situation. The next day, he sat in front of the temple and thought, whatever destruction was due to happen to the temple has happened. Now his duty was to collect as much funds he could and begin the reconstruction of the temple. As he thought on these lines, again he heard the godly voice—"If I desire am I not able to construct a seven storied temple made of gold here itself? It is due to my wish that this temple is lying in a dilapidated and shattered state."

Swamiji was in a predicament after hearing these godly words. What is the power of this saint in face of the power of this goddess? A human being's pride about his strength, education, knowledge, everything can turn into dust in a second. Swamiji's ego began to insult him—'you are nothing, nothing. You are just a machine in the hands of Mother Kali. Whatever is happening is the outcome of her work, Swamiji stayed there for six days. During those six days, Swamiji was totally engrossed in the prayer and worship of the mother goddess.

On 6th October, when he reached Srinagar, he was totally transformed—shaved head, naked foot and a stick in hand. He got engrossed in the thoughts and worship of Goddess Kali. Whenever he said something, he talked about Goddess Kali's wondrous image and qualities and recited poems written by him in honour of the goddess. His disciples were greatly worried at such a condition of Swami Vivekanand who used to be action oriented. They expressed their desire to take Swamiji to Calcutta. In order to suppress their worries, Swamiji said—"My desire to act, my love towards my motherland, everything has got dissolved. Hari om! I had forgotten that I am just a machinery and she the operator of the machine. Mother-Mother-She is omnipotent, she is the one who controls the action. Who am I? I am just an ignorant child of that Mother Goddess."

Arrangements were made for their transfer from the mountainous region to the plains. Now Swamiji did not take much interest in any kind of planning as before. He also talked less with his disciples and other people. On 11th October, all of them reached Baramula and from there they set off to Lahore. The disciples wanted to visit some places of historical importance in India. Hence, they called Swami Shardanand and Swami Sadanand from Almora. Swami Shardanand accompanied the disciples to visit Delhi, Agra etc. and Swami Sadanand accompanied Swamiji to return back to Belur.

The sudden arrival of Swamiji at Belur without any prior intimation made the people very happy. But what a drastic change has taken place in his appearance within a short span of time? Pale countenance, blood clot in his left eye, swell legs, weak body structure. He looked somewhat indifferent. No conversation with anyone. Sometimes he sat silent as if in a shocked state, sometimes with face turned towards East in padmasana posture. His open but fixed eyes seemed to be not looking at any outside view but some inside things.

The inhabitants of the Mutt were greatly worried by this condition of Swamiji. They were afraid that by practicing such harsh form of Samadhi he might leave his body. The sannyasis made all possible efforts to attract him back to the normal world from that world of spirituality where he was totally lost. Some tried to narrate attractive stories to him and some tried to discuss with him the arrangements required for the Mutt and problems associated with the construction of Sri Ramakrishna temple. But he in a serious and indifferent tone would reply—"What do I know? Whatever Goddess Kali wishes will happen."

Once, one of his disciples touched his feet reverentially and asked—"How come this blood clot in your eyes?" "That is nothing", replied Swamiji and sat silent. Then the disciple mustered some more courage and asked, "Will you not tell me your experiences during your journey to Amarnath?"

This time Swamiji was a bit surprised and his eyes wide opened. He said, "Since I have been to Amarnath, for 24 hours my mind is overpowered as if by the presence of Lord Shiva. Gradually, he related the hardship and wondrous experiences he had during his pilgrimage to Amarnath and his stay at the temple of Goddess Kshir Bhawani. After this, he somewhat returned back to the real world. Sometimes he discussed the shastras, sometimes about the on going construction work of the Mutt and the temple.

In the meantime, Swamiji began too weak day by day. After returning back to the Mutt, he protracted cough as well as asthma. In order to give proper treatment for his ailments, Swamiji was taken to Calcutta at the house of Sh. Balram Babu. There renowned doctors checked him and started giving appropriate treatment to him. This house located in Calcutta's Bagh Bazar locality crowds of people gathered from morning till evening to meet Swami Vivekanand. This became an hindrance in his proper treatment. Almost everyday there occurred a delay in partook of his meals and medicines. As per the advise of the doctors, his disciples fixed a time when public could meet Swamiji. But Swamiji who was the epitome of love, never disheartened anyone. Whosoever came to meet him at whatever time, he met with them. He never differentiated between a pious person or a sinner, a family man or a renouncer.

This nature on the part of Swamiji sowed the seeds of doubt in some disciples' minds. They thought that Swamiji lacked the capability to identify people and that was why he welcomed everyone at his Mutt. Once while Swamiji was taking a stroll, one of his female disciples discussed about this in an aggressive tone. Swamiji understood the situation and in an emotional tone replied—"Dear, do you say that I am not able to identify human beings? Who told you this? Whenever I look at a person I not only see the activities going on within him but I also get a glimpse of his past life. I also gain knowledge regarding his sub conscious mind. I assess things which he himself might not be knowing. But still I bless such people, do you? Those sad souls might have knocked many doors for the sake of mental peace. But they received rejection everywhere. At last, they have come to me. And even if I also behave in a dejected manner then where will those poor souls go? Who will support them? That is why, I do not keep any differentiation between good people and bad people. They are the worst sufferers. This world is full of miseries."

Slowly Swamiji's health began to revive due to his talks, treatment and care. Sometimes he walked towards Belur Mutt for a change of atmosphere. The construction work of the Mutt and the temple was on the verge of completion. Whatever work remained, Swami Vigyanand was getting them completed under his supervision as per the advise of Swami Vivekanand. Swamiji nursed deep affection towards Belur Mutt. He had big imaginations about its layout and its working system. As he strolled in the front lawn of the Mutt, Swamiji expressed his imagiantion in words to his disciples and Guru brothers—"This would be the place for sadhus to stay. This Mutt would be the main centre of meditation, worship and discussion of philosophy, and it is my desire. The power that will take birth here would spread all over the earth and will bring about a sea change in human life. The highest of all ideals beneficial for human existence will take birth here in the form of merger of knowledge, devotion, yoga and karma."

Raising his hands towards the south he further said— "That southern part of the Mutt will be the centre of learning. Knowledge regarding grammar, philosophy, science, poetry, etc. will be imparted there. The temple of learning will be established in line with ancient schools. Young Brahmacharis will stay there and acquire knowledge on various topics. Their food and clothing needs will be taken care of by the Mutt. All those young Brahmacharis will stay in the Mutt for five years and after acquiring knowledge they can choose their own way of life. Either they can enter into familial life or they can choose to remain sannyasis under the supervision and permission of senior officials of the Mutt. If any of the Brahmacharis behaves immorally then the chief of the Mutt has the power to rusticate him from the Mutt. Every student irrespective of his affinities regarding religion, caste, creed etc. will be imparted education here."

Swamiji, thus always kept on discussing about the rights and duties of the inhabitants of the Mutt. In addition he also drew an outline of the place of residence of Brahmacharis, their life and activities. At one corner of the land, Swamiji wanted to set up a sewashram wherein poor, ill people could be taken care of. Once Swamiji told one of his disciples—"I am leaving the southern part of the Mutt for now and will set up a small hut underneath that Bel tree. You go and search for one-two blind or handicapped persons and indulge yourself in serving and taking care of them. You yourself go and collect alms for them, cook them yourselves and feed them with your own hands. When you will do this for some days, just see how many people will join you in this endeavour and give you money in charity."

In the first week of November, Swamiji's western disciples who were on a tour to historical places of Delhi and Agra returned back to Belur Mutt after their tour. Soon after reaching Belur, Sister Nivedita got herself engaged in educating the women. In order to get acquainted with the lifestyle of Hindu women she went and stayed at Bagh Bazar alongwith Mother Sharda and other female devotees. Mother Sharda and others behaved respectfully with her and took good care of her. Swami Vivekanand used to discuss about the condition and problems of Indian women with Sister Nivedita. They always interchanged views about the new educational system to be introduced so as to educate girls and thereby make contribution towards the construction of a new society. Sister Nivedita was a renowned woman educationist in England. Swamiji was aware of her knowledge and interest in the field of female education and he wanted to utilize her expertise in educating Indian women. Hence, Swamiji entrusted the task of educating Indian girls on her shoulders. Arrangements were made for setting up a school for girls in Bagh Bazar, Calcutta under the supervision of sister Nivedita.

On 12th November, the holy day of Kali Puja came. Mother Sharda along with other female devotees came to Belur Mutt and took part in the celebration. Mother Sharda blessed all ' those who were present there after completing the rituals associated with the worship of Goddess Kali. The inhabitants of the Mutt felt confident about the fufilment of their objectives. After the completion of Puja and the other ceremonies here, Mother Sharda along with Swami Vivekanand, Brahmananda and Shardananda went to the girls school established by Sister Nivedita. There, after completing the foundation laying rituals, she sought the blessings of the Goddess in the ideal management of the school. Sister Nivedita felt satisfied by Mother Sharda's ritualistic worship to seek the blessings of the Goddess. Later on referring about it she wrote—"At that moment whatever words of blessings she gave in respect of educated Hindu women, I could not have imagined anything more significant than those words."

That girls' school run by sister Nivedita was also a centre of attraction for Swami Vivekanand and he always gave his advise regarding its rules, syllabus, curriculum etc. Sister

Nivedita was totally engrossed in the activities of the school. She didn't have even the breathing time for anything else. Her life had become one of hardships leading the life of a saintess, partaking limited food and sleeping on hard surface. Swamiji was well aware of all this. He was making all possible efforts to make her life simple. Sometimes he made Nivedita eat with him and sometimes he prepared meals which she liked with his own hands and made her eat in front of himself. Whenever she came to meet him at the Mutt, Swamiji asked her to cook something special and all the Guru brothers and disciples partook the food together. In this manner, Swamiji tried to break the shackles of the fundamentalistic views and beliefs that the Guru brothers possessed about religion, culture, etc.

6th December is a memorable day in the history of Belur Mutt. On that day, Swamiji and other Guru brothers got up early in the morning. After the morning chores, all of them went for bath in the Ganges. The December cold and the cold wind blowing near the banks of the Ganges created shivers in their body. There was no signs of sunrise in the east. At that time, Swamiji took bath and covered himself with a new saffron cloth. Then he returned back to the Mutt and at the temple kept the pot containing the mortal remains of Sri Rama Krishna, offered floral tributes and worship as per the rituals and entered into meditation. That was the day decided for setting up the mortal remains in the newly constructed Belur Mutt. All the sannyasis of the Mutt were standing in front of the temple door of Sri Ramakrishna waiting for the breaking of Swamiji's trance. Swami Vivekanand opened his eyes after many hours.

All arrangements for transferring the temple had already been made by the Guru brothers and disciples. Vivekanand was leading the way walking in front of the group of sannyasis. On his right shoulders, Swami Vivekanand carried the pot containing the mortal remains of Sri Ramakrishna decorated with flowers. The sound emanating from the blowing of conch shell and hailing of Sri Ramakrishna reverberated all around. Swamiji's countenance shined with the feeling of joy and success. His eyelashes were fluttering with joy. He said to his Guru brothers and disciples – "Gurudev had once told me 'wherever you take me on your shoulders, I will happily accompany you, whether it is underneath a tree or a hut, I will stay there.' I had firm trust on his blessing and now I am taking him to my future Mutt. Dear, be sure of one thing, as long as in his name his followers safeguard piety, spiritualism and ideal of love, till then Sri Ramakrishna will protect this Mutt with his divine presence.'

In the front lawn of the new Mutt a beautiful stage was set up. Vivekanand and other sannyasis together kept the pot on the stage. Then all of them paid obeisance to Sri Ramakrishna by prostrating in front of the pot. After performing the worship as per the ritual, Swamiji lit the pyre and chanting the vedic hymns in a sweet tone completed the havan. The deity was offered sweet made of rice and milk (kheer) and the same was distributed among the devotees. Pointing towards the Mutt Swamiji said to the sannyasis, "You pray to Gurudev with body, mind and soul that the great reincarnation of the age, remain in this holy place and everyone make thus the main centre of all religions." All of them prayed for the same with folded hands.

That day the world of the devotees of Sri Ramakrishna was pervaded with total spiritual fervour. All of them were discussing spiritualism. Swamiji said – "With the wishes of Sri Gurudev, today we were able to establish this Mutt. For twelve years, the worries that were eating me have come to an end." Swamiji had a wonderful imagination. He told his Guru brothers, disciples and the others who were present – "This Mutt will be the centre of knowledge and meditation. All the devotees who are leading a familial life will settle around the premises of this Mutt along with their family members and the sannyasis will stay in the middle. Towards the southern portion of the Mutt, accommodation will be made for the disciples from America and Europe." After a brief pause, he again resumed – "Everything will be alright at the right time. I am just laying down the foundation. Later on God knows what will happen certain things I will do. Some thoughts I will hand over to you before going. You will have to materialize them. What is the use of just listening to big philosophies. You will have to apply them practically in your day-to-day life. First of all, you will have to understand them and then apply it in your life. Understood? This is called practical religion. He put forth the proposal of building an eating hall at one corner of the land. The first and foremost duty of the Mutt dedicated to Sri Ramakrishna was to give food, impart education and then knowledge. After a minute's silence, looking towards the Ganga with dreamy eyes he said in a loving and sweet tone – "who knows when the lion slumbering inside any one among you gets awakened?" If Goddess Kali instills the fire of her Godly power in the soul of any one of you, then thousands of eating halls like this will come up all around this country. Do you all know—knowledge, devotion and strength are present in every human being. But the quantum of expression varies from person to person and that is why we call some big and some small. It seems that there is curtain between ourselves and that wholeness. When that curtain is removed then only the true image of man wholly developed human being comes to the fore. Then whatever we desire or wish for will get fulfilled.

In order to propagate the teachings of Gurudev Sri Ramakrishna, Swamiji had been thinking of bringing out a daily newspaper in Bangla language. But there was a problem of deficiency of fund. One of Sri Ramakrishna's devotees who was a familial man was kind enough to hand over Rs. 1000 to Swami Vivekanand. With the help of that money a press and other materials required for printing was purchased. Due to the scarcity of money instead of a daily newspaper, a fortnightly began to be published. Swamiji named the fortnightly as 'Udbodhan' and entrusted the task of coordination with Swami Trigunatitanand.

The first edition of 'Udbodhan' came out on 14th January, 1899. Swamiji himself wrote the preface to it. It was decided that all of Sri Ramakrishna's disciples whether Sannayasis or family men will write articles for it. The objective of the magazine was to spread a new school of thought for the family men. Swamiji said – "Through this magazine, for the physical, mental and spiritual progression of mankind, without pointing towards their wrong, slowly and gradually they will be on the path of development. By pointing their mistakes we will be hurting their sentiments and they will become discouraged. We have known and seen Sri Ramakrishna those who seemed to be of no use, Gurudev used to encourage them and gave a turning point to their lives. Teaching style was really wonderful. Swamiji emphasized the fact that there should be nothing written in the magazine which would hurt the sentiments of other religious fathers. They should express the supreme ideals of the Vedas and the Vedanta in a simple manner.

One day, Swami Vivekanand along with Swami Yogananda, Shri Sharat Chandra and Sister Nivedita went to see the Calcutta zoo. The superintendent of the zoo Rai Bahadur Ram Brahma Sanyal, extended a warm welcome to Swamiji and his disciples and took them to show the zoo. Ram Brahma Babu himself was a scholar of botany. He showered different types of plants and trees and described about their life span, their evolution, history, etc. Though Swami Vivekanand supported Darwin's 'Theory of evolution', he did not consider his assumption about the stages of evolution as the final one. Superintendent and Swamiji entered into an argument about this. Swamiji said that the topic has been discussed at length in the Sankhya philosophy. According to Swamiji, the thoughts put forth by the ancient Indian philosophers about the theory of evolution was more authentic. After visiting the zoo, they talked and reached the home of the superintendent. There they were given light refreshment at the superintendent's home and took leave from there.

By staying in the company of sannyasis, disciples and devotees in Calcutta, Swamiji could not have a life of rest and salvation. His deteriorating health condition compelled him to go somewhere outside Calcutta. On 16th December, Swamiji informed the sannyasis that he will go to Vaidyanath Dham for sometime. And with the advent of summer he will go to Europe and America. As per his plans, on 19 December he along with one of his disciples Harendranath went to Vaidyanath Dham and stayed as guest as Prijanath Mukherjee. There the life was calm and peaceful. Swami spent most of his time in self-learning, thinking and meditation and spent his morning and evening time in wondering around. One day, as he was on his morning stroll along with his disciple, he saw a person lying on the road side writing in cold. When they went near that person, they found that he was an orphan beggar. The torn clothes that he was wearing had become dirty and foul smell was emanating from them. Nobody could have gone near that person. Swamiji became disturbed by his poor and miserable condition and began to think of ways to help him. He himself was staying as guest at that place. Then how could he have provided care to that poor fellow.' If he took that fellow to Priyanath Mukherjee's house, how will he feel and respond. Many such doubts raised heads in his mind. At last a voice came from within which convinced him that he should take the person along with him whatever the repurcussions, He brought the ill person along with him to his home with the help of his disciple. He himself sponge bathed the person after removing his clothes and made him wear another dress. He was provided with medicines and as a result of their care the patient recovered from his illness very soon. When Priyanath Mukherjee saw all this his reverence for Swamiji doubled. As much knowledge he saw within Swamiji that much greatness he found in him.

Even in the absence of Swamiji the work at Belur Mutt continued as before. On January 2, 1866 all the sannyasis who were staying at the farm house of Nilambar Mukherjee came to stay at the newly built Mutt. At the request of sannyasis, sister Nivedita gave lectures on Zoology, Botany, English literature and other topics at the Belur Mutt. The inhabitants of the Mutt informed the activities of the Mutt to Swamiji through letters. Even the peaceful life and calm atmosphere at Vaidyanath Dham could not bound Swamiji there for long. He felt bored due to extreme rest. He was aware that only a few days of life was left for him and he had to accomplish so many work. After about a month on 3 February, Swamiji again appeared at Belur Mutt suddenly. He stayed wherever he felt like. Whenever he longed for solitariness and engaged himself in prayer and meditation, he went and stayed at Balram Babu's house. When he felt like staying with sannyasi brothers, then he went to the Mutt though his health had been deteriorating, his mind was full of novel plans.

After returning from Vaidyanath Dham, Swamiji called a meeting of Guru brothers and disciples and said to them that in the same manner as the disciples of Gautam Buddha who spread his teachings by traveling different countries, they should also core out of Calcutta to spread the teachings of their Gurudev throughout India as well as abroad. Swami Virjananda and Swami Prakashananda were instructed to go to East Bengal, Dhaka for propagational work. Swami Virjananda was a bit hesitant to take up this responsibility. He said in humble manner, "Swamiji, I do not know anything, what will I say to the people?" Vivekanand replied in a serious tone – "Go, and say this that I do not know anything. This in itself is a great message."

In Swami Virjananda's view, the propagational work was indeed a difficult one and he wanted to spend his time in meditation and thinking. And he appealed to Swamiji to give him some more time to indulge in meditation and worship so that he could attain self-realisation. Swami Vivekanand became furious to hear Virjananda's words. He roared, "You selfish fellow. You are wishing to attain redemption for yourself. You will go to hell. If you want to be wholly one with the Brahma then first work for other's redemption. Destroy your desire for self-redemption. That is the only important means towards self-realization.

He sat silent for sometime and then in a loving tone he talked to his disciples and gave them an insight about the duties of a brave action oriented sannyasi. For the welfare of the world, a sannyasi should totally involve himself without any desire for rewards. For this, if he has to go to hell, then also he should not hesitate. Then he along with Swami Virjananda and Swami Prakashananda went to the puja room. There Swamiji sat in meditative pose for quite a long time. When his trance was broken and he opened his eyes, Swami Vivekanand said to them, "I will transmit my power into you. God himself will stay with you forever, you do not worry about anything." That day, Swamiji made both the disciples understand about the propagation work. The very next day on February 4, 1899 both Swami Virjananda and Swami Prakashananda sought Swami Vivekanand's blessings and set off to Dhaka. Three-four days after their departure, Swamiji sent Swami Sharadananda and Swami Turiyananda to Gujarat for propagational work.

After the departure of these four Guru brothers, Swami Vivekanand taught other Guru brothers and disciples about sannyasa and Brahmacharya. In his opinion, true service required both these essential pre-requisites. If a human being is able to achieve these two qualities then unsurpassable power will be originated and he can do anything. His style of teaching was unique. He kept a close watch on the success and failures of his disciples. He never got himself attracted towards a person who possessed sharp intellect and he never developed any sense of hatred towards a foolish person. He always kept a close watch on how devotedly, truly and excitedly a person did his work. He behaved with everyone with equality. He never allowed them to feel disappointed or dejected. He always kept on encouraging them and instilling in them energy and confidence in themselves.

Once Swami Vivekanand was setting on a cot spread under the mango tree in front of the Mutt. On the ground, some disciples were sitting. He was making them understand that Brahmacharya is the basis of every power. With gaining control over mind, one can attain will power. Hence, the flame of Brahmacharya should always remain in our nerves. With the powers granted by Brahmacharya, a sannyasi can do selfless service for the welfare of the country. He said, "First believe in yourself and then in God. A handful of powerful people can make a difference to the world. We need a heart which is sensitive, a brain which can absorb thoughts and a strong arm which can do work. The history of the world is the history of a handful of people who had trust in themselves. With faith, the godly powers within men get awakened, then you can do anything."

A few days after coming back from Vaidyanath Dham, one night Swami Vivekanand called the meeting of the sannyasis in the Mutt. There he gave his opinion about the sannyasis eating and drinking habits. He stated that the impact of appropriate and inappropriate food on brain is inevitable. He put forth his thoughts about what kind of food sannyasis are supposed to eat, what quantity and at what time. According to him, sannyasis should partake sattvik food. But after the completion of the training period, after attaining complete control over the mind, they can partake food according to the needs of the body. In such a condition the objective of intake of food should not be to quench the taste buds or desire for tasty food but to make the body healthy and utilize the body for public welfare. Swami Vivekanand again and again made it clear to them that the body and mind of sannyasis are not meant for themselves, but for others, Swamiji never exercised any kind of dominance over his disciples nor tried to suppress them with his impressive personality. He even said to them that those sannyasis who find the controlled life difficult or do not have trust in it, they are free and can renounce his life as a sannyasis and embrace familial life. Even being a family man he can serve others.

After putting forth some guidelines regarding the eating habits of young sannyasis, Swamiji made an attempt to bring out some changes in their lifestyle. Swamiji's disciples who were family men also came to the ashram to meet him. But Swamiji did not like that. He wanted to keep the Bal Brahmacharis away from the family men. He said to the sannyasis – "I am finding a smell of unrestrain from the body, the clothes of family men. Hence, I have made this rule not to sit or sleep on the beds of family men. Earlier I have read about it in the shastras but now I am witnessing this truth alive that why the sannyasis are not able to bear the smell and touch of family men." Swamiji explained the point more explicitly. Young Brahmacharis should keep themselves away. They should practice strict regulation and at the appropriate time they will be enunciated into sannyasa. Once the sannyasis attain total control over their senses, then they should be allowed to mingle and work in close coordination with family men.

Swamiji's this opinion does not mean that he looked down upon family men and women. The reason behind laying down this rule was that during their training period, young sannyasis do not get attracted towards any such inappropriate temptation. The training period of these young sannyasis was the period of character building. Hence, a tab was kept on their dressing, eating, and living habits and behaviour. They were under strict supervision. Once some new members of the Mutt expressed their desire to stay with Mother Sharda at Calcutta and serve her. Even though, Mother Sharda was equally reverential to Swami Vivekanand as Gurudev Sri Ramakrishna, still he did not give them permission to go there because female sannyasis also stayed in that ashram along with Mother Sharda and female devotees visited her to attain knowledge. Inspite of all these restrictions against mingling with family men and women, Swamiji always appreciated the efforts made by family men and women.

One day, Swamiji put forth the proposal for setting up an ideal school for unmarried girls and Brahmacharini widows, which would be different from common school resembling an ashram where they will be provided boarding and fooding.

In Swamiji's opinion, girls who have attained education from this school would after getting married and settling down would be a source of inspiration for their husbands and will give birth to ideal children and become ideal mothers. But he wanted to lay down the condition that their parents do not let them entre into a marriage alliance before they attain the age of 15 years.

In this manner, Swami Vivekanand kept on giving directions to the sannyasis at every step regarding their duties such as giving food to the poor, helping the ailing and the poor, looking after these who are ill, opening hospitals and orphanages, cleaning untidy colonies, opening educational centres etc. Once, Swamiji was strolling along the banks of the Ganges during evening time. He was accompanied by some sannyasis also. Swamiji's countenance was very serious but his voice very sweet and soft—"Listen, dear Sri Ramakrishna came for the welfare of people and left the world. Me, you and everyone in this world should leave their body for the welfare of this universe. Believe me, every drop of blood that will drain out of our heart will give birth to great heroes in the future who will brighten up this world.".

During those days Swamiji did not make any public appearance or gave any speech. But many people, especially college students came to meet him and talk to him. Swamiji discussed literature, philosophy, history, science etc with them. Swamiji's heart became hostile towards their weak physique, immoral character and unethical behaviour. He time and again drew their attention towards their physical and mental well being as well as social service.

He used to tell to his disciple always that "I want to spread such a religion that would prepare 'human being'." Hence, he stopped giving public lectures and settled down at the Mutt and developed his time in imparting training to his disciples. One day, somebody asked Swamiji – "Swamiji, you with your oratorical skills impressed the Europeans and Americans. But after returning back to India, you have lost interest in it, what is the reason?" In reply, Swamiji said – "In this country, first of all ground needs to be prepared. Then only we can sow the seed and the tree will grow. The western world is ideal for sowing this seed. The people there have reached the last threshold of luxurious living. They have become so surfeit with comfort and luxury that now they are looking around for peace. In your country neither there is comfort nor a system of concentration and devotion. Once you have reached a satisfactory level of comfort, then only you can concentrate on yoga. What is the use of speaking or lecturing to people with weak body, weak mind and ill-health conditions in their motherland."

Swamiji further made it clear that first of all he wants to search out some renouncing men who instead of thinking about his own family is more considerate about others who are not related to him. Hence, I am engaged in gathering young sannyasis who after attaining training would do door-to-door campaign making them aware of their sorry state of affairs and the ways to free from them.

He was making them understand in a soft tone and loving manners. Suddenly, he became overwhelmed with emotion and began to stroll there in an impatient manner. After a few seconds, he said in a harsh voice – "Don't you see that the dawn has broken out in the east and the sun is about to rise. Get yourself ready right now. What will happen by getting entangled in family life? Now your work is to go from place to place, village to village and make them understand to shed off their inertia and laziness. Tell them about the miserable present pervaded with illiteracy and unreligiousnss. Ask them to get up and awaken. Make them understand the great truths that are hidden in the shastras in a simple language. All these days Brahmans have been exercising their monopoly over religion. Go and tell them that they also have equal right over religion. Give this fiery chant to the person belonging to the lowest caste and give them advise regarding essential topics such as business, commerce, agriculture etc. Otherwise all your education would prove to be a sheer waste. The knowledge you have attained about Vedas and Vedanta would prove to be of no use at all. What is the duration of this life? Since you have made appearance on this world, leave your mark here. Other things like tree, stone etc also take birth here and gets destroyed. Do human being ever wish to take birth and leave the world in that very manner?

Prove to me by your acts that your learning of Vedanta has been of some use. Go and tell everybody that you have eternal strength inherent within you. Awaken that strength. What will happen with your own redemption? The very desire for redemption is selfishness, leave meditation, leave your desire for redemption. Engage yourself in what I am doing. Have you not seen, Nivedita, in spite of being a British has learnt to serve you people. And you cannot do that for your own countrymen. Wherever there is famine, wherever humanity is suffering miseries, wherever there is scarcity, go there. What could be the ultimate-death? Worms like me and you are born in thousands and die in thousand. What gain or loss is that for the world? Die with a great objective. You people are the hope of the country. I feel sorry when I find you sitting inert. Go and engage yourself in action. Do not delay, death is fast approaching near day by day. Don't sit thinking that you will do it later. If you sit inert, then nothing would be possible for you."

In addition to the citizens and students of Calcutta, scholars and people from Bengal and other parts of India also came to meet and talk with Swami Vivekanand. Once the editor of 'Hitvadi' magazine Pt. Ganesh Deoskar came to meet Swamiji at Belur along with his two friends. During that time the situation in Punjab was very bad. The whole province was facing shortage of crops. When Swamiji came to know that one among those three belonged to Punjab, he began to talk about Punjab with him. It was indeed very surprising that a province irrigated by five rivers was facing scarcity of food. Swamiji discussed the food situation and other problems and necessities of Punjab and the ways to solve them.

When the guests got up to go, Deoskar said to Swamiji— "Sir, we had come here to listen your advise regarding various aspects of religion, but unfortunately our conversation turned to general things. The whole day got wasted." Hearing this Swamiji replied in a serious tone— "Oh good men, even a dog in my country is hungry, my religion is to provide it with food and look after it. Everything else is not religion or it is false religion." All three of them could not speak further after hearing Swamiji's reply.

Another such incident took place later. During those days, a renowned scholar from Uttar Pradesh came to Swamiji to enter on debate on Vedanta. During that time, Bengal was under the grip of severe draught. Swamiji was busy in serving the people there day and night. He did not have time to discuss the meaning of shastra with the Pandit.

Expressing his inability to talk to him due to time constraint, Swamiji said—'Pandit ji, first of all we should take efforts to revive the miseries spread all over, so that none of our country man wail due to hunger. After that you come to me to enter into a debate on Vedanta. The gist of the Vedanta religion is to lay down your body and life for saving thousands of people dying of hunger."

In addition to reflecting his views through conversation, he expressed his views regarding building of new India through letters. He emphasized on the fact that only that society can be on the path of progression which embraces the changes taking place according to time. In a letter addressed to Ms. Mrinalini Basu on December 23, 1898 Swamiji wrote—"If it is decided that fame and honour can be achieved by following the laid down rules and if it is considered that practicing the strict rituals is the means towards piety, then tell me who is more pious than a tree and who is a true devotee or a great soul. Have you seen a pebble breaking the rule of nature? Has anybody seen a cow or an ox committing any sinful act?"

Further, explaining the objective of education he said— "What do you mean by education?" Is it just learning? No! Is that acquisition of different types of knowledge? No, not that. The one who like an automatic machine keeps on doing good work is of no good as compared to the one who with his will power and power of intellect does inappropriate work. In my view such a person is more honourable. The person who resembles a clay idol, a lifeless machine or a heap of stones, can he be of any good to the society. How can such a society be on the path of progression? If any kind of welfare was possible in this manner, then in exchange for remaining thousands of years slaves, we would have become the most powerful nation. And instead of becoming a storehouse of foolishness, it would have been an eternal source and origin-place of knowledge and education."

Vivekanand did not like the fact that a handful of people belonging to the higher stratha of society imposing rules and regulations or practices according to their own whims on the society. Hence, he never supported many things initiated in the name of social development because in his opinion all those activities were done keeping in view the needs of only the higher strata.

People would accept whatever they think is good for themselves. The only prerequisite for it is to impart them education in the proper manner, so that they can take their own decisions.

In another letter addressed to Smt. Mrinalini Basu on January 3. 1899 he wrote: "Who is society? Those who number in lakhs? Or people like you and me who are five-ten in number belonging to the higher strata? Even if it is true why should we feel proud of ourselves and lead others way? Are we all knowing? Each one should make progression on his own. Each one should uplift himself. Freedom in every field i.e., moving towards independence is real manliness. To assist more and more people towards physical, mental and spiritual independence and be on that path on your own is actual manliness. Whichever social rule is a hindrance in attaining independence should be destroyed at the earliest. The rules that lead people towards freedom should be given importance."

Time and again Swamiji tried to make it clear that the kind of society that he dreamt for India should be based on the feeling of equality, freedom and brotherhood between two individuals. At the same time he also made it clear that this feeling should not be limited to members within a specific caste. Vivekanand especially viewed that the merger of healthy traditions of both Hindus and Muslims in India can lay the foundation of a new India. In a letter addressed to Mohd. Sarfaraz Hussain, Swamiji wrote--"Whether we call it Vedanta or call it by any other name, but the truth is that Advaita is the last word for religion and philosophy and through its perspective only we can look at religion and caste with an affectionate eye. I firmly believe that the future religion of enlightened humanity would be the same. Hindus will get the honour of discovering such a religion. The reason being they are more ancient than Arabic and Hebrews. At the same time development of practical Advaita in Hindus is still remaining.

As opposed to this, in my experience if followers of any religion in the practical world who can bring even a part of this into practice then it is only the Islamic religion. Though, in general, they are unaware of the serious meaning of this philosophy, and about which Hindus are clearly aware of.

Hence, I firmly believe that the Vedanta philosophy, in spite of being generous and supreme, without the help of

Islam is useless and devoid of any value for the mankind as a whole. We want to take the mankind to that position where there is no Vedas, the Quran or the Bible existent. But this is only possible with the merger of all three of them. The human being should be taught that all religions are the different forms of that single religion, hence, every individual can choose his path according to his desire.

The only hope for our motherland is the merger of these both great religions i.e. Hinduism and Islam.

I am able to behold the wholeness of the future India with my mind's eye. I am able to see the birth of a radiant and indomitable nation with the vedanta intellect and Islamic body which would be the outcome of all these rebellions and conflict.

In addition to conversation and communication through letters, Swami Vivekanand tried to spread his message through essay. In this context, his essay titled 'Present India' which was published in a Bengali Magazine named 'Udbodhan' in 1899 has a special significance. It makes it clear that Swamiji had conducted an indepth study and research of History and he had formulated his own philosophy about the subject. It seems that he had studied the works of the renowned European philosopher Karl Marx. Even if he had not read them, there is doubt that the thoughts of Karl Marx and Swami Vivekanand about the evolutionary progress of society had a striking resemblance. The only point of difference between them was that Karl Marx was an atheist but Swamiji saw God in every individual. If we overlook this significant difference, we can see a description of class conflict in Swamiji's essay, which has the stamp of his Indian experiences and which has been analysed in Indian context and language.

"As in the ancient age, in face of the power of the kings the power of Brahmins had to face defeat in spite of their efforts, the same thing happened in the present age. With the rise of the power of Vaishyas so many kingdoms got destroyed. If at all some kingdoms got saved, it was because these traders who sold oil, sugar, liquor got an opportunity to show off their riches and supremacy.

This new super power whose route is the ocean, with whose impact news can be taken from one country to the other and with whose efforts articles from one country can reach to another country with ease and with whose orders even an emperor begins to shiver, the British empire is established on the top portion of those huge waves in the form of all victorious Vaishya power.

Hence, the victory of England over India—as we have been hearing since our childhood—is not the victory of Jesus Christ or the Bible, or is it like the victory of Pathans, Mughals, etc. The actual England is behind this huge force comprising Jesus Christ, the Bible and other aristocratic ornamentations. The flags of this England are the chimneys of cloth mills, their army is the trading ships, their battle ground is the market of this world and their queen the all embracing goddess Laxmi herself."

This was the description of the condition during that time. As far as the question of future was concerned, Swami Vivekanand had no doubts that after Vaishyas, it would be the turn of 'Shudras'—the labour class to rule the country. The movement that was going on in Europe at that time was an indicator to this. Vivekanand said that "a time will come when Shudras along with their qualities will enjoy significance not in the manner as they are doing now by acting like a Vaishya or a Khastriya. They will enjoy power and importance along with the qualities underlying their caste. In the western world, its redness is already evident in the sky and people are really afraid of the outcome of such an outburst. Socialism, anarchism and Nihilism are the flags that will lead this rebellion."

The main objective of this explanation of the world history was to understand the contemporary Indian conditions. In Vivekanand's view, the condition of India at that time was very miserable. The whole country could be compared to the Shudras or the labour class devoid of power or strength. In the words of Vivekanand—"What to say about the condition of this country? The condition of Shudras apart, the Brahminism of India is now in the hands of white teachers and its worship is in the hands of British emperors, its Vaishya (trader)—like qualities also rested with the Britishers. For the Indians the work of only carrying the load like a donkey or works done by Shudras (lowly caste) are left to be done. Thorough darkness has stung everyone alike. There is no firmness in any efforts, no courage in the enterprise and no strength in the heart. No body is feeling hatred towards dishonor, disinterestedness towards slavery. There is no love in the heart and no hope in life. And look what is left now is hatred, ill-feeling towards one's own country men, longingness to destroy the weak and the desire to butter or praise the strong ones like a dog. At the moment, satisfaction, wealth and prosperity is in affectation, devotion in pursuing selfish interests, knowledge in compiling materialistic non-durable things, yoga in undertaking devilish activities, action in practicing slavery, civilization in initiating the westerners, oratorical skills in talking foul and improvisation of language in buttering the rich or propagating vulgarity." In Swami Vivekanand's views the main cause of India's degradation is that self-respect is diminishing among Indians and they are experiencing glory and self-esteem in blind imitation of the western world. In his words—"This is the grave cause of fear that the desire to initiate the Europeans has become so strong and deep rooted within us that we are not thinking about its merits or demerits or able to assess its repurcussions. Whatever the white people praise that is considered to be good and whatever they condemn is considered bad. What a pity? What could be more foolish than this?" In such a situation, Swami Vivekanand firmly believed that the sense of self-honour should rise in the minds of Indians. In his essay titled 'Present India' (Vartman Bharat), Swamiji staunchly expressed his view:—

'Oh India! You will attain your rights by to confirming to others' views, by copying others, by becoming slaves to others or by practicing this hateful cruelty? Will you achieve freedom with the help of this shameful intimidation? Oh India? Do not forget that you are a worshipper of Lord Shiva. Do not forget that the ideal of your wives are Sita, Savitri and Damayanti. Don't forget that your life is not for physical comforts or for your personal happiness. Do not forget that you have been kept since your birth for sacrifice for the Goddess. Do not forget that your society is a mere shadow of that enormous goddess. Do not forget that the downtrodden, ignorant, poor and the lowly classes are your own blood and brothers. Oh brave hearts! Take the help of courage. Say out proudly that you are an Indian and every Indian your brother. Shout out to the world that the ignorant Indian, the poor Indian, the Brahmin Indian, the Chandal Indian, all are my brothers. Say out proudly that all Indians are my brothers, all Indians are my life and all the Gods and Goddesses* *of India are my Almighty Lord. The Society within India my childhood pram, the garden of my youth and the Varanasi (place of pilgrimage) of my old age. Brothers, tell that the soil of India is my heaven, welfare of India my welfare and keep on telling day and night—"Oh Lord Shiva, Oh mother Goddess of this world, give me humanitarianism. Destroy my weakness and fear and make me a man, a human being!"*

■■

The Second Foreign Trip

It was a damp, humid evening of June 25, 1899. Swami
Vivekanand along with his well wishers departed for
Calcutta's Princess Port. The ship-Golkunda was standing
ready there. Many people had gathered there to see off
Swamiji. Swamiji met everybody, exchanged courtesies and
love and went inside the ship in a hurry. There was
commotion of passengers inside the steamer. The first
warning horn of the ship's departure got merged in that
noise. But the pace of the passengers and coolies coming
inside and going out increased. Swami Vivekanand along
with Swami Turiyananda and disciple Nivedita went towards
the deck and took a comfortable position there. The second
horn of the ship sounded and the ship began to move away
from the port slowly. Swami Vivekanand held up his right
hand and waved it bidding good bye to his friends and followers
standing on the port. That was his second trip abroad. For
quite some days, he had been thinking of making a visit to
America and England once again so as to oversee the
propagation of Vedanta there and to meet his old
acquaintances. But due to his ill-health conditions, this kept
on delaying. When he recovered a bit from his illness he
decided to accomplish this task.

Slowly and gradually the Calcutta port, the people
standing and the whole atmosphere there became blurred
and finally became invisible. Swamiji felt sad for a second
at the thought of distancing himself from such a heaven
like motherland. The Ganges was left behind. The ship left
behind the crystal clear white water and began to move over
bluish ocean water. Wherever the vision could reach only
one thing was visible, the unending heaves dancing to the
tune of the breeze. Slowly the pace of dancing increased.
The posture of the waves took wonderful forms. It seemed
as if the waves were planning to present the 'Tandava' dance

by mustering the support of wind. The roar of the waves, the foamy tides like thousands of hands playing with a single toy—the condition of the steamer was such. Some of the passengers had become sick with the commotion caused by the waves around the ship. Some experienced headache, some giddiness, and some a sense of surfeit. Some layed in their cabins without partaking any food. Sea sickness troubled the passengers in some way or the other. Swamiji also felt unwell. He was thinking of writing an article for the magazine 'Udbodhan' but he was not able to write because of the commotion of the ship. It was hot inside the cabin. A narrow space for accommodating four people. He felt the place suffocating. There was no other scope for doing anything else than taking their luggage and sleeping at night. Swamiji along with his disciple and Guru brothers spent the whole day outside in the verandah of the deck. The other passengers also did the same.

Slowly the tides subsided. After the violent dancing, the winds became calm as if they have entered into slumber. At the stipulated time, 'Golkunda' reached the Madras port in the morning of 28 June. The Guru brothers in Madras were given prior information about Swamiji's programme through telegraph. Hence, thousands of eyes were waiting impatiently at the Madras dock to have a glimpse of Swamiji. The workers of Ramakrishna Mission made all possible efforts to make arrangements for making Swamiji deboard from the ship for some time but failed to do so. During those days, Calcutta was under the grip of plague and as per the plague laws any one who was coming from Calcutta was prohibited from landing in Calcutta. But this prohibition was not applicable on white Britishers. The laws made by Britishers were not applicable on them. In their perception, all black people were dirty people and the possibility of spreading of germs of plague was through them only. Respectable and renowned people of Madras wrote letters to the British officials requesting them not to impose this prohibitory law on Swamiji for a few hours so that he can land on Madras. But all of them fell on deaf ears.

This behaviour on the part of British officials made it evident that they were not happy with Swamiji. Such an incident of displeasure happened some days before in Kashmir. The king of Kashmir had given to Swamiji a piece of land near river Jhelum in charity to build a Mutt. But just before the beginning of the construction work, the British resident there cancelled the proposal of grant of land. Swamiji had felt greatly hurt by this incident and now the same thing was repeated once again.

Anyway, some of Swamiji's ardent devotees, hired small boats and reached near Swamiji's ship and met him. Swamiji stood on the deck and blessed everyone who came to have a glimpse of him with a happy countenance. The gifts in the form of coconuts, fruits, sweets brought by Swamiji's friends and disciples accumulated on the ship. One of Swamiji's foreign friends, Shyam Aiyer had returned back to Madras after completing his Barrister's course in Madras. He was also present at the port to meet Swamiji along with others. It was the month of June and in Madras it was hot and sunny during this month. In spite of scorching heat, people including old, young, women and children waited there beating the heat. Swamiji was repeatedly requesting them to return back to their homes.

After much request, some women, children and elderly paid heed to him and left the place. Standing on the deck from morning till evening, exposed to the scorching sun made Swamiji also tired. He felt as if his body had become stiff and his hands and feet benumbed. He felt giddy and at this he bid adieu to his friends, followers and disciples and retired to his cabin to take rest. Alasinga Perumal did not get an opportunity to seek Swamiji's advise and suggestions regarding the Brahmavadin magazine. Hence to enjoy Swamiji's company for some time he boarded the ship by taking ticket upto Colombo. In the evening, the alarm to warn the ship's departure was sounded along with which a huge echo of applause and hailing reverberated the atmosphere. Swamiji peeped out from his cabin window. Thousands of men, women and children were shouting, bidding adieu to Swamiji.

Journey from Madras to Sri Lanka took four days. By night, the ship had steered ahead a long distance away from the Madras port. The shaking of the ships due to the huge waves had begun once again as before. Its intensity kept on increasing second by second. It was the time of monsoon and as the ship moved towards the westerly direction the intensity of the storm increased which was quite natural.

The frightening motion of the ship and the sound that emanated when the waves hit the ship made one feel that the nuts and bolts that affixed the ship and kept it intact might have got loosened. The passengers were in a state of shock unable to move from their respective positions where they were in. Nobody experienced the pangs of hunger or any other desire. Alasinga Perumal was a Madrasi Brahmin who liked Mysore 'Rasam' (a delicacy), his head bending forward, long tied hair at the back, naked feet, wearing a dhoti upto the knee and sandalwood paste applied on his forehead. Other than the ticket he was carrying two luggage. One contained some important papers and his dress and the other contained some eatables so as to avoid eating anything on board of the ship which he considered would make him impure. For four days, he had to consume this till he reached Sri Lanka. In this way, reflecting total Brahminism in his personality he strolled on the ship deck. He was not affected by sea sickness. Swamiji was deeply impressed by his devotion, self-confidence, dedication, selfless service and hardworking quality. He had during Swamiji's earlier foreign trip also travelled with him till Sri Lanka. Then people belonging to his caste had made an uproar against this and objected to his foreign travel and even threatened his expulsion from the caste. But he remained unperturbed and went ahead with his plans. When he was in the company of Swamiji, age old values and customs that he believed in remained suppressed. He never entered into a debate with Swamiji on this. Some times he himself got irritated by his fundamentalist beliefs. Swamiji understood his situation and loved him all the more.

The ship reached Colombo after four days and Swamiji could not accomplish any special task. He indulged in conversation or discussion regarding certain issues. The ship was nearing the Colombo port. The port was clearly visible from the ship and Swamiji could see thousands of people waiting there to extend a warm welcome to Swamiji. Among that huge crowd Swamiji searched out his beloved devotees such as Sir Kumaraswami and Arunachalam. Kumaraswami was present there with his British wife and son. His son was very good looking, feet naked and Vibhuti applied on the forehead. Some foreign disciples and friends were also present there—Mrs. Higgins and Mrs. Countess were present

Swami Vivekanand: A Biography

there wearing saffron coloured sari in Bengali style. His friends and disciples in Colombo had already taken permission for alighting from the ship. The good news was that the Plague law was not applied there. Hence, Swami Vivekanand could meet his friends there and travelled there freely without any restrictions. He visited the Buddhist Girls' school, and its hostel and other schools, Buddhist Mutts and temples. Alasinga had to return back to Madras from Colombo, so he also discussed important things with him also.

Early in the morning of 28th June, Swamiji's ship left the Colombo port. Now it increased its speed moving in the Western direction. They were face to face with the real monsoon. Storm was showing its actual destructive form. Day time looked like night due to the deep darkness, wind blowing at a high speed and incessant rains. Huge waves roared and hit the ship. The deck of the ship remained vacant throughout the day. It was very difficult for any body to stay at the deck for long. Some people sat on the dining table for meals. The things kept on the table turned topsy-turvy. The sound of the waves hitting the ship kept on increasing. People felt as if the ship will break into pieces. The captain of the ship was a very jolly kind of person. He took some leisure from his schedule to narrate stories to the passengers. Swamiji also extended a helping hand in this. In this manner, all were able to overcome the hardships and terrific nature of the journey. It was difficult to do mental work sitting inside the cabin. But still Swamiji did something or the other for the 'Udbodhan' magazine.

From the Colombo port, two Chrisitan priests had boarded the ship. One of them was an American, he was married. His name was Bogosh. He had a charming personality. During their seven year old married life they had begotten six children. They considered it to be the God's grace and blessing on them. Whenever the weather became clear, Mrs. Bogosh left her six children on the deck. Some ran, some played and some crawled on their knee; sometimes they smiled, sometimes shouted and sometimes cried. Their presence on the deck made it difficult to even walk on the deck lest those children got injured.

Doing some reading or writing work was out of question. The priest sat at some corner of the deck along with his wife indulging in romantic conversation. They were least worried about their children. Sister Nivedita took care of them and had taken up the role of their mother. Sister Nivedita had taken up the responsibility of feeding them and playing with them. A small girl named 'Tutal' who had lost her mother and was going to England along with her father had become her seventh child. Nivedita's motherly affection drew the children all the more towards her. Nivedita had lightened the work of the priest and his wife and hence, they were greatly pleased with her. But Swamiji developed a feeling of hatred and shame at the act of Mr and Mrs. Bogosh. He began to think that if all the 10 crores of British population died and only a few priests were left then within 20 years, 10 crores of population will be born. Due to severe storm, the progress of the ship had retarded to a great extent. As a result, Golkunda reached Adan in ten days instead of six days.

When the ship reached the Adan port it was already evening. In spite of existence of no differentiation between white and black there, no body was allowed to alight there. During his first foreign trip, Swamiji had visited some places of tourist attraction there. From the deck of the ship the brown-red coloured mountains devoid of any trees or plants was clearly visible, the lull roads were also visible. The hotel in half moon shape on the sea shore and some shops were also visible. There were many other ships on the port of Adan—some were passenger ships and some goods ships.

After some hours, the ship moved through the Red sea. Swamiji explained the geography and history of the places through which the ship passed to his disciples. Swamiji was well aware of the folk tales associated with the Egyptian sphynx and pyramids. As the ship travelled through the Red sea, the passengers experienced extreme heat weather. Still they spent the time in a joyous manner. Red sea was over and they entered Swais river. The ship was moving through a narrow river. Only one ship could cross the Swais river at a time. Restrictions were there in this regard to avoid collisions between ships. On both the river banks, they could see people indulging in water sports. The passengers were really fed up of watching just the blue sky and the blue water so many days. Now they were able to see the green earth on both sides and birds chirpings in the sky. They also enjoyed the shouting and games that the people on both sides of the river indulged in. After sometimes the ship entered the Mediterranean sea. The remains of ancient civilizations of Asia and Africa, everything were left behind.

For Sister Nivedita, this journey in the company of Swami Vivekanand was extremely educative. Swamiji kept on imparting knowledge regarding Indian literature, culture, religion, philosophy, history etc. by discussing on these topics with his disciples.

Sister Nivedita in her book on Swamiji titled *'Half Earth'* has referred to this journey with Swami Vivekanand as the most significant and outstanding. She has expressed all her conversations with her teacher and the kind of impact they have on their heart and soul in a very interesting manner. "From the beginning till the end of this sea journey, many emotions and stories originated and flowed. No body could even guess at what moment Swamiji's door of knowledge may suddenly open and new messages of truth emanated in a powerful language. On the first day of the sea journey, during the evening time we were in conversation when Swamiji suddenly said—"See, as the days are passing, it is becoming clear to me that the most outstanding worship is the attainment of humanity. I will spread this novel message throughout the world. If somebody wants to demonic act, do that also like a human being, if you want to be a cruel person, become a great one."

He kept on talking on different topics or narrated different topics. Most of the time he sat in a serious posture, in a pensive and silent manner. But sometimes it seemed that he was unable to stop the emotions ready to flow out and at last opened the door of his experiences in a helpless manner. Sometimes what he said used to be beyond sister Nivedita's understanding. Swamiji's topics of conversation kept on changing as per his mental conditions. Sometimes he referred to physical love and creation to be the root of all creations. He stated that both in India's Vaishnava religion and the Christianity of the West physical love and creation have been granted recognition. 'A very few people have the courage of worship death or Goddess Kali. We are the only ones who have worshipped death, we have embraced the frightening ones because they are enormous. We should not seek blessings to diminish this enormity. We should accept suffering for the sake of suffering.'

He always kept on emphasizing that to reach the heights of greatness, one should have the strength to face miseries. How many people are there who lose their lives after enjoying different types of worldly comforts. They are of no use to the world. Referring to the context he gave examples of many ardent devotees of God and tears came to his eyes and throat became heavy. When he found himself overwhelmed with such an emotional situation he either changed the topic of conversation or suddenly got up and went away to some other place.

As the ship moved ahead through the Mediterranean sea, foggy mountain ranges near the beach of Italy became visible. When the ship reached Cecily it was already evening time. Faded golden rays of the sun began to swim on the ocean water. The ship slowed down. When the ship was passing through Messina port, the redness of the evening had dissolved. The first phase of night. At the distant sky the weak outline of moon was visible. The moonlight was not in its complete brightness. But still with its twinkling light, the passengers were able to enjoy the natural beauty of the place and people were really attracted by it. As the ship slowly moved besides the Etna Volcano, the shivering smoke went upwards to merge with a void. Swamiji, strolling on the deck explaining the philosophical beauty of Messina to sister Nivedita said, "Messina will thank me, because I am the one who gave this incredible beauty to it." Swamiji believed from the very beginning that human brain is the mine of knowledge and beauty perceptive power. Through the means of education we bring out these wonderful things from this mine, adds shine to it, decorate it and sparkles it to make it useful.

Swamiji was on the deck, next day in the morning. The Cecily island was left behind. There was water, water everywhere, on all four sides. He stood aloof from others and was lost in some deep thoughts. Then as soon as a mood swing occurred, he returned back to his group and related interesting ancient historical stories and instilled life like fervour in those topics of discussion. As he talked about the rise and fall of different countries, a ray of hope shined in his eyes. It seemed as if he will bring about a sea change in India. At that moment, he forgets about the real problems being faced by contemporary India. He forgets the fact that it will take a long time to redeem India from the deep pit of

Swami Vivekanand: A Biography

illiteracy, misery and poverty. He behaved in such a manner as if he had in his possession some magical wand, waving of which would transform the Indian scenario.

As Swamiji strolled on the deck, sometimes he came to a hall all of sudden. His vision tried to look something beyond the horizon. The dream of new India shone on his countenance. What happened to him suddenly? Holding on to the arm of the chair lying beside him, he just throws himself on the chair. The whole body without any movement, his face turned pale without any sign of blood, eyes empty of any expressions. It seemed as if he had become aware of the reality, his limitations and the short durability of his life. He was experiencing a child like helplessness. His co-travellers understands his deep rooted love towards his motherland. Within sometime Swamiji regained back his normal self.

This happened almost always. His disciples were aware of his unpredictable behaviour. He never used to get tired of relating stories about the life of Gurudev Sri Ramakrishna and other such saints. He relied on his disciples and devotees very much and always used to say that even after him his disciples and devotees will carry out the activities of Ramakrishna Mission. In this manner, Swamiji's sea journey passed with the rise and fall of different tides of thoughts. During this period, he also wrote many articles and essays to be published in 'Udbodhan'.

On July 31, 1899 Swamiji's ship reached London's Tilvery dock. There were many of his friends and devotees present there to welcome him. Two American disciples of Swamiji Christine and Mrs. Funky were also present there. They had heard the news about Swamiji's arrival in London, in America. They could not resist their curiosity to meet Swamiji, so they reached London from Detroit. Swamiji stayed at a place called Wimbledon a few distance away from London. That time Swamiji did not give any pubic speeches in London. But his old English acquaintances, friends and devotees did not let him stay in peace. The two weeks that he stayed in London was spent in seminars and meetings. When he was still in London, he received many invitations to take part in conferences and seminars in America. His American disciples were also in a hurry to take him to America. In Britain, Swamiji's health was not in good stead and he was not able to accomplish any work according to his wish. Hence, he decided to depart to America at the earliest.

On 16th August along with Guru brother Turiyanand and two of his American disciples he set off to New York. Sister Nivedita stayed back in London for some important work. About this sea journey from London to America, Mrs. Funky had written—"The memories of those ten days spent on sea were not to be forgotten. The morning time was spent in reading the Gita and explaining it. Along with that reading of Sanskrit poems and stories and their explanation and translation, chanting of ancient prayers. The sea was peaceful and the night was illuminated with moon light. The evening was really wonderful. Swamiji, in a royal image, strolling on the deck and sometimes taking the halt and turning towards us to talk about the beauty of nature. Once he suddenly stood up and said—"When this empire of illusion has this much of beauty inherent in it then how much beauty will be inherent in the truth behind this illusion. . . . . ." An extremely beautiful evening, up above in the sky the moon was in its full form, the night with an extreme soft-golden brightness had a secretive attraction in it. He stood silent relishing the beauty of the nature. Suddenly he turned towards us and pointing his hands towards the sky and the ocean said—'Recitation of poem is of what good when the whole meaning in it spread all of over here.' "

It took ten days to reach America from London. But it seemed as if these ten days begot the wings of wind. Nobody could explain how these ten days passed so quickly. At New York, Swamiji stayed as guest at the house of the Ligate Couple. They extended a cordial welcome to Swamiji and his disciples. That very day, in the evening, he along with Swami Turiyanand, went to the village of home of the Ligate couple about 150 miles from New York on their request. Swamiji's health had been deteriorating for the past few years. When the Ligate Couple noticed Swamiji's lack of energy and enthusiasm as compared to his last visit, they became very sorrowful. They put a stop on all his public engagements and made all arrangements for his treatment and nursing. After one month, sister Nivedita also came back to Swamiji after accomplishing her work in London. Swami Abhedananda was looking after the work of propagation of Vedanta in America. When he heard about Swamiji's arrival in New York, he went to meet him. When Swamiji heard about his description of the propagation of Vedanta in America, he was very much happy. He felt happy to hear that the process of arrangement of a permanent hall for teaching Vedanta was going on. Abhedananda formally inaugurated the Hall on October 15, 1899 and within 9 weeks the Vedanta class began to held daily. In addition to explanation of Vedanta scripture, question-answer session was also organized. Swami Turiyananda began to teach children at Mount Clair. There he narrated tales from Hitopadesha and other ancient scriptures to the children. He extended a helping hand in the work of Vedanta Samiti established by Swami Abhedananda.

The rest and treatment had a positive impact on Swamiji's health, during this period. When he felt that his health has regained a bit, it became impossible for him to stay indoors in the village house. In spite of the Ligate couples' repeated requests, Swamiji took leave from them and reached New York on November 5. After two days, Swamiji attended a question-answer session amidst the pubic. Swami Abhedananda introduced to him the new members of the Vedanta Committee. In the library of the committee, Swamiji was given a commendation letter in the presence of many common people, friends and devotees. As thanks giving, Swamiji gave a beautiful speech.

 Now Swamiji's life had become very busy there. Amidst his busy schedules, Swamiji used to be haunted by the few days of his life that were remaining. He was able to see the dark shadows of death hovering around him. One day, he said to Swami Abhedananda—"Oh brother, my days are counted. Maximum I will live for three or four years from now." Swami Abhedananda instantly said to him that Swami Vivekanand should not nurse any such thoughts in his mind and that his health had shown marked improvement. And that if stayed in America some more time he will be able to gain back his lost health once again. He further said that it was just the beginning and their area of work was so huge and the distance they have to cover so long that such depressing thoughts would cause damage to their efforts. But Abhedananda's views had no effect on Swamiji. He resumed his talk saying—"Brother, you are not able to understand me. I am feeling as if from within I am assuming a huge form. My ego is going on increasing to such an extent that sometimes I have the feeling that my body does not have the capacity to bind me within its bound. I am about to burst. This cage of truth, flesh and blood cannot hold me for long now."

But Swami Vivekanand was not among those who got despaired by the thought of death nearing them. He had less time and more work in front of him. He did not get the opportunity to enjoy each breath or each moment of his life till the end of his life. On November 22, he set off on a long and difficult journey from New York to California. At California, Swamiji and his disciples became guest at the house of a 70 year old lady Mrs. Blossets. Swamiji's old American disciples Ms. Josephine Mc Leod made arrangement for Swamiji's stay there as she was well aware of the old lady's devotion towards Swamiji. It was at her request that Swamiji was invited to California.

When Ms. Mac Leod reached Mrs. Blosset's house for the first time before Swamiji's arrival there, the former saw a portrait size photo of Swamiji displayed on the wall and to know the mind of the old woman she asked her whose photo was that. In her elderly shivering but devoted voice she had replied—'If there is any supreme soul on this earth then this is that human being. I saw this person during the World Religion Congress held in Chicago in the year 1863.' After this, Mrs. Blossets narrated the success stories related to Swamiji in connection with the Chicago World Religion Congress.

When Swamiji came to stay at her house as her guest, her happiness knew no bounds. There Swami used to be too busy with her religious talks and speeches. But that old lady did not attend any of such programmes. She used to be too busy with preparing delicacies of Swamiji's choice. She felt satisfied by preparing and serving food with her own hands for Swamiji and his disciples.

Swamiji stayed in California for about seven months. Luckily the climate there then suited Swamiji very well. Hence, he utilized the situation by working hard and touring cities like Los Angels and other places in California. At some places he was supposed to deliver speech and at some places question-answer session and at some places seminars.

Thousands of audiences used to present in the meetings related to Vedanta philosophy. In addition, he taught Raj Yoga to girl and boy students interested in the topic.

During this period, on being invited by the chief of Auckland Unitarian Church, Dr. Benjamin Mills, Swamiji gave eight continuous speeches at the said church. Swamiji's knowledge got mention and coverage in local newspapers. Dr. Benjamin organized a religious conference in honour of Swamiji. Many missionaries and people belonging to different religious affinities attended the conference. Swamiji was praised for his religious insight. Praising Swamiji, on the occasion, Dr. Benjamin Mills said, "In fact, Swamiji is an extremely intellectual person that big lecturers and professors from our university are mere children in front of him."

After Auckland, Swamiji gave series of speeches at San Francisco, the capital of California. There also a Vedanta Samiti was established. Swamiji entrusted the task of Vedanta propagation there with Swami Turiyananda. Before Swamiji's departure from California, one of his American disciples, Ms. Mini C.Book gave 160 acres of land in charity to construct a permanent Mutt. The land situated at St. Anton Valley in the Santa Claura country of California was a peaceful location away from thick population. The railway station there was just 50 miles and the Post office just 3 miles from the place.

In the beginning of August, Swamiji along with his disciples and devotees set on to see the land. Luckily the weather was very pleasant. The loneliness of the route added to the beauty of the nature. Swamiji enjoyed the beauty of the nature's bliss to its utmost level. The wind was as if granting energy to them. Then path though wild and tough was really enjoyable. The solitariness of the place was its uniqueness. Hence, Swamiji named the future ashram to be built there as 'Shanti ashram' or 'Peace Retreat.'

The green lands in the vicinity was as if boasting the fertility of the land in a silent manner. But for miles together, no source of water was visible. Still the sannyasis were in a state of excitement. They set up tents of tarpaul. Swamiji entrusted them with different responsibilities as he also assisted them with various activities. Though from a distance, arrangement was made for drinking water also.

Within a few days, a small piece of land was thoroughly cleared of grass and bushes and a small but was built, a well was dug. Swami Turiyananda and his 12 foreign disciples reverberated the whole atmosphere with the chanting of Vedic Mantra. The environment devoid of any fragrance became enveloped with the smoke and sweet fragrance of incense, Swamiji had a heartfelt desire that America should also have a synonym to India's forest ashram. This dream got fulfilled in the form of Shanti Ashram. But the sad part of it was that Swamiji could not see its developed form—huge building, attractive garden and its huge number of students, in his life time.

The Shanti Ashram did not show any sympathy to Swamiji's ill-health. Whatever improvement was evident in Swamiji's health after his arrival in America, everything drained out from his body. The construction and establishment of Shanti Ashram had taken a toll of his health. Hence Swamiji took off from his busy schedule to take rest for which he went to a village called Camp Teller. After three weeks of rest, he reached New York meeting on route his friends in San Francisco, Detroit and Chicago. During this period, he did not make any significant public speech. After entrusting the task of Vedanta propagation at California with Swami Turiyananda, when Swamiji was taking leave at San Francisco, tears came into the eyes of every disciple. With a heavy throat Swami Turiyananda enquired about the nature of the newly entrusted responsibilities on him. Swami Vivekanand instantly gave a reply—"Go and establish the ashram in California. Hoist the flag of Vedanta there. From this moment onwards, erase every memory of India from your brain. Above all, lead a meaningful life. After this, every thing will happen as per the mother's wishes."

After returning back to New York, Swamiji stayed at the permanent building of the Vedanta Samiti. Now he had developed a kind of disinterestedness towards speech, oration and pubic education. Most o the time he spent alone and sometimes spent some hours with his friends. He received a message from the Ligate couple from London that they will go to Paris in July. They invited Swamiji also to Paris. At the same time, Swamiji also received an invitation from the Religious Congress of the Paris Exhibition. The

Swami Vivekanand: A Biography

medium of communication of this religious conference was French language. Hence, two months prior to its beginning Swamiji began to learn the language and within a short time span, he commanded full control over the language.

Swamiji reached Paris in the last week of July. There again Mr. and Mrs. Legate made him their guest. Ms. Josephine Mc Leod had reached there at her sister Mrs. Legate's house much earlier. In Paris, the Ligate couple owned a big, spacious beautiful and comfortable home. Swamiji stayed with them for few weeks and then began to stay with one of his friends Gerald Noble, but he had his lunch with the Ligate couple itself. The Ligate couple invited the representatives and members who have arrived in Paris to attend the conference for lunch at their place. Hence, Swamiji got an opportunity to meet some renowned people there. One of them, with whom Swamiji developed deep friendship was the Principal of Edinburgh University Patrick Gades; famous catholic priests Father Pear, Yare Mant and Mansyo Juboa, renowned canon maker Hirem Maxim, famous European singer Madame Karl, famous actress Sara Burhurt and Indian scientist Jagdish Chandra Basu.

The house of Ligate couple was a centre of attraction during those days. Talented people from various walks of life and fields of art like philosopher, scientist, politician, social worker, singer, teacher, painter etc. assembled here.

In the religious conference to be held in Paris no thought or philosophy on spirituality was stated to be discussed. There only discussion of the historic development of various religious groups was to be held. Hence, there was a scarcity of Christian priests there. The members of the conference were mostly scholars who have devoted their life totally in research on the origin and development of different religions. Because of ill-health, Swamiji could speak only in two meetings, but he made it sure to be present in every meeting. He was able to win over everyone due to his royal personality, scholastic speeches and sweet humble nature. Some Christians present in the meeting expressed their view that Indian civilization, literature, philosophy and astrology has Greek influence on them. But Swamiji proved them wrong by citing a comparative explanation of the facts inherent in Hinduism and Buddhism. He said that even if somebody drowned himself in the eternal ocean of ancient

Sanskrit literature even then he won't be able to find even a shadow of Greek influence. As opposed Greek civilization and literature is influenced by India.

During Swamiji's stay in Paris, he became very close to the then popular singer Madame Karl with whom he had become acquainted during his first visit to America. Now their acquaintance turned into strong friendship. Karl was not only a singer but also a scholar of philosophical literature. She always entered into a debate with Swamiji on various topics pertaining to religion and philosophy. There is no true teacher in the school of life than sorrow and poverty. Madame Karl's childhood and youth was spent in hardship and poverty. In spite of all hardships with devotion and hard work she attained a respectable position in the society. Later on Swamiji referred about Madame Karl as a "strange union of beauty, youthfulness, talent and divine voice."

Madame Karl was one among Swamiji's true devotees and friends. She was present at the Chicago World Religion Congress. During those days, she was in the grip of mental tension. In such an indefinite mental state, she decided to meet Swamiji. Before taking her to the place where swamiji had been residing she was forewarned to remain silent till Swamiji asked him question. She later described her first meeting with Swamiji in an interesting manner.

"I went inside the room and stood silent. He was sitting on the floor in a meditative posture. His long saffron outfit was lying on the floor. His head covered with saffron head was cast downwards and eyes centred on the floor. After some times, without looking at me he said—'Dear, your heart is unstable. Be calm and peaceful. It is the first priority.' After this the calm and uninquisitive man, who even did not know my name began to tell about the reasons of my most secret problems and turbulence. He talked about such things, which in my thought was not known to even my closest of friends. This incident was almost magical and superhuman. At last I asked him—'How do you know all this? Who talked about me to you?' With a peaceful smile he looked towards me as if I have asked a simple question like the ones asked by kids. Then he replied—'Nobody told me anything. Do you think that it is essential to hear all this? I have read your heart like an open book? It was time to bid good bye. As I stood up to leave, he said—"Try to forget the past things.

Again make your soul happy. Take care of your health. Do not try to hide your sufferings deep within you. Try to divert your emotions in some form or express them outwardly. It is very necessary for your spiritual health. It is the demand of your art."

Madame Karl after this first introduction to Swamiji returned back greatly impressed by his personality, words and his wonderful spiritual power. She felt that after getting a glimpse of Swamiji all her complex problems that had been haunting her for years had got solved, mental tension and turmoil had disappeared to nowhere. Later on she wrote about that situation—"Later on when my acquaintance with him became strong, I saw that he kept worries and excitement of his audience at bay and made there minds calm so that they could listen to his words properly and follow them." Madame Karl's spiritual life was deeply influenced by Swamiji. He pulled her to a new world of emotions and gave a new vigour to her religious beliefs which were on the brink of death.

Madame Karl was planning a tour to Egypt from Paris. She requested Swamiji to accompany her for the tour. Swamiji accepted the invitation. During Swamiji's stay in Paris, Ms. Mc Leod had taken him to all places of tourist interest in Paris. Now there was nothing left in Paris for him to see. Hence, Swamiji set off to Egypt along with Madame Karl and Ms. Mc Leod. On route they stayed in Vienna for two days, nine days in Kustuntunia and four days in Athens and met many people and then they reached the capital of Egypt-Cairo. As they were wandering there once they lost their way as they were engrossed in conversation and reached a dirty slinking street. There some half naked women were standing on the doorsteps of their houses and some were peeping from the windows. Some such women were sitting on the bench of the street. They burst into laughter on seeing Swamiji and they called him near them through action. One of the women in Swamiji's group asked them leave the place immediately. But Swamiji did not pay heed to her and went towards the bench where the women were sitting and said—"Unfortunate children. In the course of worshipping beauty they have forgotten the God. Just look at them." He experienced extreme sorrow as he stood in front of those down cast women. Tears came rolling down his eyes. The women began to look at each other in a sense of surprise. Then one among them got up and came near Swamiji and bowed down before him, embraced him and kissed the end of Swamiji's saffron outfit that touched the ground and said in Spanish—'The person who knows God!' One woman sitting on the bench covered her face in shame and fear as if her polluted soul was unable to bear the extremely pious and divine eyes of Swamiji, as if the secrets hidden beneath her heart were getting revealed.

At Cairo, Swamiji was getting keen to reach India. In the meantime, he received a bad news from India that the founder of Mayawati Mutt, Mr. Xavier had left the earthly abode. The news was shocking to Swamiji which all the more weakened his spirit. Now he decided to return back to India at the earliest. Madame Karl reserved a first class ticket for Swamiji for his return journey to India. The time to take leave was nearing and finally Madame Karl and Ms. Mc Leod tearfully bade good bye to Swamiji, seeing him off as he boarded the ship to India.

In the same ship a young American Missionary, Reams Caskins was also on his way to India. He was acquainted with the name of Swamiji but he had never got an opportunity to meet him. On board the ship, he came to know that his co-passenger donning the outfit of a saint is Swami Vivekanand. In the eating hall both exchanged wishes but none of them took an initiative for conversation. Caskins felt agonized. From the time of Chicago World Religion Congress when Swamiji established and proved the supremacy of Hinduism over other religions and criticized the Christian Missionaries for the activities undertaken by them in India, he had developed a sense of rebellion against Swamiji. He wanted to enter into a debate with Swamiji on various topics but he did not muster courage to talk to him in face of his humble and serious personality. But his heart longed to start the conversation which was evident from his eyes.

Swami understood his feeling and asked one day—'Are you from America?' He replied 'Yes'. Swamiji asked—'A missionary?' He again relied—'Yes'. Again Swamiji put up the question—"You are propagating your religion in my country?" Caskins turned Swamiji's question to him from high side—'Why are you propagating your religion in my country?' Within a wink of the eyes shine of friendship and cordiality striked. Both of them burst into a peal of laughter which continued for some time. Then both of them shook hands striking friendship.

Swamiji always talked with Caskins for sometime after he was over with his thinking and meditation. One day as both of them were talking, Swamiji got excited and said in a loud roaring tone—"Let England teach it the nuances of the art of politics because Britain is the leader in this art. Let America teach us agriculture and science. Because the wonderful manner in which you are accomplishing your job, we are at your feet. But no country can boast of imparting religious teachings in the way India does." As he said these words Swamiji's face became red and his tone harsh. This short meeting in the ship bridged the distance between Swamiji and Caskins. Both of them became very intimate with each other. In Caskins view 'Swamiji was more of a patriot than a philosopher.' In fact, he wanted to uplift the humanity which was suffering miseries. When he was in good mood he talked on such touchy issues which were not typical of any particular country. Those talks usually were about the critical state of humanity—the humanity in the grip of hunger, poverty, nakedness and in the process Swamiji used to get overwhelmed by emotion.

Swamiji was never able to forget the fact that his own motherland was the main centre of such a humanity. When he was out of India touring other countries, these Mutters pinched him a lot. The letters that he wrote to his friends, disciples and devotees in India while he was abroad reflected his real state of mind. After reaching America on October 30, 1899, in a letter addressed to Mary Hale he wrote—Some hundred modernized, half educated and men devoid of nationalist feelings are the show piece of British India at present. Nothing else. Interpreting the British policies in India he further wrote—

"This is the present situation. Now they will not let education spread any more, the freedom of press has already been throttled (we have already been disarmed) and the little opportunity of self rule which had been granted earlier is also being snatched away from us. We are waiting as to what will happen next. Those who indulged in constructive criticism were meted out with the punishment of 'Kala Pani' and others are being imprisoned without any court proceedings and some people do not have any idea when they will be beheaded."

For some years, India has been passing through a phase of terrorized administration. English soldiers are killing our countrymen, dishonouring our sisters and living a life of luxury with our resources. We are in a state of utter darkness. Where is God? Mary, you might be an optimist but is it possible for me to be one? Suppose you just publish this letter in any newspaper, British Government with the help of the newly enacted law will drag me to India from here and without any legal procedure kill me. And I am sure that all your Christian government will be happy with it because I am a non-christian. Do you think that I can sleep in peace and be an optimist?

This severe criticism of British rule by Swami Vivekanand do not mean that he considered Britishers to be responsible for all the ills happening in India. In fact his thoughts were opposed to this and he time and again emphasized that the root cause of India's downfall was its own weakness and that it was futile to blame the Britishers.

Swamiji was clear in his mind that Indians will attain political rights only when they are completely capable for that. In his opinion, this capability cannot be achieved by putting forth proposals for political rights but by serving the suffering people of the society and then proving their own worth. Severely criticizing the modus operand: of Indian National Congress at that time he wrote a letter to Akhandananda—"Where is your Congress in this time of severe fame, flood, disease and plague? Is it just sufficient to say to hand over administrative power to us? And who will listen to them? If a person does his work then where is the need to open his mouth to demand anything? If 2000 people like you were working in different districts, then the British government would have themselves called upon you and talked about administration."

What is significant here is the fact that at that time when Congress had in it members belonging to educated and rich upper middle class families, Swami Vivekanand called his disciples to work in the middle of farmers and labourers. In the same letter he further wrote—"You have wrote about opening a centre at Bhagalpur. This thought of educating the students is undoubtedly a splendid one but our mission is meant for the poor, downtrodden and illiterate farmers and labourers and after doing everything possible for them, if time is left then you can do something for the upper class of the society."

Vivekanand wanted to sensitize the farmers and the labourers about their conditions and at the same time create awareness about the powers inherent in them and then leave them alone to chart their own course of progress. He did not believe that their upgradation is possible with the help of rich class. But he was not in favour of class conflict. He further wrote to Akhandananda—'Teach a few village girls and boys the basic tenets of education and settle some great thoughts in their minds. After this, villagers in every village make contributions to set up a union, thereby proving the meaningfulness of 'Uddharedatmaratmanam' which means 'uplifting one's soul with one's own profession.' We are helping them so that they are able to help themselves. It is their efforts that give you daily meals. The moment they gain awareness regarding their situation and understand the need of assistance and development, then you will know that you were on the right path. Whatever small service that rich people do to the poor are not permanent which in fact causes destruction for both the parties in the end. The society of farmers and labourers are on the brink of death and the need of the hour is that the rich should help them gain their strength once again and nothing else. Then let the farmers and labourers face their problems and chalk out solutions thereof. But he cautions that there emerges no seed of contention between the poor and the rich. Be careful that nothing adverse is told against the rich—a knowledgable person should do his work with his own labour."

In conclusion to his letter to Swami Akhandananda he wrote, "I hate arguments, counterarguments, fundamentalism communal indifferences like person in this old age of mine. Be sure that one who will work, he will be the ornament of my head." This was not a sheer advice for others. But he himself practiced it. Whether in his own country or abroad, he kept on working according to his capability. Work, work and work – Swami Vivekanand did not consider anything other than this. During his second trip abroad he had to suffer so many hardships which is evident in the letter that he wrote to Josephine Mc Leod on March 7, 1900 from San Francisco. "Shortage of money and thorough hard work but still no outcome. The condition is bad than in Los Angeles. If you have to shell out nothing then people come in huge numbers to hear my speech but when the question of shelling out money arises then no body attends, that is the condition."

Still people had a misconception that Swamiji undertook tours to Europe and America in search of luxury and comfort. One among them was a British named E.D. Sturdy. Earlier he was deeply impressed by Swami Vivekanand. But later on he began to campaign against Swamiji. In reply, on November 1899 Swamiji wrote a letter from New York in reply to Sturdy's false propaganda against him which depicts a very touching picture of Swamiji's life in Britain.

"I remember your house in reading, where I have to survive on the boiled cabbage and potatoes rice given to me and the chutney your wife served to me swearing upon me. I do not remember whether you gave me a cigarette to smoke. Nor I remember of having ever complained to you about the food or your wife's swearings. Although I entered your home like a thief, always shuddering with fear and keeping on doing work for you daily.

The next memories of mine are associated with the house situated on St. George Road owned by you and Ms. Muller. There also I do not remember of enjoying any comfort or luxury in terms of meals or even room.

The second place where I stayed was that at Ms. Muller's house. Though she was very good to me, I had to survive on fruits and dry fruits. The other memories are associated with that dark dingy room in London, where I had to work hard day and night and usually have to cook food for five-six people and where most of the nights I have to survive on bread and butter.

I remember once Mrs. Muller called me for dinner and gave place to spend the night even but the very next day itself condemned the smoking black barbarous fellow."

Sturdy perhaps referred about the ideals of ancient India. Replying to it, Swamiji wrote in an emotional tone – "You told thousands of things about ancient India. That India is still alive...It is not dead and that India which is alive, even today without the fear of anyone or without the sympathy of a rich person, unconcerned about any opinion, whether within her own country where she is bridled and there where the other end of the bridle is in the hands of her ruler, has the courage to send across her message. That India is still alive. That unchangeable India with eternal love and permanent dedication, not only in terms of rituals but in terms of love, dedication and friendship."

What power is inherent in those worlds. But when Vivekanand was writing them the strength of his body was draining out. From the time he returned back from his first foreign trip, he felt as if the shadow of death was hovering around him. In November 1898 he wrote to the king of Khatri from Belur Mutt – "As far as my health is concerned, my heart has become weak. I do not think that change of air would be of any good. Whatever be the case, I feel that all my life's works have come to an end. My life's boat moved in the flow of good and bad, happiness and sorrow till now. The big thing that I have learned in my life is that there is nothing other than sorrow in this life. Only the Mother (Goddess Kali) knows what is good. We all are puppets at the hands of action and work according to its orders. The only basis of life which is really invaluable is love, eternal love,... The one who attains it is the luckiest of all."

This letter betrays Swamiji's state of mind. It shows that he was clearly aware that he had to live in this world for some more time only. It also reflects his sad demeanour. But this state of mind did not continue till his end. Though his health deteriorated day by day, his mental turbulence and turmoil vanished. In February 1899 he wrote a letter to Josephine Mc Leod from Belur Mutt – "I am not experiencing sorrow anymore. I have come to terms with my fate. I have suffered with physical and mental tension during my life. But I have unlimited blessing of Mother upon me. I have enjoyed the joy and blessings more than my share. I am not fighting to cause failure to Mother but I am keeping on fighting so that she watches me in action and I breathe my last in the battle field."

With this firm decision Swami Vivekanand kept on working. But as his health deteriorated, different kinds of doubts about the objectives of life raised their hands in his mind. After reaching America, on September 2, 1899 he wrote in a letter – "Life is a union of conflicts and myths…the secret of life is not worldly comfort but learning through experiences. But unfortunately, the moment we begin to gain actual knowledge, that very moment the call to go out of this world comes."

Sometimes he used to get bored with his busy life and yearned for peace. Sometimes he felt irritated at himself that he embraced such a busy life when his life was full of love and devotion. In a letter written from Los Angeles on December 12, 1899 he wrote – "I have committed many mistakes in my life but the reason for each one was overt love. Now I have begun to hate love. Oh, if I have no devotion at all in my possession. In fact, I want to be a hard core Vedanti devoid of any emotions. Now let it be, this life is about to end. I will try it out in my next life." Analyzing his life he further wrote – "I am thirsty of peace but because of love my heart could not achieve it. Conflicts and sufferings, sufferings and conflicts…! But whatever was to happen, just happened, there is no solution for them…"

As Swami Vivekanand saw his end near, he made up his mind to distance himself from the responsibilities of Ramakrishna Mission and the Mutt. He wanted the Guru brothers to take up the responsibilities till he is alive so that they do not face any difficulties later on. In the beginning of the year 1900 he withdrew himself from all the designations associated with the Mutt and the Mission and whatever funds he had collected for it he formulated a trust for the same.

In a letter addressed to Swami Brahmanand on 12 March he wrote – "You all are saints and great men. Just pray to the 'Mother' that now all these difficulties do not remain on my shoulders. Now I need some peace. I do not have the strength to shoulder these responsibilities. Whatever life is left of I want to take rest and have peace of mind." In a letter addressed to Ms. Mary Hale on 22nd March, he expressed his heart in a more clear manner – "As far as I am concerned, I am tired of continuous traveling hence, I want to return back home and take rest. Now I do not want to do any more work. My case is like that of a scholar for whom retirement is impossible. I never get that. I am desirous of getting it especially since I am totally broken and tired of working this much. Whenever I receive a letter from Mrs. Xavier from her residence in the Himalayas, I feel like flying towards the Himalayas. I am really tired of stage, work, permanent travel, meeting with new people and oration."

On 28th March, Vivekanand wrote another letter to Mary Hale and expressed his increasing disinterestedness towards, the worldly things. "I am raising above the stink of happiness and sorrow in the form of happiness and sorrow. For the meaning of all such things is losing sense. This world is a dream, which will break at an early stage or a later stage. Here there is no value of anyone's laugh or weep. This is just a dream." He further wrote – "I am attaining that peace, which is beyond intellect which is neither happiness or sorrow but above both. The physical and mental ailments that I have been suffering during the past two to three years has helped me to attain this. Now I am nearing that state of peace, eternal silence. The most important thing that I can attain is the soul. I am free. I am free. Hence, I need nothing else to be happy. I have been alone since eternity and hence I was free, I am free and will remain free forever. This is the opinion of Vedanta. All these day, I have been propagating philosophy. But it is a reason to be joyous, my dear sister, that now I am experiencing it almost everyday. Yes, I am experiencing it."

Now with that experience Swamiji slowly attained peace and felt no anxiety as before. The letters written during that time shows that he was totally ready to embrace death at that time. In a letter written to Josephine Mc Leod, he wrote – "I am healthy, mentally more healthy. Instead of physical rest I am experiencing dire need of rest for my soul. Victory or defeat is inevitable in a conflict. I have packed my things and waiting for my redeemer. In this condition, old experiences are getting enlivened and coming before my eyes. As he was traveling from one place to another in America, memories of his youth came up before his eyes in a vivid manner and he felt as if Gurudev Ramakrishna was calling him.

"Do not forget that I am that same boy who with full concentration but wondrous emotions used to hear the surprising words of Sri Ramakrishna in Dakshineswar under the Panchvati tree. This is my true nature, action, industry, service to others are all superficial aspects. Now I am again hearing his sweet words. That ever acquainted voice that give me goose bumps. The relationship is breaking and the lamp of love is about to die. Action is becoming disinteresting. The attraction towards life is also diminishing and now just the sweet serious words of my Guru is to be heard. I am coming Lord. He is saying – "Let them bury the dead and you become my follower. I am coming, my lord of love."

As he was getting ready to bid adieu to life, Swami Vivekanand did not have any guilty feeling. In a letter to Josephine he wrote – "I am happy that I am born and happy that I suffered all these miseries; I am happy that I have committed great mistakes and I am happy that I am going to get merged with the peaceful ocean of redemption. I am not leaving anyone in foundation for myself nor I am I taking any foundation." Now he developed a feeling of indifference towards his image as a leader. If at all he had any liking towards himself, it was his image as the disciple of Ramakrishna and that too as a young boy in the beginning when he sat near Ramakrishna's feet. In his words – "Even if I get redemption in the body, that first man has already gone, gone for ever and will not come back. The teacher, Guru, leader Vivekanand has gone, now what remains is that boy, favourite disciple of the Lord and the servant of Lord. For him the work he accomplished as a Guru and a leader, for which he undertook so much of pains, had no significance for him. In comparison to that life full of life, the imagination of life after death seemed to be more attractive to him – "the selfishness behind my work, the ego behind my love, the fear behind my piety and the desire of power behind my guidance of right path everything is now getting dissolved and I am flowing. In that wordless, unknowing and wonderful world I am coming as a viewer not as an actor.

Behind this happy welcoming of death, Swamiji was prevailed by the feeling that there is nothing in this world. In a letter to Mary Hale written on June 17, 1900 he wrote – "If at any moment I felt the futility of worldly things that was now at this moment. This world is worth hating, criminal and equivalent to a dead. Whosoever thinks of helping it is a foolish person. But we should make efforts for redemption while doing good or bad. I hope that I have done so. Lord take me to that redemption. I have renounced thinking about

India or any other country. Now I have become selfish and want my own upliftment. The one who expressed the Almighty through the Vedas, which is expressed in the heart of each one, I take shelter under him with the hope to free myself from all boundation.

On 23rd June he wrote to Mary Hale again – "I am bent upon getting freedom from every sort of sentiments and emotional overflow and if you find me sentimental ever again, hang me to death. I am the follower of Advaita philosophy, our aim is knowledge devoid of any emotions, without any affection because all these fall under the category of earthly elements, myths and boundation. I am just truth and knowledge."

In such an emotional state, if at all Vivekanand felt joyous about something was the fact that he was able to see the end of his life very near to him. On 14th October, 1900 in a letter to Ms. Christian in Paris he wrote – "In the same manner as the bird taking a nap on the branch of a tree awakens by day break and flies high up in the sky singing, my life is also coming to an end. I feel that now the Mother of the Earth will take me through the life's path slowly without any sort of interruption. Now there is no need to travel on an obstructive path. Now life will be a bed of roses. Are you getting it? I am totally sure about it."

Only a few days were left in the execution of this imagination on the part of Swami Vivekanand.

■■

Mahaprayana (The Final Journey)

The chilled night of December 9, 1900. The silence of midnight has enveloped Belur Mutt at 10 o'clock in the night. In the corner of the Mutt, a faded light was winking. Perhaps somebody is sitting over there. In the inner verandah, the sannyasis were sitting on the floor for dinner. In front of the main gate of the Mutt a carriage came and halted. The gardener sitting on the corner saw the carriage stopping and somebody wearing a long coat and hat alighting from the carriage. He ran inside to bring the gate key. But when he opened the gate the carriage was empty. With lantern in his hand he inspected the place but nobody was visible there. There the person was standing in front of the dining hall by slightly pulling his hat towards his face. One sannyasi holding a small earthern lamp in his hand came in front of the person. Oh that was none other than their own beloved Swamiji. Within a second, all the Guru brothers gathered around Swamiji. They began to shout in a unified voice – "Swamiji has come", "Swamiji has come." Swamiji burst out into a peel of laughter and said that he had heard the sound of bell for dinner and had jumped over the boundary walls to reach the dining hall before everything got over. Then he said – "I am feeling hungry. Give me something to eat." He was made to sit on the wooden board and served with pudding. Swamiji relished the *khichdi* as he was having it after a long time and went on talking with his Guru brothers.

Swami Vivekanand's joy knew no bounds after returning back to Belur Mutt after a long gap. He was happy to know that even in his absence the work in the Mutt continued in a planned manner. He had to accomplish many tasks in Belur. He could not resist his curiosity to make a visit to Mrs. Xavier who after her husband's death, who was the president of Mayawati Ashram, was looking after the work of the Ashram. Hence, no sooner than he reached Belur, he made preparations to go to Mayawati. The route from Kathgodam to Mayawati was blocked due to snowfall but Swamiji continued with his journey. He completed the journey with great difficulties. By the time Swamiji reached his destination, he felt ill. He was already weak. It was due to the difficulties of the journey. But by the time he reached Mayawati, Swamiji forgot the difficulties that he faced en route. He said to Mrs. Xavier – "In fact my health got deteriorated now but my mental state is strong and active as before." Swamiji stayed at Mayawati Ashram for about 15 days, but because of snowfall and fog, Swamiji could not enjoy the open air by taking long strolls. People queued at the ashram to meet him, still whenever Swamiji was free and alone he wrote many essays for the 'Udbodhan' magazine. One day, he called his disciples Swami Swarupanand and gave him inputs regarding the coordination and publication of the magazine 'Prabuddha Bharat.'

The sannyasis residing in the ashram converted a room inside the ashram into a temple. There they set up an idol of Shri Ramakrishna and offered with flowers, fruits, incense etc. They sang devotional songs. Swamiji felt sad at the physical worship being undertaken in the Advaita ashram. In the evening when all of them assembled for the 'Havan' at the altar of fire, then he told them that whatever they have been doing was inappropriate. But he did not order them to stop physical worship with immediate effect. He did not want to hurt the sentiments of the sannyasis. But the residents of the ashram realized their fault and discontinued with their routine of offering physical worship to Sri Ramakrishna. But one of the inmates did not like this. Turning very much emotional at this incident, he tried to gain permission of continuing with physical worship of Sri Ramakrishna from Mother Sharda. But Mother Sharda wrote – Sri Ramakrishna believed in Advaita and propagated it. Why don't you follow Advaita being his disciple. All his disciples are followers of Advaita philosophy." When Swamiji returned back to Belur from Mayawati, he told to his Guru brothers and disciples there – "I was thinking that there would be at least one Mutt of ours where in physical worship would not be practiced. But after reaching there I found that the old man was sitting then in yogic posture."

At Belur Mutt, Vivekanand constantly received invitation from Dhaka. Due to ill health, Swamiji kept on postponing it. In the meantime, his mother expressed her wish to go on a pilgrimage to East Bengal and Assam. During his foreign trip itself Swamiji had decided that he will spend the rest of his life in serving his mother. On 17th January, 1900 in a letter he wrote – "Now I am quite clear that I should free myself from all worries regarding the Mutt and spent some time with my mother. She had suffered so much due to me. I should try my level best to make her last days free from all worries." On 7th March, he departed for Dhaka along with some of his disciples and mother.

At Dhaka Station the welcome committee extended a warm welcome to him. Renowned people invited him and his groups to their homes. At the insistence of people, he gave two speeches. On the day of Budhashtami, Swamiji along with his mothers and other companions went to Langal Bandh on a boat and took bath in the holy river of Brahmaputra. That night Swamiji protracted fever due to fatigue. Everybody was worried about returning back to Calcutta. But as the morning dawned he seemed to regain back his health to some extent.

People gathered to have a glimpse of Swamiji. One day, a woman came to meet Swamiji in full make up. When the sannyasis came to know that she was a prostitute, they denied her entry to meet Swamiji taking into consideration her impious lifestyle. When Swamiji came to know about it, he himself went to her and asked what she wanted. The woman was deeply moved by Swamiji's behaviour and touched Swamiji's feet and related her miseries. She said that she was fed up by recurrent attacks of asthma and if Swamiji gave her some medicine with his own hands she was sure to revive from her illness. Swamiji with the simplicity of a young boy replied – "Look here, mother. I myself am suffering from this illness and could not free myself from it all this year. If at all I could have done something to help you." As he said this his throat became heavy. The sorrow of others miseries made him forget his own sufferings. But this incident had a great impact on the woman and the other present there.

Swamiji accepted food from any one irrespective of caste or creed. The Hindus in Dhaka did not like this. They began to oppose this. Swamiji told them – "Brothers, I am sannyasi living on alms, then how can I think of caste. According to the Shastras, "Sannyasis will live their lives by begging for alms. Even he can seek alms from the house belonging to the lower strata of society."

From Dhaka, Swamiji and his group went on to Kamrupa, Chandranath, Guwahati. The length of the tour had taken a toll on Swamiji's health. Thinking that the climate in Shillong will be somewhat effective in Swamiji's recovery, Swamiji's group proceeded to Shillong to stay there for sometime. During those days, the chief commissioner of Assam was Sir Henry Cotton who was the well wisher of India. He had been nursing a wish to meet Swamiji since long. He made good arrangement for the stay of Swamiji and his group. On his request, Swamiji gave a speech. Most of Assam's scholastic society and some English and Americans were present there. All of them praised Swamiji for the speech. Sir Cotton honoured Swamiji in the presence of all present and asked – "After visiting famous countries in Europe and America, why have to come here? What do you want to see in this forest?" Joining both his hands, he burst out into laughter – "The place where a saint like you resides is a place of pilgrimage. I have come here to visit this place of pilgrimage."

Though the climate in Shillong was pleasant, it did not prove to be any beneficial for Vivekanand. He was totally in the grip of asthma. One night, his condition became very serious. Everybody felt as if Swamiji was about to leave them forever alone in the world. A boy sannyasi stood near the side of his head touching his forehead. He prayed to God with total concentration requesting the Almighty to revive Swamiji and in turn transfer his illness to him. The prayers offered with true heart had such a power that by day break, there was a pretty good sign of recovery evident in Swamiji's health. Slowly the asthmatic attack subsided. Within a few days, Swamiji regained back sufficient health to continue with his journey and then they all set off on their return journey to Belur.

By the time he reached back Belur Mutt, Swamiji had revived from Asthma but now he had protected wine related illness. As a result, swelling became evident all over his body. His treatment was entrusted to an Ayurvedic physician.

The sannyasis of the Mutt exercised complete supervision on Swamiji so that he did not indulge in hard work and follow the strictures associated with intake of Ayurvedic medicines. The Guru brothers kept him away from all types of mental excesses such as meditation, samadhi, etc. They entertained him with jokes and simple conversation.

In this illness, Swamiji's diet and sleep had decreased to a great extent. During those days, a new "Encyclopedia Britannica' was brought for the Mutt. The make and colour of the thick heavy books were really attractive. Swamiji's face shined with child-like curiosity at seeing the new and beautiful books. Considering his physical condition, he sadly said – "It is difficult to read this much of books within a life time." But during the silence and loneliness of night when he was unable to sleep, Swamiji made these books his friends. Within a few nights, Swamiji completed reading 10 volumes of the encyclopedia and when he began reading the 11th volume one of his disciples came to know about it. When the disciple expressed his surprise at Swamiji's unusual feat, Swamiji said – What are you saying? From these ten books ask any question which you wish to ask, I will answer them all." The disciple was surprised and asked – "Have you read all of them?" "Why not? Do you think that I am saying true without reading it?" Swamiji answered with a smile on his face. After this the disciple asked many questions from all the ten volumes and Swamiji gave correct reply to all of them. Many a times he quoted pages as given in the book. The disciple kept on looking at Swamiji as if wonderstruck and then taking the books in his hand said – "This is not human power."

Rest, strict follow of rules and appropriate treatment brought about a positive improvement in his health. He was happy with the solitary confinement he had been enjoying in Belur Mutt. In the peaceful and solitary environment around the Mutt, Swamiji did not lack company. The inseparable members of the ashram, attracted with Swamiji's loving behaviour gave company to Swamiji. Those were the birds and animals in the ashram – the faithful dog 'Bagha', the snow-white goat named 'Hansi', the sheeps, cows and their young ones, the swans swimming in the pond, the pair of dover, deer, etc., when the sannyasis of the ashram took a dip in the holy Ganga, 'Bagha' the dog also took a dip in the holy river.

In Swamiji's room, there was a sofa kept on one side of the wall which was presented to him by a foreign friend. Whosoever came to meet Swamiji, sat on the sofa. Hansi the goat also had a great liking for the sofa. Most of the time she used to lie on that sofa in Swamiji's room. Swamiji had tied small bells around the neck of the goat kid 'Matru'. Almost every evening, he played with 'Matru' and always used to say that all of them were their relatives in his previous life. He talked with the animals in human language. The animals expressed their love in a silent manner which Swamiji understood very well.

The young 'Matru' was embraced by death very soon. Expressing his shock Swamiji said – "How strange? Whomsoever I have that dies early." At the Chicago world religion Congress, the person who hoisted the flag of India at a great height, the one who gave scholastic explanation and speeches on topics pertaining to religion, theology, philosophy, literature, culture and civilization in different countries of the world. Is that very person praying with animals with a child like innocence? Many a time it was a cause of disbelief for many. The image of an all renouncing saint becomes diminutive in such a situation. What becomes evident is the image of a common man, installed with affection for the creatures of the world.

Vivekanand's alert eyes kept a close vigil on the smallest and minutest of things happening in the Mutt. His day-to-day worries included provision of water and food for animals and birds; cleanliness of their abodes, their sufferings and illnesses, the plants and vegetables grown in the kitchen garden, the pests invading the plants, cleanliness of kitchen and the premises around, purity of drinking water, etc. He gave constant information about the activities of the Mutt to sister Nivedita. Once he wrote to her – "When it rains, water gets accumulated in the compound of the Mutt. A drain is being dug to enable the release of water. I am returning back after assisting them in this work. At some places the water logging is more. My huge stroke and swans all are in a state of joy and excitement. The deer taken care of by me had run away. We searched it out with great difficulty. Unfortunately, yesterday a swam died. For almost a week, it had been facing difficulty in breathing. Witnessing all these incidents one old saint was saying that – 'Sir, in this Kali

Yuga when due to cold weather and rain swans suffer from cold, frogs begin to sneeze, then it is meaningless to stay alive in this world.' One night, one female swan began to shed its feathers. As nobody knew the solution for it, a mixture of water and carbolic acid was taken in a vessel and the swan left in it for a few minutes thinking that either it will recover totally or die. But it is now alright."

In this way looking after birds and animals, working in the kitchen garden, etc were Swamiji's favourite pastimes. He behaved with the workers of the Mutt as if they were his relatives and helped them with their work. Sometimes while inspecting the kitchen he himself landed up cooking and asked the cook to go out. At times when he felt hale, hearty and relaxed he indulged in cracking jokes with the Mutt inmates.

Even in such lighter moods the rules and discipline of the Mutt were strictly followed. Swamiji himself got up at 4 in the morning and rang the bell to awaken other sannyasis. One day Swamiji was not feeling well and entrusted the task of awakening the sannyasis to a disciple. The silence of the early morning hour got disturbed by the ringing of bell. When one of the sannyasis did not get up, the disciple who was ringing the bell went near the sannyasi and began to ring the bell near his ear. When later on Swamiji heard about it he said to his disciple laughingly – "You have done the correct thing." After this, it was the turn for yoga. In the morning and evening, Swamiji came downstairs from his room situated on the second floor to take a walk in the garden in front of the Mutt.

When people came to know that Swamiji's health was not well as he will stay in Belur Mutt for some times, then people from Calcutta and nearby areas came to meet him. One day before noon some ten-twelve young students from Calcutta came to meet him. The students directly went upstairs on the second floor and wanted for Swamiji in the corridor itself. After some time Swamiji came out from the room. When he was in the midst of students he also got transformed into a student behaving in an excited and curious manner. He was talking to me, rubbing the back of another and patting the shoulder of third one. Swamiji wore a thin gold chain around his neck, it was connected through a string with his pocket watch. One of the students touched the chain with his fingers and praised it. The very next

Swami Vivekanand: A Biography

moment Swamiji took out the chain along with the watch and handed it over to the student saying that "You liked it very much so now it is yours. But dear, never sell it off, preserve it with you like a gift." The boy's joy knew no bounds though he felt guilty for speaking in that manner.

Educated and liberal religious thinkers frequented Belur Mutt. And on the other hand those grown up amidst the false beliefs of Hinduism tried to defame Belur Mutt. People ignorant about the hidden truths of religious texts, believers of the prevalent beliefs and rituals while passing in front of the Belur Mutt in small boats made adverse comments on it. They created imaginative stories about the rituals devoid of untouchability and other fundamentalistic beliefs and made it public with the intention to defame the Mutt and Swamiji. Some sannyasis overheard these comments and sorrowfully related what they heard to Swamiji. Swamiji replied in an uninterested manner – "Elephant goes to the market, thousands of dogs bark, the saint is unperturbed even when the world condemns him."

In his short life, Swamiji had endured many such condemnation from his own countrymen as well as foreigners. In one way, he had attained freedom from all that. Sometimes he used to say – "During the propagation of new thoughts, it is natural for the old believers to put up stiff opposition. Every religious propagator around the world have to face this situation and emerge victorious."

That year (1901) he could not resist his wish to celebrate Durga Puja in a pompous manner. Though he was a follower of Advaita philosophy, sometimes the advaita culture came to the fore. But the sannyasis who have renounced everything had no right to offer prayers and worship. Hence, Swamiji could not decide anything as to what should be done on the occasion of Durga Puja. Only ten-twelve days before the Puja did the inmates of the Mutt come to know from Swamiji that they were going to worship the idol of Goddess Durga during Durga Puja. In the meanwhile, one of Swamiji's Guru brothers dreamt that the ten handed Mother Goddess was on her way from Dakshineswar to Belur Mutt flowing over the Ganga. The next day in the morning when Swamiji presented his decision regarding Durga Puja celebration, then the Guru brother expressed the dream he had the night before.

In this regard, the permission of Mother Sharda was

essential because the worship was to be accomplished in her name. Mother gave here acceprative her acceptance. Order was booked for making the idol of Goddess Kali. Money began to be collected for various expenses to make the puja a grand success. The main objective of the puja was to provide delicious food to the poor and needy to their heart's fill. In addition many known and unknown Brahmins were invited for the puja and meals. Some Brahmins who nursed a feeling of hatred towards the inmates, now realized that they were wrong after witnessing the sense of devotion in them. They now became sure that these believers of Advaita philosophy were indeed Hindus. The peaceful atmosphere of the Mutt turned into one of gaiety and fervour due to the celebration arrangements. The whole Mutt complex looked colourful with decoration of flowers, leaves, papers, etc. Beautiful notes of music emerged from Shahnai (a pipe like musical instrument). It seemed as if the waves danced to its rhythm. The sound that emanated from the meeting of drums shook the other end of the river bank.

Worship of Mother Durga was completed without much hindrance for the first three days. On the night of 'Saptami', Vivekanand protracted fever. Hence, he could not attend the puja the next morning. In spite of restrictions from Guru brothers and disciples, he came out of his room in the evening on the 'Mahaashtami' and offered prayers to Goddess Durga and returned back to his room. On the 'Navami' night (ninth day of the puja) he sat in front of the idol of the Goddess and sang two devotional songs in a highly emotional manner. Sri Ramakrishna used to sing those songs frequently.

That year Swamiji organized idol worship of Goddess Lakshmi and Goddess Kali according to the rules laid down in the Shastras. The very next day of Kali Puja, Swami Vivekanand received a message from his mother that she wanted to take him to the Kali Ghat to offer prayers to goddess Mahamaya. When Vivekanand used to be ill during his childhood days, his mother had made an offering to Goddess Mahamaya. Till that day she was unable to fulfil that. Now again when Swamiji became frequently ill, she felt that she should fulfil the offering made to the Goddess at the earliest Swamiji understood his mother seelings and accompanied her to the Kali Ghat. As per his mother's order he took a holy bath in the Ganges and entered the premises of the

Kali temple in wet clothes itself and prostrated before the idol of the Goddess like a young child. The mother had offered this very thing. After that he took seven parikramas of the temple and did a *havan* (fire offering) in the open himself. That day a huge crowd gathered at the temple premises to watch the self-strong radiant saint perform the worship rituals. After accomplishing the rituals at the temple when Swamiji returned back to Belur Mutt, he said to the Sannyasis – "The people in Kali Ghat are so liberal even now. In spite of the fact that I had made a visit to foreign countries no body made any objection with regard to my entry into the temple, but they extended a warm welcome and reverentially took me inside and gave all necessary help.

Swami Vivekanand who followed the Advaita philosophy, during his last days, indulged in idol worship, according to the Shastras and he used to said in a firm manner – "I have not come to destroy the decorum of Shastras but to make it wholesome.

After the Durga puja celebrations, Swami Vivekanand once again became ill and his body was totally weakened by different ailments. Once again he was given Ayurvedic treatment. He was not to intake water and in place of water he was given milk.

Many kinds of restrictions were made in respect of his food. But whenever he was able to muster some strength in his body, he used to sit up in his bed and discussed about students union and ways and means to build a strong character and body with his disciple. With sufficient rest, treatment and care his illness was somewhat controlled. Still he used to go out of his room only when extremely necessary.

During those days worship, prayers and meditation were done with full devotion in the Mutt. Every day after taking bath Swamiji went to the temple, offered prayers to Sri Ramakrishna and then went ahead with the inspection of the activities going on in the Mutt. In the same year i.e. in the end of 1901, two famous scholars from Japan came to Belur Mutt to meet Swamiji. A seminar on religion was to be organized in Japan. They had come to invite Swamiji to attend the seminar. One of the representatives of the Buddhist Mutt said to Swamiji – "If a renowned person like you assist us in our endeavour then our objectives will be fulfilled successfully.

You should indeed help us. Japan badly requires religious enlightenment these days. We do not know any one else other than you who can do this. Dr. Okakura who accompanied this person described the contempary condition in Japan and kept on insisting to accompany them to Japan. Swamiji was also very keen to spread spirituality in Japan the forgot about his ailments and accepted the invitation.

The wonderful personality of Swamiji, made both the scholars from Japan to stay in the Mutt itself for many days. They discussed about religion especially Buddhism and about the life of Lord Buddha. Swami totally thwarted the view put forth by western scholars that the Buddhist philosophy was totally opposed to Hindu philosophy. He said that there were many similarities between the teachings of Lord Buddha and that of Upanishads. Hence, Buddhist philosophy was based on the knowledge of Upanishada. The Japanese scholars were greatly surprised by the explanation of Buddhist philosophies. They were surprised to know that Swami had read almost every book pertaining to Buddhism. They were not able to arrive at a decision as to whether Swamiji be called a Buddhist or a Hindu saint.

In January 1902, accepting the invitation of the Japanese guests he accompanied them to Bodh Gaya. After many days, in that age, Swamiji got an opportunity to once again sit under the Bodhi tree in a meditative posture. Swamiji's joy knew no bounds. The images of the past visit became vivid before his eyes. The emotional student 'Naren' had sat under this very tree with closed eyes in search of truth. That day the truth that emerged within him was that he was wondering far away there leaving god-like people behind. At last, he had to take shelter at the feet of that mad man. What he told had turned out to be true.

After Bodh Gaya, the next destination of the Japanese scholars was Benaras. After visiting the places of tourist and historical importance there at Benares for two-three days, the Japanese scholar took leave of Swamiji. While leaving also they reminded Swamiji to decide the day of departure to Japan and inform them accordingly.

Swamiji felt a great attraction towards Kashi. Many great scholars and students in Kashi were keen to hear Swamiji's speech. During those days, Brahmins looked down upon people who had made a trip abroad. In many temples,

Swamiji was not supposed to enter. But in spite of all this, these people extended a warm welcome to Swamiji and gave priority to his words. He also accepted the invitation of king of Bhinga. The king asked Swamiji to set up an ashram in Kashi. The king gave money meant for one year's expenses to Swamiji and gave assurances of assistance in the future. Swamiji promised to establish a Mutt in Kashi. After returning back to Calcutta from Kashi, he sent Swami Shivanand to establish an ashram in Kashi.

While in Kashi, Swami Vivekanand experienced a strange kind of happiness. There was a secret behind this. Inspired by Swamiji's teachings and advise, the youth union was established. The members of the union organized social welfare activities with great interest. Their first duty was to look after orphans, ailing pilgrims. They took a small building on rent on the banks of the Gangas and there they brought the ailing, the old, handicapped etc and made arrangements for their medicines, care, etc. Swamiji also experienced vigour in the company of those youngsters. In the first report published about the Ramakrishna Sevashram, Swamiji also made an appeal to the public for financial help. Even today the ashram is famous in the same name – 'Ramakrishna Sevashram'.

After spending some active and joyous days in Kashi, Swamiji returned back to Belur Mutt. It was the month of April and it was the height of summer heat. Swamiji sometimes went to distant place, strolling in the morning and the evening hours, himself or accompanied by a Guru brother or disciple. One day, in the evening one of the disciples who was taking a stroll on the banks of the Ganges saw a sannyasi walking towards him at a distance. When he came near the disciple he realized that the saint' was none other than Swami Vivekanand. He was totally immersed in his own thoughts and was eating roasted peas. When he saw his disciple he said in a loving manner – "Have some roasted peas. It is quite spicy." The disciple readily took some peas and partook it and both of them walked towards the Mutt.

During those days, some Santhal labourers – both men and women, were employed to plough the soil around the Mutt and make it plain. Swamiji, most of the times, went and sat with those labourers and talked with them enquiring about their life, children, and other personal things. He laughed with simplicity at their joyous incidents and his heart cried miserably for their sorrowful incidents. One day, some renowned persons from Calcutta came to meet Swamiji at the Mutt. At that time Swamiji was very much indulged in talking with the labourers, when he was informed about the people who had come to meet him, he did not pay much attention and said – "At this moment I cannot meet anyone. I am enjoying my conversation with these people." There was one person named Keshta among the labourers whom Swamiji loved for his simplicity. Kashta also utilized every opportunity to talk with Swamiji.

One day, Keshta said to Swamiji –'Oh my Swami, when we are engrossed in our work please do not come here because by talking to you we are unable to complete one work and the one who inspects our work later on scolds us." Tears came to Swamiji's eyes when he heard this. He said – "No, no. He won't say anything to you. You just tell me some thing about your native place." And this way they indulged in long conversations. One day Swamiji asked Keshta – "Would you people like to have meals at our place one day?" Keshta replied – "We cannot eat things touched by you. By eating the salt touched by you we will lose our caste." Swamiji said – "Why will you eat salt? We will prepare food without salt for you, then you can have it?" Keshta and his co-workers agreed with Swamij's proposal.

One day, a saltless feast was prepared for them at the Mutt. Swamiji served those poor with all the delicacies with his own hands. While eating Keshta said – "Oh Swami, from where did you get all these delicacies? We had never had such kind of food in our life." Swamiji keeping out more food to their plates said – "You people are Narayanas, the image of God. Today I have offered food to the God. That day Santhals were given off from work. After lunch, they asked to take rest. When they were taking rest, Swamiji said to his disciples – "I feel that they are real Narayana. I have never seen such simpletons and innocent people whose love is so honest. We discussed about their poverty ridden miserable life with his disciples and made them understand that real sannyasa is to help such people."

"Many people of our country do not get ample food to fill their stomach, but even after seeing that and knowing that how we are able to intake food." Saying this he turned very

Swami Vivekanand: A Biography

emotional and began to stroll at a fast pace. Then he stopped for a while and said, "I feel like selling off this Mutt and everything and distribute everything among those poor fellows. Our country does not think about these poor and miserable lots. Those people who are the backbone of our country, with whose efforts crops are grown and if they do not work for even a day we all become restless – why don't we have any sympathy towards them, why don't we show concern towards them in happiness and sorrow. Is there no body in our country? Just see, unable to gain the sympathy of Hindus, thousands of people are getting converted into Christians in the Madras province. Do not think that these people are becoming Christians only for the sake of their stomach. Day and night we keep on saying 'Do not touch, do not touch.' What religion is left in our country. Only two groups that of touchables and untoucables have remained. On these people do not know about the ways of the world. That is why they are unable to arrange even food and clothing even after working so hard. Come, let us do something to open their eyes to the truth and the reality. I am able to see with my divine vision that the God within them and within me are the same, the same kind of power is existent in both. The only difference is that of development and progress. Unless blood gushes in all members, have you seen any change happening in any country? Even if a single body part is weak and all other parts strong, the body cannot accomplish any big task."

As Swamiji talked, he became seriously pensive. Night had fallen. Swamiji, silent and engrossed in some thoughts, climbed the stairs to his room upstairs. He was followed by a disciple. Swamiji laid down on his bed. When he saw the disciple standing near his bed, he asked him to massage his feet. In the afternoon, he had walked more than normal days and because of that his body was aching. The disciple sat near Swamiji's feet and continued with the massaging. The opportunity to spend sometime alone with Swamiji raised many doubts that he wanted to get clarified from his teacher, in his mind. But he could not muster courage to ask those questions because Swamiji in a serious disposition. After sometime he slowly put forth his doubt before Swamiji that in this country where there is heterogeneity of religions and thoughts, it is very difficult to bring about singularity in the minds of people to fulfil some objective.

Swamiji's face turned red, veins became tight. Somehow controlling his emotions and words he said – "If you consider any work difficult, then do not come here." But he could hide the anger in his tone. He paused for a while and then in a calm tone explained that he should leave his thoughts about caste and creed and serve the weak, poor and the miserable lot. He should not think about the outcome but continue with his action. With the blessings of Sri Ramakrishna everything will be in place.

As he talked Swamiji became somewhat indignant. Then he said – "The condition of this body is like this. None among you is taking up the gauntlet to extend any keeping hand in my efforts. What will I do?" The darkness of pessimism was clear on his face. The disciple convinced – "Swamiji, all these Brahmacharis, men who have sacrificed everything for you, is at your back. I am sure that each one among them is ready to give their lives. Then why are you thinking in this manner? Swamiji became overwhelmed with emotions and gave words to his desires. He wanted such a youth wing who are healthy both mentally and physically, of strong character and intelligent. He wanted youths who are ready to lay down their lives for the country and who were ready and prepared to walk on the path of thorns. He strongly believed that only such youths can be instrumental in constructing a new India.

In February 18, 1902 the birth anniversary of Sri Ramakrishna was celebrated with gaiety and fervour. Many devotees assembled there from distant place to attend the celebrations. The huge open space in front of the Mutt was crowded with people. On the one hand devotional songs and chanting of Mantras were in progression and on the other, Prasada was being distributed. A large number of poor men were fed. But a shadow of gloomness pervaded the otherwise environment. There was a kind of emptiness inspite of presence of so many people. Swami Vivekanand was in the grip of severe fever and was totally bedridden with weakness. There was swelling in his feet which rendered him incapable of standing on his own. Weakness had pervaded all over his body. He expressed his desire to be amidst the people and celebrations. But his doctors did not let him go downstairs.

He was strictly prohibited from talking. The disciples sat outside his door turn-wise and restricted the entry of visitors into his room. The guests were greatly disappointed by this.

One disciple was sitting near Swami's feet and massaging his feet. The disciple was sad seeing the condition of Swamiji. Swamiji understood his feelings and said – "What are you thinking?" If you have taken the garb of body, it is sure to get destroyed. If you are able to instill my ideas in people even to some extent, I will feel that my attaining this body had proved successful." At that moment, talking about various things, he expressed his thoughts about organizing Sri Ramakrishna's birth anniversary celebrations. He wanted that Sri Ramakrishna birthday be celebrated in a novel way in the future and the celebration continue for three to four days. On the first day reading of Shastras and teachings, the second day discussion on Vedas and Vedanta, third day question-answer sessions, fourth day explanation and analysis, devotional songs, chanting of mantras and serving the poor.

The sound of devotional songs accompanied by musical instruments was to be heard from downstairs. Swamiji got up from the bed with the support of the disciple and stood holding on to the railings of the window and watched the happenings downstairs. Hope and excitement spilled from his eyes. The face down with pain suddenly bloomed up. Within two minutes, sweat became evident on his forehead. He was once again overtook by weakness and he once again fell back on his bed. After a second, regaining back his stability Swamiji asked – "How many people would be there downstairs?" About 50,000, answered the disciple. Swamiji said – "No, not more than 30,000."

It was evening. The weak, unlively rays of the setting sun was making an unsuccessful attempt to light up the room. Outside the room, crowds of people gathered to have a glimpse of Swamiji. Some Guru brothers requested the people with folded hands not to disturb Swamiji as he was supposed to take complete rest. Almost all of them returned back disappointed. The next day when Swamiji came to know about it he became disappointed. He called the Guru brothers and disciples and said – "See, what good will keeping this body do? Let it get destroyed in the welfare of others. Sri Ramakrishna endured the pain and illness he had protracted but he continued giving advise for the welfare of others till the end. Should I also not do the same thing? I do not care whether this perishable body remains or gets destroyed. Conversation with researchers of truth is the most joyous thing for me, you cannot even imagine the kind of enjoyment that it will give to me."

With months of treatment, rest and regulated food, Swamiji's health improved a lot. But Swamiji's treatment involved great expenditure. Swamiji could not bear the fact that so much of money was being spent on his treatment. During this period, in the month of April, Ms. Josephine Mc Leod who was on her way to Europe from Japan, took a few days' break in India to meet Swamiji. Swamiji had not completely revived from his illness. Swamiji was happy to have his friend-like American disciple as guest at Belur Mutt. One day during the course of conversation he presented his financial condition before her – "There is nothing for me in this world. I do not have any money left with me. Till now whatever I have got, I have distributed."

Josephine felt pity at Swamiji's condition. She assured Swamiji that as long as she stays alive, she will give 50 dollars (equivalent to Rs. 250 at that time) for Swamiji's personal expenses. A frown came over Swamiji and worry became evident on his forehead and he asked—"Is that sufficient for me?" "Yes, why not?" Replied the disciple and smilingly gave 200 dollars to Swamiji. Another day, during the course of conversation Swamiji said to Josephine – "I do not think that I would be able to see my 40th year." The disciple was a bit frightened by the seriousness on Swamiji's face. But trying to pacify him she said – "But Swamiji, Buddha accomplished his most important and significant mission in the period between 40 to 60 years of age." The seriousness on his face now got transferred to his eyes. He said – "I have given my message to the world. Now I should go." The disciple once again became overwhelmed with a sense of fear and said, "Why at all should you go?" Swamiji replied – "Under the shadow of a huge tree, small plants cannot grow up. To give space to them, I should go." The disciple could not say anything further and change his attention from the topic. She tried to discuss about something else.

The lamp, before blowing out, gives extraordinary light for a moment. Almost a month before Swamiji bade good bye

Swami Vivekanand: A Biography

to this world, he looked very healthy. Though he was crumbling from within, nobody knew about it. Slowly he had resumed with his morning and evening walks also. He had begun to participate in discussion on Vedanta along with other Guru brothers and disciples at the stipulated time. But interest in Ramakrishna and other Mutt related activities had begun to recede. He never expressed his opinion on anything. He asked the Guru brothers to take decision on important aspects pertaining to the Mutt.

In this manner, Swamiji withdrew himself from almost every field of life. Now only aim left in his life was to sit in Samadhi. Most of the times people found him engrossed in thinking and meditation. The Guru brothers and disciples were greatly worried by such a drastic change in his attitude. Many years ago Gurudev Ramakrishna had made the prediction that after accomplishing his work, Naren will attain Samadhi and when he will know very well that who he is, then he will not be able to remain bound in the clutches of the body. Those words of Gurudev seemed to become true. Whenever Swamiji went into Samadhi the Sannyasis of the ashram tried to pull him back to the real world but most of the time they failed in their endeavours.

Sister Nivedita had written – "A few days before bidding adieu he discussed past incidents with Guru brothers. One among them asked Swamiji during the course of one such conversation – "Swamiji, have you realized who you are?" Instant came the reply – "Yes, I have realized now." Such an unexpected answer sent a shock wave among them. None among them could muster courage to question any further. But all of them got a premonition that Swamiji won't be with them for long.

A week before Swamiji attained Nirvana, Swamiji was taking rest in his room. One of his disciples who was a family man had come straight from his office to Belur Mutt to meet Swamiji. As soon as he entered the room he paid obeisance at Swamiji's feet and asked about his health. Swamiji was staring at the costume worn by the disciple. Swamiji shot the question to the disciple – I am fine but tell me why don't you wear collar when you wear coat-pant." After this Swamiji said, "Give two collars from mine tomorrow morning to him." After that the disciple went to the other room, changed his official clothes, washed his hands and face and returned back to Swamiji's room with the intention to carry on with the conversation.

Even before the disciple had taken his seat, Swamiji continued with the topic he had left before – "By renouncing food, clothing and caste rituals, slowly and gradually casteism gets dissolved. Knowledge can be attained from anyone but the kind of knowledge which vanishes culture that does not take you on to the path of progress but on to the path of downfall." The disciple answered in a hesitant manner – "It is essential to comply with the orders of the officers with regard to the dress. Swami laughed and explained – 'Who says you should not wear this dress in the office. But after returning back home, became a Bengali Babu – the dhoti, kameez or kurta and shawl over the shoulders. Understood!" The disciple nodded his head in consent. Swamiji again explained – "You people go to others house wearing that kameez. But in the west, going to others' houses in such outfit is considered uncivilized. Without wearing the coat no civilized person would let you inside their homes.

What blind imitation have you learnt about that costume. The dresses worn by young boys these days are neither indigenous nor foreign, it is a strange mixture." The disciple had come from a distant place to meet Swamiji hence, Swamiji did not disappoint him. That day they continued with their conversation till late in the night.

The next day, Vivekanand asked Swami Shudhananda to bring the calendar (Panchang). After receiving it, Swamiji kept on turning and overturning it. It seemed as if he was searching something in the pages and take some decisions. Perhaps he found what he had been searching. He closed the Panchang and kept it aside and began to see something at a distance beyond the windows.

Human memory forgets things at the appropriate moment. People are not able to see the truth of the incidents happening in front of their eyes. The incident of asking for the Panchang had taken place earlier also in the lives of the sannyasis. When Swamiji left the earthly abode just one week after he had asked for the [Panchang] the sannyasis recollected the same incident that took place just a week before Gurudev Sri Ramakrishna passed away. He had also asked one of his disciples to bring the 'panchanga' and he consulted it and decided some special date and returned it back to the disciple and said – 'Ok. Now there is no need of this.' Swami Vivekanand also followed the footsteps of his Gurudev. But only if any one could have undertstood the significance of this symbolic act. Three days before his death while strolling in the company of Swami Premananda, Vivekanand pointing towards a specific point on the bank of river Ganga said – "When I leave my body, then my cremation should be done there." Today a temple is situated at the place in Swamiji's honour. His behaviour and conversation during the last days of his life were somewhat enigmatic and at the same time meaningful. People analysed what Swamiji said then only later.

It was July 2, 1902, Wednesday. The day was that of 'Ekadashi'. Swaiji had kept a fast on that day. Sister Nivedita had come over to Belur Mutt to seek some advise regarding her school. She was asking whether she should start teaching Science in the school or not. She was of the opinion that the subject of Science should be taught essentially. After thinking for a while Swamiji in a half-hearted manner said – 'Perhaps you are correct. But my mind is busy with some other things. I am getting ready for death. Strange kinds of talks." Outwardly Swamiji was looking perfectly alright, but what has happened to him? Why is he so lost and unhappy. Perhaps he needed some loneliness. Sister Nivedita got up to go. 'But you should definitely eat something', saying so he himself got up and began serving food for his favourite disciple with his own hands.

The breakfast for the day was ready–plain rice, boiled potatoes, boiled seeds of jackfruit and cold milk. According to the ancient Indian tradition, Nivedita sat on the wooden platform laid on the floor. Swamiji served rice, potato, seeds of jackfruit on her plate. He seemed very happy and there was a smile on his face. Sister Nivedita and other disciples were surprised to find such a changed image of Swamiji. Sister Nivedita finished eating and got up to wash her hands. But Swamiji himself poured water to her to wash her hands. She became hesitant and before she could make out what was happening, Swamiji began to wipe her hands with a towel. The disciple remonstrated – 'I should have done this for you, Swamiji, not you for me.'

"Jesus Christ washed the feet of his disciples" – the calm but serious words of Swamiji surprised Nivedita – "But that was when he met them for the last time." The words got struck in the throat. She opened her mouth but words did not come out. In fact that day she met Swamiji for the last time and talked for the last time.

Friday, July 4, 1902. Swamiji got up very early in the morning. Since the time he had become ill, his routine of getting up early in the morning had changed. He got up and came downstairs and sat along with the sannyasis for meditation. After sometimes, he sat sipping tea with them and talking about past incidents. Suddenly he got up and walked towards the Kali temple as if he was reminded of something that he had forgotten. He entered the temple and closed the doors and windows from within. What happened to him suddenly! He had never done such a thing before. The Guru brothers and disciples were surprised. They were at loss as to what to do. After spending about 3 hours from 6 am to 11 am he came down from the temple. It seems as if he was in some other world of his own, eyes were lost somewhere. He was mumbling a song devoted to Mother Kali. No one could muster the courage to go and talk to him in such a semi conscious state. Swamiji kept on singing the devotional song and strolled outside the Mutt.

The beauty of the music removes the curtains of the past. The Guru brothers are able to see the images of the past imprinted in their memory. The young Naren was singing the very same song in the temple of Dakshineswar. Gurudev Ramakrishna was looking at the boy with a serious countenance and big eyes continuously. Tears were coming down Guruji's eyes. What a piteous scene! As Swamiji walked he was mumbling something. The Sannyasis standing at a distance could hear something but not very clearly. But Swami Premananda who was standing near him could hear it – "If there had been some other Vivekanand then we could have understood what Vivekanand had done. But at the ripe time many Vivekanand will be born." Premananda was in a state of shock. No, no. Swamiji is in a semi conscious state, that is why he is talking like this. In his normal state, he had never said such things. After sometime his trance was broken.

At the time of meals, that day, after so many months, Swamiji sat along with other Guru brothers in line for the food. Since the time he had been keeping ill, the time and place of his partaking food had changed. But that day there

Swami Vivekanand: A Biography

was a reason for Swamiji to sit with them for having his meals. At that time, a marked change had come over Swamiji's mental condition. He was looking very happy and indulged in light conversation with everyone. Vivekanand, whom the inmates of the Mutt unstressed sometime ago had disappeared into nowhere. He seemed like some one else who was relishing the food amidst cheerful conversation. During the course of conversation he expressed his desire that the next day being Saturday they should make arrangements for special puja and worship at the Kali temple as it was an auspicious day. He gave orders to some sannyasis to make arrangements for certain articles required for the puja.

Swamiji was looking very happy. He said that he was feeling energetic and healthy that day than all other days. At one o'clock, he called all sannyasis and began to teach Sanskrit grammar. The subject was very boring but Swamiji's way of teaching made it interesting. The laughs of Sannyasis could be heard frequently. Three long hours got lapsed in no time. None of them could make out how.

After the class, Swamji looked somewhat tired. He went to his room for rest but he was unable to take proper rest. Talking in the company of Swami Premananda, he proceeded towards Belur market for his evening walk. On the way, he related many interesting incidents touching the past, present and the future. Sometimes about Gurudev Ramakrishna and sometimes about the birds and animals of the ashram or about the setting up of a vedic college. Both of them returned back to the Mutt.

The evening had spread its dusky atmosphere all over the Mutt. Swamiji talked and laughed with the sannyasis a while and then went upstairs. The lamp kept on the table was spreading its faded light inside the room. All the doors and windows of the room were open. Swamiji went and stood near the window opening towards the Ganga. It was a no moon night. It was very dark outside. But the sky was clear. Innumerous stars were shining in the sky. Swamiji was looking at the Dakshineswar temple across the river. A silent invitation, a silent call from someone was making Swamiji restive. He went to the door and gave instructions to the Sannyasi standing there not to enter inside till he made a call. He sat down in the centre of the room and entered into Samadhi. His eyes were closed and no body knew that behind that closed eyes he was enjoying the sight of the ultimate truth, the eternal beauty of the divine Shiva. A divine light enveloped his countenance. A feeling of affection got pervaded all over his face and the boundation of action broke. Religion, philosophy, Shastras, temple, Mutt everything got entangled in a turbulence and dissolved into nowhere disappearing into some divine source of light.

At 8 o'clock in the night Swamiji got up from his seat with Rudraksh in his hands. The sannyasi standing at the door wanting for his orders became alert and hurried towards Swamiji. 'It is very hot just fan me' saying so Swamiji laid down on the Muttress on the floor. He closed his eyes as soon as he laid down. Soon he was asleep and sannyais continued fanning Swamiji.

Almost an hour had lapsed and Swamiji continued sleeping. It was something very strange. Swamiji never slept at odd hour in such a manner. Perhaps he had entered into Samadhi in the sleeping position – The sannyasi who was sitting beside Swamiji thought. The bell for dinner at 9 pm caused a disturbance in the otherwise peaceful atmosphere. The Sannyasis sight was fixed on Swamiji itself. There was a slight shivering on both his arms, then two weak but deep breathe – his chest expanded and contracted with it. The very next moment the head he had rested on the pillow in a straight manner fell downwards in a sudden jerk, what is happening? The sannyasi went downstairs in a state of shock.

As soon as the news reached the Guru brothers, two main sannyasis Swami Premananda and Swami Nishchayananda rushed to Swami Vivekanand's room followed by other Guru brothers and disciples. Swamiji's body was totally motionless and without any pulse beat. Both the Guru brothers tried to shake him and pressed his heart and hands. Sweat came upon their face as they found themselves unsuccessful in their attempt. Swamiji's heart beat and pulse had stopped. They were unable to believe the harsh truth. They hoped that it was some other form of Samadhi. Whatever be the case they longed that Swamiji would return back to consciousness. Swami Premananda and Nityananda began to mutter the pious name of Sri Ramakrishna in the ears of Swamiji. In the meantime, a renowned doctor of Calcutta was called in. He checked Swamiji's body thoroughly and expressed his conclusion that Swamiji will not regain back his consciousness at any cost.

Seven years ago Swami Vivekanand had prayed to the Mother Goddess Kali:

Mother, take me to that bank
Where there is no conflict like this
Beyond this pain, tears and physical comforts.
The greatness of the bank
is not expressed by the sun, the moon or the planets
But just reflects the light of it.
Oh mother, the deceptive dreams covering this eye
do not obstruct me from seeing you.
My game is coming to an end mother
Just break all these shackles
And redeem me.

That day Goddess Kali heard the prayers of Swami Vivekanand.

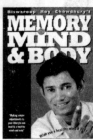

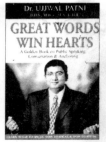

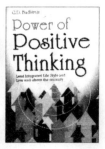